FEMINIST
PSYCHOANALYTIC
PSYCHOTHERAPY

FEMINIST PSYCHOANALYTIC PSYCHOTHERAPY

CHARLOTTE KRAUSE PROZAN

JASON ARONSON INC.
Northvale, New Jersey
London

Production Editor: Leslie Block

This book was set in Garamond by Lind Graphics of Upper Saddle River, New Jersey, and printed and bound by Haddon Craftsmen of Scranton, Pennsylvania.

Library of Congress Cataloging-in-Publication Data

Prozan, Charlotte Krause.
    Feminist psychoanalytic psychotherapy / by Charlotte Krause Prozan.
        p.   cm.
    Includes bibliographical references and index.
    ISBN 0-87668-456-8
    1. Women and psychoanalysis.   2. Feminist therapy.   I. Title.
    [DNLM: 1. Psychoanalytic Interpretation.   2. Psychoanalytic
Therapy.   3. Women—psychology.   WM 460.5.W6 P969w]
RC451.4.W6P73   1992
616.89'17'082—dc20
DNLM/DLC
for Library of Congress   91-47122

Manufactured in the United States of America. Jason Aronson Inc. offers books and cassettes. For information and catalog write to Jason Aronson Inc., 230 Livingston Street, Northvale, New Jersey 07647.

This book is dedicated to my father Emil Lackow,
my mother Manya Prozanskaya Lackow,
my children Karen and Jeff,
and my grandsons Alex and Kevin

CONTENTS

ACKNOWLEDGMENT

The writing of this book was made infinitely easier by my learning to use a computer. For ordering the computer, teaching me to use it, and being available p.r.n. for advice in innumerable crises, I am most grateful to my son-in-law, Eric Andresen. His calmness, his patience, and his always knowing just what to do to solve the problem were greatly appreciated. I am truly fortunate to have Eric in my family.

Ephraim Margolin and Tom Christie both brought some valuable references to my attention from their fine libraries. A word of thanks to the librarians at the San Francisco Psychoanalytic Institute, at the Institute for Human Sexuality in San Francisco, and the San Francisco Public Library, and also to the helpful researcher at the Kinsey Institute. Zenobia Grusky assisted with the research on Helene Deutsch.

My woman's consciousness-raising group was a profound experience of both intellectual stimulation and emotional support. For seventeen years of sisterhood, I thank Joan Dunkel, Gloria Sparrow, and Adine Panitch.

Warm thanks to my consultant of twenty-five years, Jerome D. Oremland, a psychoanalyst and gifted teacher, a gatekeeper who truly kept the gate open for me with his knowledge, skill, and experience.

A whole year of thank yous to my husband, Guy Smyth, for his enduring patience and for always being there for me. I thank him for being skeptical, at times to the point of irritation, and for his good questions and thoughtful comments. Talks with him provided much stimulation for my thinking and forced me to clarify my ideas.

My editors, Anne Patota and Leslie Block, were always patient and supportive as well. Their many helpful ideas have added to the organization and clarity of my writing.

The enthusiasm and good suggestions of my publisher, Jason Aronson, are much appreciated. It was his idea for me to write this book, and it was his recognition of the importance of integrating psychoanalytic and feminist approaches to psychotherapy that has enabled me to translate my years of work as a feminist and psychoanalytically oriented psychotherapist into this document.

INTRODUCTION

This book reviews the history of the feminist and psychoanalytic theories of female development and personality. Its companion book, *The Technique of Feminist Psychoanalytic Psychotherapy,* illustrates how an integration of these theories can be applied in clinical practice. I do not regard the two theories as competitive views of female psychology, but rather see each as making valuable contributions to our understanding of women and treatment of female patients. Each theory enriches the other when they are integrated, and, conversely, each suffers when the valuable insights of the other have been ignored, misunderstood, or rejected.

I do not call myself a feminist therapist, because that term may be interpreted as a rejection of analytic technique. I am rather a therapist who is a feminist, and who brings this new mentality to my work, incorporating it as I do other bodies of new research and writing that I find valuable. The questions I ask and the comments and interpretations I make include a feminist position that I integrate into a traditional psychodynamic analysis, thereby broadening and enhancing both. I work with the patient to understand how the interplay of family history, internal dynamics (such as repressed memory and fantasy), and societal forces have combined to inhibit her autonomy and achievement, with the anger, anxiety, and other personality distortions that may result.

This integration is an additional layer of treatment, to be added to the therapist's previously learned skills in diagnosis, analysis of symptoms and pathology, and analysis of the transference. It is a new perspective that I believe is essential in helping women achieve the full potential benefit from psychoanalysis and psychotherapy. Using the techniques of free association, dream analysis, and analysis of the transference and countertransference offers women the most hopeful, effective, and deeply profound method for freeing themselves from the constraints of a traditional female upbringing.

In the early days of the women's movement, new women patients and members of an audience would ask me if I were a Freudian, and the tone made it clear that being a Freudian meant belonging to the enemy. Phyllis Chesler (1970), in an article harshly critical of psychotherapy, sees marriage and psychotherapy as parallel dependency structures for women. (See also Chesler 1972.) Chesler feels that the two are the major socially approved institutions for middle class women, who enter both with a similar sense of urgency and desperation and without questioning their own motives. Each institution, she states, is based on a woman's helplessness and dependence on a strong authority figure—husband or therapist (male or female)—and thus the woman is repeating her relationship with her father in a male-dominated society. Chesler fails to appreciate the strength of the authority of the mother for both men and women, and that the transference in psychotherapy may resemble the relationship with the mother just as strongly.

The article goes on to describe psychotherapy as a form of control and oppression for women—surely a distortion of its aims. A woman in therapy can come to see how she allows herself to be oppressed and how she infantalizes herself. Through therapy she can gain the strength and understanding to change this inappropriate mode of relating to men, and probably to certain women as well. The dependency that develops in the psychotherapeutic relationship may have particular meaning when dealing with women patients. If not interpreted often and with accuracy, it can perpetuate infantile modes of relating, sustain a low self-image, and discourage termination. In order to raise our consciousness in this area we must deal with our own feelings of dependence and our own defenses against these feelings. We also need to be very aware of the real factors within our culture that mitigate against independent womanhood, factors that in subtle and sometimes not so subtle ways keep women isolated and dependent and perpetuate feelings of helplessness in relation to husbands, lovers, parents, employers, their own children, and life itself.

As I began to try to integrate feminist theory into my work, I found it useful to distinguish between the two areas of contribution made by Freud: (1) the technique of psychoanalysis and psychoanalytically oriented psychotherapy, and (2) the developmental theory—that is, the theory of the unconscious, the role of the superego, the importance of repression and so on. In my work I adhere to traditional technique; the development and interpretation of the transference is our best tool for helping our patients to uncover their fears and doubts, their anger and envy, and their need to be understood, appreciated, and loved. By maintaining a professional distance and by not revealing our own lives and opinions, we facilitate the projections that enable the therapist and patient to look inside and discover the sources of the patient's misery. A new patient once said to me, "Since I don't know anything about you, I don't have to alter what I say to fit what I know about you."

Chesler accuses the practitioners of this traditional mode of psycho-therapy of attempting to maintain a superior position to the patient and of using an authoritarian approach. The real function of neutrality, however, is to protect the patient. Why should patients be burdened with my life when they are coming to me for help with their own? The atmosphere of neutrality is designed to discourage therapists from narcissistically using our patients to meet our own needs: to fulfill our thwarted ambitions or to confirm our way of thinking and being in the world. What we should not be neutral about is the health and welfare and progress of our patients. For example, we should not remain silent if a woman is reacting passively and masochistically to a damaging relationship or to a life situation that threatens her self-respect and depresses her. This may seem contradictory, so I will attempt to clarify it. In any clinical situation where the patient is behaving in a self-destructive manner, the behavior must be confronted by the therapist. This principle could apply to alcohol or drug abuse, illegal activities, or submission to physical or psychological abuse. According to Langs (1973):

> Failure on (his) part to confront his patient with dangerous or destructive behavior constitutes a sanction of the action; it will promote acting out and acting in, and generally poor controls. Thus, confrontations must be made when indicated; failure to do so nonverbally supports the patient's disturbed behavior. However certain dangers must be kept in mind: such confrontations must not be made too quickly, intolerantly, or in a morally condemning tone. The patient must be allowed freedom of behavioral exploration; confrontations must not be used to control or direct the patient. It is essential that the therapist be aware of the implications of maladaptive behavior and explore them with the patient tactfully. . . . Correct confrontations modify the patient's defenses and permit new, meaningful material to enter consciousness. [p. 421]

The difficulty here resides in the judgment of what is self-destructive. The therapist is clearly making a value judgment. It is in this area that there is likely to be a clear difference between a feminist orientation and a traditional orientation, because of the high value placed by feminists on a woman's autonomy, her right to make nontraditional life choices, and the necessity in terms of her self-esteem to object to demeaning or abusive treatment.

Another criticism of traditional therapy, that it aims to adjust the patient to an unjust society, cannot be countered by getting the patient to conform to what we as feminists or socialists or antinuclear activists envision as a just society. Each patient must choose her or his own goals. If a patient's goal is to catch a rich man who will support her, we may analyze this wish to be taken care of, but we should not intrude. If we do, we are making a moral rather than a psychological judgment. Here, the feminist value of autonomy should not apply, because we cannot define the choice as self-destructive, but merely distasteful.

However, the therapeutic process and the therapeutic alliance can teach the patient the values of honesty and of exploring feelings. The cooperative nature of the relationship with the therapist can teach the advantages of understanding and being understood, as well as the opposite, the self-destructive effects of suspicion, mistrust, and competitive fears and practices. These values have a ripple effect on the patient's relationships with others, especially his or her children, spouse, and co-workers.

Developmental theory, as described by Freud, Helene Deutsch, and other writers on the psychology of women, is a different matter. Our theoretical understanding of what is normal and what is pathological for a woman is naturally going to have a significant effect on our work with her. Freud saw penis envy as the central issue in women's psychology. This concept has stirred much resentment in the feminist community and among some women therapists, but it does have some value and can be adapted to be useful in our work with women. Deutsch's work, which describes female psychology in terms of masochism, narcissism, and passivity, also contains some valuable material but is based on a number of assumptions with which I disagree. What she calls a masculine or "active" woman I would call a healthy adult. What she calls feminine, as in her ideas about receptivity, I would view as undifferentiated. Karen Horney, however, makes valuable contributions to our thinking about women, incorporating a cultural perspective.

A feminist orientation to psychotherapy, practiced by male or female, gay or straight therapists, involves most importantly an image of women radically different from the traditional images of women in our society. I see women as having the potential for being emotionally and physically strong, nurturing and creative, intelligent and competent; and for living meaningful lives within a family, in individual pursuits, or in a combination of both. Feminists believe that women have been prevented from developing their full potential by social mores and not by their anatomy, because society has confined them to the roles of wife and mother, subordinate to and financially dependent upon their husbands. Anatomy need not be destiny when birth control and other medical advances have improved our health and given us choices in childbearing. To his credit, Freud recognized women's strong sexual drive and the danger that repressing it could result in neurotic symptoms.

Feminists recognize that anger is a natural and healthy reaction to the distorted view of women as weak, intellectually inferior, and silly. They feel pained at how these beliefs are internalized by women, destroy self-esteem, and thus make women vulnerable to economic, political, social, and sexual exploitation. We need to be clear about the difference between the genitals and the brain. There is, I believe, much unconscious confusion here on the part of many men and some women. A woman can feel well satisfied with her female body parts and functions (although she may wish to be prettier or have larger breasts or smaller hips), enjoying both her sexuality and motherhood, and yet strongly resent any inferences that her brain or her morality is inferior. Her anger is not about what she lacks, but at the lack of recognition of and respect for what she has.

I began my own psychoanalysis in 1965 and my training in psychoanalytically oriented psychotherapy in 1967, when I began my private practice. In 1970 I joined a feminist consciousness-raising group that continued to meet until 1987. In 1975 I joined a consultation group of psychoanalytically oriented women therapists who were feminists, and this group also continued to meet until 1987. The past twenty-five years have been rich and vital ones in my professional growth and, simultaneously, in the raising of my consciousness of the ways women can be emotionally crippled by internalizing patriarchal values of male superiority. This book is the culmination of twenty-five years of intense study and practice of psychotherapy and twenty years of personal involvement in the women's movement and with other psychotherapists working to apply these new ideas to help our women patients. Therapists, friends, and patients have all been sources of stimulation and partners in the struggles and satisfactions of these years.

It should be stated that my patients, friends, and co-workers all reside in the San Francisco Bay area, an area notable for its high level of educated people, its political activity, and the large foreign and out of state population drawn here. Thus, my patients may not be "average" women. The women who come here from other parts of the country are often the seekers, those not satisfied with the status quo in their home towns and cities. San Francisco and Berkeley have a history of both political radicalism and sexual freedom, which, I believe, contributed to making this area a place where the women's movement flourished. This fact has an effect on therapist and patient alike.

In many ways society has made tremendous strides in the past twenty years in its view of women. We have gone from Playboy Bunny to the

United States Supreme Court. But Playmates still exist, with the dissemination of more and more degrading images of women in pornographic magazines, films, and videos. How can we understand these contradictions? One of the themes of this book will be the tremendous ambivalence toward women, especially women in power, that is experienced by both men and women. The number of women raising children alone continues to grow, as do the numbers of women and children living in poverty. For many women, the progress of feminists is a cruel hoax. Many issues reach across race and class boundaries. Fear, loneliness, low self-esteem, and dependency on men for status and approval cut across these lines, so that much of what I write about can be useful to therapists in clinics and social agencies as well as to private practitioners.

I discuss a great many writers from both psychoanalysis and feminism in this book, but there are many writers I have not mentioned. So many valuable books and articles exist, it was impossible to include them all. I have tried to select the authors whom I have found most stimulating, who have made the most significant contributions, and who are representative of certain streams of thought in this field. Many outstanding writers had to be omitted.

This book provides the theoretical background for a second book, *The Technique of Feminist Psychoanalytic Psychotherapy*, which focuses on clinical material. These books deal with issues of race and class mainly when they occur in the background of a private psychotherapy patient. Key issues, such as incest, wife battering, overeating, mother–daughter relationships, transference and countertransference issues between female patient and female therapist, patient–therapist sex, the fears of women, women at mid-life, aging, and abortion are discussed and illustrated with extensive case material. I recommend feminist psychoanalytic interpretations for many of the dilemmas common to women in therapy. I also show how the knowledge and application of both psychoanalytic and feminist theory can enhance the scope and the skills of the therapist and enrich the therapeutic process. The theoretical topics raised in this book will come alive in the therapeutic hour.

My hope is that male psychotherapists will read these books. It has been discouraging to me when attending conferences related to women in psychotherapy to note the paucity of men in the audience. Surely men are seeing women patients and need to familiarize themselves with the insights gained about women's psychology in these very productive years. A failure to do so will leave men ill suited for working with modern women.

It is my hope that these two books will provide both the theoretical background and the clinical framework for therapists to help their women patients who need a modern approach to the changing roles, goals, and conflicts inherent in women's lives.

1

THE PSYCHOANALYTIC THEORY OF FEMALE DEVELOPMENT

. . . science as something existing and complete is the most objective thing known to man. But, science in the making, science as an end to be pursued is as subjective and psychologically conditioned as any other branch of human endeavor.

—Albert Einstein

It is surprising that, in a field that places so much emphasis on introspection and internal dynamics and gives so little consideration to the forces of culture and society, the most repeated explanation for Freud's views on the inferiority of women is a simple reference to the Victorian times in which he lived. Even the recent and highly admired Peter Gay biography (1988) reiterates this truism: "Freud's attitudes toward women were part of larger cultural loyalties, his Victorian style" (p. 608).

In my view, this is only one of several factors that can help us place Freud's erroneous theories of female psychology in context. After all, "cultural loyalties" did not prevent Freud from shocking society with his theories of infantile sexuality, bisexuality, and the determining power of the unconscious.

THE INFLUENCE OF CULTURE AND RELIGION

At age 12 Freud planned to become a lawyer and go into politics. But by age 17, "Freud suddenly retreats from his search for power over men. He turns to the more sublime power over nature, through science, and he decides to study 'natural history'—biology to us today" (Jones 1953, p. 30).

I don't want to enter into the debate about whether or not psycho-analysis is a science, as that is not relevant. What is relevant is that Freud considered himself a scientist, was trained in medicine, and believed that his search for the truth was rational and objective, as in all scientific research. The question is: Has science, until quite recently an almost exclusively male preserve, been rational and objective about the physical and mental condition of women; or have scientists been unconsciously affected by the prevailing myths of their times, as promulgated by the Church, political and economic considerations, and, yes, even emotional biases? To the latter, my answer is yes on all counts.

When I was in the eighth grade at a junior high school in Santa Barbara, California, the girls and boys were divided for one period each day, when the boys took science and the girls took home economics. I have no memory of feeling there was anything wrong or unfair about this. I merely accepted it as a given and proceeded with my girlfriends to hate our home economics teacher and the class. One of the major components of our curriculum was learning to set the table properly, and this skill has served me well through the years. We also received an occasional lecture on sex, which included such statements as "when a girl allows a boy to kiss her it is like taking a pickle out of the pickle jar—the first one is difficult, but then the rest are easy." Another gem was that having a baby is like having a bowel movement, only much harder. One day, as part of her crusade against sex, our teacher described the dangers a woman faces in childbirth if she has gonorrhea. The girl sitting opposite me fell out of her chair in a dead faint. Naturally this caused quite a stir, but it had the positive result of slowing down our teacher in her fear campaign.

I relate this story to ask how it came about that girls were excluded from knowledge about science. Collections of old children's books com-monly include a *Boy's Book of Science*. I don't know what the boys learned in science class, as I never asked them. But I feel certain that every girl in my school got a clear message that this knowledge of science could serve no purpose in her life, that she was unfit for it, and that it was unfeminine.

THE CATHOLIC CHURCH AND THE PERSECUTION
OF WOMEN

It is hard to locate the beginning of misogyny in the Western world. But surely the Old Testament story of Creation was a significant and influential source. Ignoring the obvious symbol of the female giving birth, with all its power and wonder, the story—believed even today by fundamentalists—

tells how a male deity, God, created a male, Adam, who then was used to create woman. There is reason to believe that, in pre-Biblical times, creation and birth were related through the phases of the moon to menstruation, and so thought to be entirely in the power of women. Women were associated with fertility, and patriarchy did not emerge until the connection between sexual intercourse and impregnation was made, as a means of controlling the succession of male power and inheritance (Lederer 1968, p. 25). It is also The Old Testament creation story, specifically the banishment of Adam and Eve from the Garden of Eden, that propounds the view of woman as evil, as temptress, as weak-minded, and as the source of all the world's miseries. It has affected the Judeo–Christian world through the centuries. Nowhere in the history of religion have women been more persecuted than during the fourteenth through the seventeenth centuries, when the Catholic Church perpetrated the burning of perhaps as many as nine million persons, mostly women (some estimates say 20 to 1, others 100 to 1), as witches (Dworkin 1974, p. 130). This was a massacre of women who refused to conform to the Church, who were suspected of independent thinking or creative powers, and feared as sexually aggressive. It profoundly changed the course of the history of women.

> The most important document revealing the real meaning of the witchcraft mania is the *Malleus Maleficarum*. In 1484, Innocent VIII issued a special papal bull empowering two Dominican monks, Jacob Sprenger and Heinrich Kramer, to try witches in northern Germany. Since inquisitors met with some resistance, they composed a handbook, the Malleus, and more or less forced the faculty of the University of Cologne to endorse it in 1486. It was also given full legal support by Maximilian, King of Rome. . . . Six out of the seven chapters of the treatise deal with sex. . . . The basic charge against the witch as a night demon and seducer springs clearly from the experiences of a repressed and celibate male clergy. [Hayes 1964, pp. 151–152]

The following quotations from the Malleus show the extent to which women were accused of being evil, disgusting, and dangerous.

> It is not good to marry. What else is woman but a foe to friendship, an inescapable punishment, a necessary evil, a natural temptation, a desirable calamity, a delectable detriment, an evil of nature, painted with fair colors. . . . The word woman means the lust of the flesh. Perfidy is more found in women than in men. . . . Since they are feeble in body and in mind, it is not surprising they should come under the spell of witchcraft. . . . She is more carnal than man as is clear from her

many carnal abominations. . . . All witchcraft comes from carnal lust
which in women is insatiable. [Dworkin 1974, pp. 131–133]

This predates Masters and Johnson by nearly 500 years. Woman,
before the repression of her sexuality, was frightening. Hayes concludes
that this represents fear of the female organ, also evident in many cultural
myths around the notion of "vaginal dentata," and goes on to describe the
Malleus as a "product of the basic male anxiety . . . the hysterical fear of
castration" (p. 153). Hayes quotes the Malleus as asking "whether witches
can, with the help of devils, remove the member or whether they can do so
apparently by some glamour or illusion" (pp. 153–154).

And what then is to be thought of those witches who in this way
sometimes collect male organs, as many as twenty or thirty members
together, and put them in a bird's nest or shut them up in a box, where
they move themselves like living members and eat oats and corn as has
been seen by many as is a matter of common report? [Dworkin, p. 135]

Freud, educated in Catholic Vienna, believed 500 years after the
Malleus that women envied men their penises and became "castrating" as
a result. It seems to me that the basis for Freud's view lay as much in the
irrational beliefs about women that had been handed down from the
Church to the universities and into the medical schools, as in the data
supplied by his female patients.

The early origins of the medical profession were linked with the
Church and with the persecution of women. The thirteenth century saw
the establishment of European medicine as a secular science and a profession. Female healers were eliminated through their exclusion from universities long before the witch hunts began. According to Ehrenreich (1973),
"The great majority of witches were lay healers . . . and their suppression
marks one of the opening struggles in the history of man's suppression of
women as healers. . . . This new European medical profession played an
important role in the witch-hunts, supporting the witches' prosecutors
with 'medical' reasoning" (p. 6).

The partnership between Church, State and medical profession reached
full bloom in the witch trials. The doctor was held up as the medical
"expert" giving an aura of science to the whole proceeding. He was
asked to make judgments about whether certain women were witches
and whether certain afflictions had been caused by witchcraft. . . . In
the witch-hunts, the Church explicitly legitimized the doctors' profes-
sionalism, denouncing non-professional healing as equivalent to her-
esy: "If a woman dare to cure without having studied she is a witch and
must die." (Of course there wasn't any way for a woman to study.)

Finally, the witch craze provided a handy excuse for the doctor's failings in everyday practice: anything he couldn't cure was obviously the result of sorcery. [p. 19]

The economic motive is seen at work here, in what we would now term "restraint of trade." Witches' "magic" actually included medical skills and a thorough knowledge of herbal remedies, abortion, midwifery with pain-relieving drugs, reproductive and psychological processes, telepathy, autosuggestion and heterosuggestion, hypnotism, mood controlling drugs, analgesics, organic amphetamines, and hallucinogenics. So thoroughly were women healers discredited by the witch hunts that by the seventeenth and eighteenth centuries, male physicians were able to move into the last preserve of women's healing, midwifery, which barber-surgeons took over with the use of forceps, while women were legally barred from surgical practice. Midwives still practice in some European countries, but for the most part women who wished to be healers have been relegated to the "womanly" role of the nurse, subordinate to the male physician. Battles are still being fought over turf as midwifery is suppressed in the United States, and as—in other issues—non-M.D.s seek psychoanalytic training and psychologists seek hospital privileges.

Europe in the seventeenth century was a place of tremendous change. The industrial revolution was transforming the continent from feudalism to capitalism. The division between the home and the workplace was begun, and the varied economic roles that women had performed were being replaced—for the middle and upper classes—by the "housewife" role, with its tremendous implications for the economic dependency of women on their husbands. The birth of modern science and medicine emerged from the "Dark Ages." What was so promising for "mankind" was unfortunately sexually and intellectually repressive for women.

A FEMINIST ANALYSIS OF SCIENCE—EVYLYN FOX KELLER

The subject of male dominance in science and medicine has been excellently explored by Evylyn Fox Keller, a mathematical biophysicist, in *Reflections on Gender and Science* (1985). Keller's subject is "how the making of men and women has affected the making of science" (p. 4). What does it mean, she asks, "to call one aspect of human experience male and another female? How do such labels affect the ways in which we structure our experiential world, assign value to its different domains and, in turn, acculturate and value actual men and women?" (p. 6). She then describes the issue from a feminist perspective on the natural sciences as the deeply rooted popular mythology that casts objectivity, reason, and mind as male, and subjectivity, feeling and nature as female. In this division of emotional and intellectual labor, women have been the guarantors and protectors of the personal, the emotional, the particular, whereas science—the province par excellence of the impersonal, the rational, and the general—has been the preserve of men. The consequence of such a division is not simply the exclusion of women from the practice of science. That exclusion itself is a symptom of a wider and deeper rift between feminine and masculine, subjective and objective, indeed between love and power—a rending of the human fabric that affects all of us, as women and men, as members of a society, and even as scientists. . . . Thus, for example, the division between objective fact and subjective feeling is sustained by the association of objectivity with power and masculinity, and its remove from the world of women and love. In turn, the disjunction of male from female is sustained by the association of masculinity with power and objectivity, and its disjunction from subjectivity and love. And so on. [pp. 6–8]

A feminist analysis of science, Keller states, would mean exploring the interdependencies between subjectivity and objectivity and between feeling and reason. It would mean including an understanding of the ways in which the personal, the emotional, and the sexual affect scientists, the "personal investment scientists make in impersonality" (p. 10). Scientists' search for knowledge involves judgments about

which phenomena are worth studying, which kinds of data are significant—as well as which description (or theories) of those phenomena are most adequate, satisfying, useful and even reliable. . . . Predilections based on emotional (as well as social and political) commitments express themselves precisely in the domain of those social and linguistic practices that help determine, within the scientific community, the priority of interests and the criteria of success. . . . This is where the truly subversive force of ideology makes itself felt. [p. 11]

It is in this light that we can understand the astonishing participation of "scientists" in the witch trials and the unfortunate conclusions drawn by Freud and supported by his co-workers on the inferiority of women.

In seventeenth-century England, debates were waged among scientists over the "true" science. In the 1640s and 1650s, interest in Paracelsian philosophy, based on the hermetic tradition and concerned with the curative powers of chemically prepared medicines, drew on a philosophy that material nature was suffused with spirit, requiring

the joint and integrated effort of heart, hand and mind. By contrast, the mechanical philosophers sought to divorce matter from spirit and hand

and mind from heart. . . . At the end of the 1650's a fiercely bitter campaign was mounted against the alchemical "enthusiasts" by a number of the leading moderate churchmen—at least some of whom were soon to become founding members of the Royal Society. [pp. 44–46]

The Royal Society was established in 1662. It represented a victory for the mechanical philosophers and a triumph for the philosophy of Francis Bacon, who viewed science as power and the salvation of mankind. Prior to Bacon, knowledge had been viewed as wisdom; therefore his insertion of power was a great departure from earlier philosophic and religious concepts of knowledge. Additionally, Bacon's vision was clearly that of the mastery of man, as scientist, over a female "nature." "It is important," Keller points out, "to see how deeply Bacon's use of gender is implicated in his conception of mastery and domination. The fact that mastery and domination are, invariably, exercised over nature as 'she' can hardly escape our attention" (p. 34). Keller quotes Bacon:

> Let us establish a chaste and lawful marriage between Mind and Nature. . . . I am come in very truth leading to you Nature with all her children to bind her to your service and make her your slave. . . . I invite all such to join themselves, as true sons of knowledge, with me, that passing by the outer courts of nature . . . we may find a way at length into her inner chambers. [Men of science] have the power to conquer and subdue her, to shake her to her foundations. [p. 36]

Surely it doesn't take a Freudian to see male and female sexual imagery in these quotations of Bacon. Bear in mind that the burning of witches is still continuing in England and is making its way into America at this same moment in history. Bacon makes it clear that science is a man's world, a world in which heroic men (scientists) conquer a female (nature). The fear of women is being systematically defended against by domination over women and their exclusion from the masculine world.

Keller concludes:

> A circular process of mutual reinforcement is established in which what is called scientific receives extra validation from the cultural preference for what is called masculine, and, conversely, what is called feminine— be it a branch of knowledge, a way of thinking, or woman herself— becomes further devalued by its exclusion from the special social and intellectual value placed on science and the model science provides for all intellectual endeavors . . . to effect biases and perpetuate carica- tures. [p. 92]

These prejudices are frequently illustrated in the writings of Freud and the early psychoanalysts, and they produced biases toward women in psychoanalytic theory, which I will describe and for which I will propose revisions.

THE INFLUENCE OF JUDAISM ON FREUD'S VIEWS OF WOMEN

In addition to the Victorian view of science and objectivity as a male preserve, a second strong influence on Freud's views of women was his Jewish upbringing. An appreciation of Jewish traditional practices and teachings about women can help us to understand these influential forces in his family and community life and from his early education in Judaism. Although Freud was an avowed atheist, he always maintained his Jewish identity, however ambivalently. In 1897, he joined the local B'nai B'rith lodge and occasionally lectured there. He was sympathetic to Zionism, although even the major Jewish holidays were not observed in his home, while Christmas and Easter were celebrated. "At the same time," according to Gay (1988), "Freud believed that there was some elusive, indefinable element that made him a Jew . . . not faith . . . nor was it national pride." He wrote to his B'nai B'rith lodge in 1926, "But enough else remained to make the attraction of Judaism and of Jews so irresistible, many dark emotional powers, all the mightier the less they let themselves be grasped in words, as well as the clear consciousness of inner identity, the secrecy of the same mental construction" (p. 601).

Ernest Jones, in the second volume of his biography of Freud (1955), also stresses Freud's identification as a Jew.

> One cannot describe the man Freud without laying stress on the fact that he was a Jew. Though never orthodox or in any way religious he held together with his people, was a Governor of the Hebrew University in Jerusalem, and took an interest in all that concerned the fate of Jewry. . . . It is doubtful if without certain traits inherited from his Jewish ancestry Freud would have been able to accomplish the work he did. I think here of a peculiar native shrewdness, a skeptical attitude towards illusion and deception, and a determined courage that made him impervious to hostile public opinion and the contumely of his professional colleagues. [p. 427]

There is another point Jones stresses in regard to public opinion and Freud's Jewishness.

There is one respect in which it unquestionably played an important part, one to which he often referred himself. The inherited capacity of Jews to stand their ground and maintain their position in life in the face of surrounding opposition or hostility was very evidently highly pronounced in Freud, and he was doubtless right in attributing to it the firmness with which he maintained his convictions undeterred by the prevailing opposition to them. [p. 398]

Jones clearly does not view Freud's thinking as bound by "cultural loyalties."

Freud was born in 1856, in Frieberg, a small Moravian town, where the family lived in a Hasidic (orthodox) milieu. They moved to Vienna in 1859 and settled in the Jewish district. He had received Jewish religious training and had learned Hebrew, although he later forgot it, because his teachers in liberal Vienna emphasized ethical values and Jewish history. His father, however, did speak Hebrew, and both his paternal great-grandfather and grandfather were referred to as "Rabbi," meaning they were respected as scholarly in Jewish laws.

It is reasonable to assume that the young Freud's Jewish education included the major elements of the Talmud, including the *Pirke Avot (Wisdom of the Fathers),* which contains the teachings of Jewish scholars on Jewish law and tradition. Jewish ethics are in fact derived from the teachings of the Talmud. Additionally, Freud was surely aware of the inferior status of women in the synagogue and in religious rituals. Most readers are familiar with the orthodox tradition of segregating women in the back of the synagogue or the balcony and forbidding their full participation in the service, presumably for apotropaic purposes. Women did not receive an education and were not even taught to read. They did not count as persons—a religious service could begin only when ten men were present. Even the morning prayers said by the orthodox male testify to the inferior status of women. The man thanks God each day for not making him a woman. Taboos around menstruation declare women "unclean" for a period of ten days of each menstrual cycle. More specifically the Talmud (Goldin 1955) instructs:

And Talk Not Overmuch With Women, Even With One's Own Wife: It is a known thing that for the most part conversation with women has to do with sexual matters. That is why Yose ben Johanan says that much talk with them is forbidden, for by such talk a man brings evil upon himself (Maimonides). [p. 55]

And in the commentary that follows:

Yose ben Johanan is not restricting necessary conversation with one's wife, be it short or long, in such affairs as household needs or expenses or suchlike matters. For so long as a husband speaks with his wife about necessary matters, no evil comes about, because then the mind is concentrating on the advice it is receiving. . . . What the Sage warns against is unnecessary conversation, unnecessary greetings, chitchat of what has been happening and things of that sort. If it should sometimes happen . . . that the husband has gotten into a conversation over such things, he ought not to talk too much. And this applies even to his own wife, so that he will not bring evil upon himself, for he is a man and should be working or studying and not be distracted (Melri). [p. 55]

These quotations seem to equate sexuality with evil and thus evil with women. The primitive notion of contamination by women leads to an avoidance of women and to their segregation. Freud never refers to women as evil, but his notion of women as having less of a sense of justice, of being less ethical than men, had its origins in his early training and experiences with Judaism. There is also the self-fulfilling prophesy that if women are relegated to housekeeping and child care, are not permitted access to knowledge through reading, and are forbidden from studying the laws, they will not have the training and knowledge for making good judgments. The "chitchat" of women implies an inferior mind as Freud's statements do. "Freud stood firm: one should not allow oneself to be distracted or disconcerted by the 'protests of the feminists who want to press a complete equality of the sexes in position and value' " (Gay 1988, p. 516).

Here we recognize echoes of the Talmudic proscription that a man should not be "distracted" by talking with women, although Freud made exceptions for the women who admired him and wanted to work with him. It is common to point to the many women who were encouraged in psychoanalysis by Freud and who were respected contributors as evidence of Freud's liberalism on the question of women's roles. This is an intriguing apparent contradiction and has been explored from the point of view of the women analysts by Chodorow (1989). Early women analysts believed that home and child care were the natural roles for women, and in their personal lives they were responsible for these traditional functions, along with their professional work. They apparently accepted the notion that women who pursued careers were "masculine." It is perhaps for this reason that many women analysts specialized in work with children, a devalued component of psychoanalytic work. A subtle hint of this was brought to my attention at a psychoanalytic conference when a male analyst introduced a female speaker as a "child analyst." She corrected him, saying courteously that she was an adult analyst. I believe that the best way to understand the acceptance of women in Freud's larger psychoanalytic circle and his apparent comfort with their participation is to recognize that he was always the unquestioned authority and leader, the "Rabbi," and clearly held the superior status. It is significant to note that there were no women members of Freud's secret inner circle, the "Committee of the Seven Rings," which consisted of Freud, Karl Abraham, Sandor Ferenczi, Ernest Jones, Hans Sachs, Otto Rank, and Max Eitingon. In an incident also worth noting, Freud's daughter Anna—having seen Helene Deutsch wearing her white doctor's coat—told her father that, to prepare herself to be an analyst, she wanted to go to medical school. Freud balked at her desire to become a physician, persuading her to follow a career as a lay analyst (Gay 1988, p. 435).

FREUD'S FAMILY OF ORIGIN

This leads to the third significant influence on Freud's views of women: his family, and especially his relationship with his siblings. Freud was the eldest of seven surviving children. A brother who would have been the second eldest died young. Then came five sisters and the youngest, a brother, Alexander. Freud was recognized as a genius by his parents at an early age and was clearly the favorite child. His mother especially doted on him. He had power over her, and even, after a while, surpassed his father. He always had a room of his own, while his parents and six siblings shared three bedrooms.

> The family accepted Freud's boyish imperiousness with equanimity and fostered his sense of being exceptional. If Freud's needs clashed with those of Anna (the eldest daughter) or the others, his prevailed without question. When, intent on his school books, he complained about the noise that Anna's piano lessons were making, the piano vanished never to return. It was much regretted by his sister and mother alike, but without apparent rancor. [Gay 1988, p. 14]

Bank and Kahn (1982) analyze Freud's sibling position:

> Freud was the classic first-born who thrived by dominating; when he could not dominate, he tried to eliminate or ignore. . . . He was treated with a respect that verged on deference. His sisters, abetted by their mother, learned early to look up to him and to stay out of his way. Sigmund considered himself superior to his siblings. . . . He occasionally tyrannized his siblings, showing toward them that sense of privilege and entitlement that first-born males seem destined to live out. His mother did little to prevent [this]. . . . His personal autocracy in the psychoanalytic movement flowed naturally from the autocratic role that he had played out among his siblings. His younger brother, his only male rival, was his worshipful follower. [pp. 213–214]

I believe it is in the light of Freud's superior position in relation to his five sisters that we can understand both another factor in his unshaken conviction of male superiority, and also his acceptance of and comfort with a number of women "followers," whose abilities and contributions he welcomed.

On the intrapsychic level, one can conjecture that his clearly derogatory pronouncements about women could have been related to his resentment and rivalrous feelings toward his five sisters. No matter how much he was his mother's favorite, the birth and breast-feeding and caring for seven infants while Freud was himself quite young and needful of his mother's attention could have been a source of anger toward women, which, due to his remarkable gifts, he was able to maneuver into a position of favoritism and domination. Nevertheless, achieving and maintaining that position involved scheming, competition, and manipulation of his parents and siblings, which surely took a toll on the young boy and engendered deep antagonism to the female sex. The notion of women as "the dark continent," of female sexuality being "extraordinarily obscure" to him, sounds more like that of a man from an all male family. With five sisters, a mother, and an aunt in his home, young Freud surely had the opportunity to be aware of much more about women than he admitted. Imagine five girl babies being diapered many times daily and seven women menstruating in one household. A male child surrounded by females must make a strenuous effort to establish and maintain his male identity, and one way to do that is to distance himself from the female world by establishing a clear demarcation line to protect his maleness. Thus a "super-male" can emerge to counteract the anxiety of being sucked into the female world. This can help explain both Freud's pseudoignorance of the female sex, and his need to differentiate and distance himself through theories of the inferiority of women.

Gay refers to Freud as having said some "deeply offensive" and "at times scurrilous" things about women (p. 501). He also states that Freud's "professions of ignorance" about women were admitted "a little too cheerfully" and appear "almost willful, as though there were some things about women he did not want to know" (pp. 505, 515).

WOMEN IN VIENNA

What about the community of turn-of-the-century Vienna in which Freud lived, was educated, and practiced? The cause of feminism in Catholic Austria was slow and frustrating. An 1867 law prohibited "female persons, foreigners and minors" from engaging in any political activity, so suffrage groups were illegal. Even the Socialists did not include extending the vote to women in their platform. Austrian wives, according to the legal code of 1811, had to recognize their husbands as "head of the family and director of the household" whose orders the wife must follow. Austrian women who sought education and independence had to face "unsparing ridicule" (Gay 1988, p. 510).

No wonder Freud wrote to his fianceé, Martha Bernays, who was five years his junior, that he couldn't think of her as employed outside the home as it was foolish for his "tender, dear girl" to be a competitor. But why, we must ask, a "competitor?" Freud could not imagine a working wife as an independent producer and contributor to the marriage, adding to the stimulation of her companionship, but only as a competitor, because he was still too deeply and unconsciously distressed by the competition of his five sisters. His fierce jealousy of Martha's attention to other men also points to deeper meaning: hence, his well-defended denial of this competition in his love letters.

In forcefully rejecting the views of John Stuart Mill on the equality of women, Freud asserts "our ideal of womanhood." "Nature has determined woman's destiny through beauty, charm and sweetness . . . the position of women will surely be what it is: in youth an adored darling and in mature years a loved wife" (Jones 1953, pp. 176–177).

The whole issue of female envy of men, as in the concept of penis envy, takes on a more personal meaning to the originator in this context as well. Of course, there are important ramifications for a girl in observing the boy's penis and the recognition of the absence of a penis on her own body. But Freud's focus on this anatomical fact was blown out of proportion by his own repressed envy of the five girl babies who displaced him, even if only partially, and whatever anxiety he experienced upon seeing their penisless bodies. The jealousy toward his first brother, Julius, born when Freud was only 15 months old, turned to guilt when Julius died, but could also be a factor in the strength of his jealousy and in the projection of envy onto women.

We have seen how the major institutions in society—medicine, Christianity, Judaism, the state through its laws, and the patriarchal family—all were united in viewing women as intellectually and morally inferior to men. From the view of woman as the sexual temptress in the Creation story, and the image of her in the Middle Ages as dangerous, destructive, powerful, and sexually insatiable, an astonishing reversal occurred in the Victorian age to a model of middle-class women as dependent, powerless, asexual, and sickly. Sex was an imposition on their delicacy, and prostitution with lower class women was the way for men to satisfy the lustful passions now defined as belonging only to the male psyche and biology.

It is this fragile, sickly, asexual woman of the middle and upper classes (of course working-class women were toiling in the fields, the mills, the sweatshops and as domestics) who came to Dr. Freud with symptoms of hysteria and about whom his theories of female psychology were formed. How different those theories might have been had he had as patients the independent thinking women who were condemned to burn as witches, or some of today's high functioning career women and mothers.

FREUD'S THEORY OF FEMALE DEVELOPMENT

Although dissent flared up sporadically, such as in the papers of Karen Horney and Clara Thompson, "Freud's views on femininity largely carried the day among psychoanalysts; from the early 1930's onward it was established as more or less canonical for his profession" (Gay, p. 502).

Readers are most likely familiar with the Freudian theory of female development. But for review, I will state some of his major ideas about women with some commentary.

During the period he was evolving his ideas about women, Freud was also writing his major works and establishing psychoanalysis as the science of the mind. Much of this work still stands today, as both the theoretical foundation of our work as psychoanalysts and psychotherapists and as the technique for our patients' treatment. For example, *The Interpretation of Dreams,* published in 1900, is still the standard text for dream analysis and would apply equally to men and women. The theory of the dream as wish fulfillment, the role of the day-residue, the manifest and latent content, the idea that causation is represented by succession, and so on, all are gender-free. Particular dream interpretations made by an individual therapist may not be free of gender bias, however.

Freud's "Mourning and Melancholia" (1917) is another example of his work that is as relevant today as when it was written and that makes no distinction between depression in men and in women. Freud's theory of depression is based on the concept of ambivalence and avoidance of the open expression of hostility against loved ones. We are especially concerned with depression because it is so common in women patients. Freud's work can be applied in our analysis of the *mechanism* by which depression occurs, though we may have our own ideas about how the culturally proscribed role of women can contribute to a high incidence of depression in women and affect the *content* of women's depression. By combining Freud's theory of the formation of depression with a feminist analysis of the sources of depression in women, we can enrich both psychoanalytic and feminist theory.

There is really no question in my mind of the genius of Freud and of his great contributions to our knowledge. Yet I am intrigued by the question of why writers in our field keep going over and over what Freud said. Why must we keep interpreting and reinterpreting obsessively what each phrase does or does not mean, like the Talmudic scholar reading and rereading the same text? Freud's writings are like the Bible for psychoanalytic thinkers, as if they are the word given not by God the Father but by Freud the Father. Can he be both revered and faulted? I think so, as in the process each of us goes through personally, gradually recognizing that our parents are only human, that they have strengths and weaknesses, good qualities and bad. To see flaws in our parents need not mean not loving them. This capacity to tolerate ambivalence, to hold both feelings of love and admiration and feelings of anger and disappointment toward the same person, is what enables an adult child to continue to love a parent, wives and husbands to continue to love each other, and parents to love their children. We must be able to "love" Freud and respect his remarkable genius in opening up an entire new world to us, the world of the unconscious, and at the same time be able to recognize his biases and his errors.

FEMALE SEXUALITY

Freud's views on female sexuality were first given expression in his "Three Essays on the Theory of Sexuality," written in 1905 and revised in 1910, 1915, 1920, 1922, 1923, and 1924. In 1924, he wrote "The Dissolution of the Oedipus Complex"; in 1925, "Some Psychological Consequences of the Anatomical Distinction Between the Sexes"; in 1931, "Female Sexuality"; and in 1932, "Femininity." Freud was consistent in his observation that bisexuality was a characteristic shared by both men and women, and he believed that bisexuality was basic to our understanding of sexuality in both sexes. However, in many other ways Freud sees the little boy and girl developing quite differently. As many writers have pointed out, Freud (1925) does present his ideas as tentative: "I bring forward some findings of analytical research which would be of great importance if they could be proved to apply universally. . . . I feel justified in publishing something which stands in urgent need of confirmation before its value or lack of value can be decided" (pp. 183–184). And again: "This opinion can only be maintained if my findings, which are based on a handful of cases, turn out to have general validity and to be typical" (p. 193).

However, it took fifty years from these 1925 statements before the value of these ideas could be debated openly.

In the 1925 essay, Freud makes the following assertions. Boys and girls have the same first love object, the mother. The boy regards his father as a rival and would like to get rid of him and replace him with his mother.

However, the fear of castration forces the boy to abandon these desires. This desire for the mother is considered active. But the boy has a passive desire in accordance with his "bisexual constitution" to take his mother's place as the love object of his father. The boy's masturbation is suppressed by his mother, thus laying the groundwork for his castration complex.

The little girl must abandon her primary love object, her mother, in favor of her father. Initially, the father is her rival for mother's love. The preoedipal attachment to her mother is crucial and may extend for many years, but is markedly ambivalent. The crucial moment in the girl's sexual development is the discovery of the penis on a brother or playmate, and the recognition of it as the "superior counterpart of [her] own small and inconspicuous organ, and from that time forward [girls] fall a victim to envy for the penis" (p. 187). When the boy notices the girl's lack of a penis it forces him to believe in the reality of the threat of castration. It also "permanently determines the boy's relations to women: horror of the mutilated creature or triumphant contempt for her" (p. 187). The little girl "makes her judgment and her decision in a flash. She has seen it and knows that she is without it and wants to have it" (p. 188). She may hope to one day acquire a penis or refuse to accept the "fact of being castrated" and develop a "masculinity complex" (p. 188).

Freud enumerates several consequences of this discovery for the girl:

1. The wound to her narcissism leads to a scar, a permanent sense of inferiority, and a contempt for all other women.

2. She develops the character trait of jealousy, which becomes more prominent than in men because it is reinforced by displaced penis envy.

3. The girl loosens her ties to her mother, whom she holds responsible for bringing her into the world "insufficiently equipped" (p. 189), with genitals that are unsatisfactory.

4. The clitoris is viewed by the girl as inferior, and therefore "an intense current of feeling against masturbation makes its appearance," due to her "narcissistic sense of humiliation" (p. 190). Freud believed that masturbation is a masculine activity and that elimination of clitoral sexuality is a necessary precondition for the development of femininity, which he views as passive. The girl must shift her erogenous zone from clitoris to vagina and switch her object from female to male. Freud views this as an exhausting psychological task, weakening and depleting the girl for life.

5. The male is active, the subject; the female is passive, the object.

6. The girl replaces her wish for a penis with a wish for a child, and "with this purpose in view she takes her father as a love object" (p. 191) and turns against her mother with jealousy. Baby equals penis. The woman can only be fully satisfied when she has a son.

7. If the girl's attachment to her father "comes to grief" (p. 191) and must be abandoned, it may be replaced with an identification with him and a return to her masculinity complex.

8. In girls, the castration complex precedes and leads up to the Oedipus complex, making it a secondary formation, whereas in boys the Oedipus complex comes first and then "succumbs" to the castration complex.

It is clear from these descriptions that Freud took the male as the normal and the female as diverging from the normal. This accounts for the criticism of his phallocentric bias. In my view, the error of Freud's theory lies in how alone the little girl is in his picture. She is left to her inadequate reasoning and childish explanations based on her immature observations. There are no parents or others to ask questions of or to explain the differences and to tell her of her own "equipment" on the inside—her ovaries and uterus—her potential for pregnancy, for suckling, and for the enjoyment of her sexuality in intercourse when she becomes a woman. Even if Freud was right in saying that when a little girl sees the penis she wants one for herself, this jealousy can be short-lived if she is educated as to the reality of her own wonderful body parts. Perhaps in Freud's time he was correct to assume that none of these questions in the child's mind would be addressed by the parents, as sex was a taboo subject and parents were not aware of these issues in childhood sexuality, having thoroughly repressed it themselves. Now, thanks to Freud, parents are sensitive to the problems for both boys and girls in recognizing anatomical differences and can raise the subject with children, judging when they are ready and for what level of explanation. Girls are now told of their external and internal body parts, masturbation is no longer so savagely punished, and there is no longer a basis to believe that today's girls will develop the pathological consequences of what can best be described as ignorance. This all assumes a family atmosphere of respect for the mother, a mother who respects herself, and a society that does not have a double standard in economic, political, and sexual activity which would be the basis for a girl's conscious envy of boys. Surely, much progress has been made in this regard since 1925.

Woody Allen dealt with this issue quite amusingly in his film *Zelig*. He imagines himself a psychiatrist who has studied with Freud but disagrees with him on the subject of penis envy. "He thinks only girls have it," says Allen.

I disagree with Freud's idea that if the girl's attachment to her father "comes to grief" it may give place to an identification with him and thus a return to the masculinity complex. "Comes to grief" is very vague. Identifications come from positive and negative attachments. Those at the most disadvantage in life are those who are unable to identify with the strengths of a parent due to anger at parental rejection or mistreatment. If identification cannot occur with either parent, the outcome is grim indeed. The young women today who become doctors, lawyers, engineers, or business women have by no means all had relationships with their fathers that have "come to grief." Quite the contrary, many of them are close to their fathers and have their love and encouragement. Giving up on the little girl's wish to become the wife to her father does not preclude other avenues of positive identification with him. One wonders what in Freud's relationship with his daughter Anna might have been reflected in these theories. We know she strongly identified with her father, became a lay analyst, but never married or had her own family. She may have been a lesbian.

The Weakness of the Female Superego

Freud continues in his 1925 essay to develop his notion of the difference in superego development between boys and girls. In boys, the Oedipus complex is "smashed to pieces" by the shock of threatened castration and its objects are incorporated into the ego, forming the nucleus of the superego. The superego is the heir to the Oedipus complex. "The catastrophe of the Oedipus complex (the abandonment of incest and the institution of conscience and morality) may be regarded as a victory of the race over the individual" (p. 192). In girls this motive, the fear of castration, is lacking. Thus the Oedipus complex is only slowly abandoned or repressed, or it may persist into adult life. The following is the oft-quoted view of Freud on the result of this failure to dissolve the Oedipus complex and the lack of the fear of castration in girls:

> I cannot escape the notion (though I hesitate to give it expression) that for women the level of what is ethically normal is different from what it is in men. Their super-ego is never so inexorable, so impersonal, so independent of its emotional origins as we require it to be in men. Character traits which critics of every epoch have brought up against women—that they show less sense of justice than men, that they are less ready to submit to the great necessities of life, that they are more often influenced in their judgments by feelings of affection or hos-

tility—all these would be amply accounted for by the modification in the formation of their super-ego which we have already inferred. We must not allow ourselves to be deflected from such conclusions by the denials of the feminists, who are anxious to force us to regard the two sexes as completely equal in position and worth; but we shall, of course willingly agree that the majority of men are also far behind the masculine ideal and that all human individuals, as a result of their bisexual disposition and of cross inheritance, combine in themselves both masculine and feminine characteristics, so that pure masculinity and femininity remain theoretical constructions of uncertain content. [p. 193]

It is clear that Freud believed in the existence of a masculine and a feminine "nature," which translate into a masculine and a feminine sexuality in which the masculine is active and the feminine is passive. Thus, any activity on the part of the female, such as masturbation, is judged as masculine, and any passivity on the part of the male is judged as feminine. Freud accepts without question the validity of a concept of masculine traits and feminine traits. He expands the biological differences to include a complete division of all qualities that have to do with individual person-ality as influenced by culture and family training, and then deals with the obvious blending by calling it "bisexual."

Parenthetically, Freud's belief in the moral superiority of men is difficult to accept, considering that the vast majority of crimes—rape, incest, murder, robbery, and most crimes of violence—are committed by men. Men are also largely responsible for so-called white-collar and business crimes and such marriage-related crimes as wife beating and adultery. Even in our own field, the percentage of male therapists who engage in the forbidden practice of sex with their patients far outnumbers the percentage of female therapists who do. Additionally, it is men who decide to go to war and commit the innumerable atrocities of war.

In his supplement to the "Theory of Sexuality," Freud (1923) asserts that until puberty, male and female signify *phallic* and *castrated,* and the existence of the vagina is unknown to both boys and girls. In "Femininity" (1932), Freud changes his view of the association of masculinity with activity and femininity with passivity, pointing out the active elements in the mother's care of her children. However, Helene Deutsch maintained this dichotomy in her writings.

Freud (quoted in Chasseguet-Smirgel 1970a) wrote the following:

But we must beware in this of underestimating the influence of social customs, which similarly force women into passive situations. All this is still far from being cleared up. . . . The suppression of women's aggressiveness which is prescribed for men constitutionally and im-

posed on them socially, favors the development of powerful masochistic impulses, which succeed, as we know, in binding erotically the
destructive trends which have been diverted inwards. Thus masochism,
as people say, is truly feminine. [p. 13]

The libido, he states, is always masculine because it is active even though
it may have passive aims. Frigidity in women stems from a massive
repression of the libido in the service of female functions.

Finally, Freud makes one of the most disturbing of his remarks about
women, from the point of view of a psychotherapist:

> A man of about thirty strikes us as a youthful, somewhat unformed
> individual, whom we expect to make powerful use of the possibilities
> for development opened up to him by analysis. A woman of the same
> age, however, often frightens us by her psychic rigidity and unchange-
> ability. . . . There are no paths open to further development, it is as
> though the whole process had already run its course and remains
> thenceforward insusceptible to influence—as though, indeed, the dif-
> ficult development to femininity has exhausted the possibilities of the
> person concerned. [p. 15]

What are we to make of this? Could it have been true for the
middle-class, neurotic woman in turn of the century Vienna? If it was true,
was it also true of the nonneurotic women Freud did not see as patients? In
either case, where is Freud's sense of despair over this terrible fate or
proposals for alleviating this tragedy? No comment. He accepts this
deplorable situation as the inevitable fate of the female sex, doomed by her
anatomy and the exigencies of her difficult oedipal triangle. His apparent
total lack of sympathy or even concern has forced us to explore the reasons
for his complacency.

THE PSYCHOLOGY OF WOMEN—HELENE DEUTSCH

Helene Deutsch, a Polish-born Jew (1884), came to Vienna to attend
medical school and became a disciple of Freud, on whom she was able to
transfer her positive feelings toward her father, whom she admired greatly.
She became a member of the early psychoanalytic circle in the 1920s.
Deutsch was attracted to Freud because she considered him a revolutionary. In the 1910s she was a socialist in Poland, where she fought for the
rights of women and organized women workers. She had a strong influence
on the psychoanalytic theory of female development and thus on the lens
through which women patients were seen. She moved to Boston in the
1930s to flee the Nazis, and had a powerful influence on American

psychoanalysis through training and analyzing a generation of younger analysts.

Deutsch was clearly an active and ambitious woman, as were the other women in Freud's circle. This raises the question of how she could then theorize that women are by nature passive, although she has modified the term *passivity* to *activity directed inward.* Deutsch claimed she never intended to say that women must be mothers or that they should not work. Rather, she felt they should be free to choose, and she believed Freud's theories helped to liberate women (Gordon 1978). Nevertheless, her writings say some very negative things about women and became the target for feminist attack. Could she have been so eager to please Freud? "I was never angry at Freud, I was only worried he should not be angry at me" (Gordon, p. 23). It is her personal history that helps explain the dichotomy between Deutsch's active intellectual life and her theory.

Deutsch published her essay "Psychology of Women in Relation to the Functions of Reproduction" in 1925, and it is expanded in her books. In this essay (as quoted in Chasseguet-Smirgel 1970a) she proposes that for the girl or woman, sexual intercourse is a masochistic submission to the penis; and that sex is only pleasurable because intercourse is a prelude to parturition, which is itself "an orgy of masochistic pleasure" (p. 20). Thus, sexuality and reproduction are inseparably linked in women, and the child in the womb represents both a part of the woman's ego and the incarnation of the paternal ego-ideal. In her 1930 essay, "The Significance of Masochism in the Mental Life of Women" (also quoted in Chasseguet-Smirgel), Deutsch states that a woman's life is dominated by a "masochistic triad: castration-rape-parturition" (p. 21). She believes that frigidity in women is due to masochistic tendencies. Thus, sexual satisfaction is seen as masculine and frigidity as feminine. Women who never experience orgasm are perfectly healthy psychologically. They find full satisfaction and happiness in maternal giving. A woman's pleasure in sex thus comes from giving her husband pleasure. A strong orgasm in a woman is disturbing to her and creates anxiety. Her role is passive-receptive in intercourse, and she is truly feminine when she does not reach an orgasm, but simply relaxes after intercourse. The vagina is truly meant for reproduction, not for sexual gratification. The clitoris is the organ of pleasure; but of course the so-called clitoral orgasm was seen by psychoanalysts as immature, so women had best not expect anything from sex.

When I first read Deutsch's two-volume *The Psychology of Women,* which was published in the United States in 1944 and 1945, I found it fascinating and illuminating. It was 1968–1969, just before my involvement in the women's movement, so I had no feminist consciousness to bring to bear on what I was reading. The only point that I knew was wrong was the two-orgasm theory, clitoral and vaginal, because I had just read the

Masters and Johnson research that proved that theory incorrect (1966). Rereading Deutsch in 1971 I saw many flaws, and reading it again in 1990 it seems very outdated, related to a time that really no longer exists for women I know or for my patients. The direct association between intercourse and pregnancy, true prior to effective birth control, is now almost completely eliminated.

Freud based his theory of female psychology on his work with women patients, on his study of the perversions, and on his observation that a girl admired and coveted the penis when she discovered it on a brother or playmate (1925). Deutsch (1944) sees penis envy as secondary in the development of the female personality. She bases her theory that femininity is largely associated with passivity and masochism on the female sexual role and states that the fundamental identities *feminine-passive* and *masculine-active* apply to some degree in all known cultures and races. She stresses the importance of a healthy narcissism to ward off and master the dangers for the ego inherent in passivity and masochism. A woman who "resists these characteristics given her by nature" (p. 225) and who is unable to find a successful means of coping with this passivity feels dissatisfaction with her own constitution.

> In our view, the masculinity complex is characterized by the predominance of active and aggressive tendencies that lead to conflicts with the woman's environment and above all with the remaining feminine inner world. . . . From a therapeutic point of view it is important to realize that the masculinity complex often conceals not a protest against but a fear of the feminine function. [p. 289]

What comes through in a current reading is a very deep concern about women and their lives and a careful thought process in analyzing various "types" of women, but also a very negative, pessimistic, and at times even hostile view of women. One wonders how Deutsch must have felt about herself as a woman and whether certain depressive and masochistic features in her own personality influenced and biased her view of women. There is a pronounced view of a woman's life as fraught with difficulties, mortifications, struggles, dangers, disappointments, protests, renunciations, escapes, resignations, and trauma. For example, a comparison of her final chapter on the "Climacterium" (1945) with a current book, *Menopause Naturally* (Greenwood 1984), points out how a positive, optimistic woman physician can describe the very same period in a woman's life with a helpfulness and hopefulness that is in amazingly sharp contrast to Deutsch's resigned and pathological view. Of course this difference may also reflect medical progress, such as hormonal therapy during menopause, a change in attitudes within the medical community, and a change in the times as a result of the feminist movement.

Hostility is a strong word, yet in her final chapter Deutsch refers at one point to unmarried women as "old maids" (p. 471) and in another place to an unmarried woman as an "old spinster" (p. 482). In my mind, these are not professional terms, nor are they put in quotation marks in her text. They are words of social derision and have no place in a book by a helping professional. Also in this chapter she refers to some grandmothers as "wicked old women. Hence the term witch" (p. 486), again not in quotes. When she describes positive attempts by women to give their lives meaning and pleasure, an attitude of pity is conveyed rather than encouragement. No matter which way her women turn, they risk ridicule and remain defective. For example: "The transformation of a vain, worldly woman into a pious bigot is very typical, as witnessed in the German proverb: 'A young harlot, an old nun' " (p. 464).

I believe Deutsch's problem lies in her not analyzing this and other German proverbs in terms of their misogyny, rather than accepting them as some kind of wisdom. Descriptions that could be interpreted as positive are seen as either foolish or unfeminine. I believe her lack of optimism stems largely from her own personal life experiences. According to an interview she gave to the *New York Times* at the age of 93 (Gordon 1978), Deutsch was still saddened by the deprivation of her own opportunities at analysis:

> After I stopped analysis with Freud [he had terminated her to make time to resume work with the Wolf Man] I wanted to finish it. Freud had not time and was already sick, so he sent me to Karl Abraham in Berlin. But Abraham wrote Freud that he is too much my friend to analyze me. And so, I am sitting here waiting for analysis. [p. 5]

According to Deutsch's biographer Paul Roazen (1985), Freud looked upon divorce unfavorably and advised her to continue her marriage. When she went to Karl Abraham for analysis, Freud wrote to Abraham urging that the marriage not be terminated. "By the spring of 1923 she felt more trapped than ever" (p. 217). Abraham was in correspondence with Deutsch's husband, Felix (Freud's personal physician), and wrote to him as follows:

> The treatment has lately been having to go through a difficult stage, i.e., through the analysis of the masochism which turns out to be a main source of last summer's crisis but also upon which all other difficulties of the past years are based. It now seems to have been possible to put a stop to those tendencies. [p. 222]

The crisis of the past summer referred to was in Deutsch's marriage. Deutsch's analyst was taking advice from Freud and was in contact with her husband, sending him progress reports. This seems highly unusual, although perhaps it was common within the earlier small circle of psycho-analysts. I would wonder, however, if a male analyst in analysis would be treated similarly; that is, would the analyst give progress reports to his patient's wife?

It may be that Deutsch's unacknowledged anger about having her analysis with Freud prematurely terminated was acted out in her cold and cruel treatment of Margaret Mahler, who began analysis with Deutsch. Mahler had been highly recommended to Deutsch by Sandor Ferenczi. In Mahler's memoirs (Stepansky 1988), Mahler describes frequent cancella-tions by Deutsch and, finally, dismissal by her as suffering from "paranoid melancholia" and hence "unanalyzable" after fifty to sixty sessions, which in effect amounted to dismissal from training at the Psychoanalytic Insti-tute in Vienna (p. 63). Mahler received a letter from Anna Freud dismissing her from her "candidate" status. Mahler describes herself as crestfallen and depressed. She said, "Mrs. Deutsch seemed intent on making me feel like a second-class citizen within the ranks of analysis" (pp. 59–60). Mahler herself suggests that Deutsch was having countertransference difficulties working with her, and that assessment is surely accurate. I suspect Deutsch's avowed hatred of her own cruel mother, plus her abrupt dismissal by Freud, was reenacted in her cruel treatment of Mahler.

Why she was not more active in seeking completion of her analysis after moving to the United States may reflect a deep problem with passivity and masochism. According to Roazen, when Deutsch wrote about the conflict between motherhood and eroticism, she was writing about her own life; just as, when she theorized about the conflict between intellec-tuality and femininity, she was writing about her own unsatisfied yearnings to reconcile them. Roazen also tells us that Deutsch "whole heartedly despised" her mother and even in old age spoke about her as "unimagina-tively bad" (p. 7). The mother, Regina Fass Rosenbach, hated Helene and beat her. Deutsch idealized her father and identified with him. Her analysis with Freud did not include working through her relationship with her mother, and it is interesting to note in this regard that her two volume work on women begins at age 10, when the loosening of a girl's ties to her mother begins. We can speculate that Deutsch's very negative and de-meaning view of women may have a lot to do with both her terrible relationship with her mother and the unfortunate circumstances of her own two abortive efforts at analysis, which did not allow a working through of these painful and angry feelings.

In describing the turning away from the mother in both boys and girls toward reality as represented by the father, Deutsch states: "In girls, an additional motive arises from emotional reactions connected with the genital trauma, since they turn their resentment of their own inferiority against their mothers and make them responsible for it" (1944, p. 244). How differently this would read with the mere insertion of one word, *imagined,* before "inferiority." A feminist interpretation would be that if a girl felt inferior and rejected her mother, it would reflect a problem in the mother's feelings about herself as a woman that left her incapable of conveying to her daughter a sense of pride, dignity, and pleasure in the female functions and in the daughter's potential for a satisfying life. I have often met with this problem in women patients and have needed to work with them on their self-effacement and low feelings of self-esteem by tracing the source to their family origins. I certainly do not share such distorted feelings, and I am sure this gets communicated to my patients as I question the truth in such assumptions. What is the evidence for the statement that girls hold their mothers responsible for genital trauma? I worked with one woman who, through dream analysis, discovered that she held her father responsible, which made sense because her father was clearly the more capable and the domineering one in the marriage and family.

In addition, the old idea of the father representing the real world, "reality," which would have had some possible validity earlier in the century, must be altered when the mother also works in the "real world" and the child is aware of the mother's earnings and accomplishments. Of course there is still the early dependent attachment based on her nursing and likely primary responsibility for nurturing the child, but as parents do more sharing of even these early parenting tasks, this whole notion needs to be revised and, in some cases, abandoned.

The reality today is that anatomy is no longer destiny, with the birth control pill and medical advancements that so improve the health of children and women. Perhaps the nineteenth- and early twentieth-century women Freud and Deutsch saw in their practices and used as data for their theories, because they were not in control of their reproductive system, were always pregnant or nursing, and lost children to disease, did associate a woman's lot in life with pain. The masochistic women I see—and they are certainly still with us—are products of severe mother–daughter disturbance, with mothers who were sometimes depressed, often narcissistic and/or borderline, and incapable of giving real love to the daughter or protecting her from cruelty by siblings or fathers. These women experience their mothers as cruel, competitive, and resentful. They sometimes did get more love from their fathers, as seems to be the case in Deutsch's girlhood, and so are able to turn to men for attention, though not always successfully because of trouble transferring the anticipation of rejection and suffering from the maternal experience to men. Sometimes difficult, competitive, and even cruel sibling relationships play a considerable role in adult masochism as well.

Deutsch's theory that masochism and passivity are both constitutional in women and that it is "instinctual" to turn from a normal active, aggressive little girl to an inhibited, passive, masochistic woman does not, in my view, give enough weight to the very powerful forces of family and society that teach children daily how they should think, feel, and behave in order to win love and approval. If a girl learns that her only honorable identity is to be a wife and mother, and that the only way she will find a man to marry her is to pretend to be helpless and intellectually inferior, that is exactly what all but the most unusual girls will do. I can still remember as a teenager reading advice books that warned me not ever to let a boy think I was as smart as he was. Only very special girls had the courage to withstand the disapproval and isolation entailed in flouting these socially prescribed roles.

The contributions of Freud and his followers are exceptional, and much of their brilliant work is still of great value and applicable today, fifty to ninety years later, an occurrence not as frequent in other medical specialties. By correcting the biased views toward women that resulted from the pioneers' inability to be as purely objective and rational as scientists hope to be and as they believed they were, psychotherapists can still use all the valuable theories and tools of the psychoanalytic method to help our patients. Feminism has made a great contribution toward the critique of the Freudian theory of female development and the female character, and in questioning society's stereotyped views of women. In the following chapters I will describe these contributions and show how an integration of the feminist critique can correct these errors and enrich psychoanalytic theory and practice.

2

THE FEMININE MYSTIQUE AND THE FEMINIST WRITERS WHO FOLLOW

I married for ambition. Carlyle has exceeded all that my wildest hopes ever imagined for him, and I am miserable.

—Mrs. Thomas Carlyle

The publication of Betty Friedan's book *The Feminine Mystique* in 1963 marked the opening of the current stage of feminist activity in the United States, referred to at that time as the "women's liberation movement." By 1970 there were enough writings of importance emanating from this new wave of feminism for Robin Morgan (now Editor-in-Chief of *Ms.* magazine) to publish a widely read anthology, *Sisterhood is Powerful,* which constituted a call to arms for American women. Its contributors, fifty-four in all, constituted a Who's Who of influential feminists at that time, of whom some had already published books, and others would later expand their articles into books: psychologists, psychiatrists, writers, poets, artists, attorneys (Florynce Kennedy and Eleanor Holmes Norton), and women's liberation activists—a stunning and powerful collection. The country would never be the same.

Sisterhood is Powerful was followed in 1971 by another anthology, *Women in Sexist Society,* edited by Vivian Gornick and Barbara K. Moran. It contained the writings of thirty-one women scholars and activists but was more heavily weighted with women from the academic world than *Sisterhood is Powerful.* Nancy Chodorow, the sociologist, appears in this collection. In addition to the anthologies, the November/December 1970 *Transaction* appeared as a special issue on the American woman, as did the *Journal of Marriage and the Family* of August 1971. *Ms.* magazine began publication with a preview issue in the spring of 1972. The themes are similar. Women have been an oppressed majority. The patriarchal system has controlled women's lives and hindered their development through marriage, the law, religion, medicine, and the educational system, and in the working world.

The forebears of these women are many and influential (Morgan 1970a). They include the early woman suffragette Lucy Stone, who wrote in 1885: "In education, in marriage, in everything, disappointment is the lot of woman. It shall be the business of my life to deepen this disappointment in every woman's heart until she bows down to it no longer" (p. 632).

In 1869 John Stuart Mill, truly a remarkable man, wrote in *The Subjection of Women*: "Women are declared to be better than men, an empty compliment which must provoke a bitter smile from every woman of spirit, since there is no other situation in life, in which it is the established order, and quite natural and suitable, that the better should obey the worse" (p. 632).

A ROOM OF ONE'S OWN—VIRGINIA WOOLF

A twentieth-century writer of great genius and an extraordinary talent for writing, Virginia Woolf wrote her long essay, *A Room of One's Own,* in 1929. (It is interesting to note that this post-World War I period also was the time Karen Horney wrote her papers on feminine psychology, in which she began the critique of Freud's theories on women that continues today.) With imagination, wit, poetry, and elegance, Woolf writes about women as writers of fiction. Woolf wonders why one sex is so prosperous and the other so poor and what effect poverty has on women's fiction. What conditions, she asks, are necessary for the creation of works of art? A woman, she concludes, must have money and a room of her own if she is to write fiction. Woolf is attempting to deal with the fact that women have not produced any of the great works. She writes of the need of men to feel superior to women, and therefore to see women as inferior and to be terribly angry at any woman who does not stay in her place.

> Women have served all these centuries as looking-glasses possessing the magic and delicious power of reflecting the figure of man at twice its natural size. Without that power probably the earth would still be swamp and jungle. . . . That serves to explain in part the necessity that women so often are to men. And it serves to explain how restless they

are under her criticism, how impossible it is for her to say to them this book is bad, this picture is feeble, or whatever it may be, without giving far more pain and rousing far more anger than a man would do who gave the same criticism. For if she begins to tell the truth, the figure in the looking-glass shrinks, his fitness for life is diminished. How is he to go on giving judgement, civilizing natives, making laws, writing books, dressing up and speechifying at banquets, unless he can see himself at breakfast and at dinner at least twice the size he really is? [pp. 35–36]

In attempting to deal with the fact that there was no female writer comparable in majesty to Shakespeare, Woolf explores the lives of women in Shakespeare's England. In one of the pithiest paragraphs of this delightful book, she writes:

It would have been extremely odd . . . had one of them written the plays of Shakespeare, I concluded, and I thought of that old gentleman, who is dead now, but was a bishop, I think, who declared that it was impossible for any woman, past, present, or to come, to have the genius of Shakespeare. He wrote to the papers about it. He also told a lady who applied to him for information that cats do not as a matter of fact go to heaven, though they have, he added, souls of a sort. How much thinking those old gentlemen used to save one! How the borders of ignorance shrink back at their approach! Cats do not go to heaven. Women cannot write the plays of Shakespeare. [p. 48]

She concludes that in fact it would have been impossible for any woman to have written the plays of Shakespeare in the age of Shakespeare, and then takes us on an imaginary trip back to the sixteenth century to meet Shakespeare's sister, a "wonderfully gifted" girl named Judith, and tells what her lot in life would have been. Woolf's Judith is as "adventurous, as imaginative, as agog to see the world" as her brother, but she is not sent to school. In her teens she is betrothed to a neighbor's son, and when she cries out against it she is beaten by her father. She runs away from home to London and, like her brother, tries to get a job acting in the theatre. She is rejected and laughed at, but the manager takes pity on her. When she discovers she is pregnant by him she becomes so desperate that she kills herself. Woolf concludes, "a highly gifted girl who had tried to use her gift for poetry would have been so thwarted and hindered by other people, so tortured and pulled asunder by her own contrary instincts, that she must have lost her health and sanity to a certainty" (p. 51).

As late as the nineteenth century, Currer Bell, George Eliot, and George Sand all concealed their female identities in order to write. Woolf quotes outrageous statements of Englishmen such as Oscar Browning of Cambridge, who declared "that the impression left on his mind, after

looking over any set of examination papers, was that . . . the best woman
was intellectually the inferior of the worst man" (p. 55). In an observation
that predates Evylyn Fox Keller by nearly fifty years:

> But it is obvious that the values of women differ very often from the
> values which have been made by the other sex, naturally, this is so. Yet
> it is the masculine values that prevail. Speaking crudely, football and
> sport are "important"; the worship of fashion, the buying of clothes
> "trivial." And these values are inevitably transferred from life to
> fiction. This is an important book, the critic assumes, because it deals
> with war. This is an insignificant book because it deals with the feelings
> of women in a drawing-room. [pp. 76–77]

Woolf reminds us that the great male writers were, with a few
exceptions, men of means and well educated: Coleridge, Wordsworth,
Byron, Shelley, Landor, Keats, Tennyson, Browning, Arnold, Morris,
Rossetti, Swinburne. All but Keats, Browning, and Rossetti were university
men, and Keats was the only one not fairly well-to-do (p. 111). It is only
because a (fictional) aunt has died and left her 500 pounds a year for life
that Woolf herself is able to give up the menial jobs she has needed for
survival and become a full-time writer: "The news of my legacy reached
me one night about the same time that the act was passed that gave votes to
women. . . . Of the two—the vote and the money—the money, I own,
seemed infinitely the more important" (p. 37).

Toward the end of the eighteenth century, the middle class woman
began to write. By the early nineteenth century, four famous names had
emerged—George Eliot, Emily Bronte, Charlotte Bronte, and Jane Austen.
According to Woolf, "Save for the possibly relevant fact that not one of
them had a child, four more incongruous characters could not have met
together in a room" (p. 69). Here I believe Woolf misses a major point. The
"possibly relevant fact" is, I believe, a most significant fact. Why, we must
ask, did this marvelous essay not ignite the women of the Western world in
1929 in the way Betty Friedan's book did in 1963? Surely the prose is
superior, the logic is as compelling, and the historical facts are as mad-
dening and inspiring. Certainly the Depression is a major factor and then
World War II, but what about the 1950s? Simone de Beauvoir's book *The
Second Sex* was first published in the United States in 1952, but still there
was no major reaction. The most important reason is children. As long as
women did not have control of their anatomy, the reproductive system,
the revolution of the sixties and the following years could not occur. The
birth control pill and legalized abortion gave women that control. In 1960
the "pill" had been tested successfully and was ready for mass distribution
to all but those women whose Catholicism prevented its use. Legalized

abortion was available in some states in the late 1960s and became federal law in 1973, with Roe vs. Wade. The publication of *Sisterhood is Powerful* and the rapid growth of consciousness-raising groups meant the new feminist movement had been launched.

Other medical advances figured strongly as well. The introduction of penicillin, the polio vaccine, other immunizations against childhood diseases, and then antibiotics changed the job of motherhood. Childhood illnesses that had required two weeks of constant nursing were now either eliminated altogether or reduced to forty-eight hours. The death of a child changed from an accepted occurrence (half for God and half for me) to an unusual tragedy. The freedom for a mother to study and to work was dependent on these medical miracles. The dishwasher was another kind of miracle that entered our homes and lightened the load. Science, which had steadfastly excluded women, gave women the gifts she needed to fight her way into the world previously barred to her if she wanted marriage and a family. That historical dilemma, that terrible choice—career *or* wife and mother—no longer was forced upon women. Formerly, women's choices were limited to marriage, the convent, prostitution, the maiden aunt role, or "old maid" schoolteacher or other traditional female career. Now only psychological change was needed to take advantage of women's new opportunities. We discovered that the hurdles facing women were as great internally as they were in the universities, the marketplace, and their families. The "consciousness-raising" group became the vehicle for making these internal changes.

THE '60S COUNTERCULTURE

Another factor worthy of consideration in understanding the changing mood in the 1960s is the emergence of *Playboy* magazine and the Playboy mentality. *Playboy* began publication in December 1953. Playboy clubs followed. Although there had been a double standard of sexual morality for centuries, this had coexisted with the stable patriarchal family. Hugh Hefner promoted a free-wheeling sexual exploitation of women as part of a bachelor style of life. Men should no longer be bound by responsibility for wife and children but could lead a life of irresponsible hedonism openly and honestly. Adultery was out, casual sex was in. The lure of such a life-style was of course tremendous. For women, however, unless one was willing to be a "playmate," which probably would leave her over the hill by 25, marriageable men were no longer as likely to believe in marriage. For married men, many could not resist the seduction of this fantasy world of unlimited sexual gratification, and they abandoned wives and children to pursue the freedom of bachelorhood. Women were forced onto the job market to support themselves, and sometimes their children as well; and the 59 cents an hour they could earn for each one dollar a man could earn was not enough to support a family. Thus, for some women the women's movement represented a financial necessity as much as a political cause. It was not so much a desire for independence as being forced out of dependency by men who no longer saw themselves as bound to provide for women and children. Maleness was proven not by success in the market-place and being a "good provider" but by success as predators of young women. So when Friedan's book appeared in 1963, the soil was fertilized by growing resentment at male freedoms and female vulnerability.

In a fine analysis of the many factors leading up to the feminist movement, Barbara Ehrenreich argues in *The Hearts of Men* (1983) that the collapse of the breadwinner ethic had begun well before the revival of feminism and stemmed from dissatisfactions every bit as deep as those motivating the women's movement. She sees the antifeminist backlash of the right-wing as a backlash not so much against feminism as against the male revolt (pp. 12–13). Psychiatry had deemed marriage and the bread-winner role as the only respectable roles for men, with those not fulfilling these tasks described as "immature" and sexually suspect. Rebelling against the "grey flannel suit" stereotype, some men chose the "playboy" ideal of the single consumer; others became "beatniks," living in a Bohemian style that often meant finding an admiring female to support their "artistic talents"; and others were drawn to the "humanistic psychology" and "human potential" movement, spearheaded by Fritz Perls, who didn't think he should owe anybody anything and proved it by abandoning his wife and children and fondling women in public. "Do your own thing" was the password and "conformity" became the illness to be cured. Adapting to reality was the neurosis.

The use of LSD and marijuana helped to dissolve the work ethic and promote self-indulgence. Many men were cured of marital and paternal responsibility by this new wave of psychology. Psychoanalysis was defi-nitely out—it took too long and did not provide instant gratification—and feminism was ignored or ridiculed. I know of someone who went to a Gestalt weekend at which the group leader struck a woman for objecting to one of his techniques, telling her, "That will teach you to talk back to a man." Permanent relationships interfered with "growth." Divorce, here-tofore viewed as a tragedy, became an "opportunity for growth," a creative change, and the 1970s gave rise to a divorce epidemic that has not let up.

Another current during these years was the discovery by medicine that the stress of work was unhealthy for men. The Type A personality, the hard-driving man who was successful but was dying of heart disease, was warned to reduce stress by not working as hard. It was not until years later that the picture was clarified and smoking, high-fat diets, and lack of exercise were targeted as the real menace to male health. In the 1980s men were working hard again, but jogging and keeping fit and trim. But the warnings to men of stress leading to illness supported the psychology of rebellion from the white-collar-male provider role that had started in the '50s.

The counterculture of the 1960s, along with the anti-Vietnam War movement, put another nail in the coffin of traditional masculinity. Draft resisters were rebelling against the notion that real men go to war to fight and kill and do not question their leaders. The hippie culture, with its back-to-the-earth philosophy, also supported the male revolt. Many communes were supported by the women who collected welfare benefits for their babies, fathers known or unknown. Drugs, sex, and a general state of hedonism freed men of responsibility, and long hair, beads, and beards symbolized their new ideology. What Ehrenreich calls the "old financial bond between the sexes" was already dissolving when feminism moved into full force in the early 1970s. The antifeminist women who opposed the passage of the Equal Rights Amendment (ERA) feared that this would mean the end of their "right to be a housewife" and considered feminists either traitors or fools to let men off the hook from having to support them. They did not believe men could be trusted to be responsible husbands and fathers if women demanded equality.

THE FEMININE MYSTIQUE—BETTY FRIEDAN

Friedan's book was a psychological approach to the plight of women in the United States in the 1950s. The "mystique" really describes an internalized ideal of femininity, of being a devoted wife and mother, which resulted in the "housewife syndrome." Friedan, a writer for women's magazines, had graduated from Smith College in 1942 with a major in psychology. She received a fellowship to study toward a Ph.D. in psychology at Berkeley, but dropped out of the program and chose marriage instead. She recalls having severe doubts about what she really wanted, and was terrified of going on. She believed she had to choose between love and marriage, and a Ph.D. The book combines her interest in both fields, psychology and journalism; specifically, how the women's magazines were used in the post-World War II period to create an ideal of women as wives and mothers with no interest in careers, politics, science, or anything that did not immediately relate to their roles as wives and mothers.

Friedan started in 1957 by doing an intensive questionnaire of her Smith classmates, 200 women of the Class of 1942, to discover the source of "the problem that had no name." She interviewed experts on women from the fields of psychoanalysis, psychiatry, sociology, anthropology, medicine, and social work for their impressions, and she spoke with women's magazine editors. She then interviewed in depth eighty women at certain crucial points in the life cycle. From these women she was able to complete the puzzle of why so many American women who "had everything" were so dissatisfied and felt "trapped." By 1962 she had her answer. The ideal of femininity actually amounted to living vicariously through the lives of one's husband and children, and it was failing to meet the needs of women for the satisfactions of the pursuit of independent goals.

Friedan describes the "happy housewife heroine" of the four major women's magazines: *Ladies' Home Journal, McCalls, Good Housekeeping,* and *The Woman's Home Companion.* An editor at the *Ladies' Home Journal* tells her, "If we get an article about a woman who does anything adventurous, out of the way, something by herself, you know, we figure she must be terribly aggressive, neurotic" (p. 45). Friedan describes attending a meeting of magazine writers and hearing a man describe to the group the needs of the large women's magazine he edited: "Our readers are housewives, full time. They're not interested in the broad public issues of the day. They are not interested in national or international affairs. They are only interested in the family and the home. . . . You just can't write about ideas or broad issues of the day for women" (p. 31).

Friedan describes the feminine mystique as follows:

The highest value and the only commitment for women is the fulfillment of their own femininity. It says that the great mistake of Western culture, through most of its history, has been the undervaluation of this femininity. It says this femininity is so mysterious and intuitive and close to the creation and origin of life that man-made science may never be able to understand it. . . . Fulfillment as a woman had only one definition for American women after 1949—the housewife—mother. [p. 37]

Friedan then deals with the issue of autonomy for women. "The feminine mystique permits, even encourages, women to ignore the question of their identity. The mystique says they can answer the question 'Who am I' by saying 'Tom's wife . . . May's mother' " (p. 64).

It is my thesis that the core of the problem for women today is not sexual but a problem of identity—a stunting or evasion of growth that is perpetuated by the feminine mystique. It is my thesis that as the Victorian culture did not permit women to accept or gratify their basic sexual needs, our culture does not permit women to accept or gratify their basic need to grow and fulfill their potentialities as human beings, a need which is not solely defined by their sexual role. [p. 69]

Like Virginia Woolf in the 1920s, Betty Friedan, not being in the academic world, takes herself to a public library—in this case the New York Public Library—and goes back over bound volumes of American women's magazines for the previous twenty years. She finds that in 1939:

The majority of heroines in the four major women's magazines . . . were career women—happily, proudly, adventurously, attractively, career women—who loved and were loved by men. And the spirit, courage, independence, determination—the strength of character they showed in their work as nurses, teachers, artists, actresses, copywriters, saleswomen—were part of their charm. There was a definite aura that their individuality was something to be admired, not unattractive to men, that men were drawn to them as much for their spirit and character as for their looks. . . . These New Women were almost never housewives; in fact the stories usually ended before they had children. . . . It is like remembering a long-forgotten dream, to recapture the memory of what a career meant to women before "career woman" became a dirty word in America. . . . It seemed to mean doing something, being somebody yourself, not just existing in and through others. [pp. 32–34]

The last story of an independent woman appears in the February 1949 issue of the *Ladies Home Journal*. It is called "Sarah and the Seaplane."

Sarah, who for nineteen years has played the part of docile daughter, is secretly learning to fly. An elderly doctor houseguest says: "My dear Sarah, every day, all the time, you are committing suicide. It's a greater crime than not pleasing others, not doing justice to yourself." The next morning, Sarah solos. . . . [S]uddenly a wonderful sense of competence made her sit erect and smiling. She was alone! She was answerable to herself alone, and she was sufficient. . . . "I can do it!" . . . In bed that night she smiles sleepily, remembering how Henry [the flying teacher] had said "You're my girl". . . . No she was not Henry's girl. She was Sarah. And that was sufficient. And with such a late start it would be some time before she got to know herself. Half in a dream now, she wondered if at the end of that time she would need someone else and who it would be. [pp. 34–35]

From both a feminist and an object relations point of view, this is a clear example of a young woman separating from her mother, differentiating, and becoming an autonomous adult. By today's standards, Sarah is a healthy adult, but by Helene Deutsch's standards, Sarah would be a woman with a masculinity complex, fearful of her natural feminine functions. Unfortunately, many psychotherapists would have seen Sarah in a pathological light until the influence of the woman's liberation movement forced a reevaluation.

Sad to say, by the end of 1949, only one out of three heroines in the women's magazines was a career woman—and she was shown in the act of renouncing her career and discovering that what she really wanted was to be was a housewife. In issues of 1958 and 1959 Friedan could not find any heroines with a career or a commitment to anything in the world other than being a housewife.

We know that during World War II women were needed in the defense industry, and millions of American women went to work as the men went to war. "Rosie the Riveter" became a national heroine. When the war ended and the men returned, they needed jobs and the women were encouraged to return to their homes. During the war, day care for their children was provided at the plants; now women were told their children needed them at home. Some combination of economic realities and a perceived threat to men from women's proven competence joined with watered-down psychoanalytic theories of women's "natural" role to send women back home from "men's jobs," and resulted in a dramatic turnaround from their pre-war growing independence. It may not be just coincidence that Deutsch's two volumes on women had their first American printings in 1944 and 1945.

Friedan's book, in a chapter titled "The Sexual Solipsism of Sigmund Freud," clearly points the finger at psychoanalytic theory:

> The feminine mystique derived its power from Freudian thought; for it was an idea born of Freud, which led women, and those who studied them, to misinterpret their mothers' frustrations and their fathers' and brothers' and husbands' resentments and inadequacies, and their own emotions and possible choices in life. It is a Freudian idea, hardened into apparent fact, that has trapped so many American women today.
>
> The new mystique is much more difficult for the modern woman to question than the old prejudices, partly because the mystique is broadcast by the very agents of education and social science that are supposed to be the chief enemies of prejudice, partly because the very nature of Freudian thought makes it virtually invulnerable to question. How can an educated American woman, who is not herself an analyst, presume to question a Freudian truth? . . . I question its use, not in therapy, but as it has filtered into the lives of American women through the popular magazines and the opinions and interpretations of so-called experts. I think much of the Freudian theory about women is obsolescent, an obstacle to truth for women in America today and a major cause of the pervasive problem that has no name. [pp. 95–96]

After summarizing Freud's theory of penis envy and quoting some of his famous passages about the inferiority of women, Friedan links these theories with the focus of womens' magazines. She quotes from *Modern Woman: The Lost Sex,* by the psychoanalyst Marynia Farnham and the sociologist Ferdinand Lundberg, which equated feminism with penis envy, and was quoted repeatedly in magazines and marriage courses:

> Feminism, despite the external validity of its political program and most (not all) of its social program, was at its core a deep illness. . . . The dominant direction of feminine training and development today . . . discourages just those traits necessary to the attainment of sexual pleasure: receptivity and passiveness, a willingness to accept dependence without fear or resentment, with deep inwardness and readiness for the final goal of sexual life—impregnation. . . . It is not in the capacity of the female organism to attain feelings of well-being by the route of male achievement. . . . The psychosocial rule that begins to take form, then, is this: the more educated the woman is, the greater chance there is of sexual disorder, more or less severe. [p. 111]

Women are threatened with a loss of pleasure from sex if they are not submissive to men and do not give up any independent ambitions. In fact, modern research has shown the exact opposite to be true. Women with satisfaction in their work life are more, not less, likely to enjoy a rich sexual life because, as should surprise no one, feelings of self worth and competence lead to a general zest and lust for life. And what about the life of a woman after age 40 or 45, when her children have been raised and have left home and her job as mother is complete? Another gift to women from science is a life that extends long beyond childbearing age. It is of special interest that human females are the only mammals who live beyond childbearing age, and thus have 30 or perhaps 40 years of emptiness if they do not develop their ambitions for achievement in other areas of life.

A woman analyst who took an independent stand on this issue is Mildred Ash, who writes (1974) that when she and her women classmates went to medical school at the end of World War II, the feminine mystique was coming into being and women were being told to return to marriage and children. She had been warned that more education would decrease her chances for marriage and believed this was so, but she wanted to receive advanced education so much that she was willing to risk being an old maid. She says that she and the seventeen women in her class were obvious marriage rejects, but that most ultimately did marry. She quotes a classmate who said, "When I went into medicine it was like taking the veil." Once out in psychiatric practice the problems of women trying to live up to the ideal of wife and mother were seen clinically. "Childbearing was the outlet for feminine women whose creativity and competitiveness were ordained by the society of the 1950's to be kept out of the market-place and the halls of ivy. Women were being misled into thinking that the entire solution to their need for an identity came with motherhood'' (p. 411).

Ash tells the story of a woman patient married to a college professor and the mother of two children. She complained repeatedly in treatment that she could not organize her household work and errands, until finally her analyst jokingly reminded her that the psychiatric fee she was paying was equivalent to half-time household help for a week, and suggested she get a cleaning woman rather than a psychiatrist. However, the patient insisted that doing her own housework was necessary to fulfill her feminine role. Ash believes that the relationship of a woman to her household help can be a recapitulation of her troubled relationship to her mother, and that this may account for resistance to hiring a woman to clean. She points out that although a woman may give up her education for marriage and family, she may return to school later and should not be exhorted or preached at to do so sooner by her therapist.

Friedan criticizes Helene Deutsch and talks about the effect of psychoanalytic theory on American society, calling it an ''all-embracing American ideology, a new religion'' (p. 115). But she does not blame the practitioners of psychoanalysis for the feminine mystique. She points to the writers and editors in the mass media, ad agency motivation research-ers, and popularizers in the colleges and universities. Her analysis is limited, however, by her failure to search for deeper motives. She proposes neither an economic nor a psychological motive for those in positions of power who propagated these distortions. It would be later writers who would explore the deep, unconscious fears of women who are powerful and independent, fears that exist in men and women alike, based on deep dependency needs for all-giving, all-loving mothers who are never angry, who have no power to reject, condemn, deny, or deprive a child, but are only an ever-flowing breast to satiate our needs.

SISTERHOOD IS POWERFUL

Naomi Weisstein

Among the writers represented in *Sisterhood is Powerful* (Morgan 1970a), Weisstein, Sherfy, and Shainess are of special interest because they wrote about the fields of psychology and psychiatry from a new feminist view-point. Naomi Weisstein is described as follows in the notes on contribu-tors:

> [She] completed her NSF postdoctoral fellowship in mathematical biology at the University of Chicago, after obtaining her Ph.D. in psychology from Harvard University in two and a half years. She was understandably surprised therefore, that none of the twelve institutions to which she had been recommended for jobs would hire her. . . . She has been in SDS since 1960, in Women's Liberation since 1966, plays piano in a women's liberation rock group, holds a yellow belt in Karate—and is no longer surprised. [p. 647]

Since then, Weisstein has been professor of psychology at the University of Buffalo and visiting professor at Princeton University. Her article, " 'Kinde, Kushe, Kirche' as Scientific Law: Psychology Constructs the Female," renamed in 1971 "Psychology Constructs the Female, or the Fantasy Life of the Male Psychologist" (in Cox 1976, source of the following quotations) is an indictment of psychology, psychiatry, and psychoanalysis for its biased, invalid, and unscientific view of women that reflects the cultural consensus and wishes of the male researchers and clinicians who compose the theories. "And they support their theory and practice with stuff so transparently biased as to have absolutely no standing as empirical evidence" (p. 93).

> Psychologists have set about describing the true natures of women with a certainty and a sense of their own infallibility rarely found in the secular world. Bruno Bettelheim, of the University of Chicago, tells us (1965) that "We must start with the realization that, as much as women want to be good scientists or engineers, they want first and foremost to be womanly companions of men and to be mothers." "Woman is nurturance . . ." writes Joseph Rheingold (1964), a psychiatrist at Harvard Medical School. . . "anatomy decrees the life of a woman. . . . When women grow up without dread of their biological functions and without subversion by feminist doctrine, and therefore enter upon motherhood with a sense of fulfillment and altruistic sentiment, we shall attain the goal of a good life and a secure world in which to live it". . . . The central argument of my paper, then is this. Psychology has nothing to say about what women are really like, what they need and what they want, essentially because psychology does not know. I want to stress that this failure is not limited to women. [pp. 91–92]

"Years of intensive clinical experience," Weisstein asserts, allow one to make up theories, but not to claim validity for a theory until it has been tested and confirmed because of the contamination problems of clinical experience. She cites experiment after experiment to illustrate her point, concluding that "since clinical experience and tools can be shown to be worse than useless when tested for consistency, efficacy, agreement and reliability, we can safely conclude that theories of a clinical nature advanced about women are also worse than useless" (p. 95).

She goes on to point to research showing that, even in carefully controlled experiments, "the hypotheses we start with will influence enormously the behavior of another organism," and she stresses the influence of social expectation:

> In some extremely important ways, people are what you expect them to be, or a least they behave as you expect them to behave. Thus, if women, according to Bettelheim, want first and foremost to be good wives and mothers, it is extremely likely that this is what Bruno Bettelheim, and the rest of society, want them to be. . . . Behavior is predicted from the social situation, not from the individual history. [pp. 97–98]

An amusing example of what Weisstein refers to as the "maiming and selective truncation of the evidence in the service of a plea for the maintenance of male privilege" comes from the study of primate behavior:

> Invariably, only those primates have been cited which exhibit exactly the kind of behavior that the proponents of the biological fixedness of human female behavior wish were true for humans. Thus, baboons and rhesus monkeys are generally cited: males in these groups exhibit some of the most irritable and aggressive behavior found in primates, and if one wishes to argue that females are naturally passive and submissive, these groups provide vivid examples. . . . [The abundance] of counter examples has not stopped florid and overarching theories of the natural or biological basis of male privilege from proliferating. For instance, there have been a number of theories dealing with the innate incapacity in human males for monogamy. Here, as in most of this type of theorizing, baboons are a favorite example, probably because of their fantasy value: the family unit of the hamadryas baboon, for instance, consists of a highly constant pattern of one male and a number of females and their young. And again, the counter examples, such as the invariably monogamous gibbon, are ignored. [p. 101]

Later work has shown that in fact baboons and rhesus monkeys are controlled by dominant female families with males playing only a peripheral role in social organization.

Weisstein's article was excellent, influential, and angry. There was a lot to be angry about and she made constructive use of her anger through the mechanism available to those in the academic world, an attack on the theory and research of those in her field. The admiration at her contribution is illustrated by the fact that hers is the only article from *Sisterhood is Powerful* reprinted in the anthology *Woman in Sexist Society* (Gornick and Moran 1971). However, I believe she makes the error many writers do of falling into the either or trap. Like Bettelheim and Rheingold, she fails to integrate. When she says "psychologists must turn away from the theory of the causal nature of the inner dynamic and look to the social context within which individuals live" (Weisstein, p. 96), I must disagree. We must do both. It is true that the inner world will be strongly influenced by what is internalized from the culture, via the family; but experience in the women's movement as in the civil rights movement shows that changing the social context, desegregating schools, or admitting women to graduate schools (as in the case of Betty Friedan) will not solve the problem alone. Internal change or consciousness-raising, as it began to be called, would be necessary before women could make the transition to independence, achievement, and pride in their bodies and brains. The failure to include the unconscious world of the individual woman weakens feminist theory.

Mary Jane Sherfy

Mary Jane Sherfy, a psychiatrist on the faculty at Cornell Medical School in 1970, first published "A Theory on Female Sexuality" (1970) in the *Journal of the American Psychoanalytic Association* in 1966. Its description of the female capacity for multiple orgasms was based on the as yet unpublished Masters and Johnson research (1966), in which Masters states that a woman will usually be satisfied with three to five orgasms. Sherfy makes a distinction between satisfaction and satiation—apparently women are unable to ever reach complete sexual satiation. In a section entitled "Historical Perspective and Cultural Dilemma," she states that "neither men nor women, but especially not women, are biologically built for the single spouse monogamous marital structure" (p. 248).

> Many factors have been advanced to explain the rise of the patriarchal, usually polygamous, system and its concomitant ruthless subjugation of female sexuality (which necessarily subjugated her entire emotional and intellectual life). However, if the conclusions reached here are true, it is conceivable that the forceful suppression of women's inordinate sexual demands was a prerequisite to the dawn of every modern civilization and almost every living culture. Primitive woman's sexual drive was too strong, too susceptible to the fluctuating extremes of an impelling, aggressive eroticism to withstand the disciplined requirements of a settled family life—where many living children were necessary to a family's well-being and where paternity had become as important as maternity in maintaining family and property cohesion. [p. 249]

Sherfy credits the then-recent lifting of the social injunctions against the free expression of female sexuality to "the genius of Sigmund Freud" (p. 256).

Natalie Shainess

Natalie Shainess, a psychiatrist and psychoanalyst, was a lecturer in psychiatry at Columbia University in 1970. Her article, "A Psychiatrist's View: Images of Woman—Past and Present, Overt and Obscured," (Shainess 1970) was excerpted from the *American Journal of Psychotherapy* of January 1969. She reexamines the case of Freud's patient Dora as an example of the bias in psychoanalysis toward blaming the woman and believing the man when there is a divergence in the story told by each, leading to therapeutic error. A modern example of this would be the Clarence Thomas–Anita Hill controversy, where ultimately the word of a woman, although a professor of law, was considered less believable than that of a man.

In the case of Dora, Freud did not believe that a kiss from Herr K., a friend of the family and a man her father's age, was truly unwelcome to Dora. In fact, he interpreted the slap Dora gave to Herr K. as a seductive provocation, telling her she was jealous and revengeful. When Dora failed to return to continue her analysis, Freud called it an act of vengeance.

Shainess writes: "Freud considered this a sexual trauma—but only in the sense that it surely must have called up a distinct feeling of sexual excitement in the girl. That it might have been unwelcome, or experienced as a frightening or devastating outrage, did not occur to him—nor that sexual revulsion might be its consequence, rather than erotic stimulation" (p. 264).

Freud chose to believe the male—her father—and failed to see how her father was, in fact, seeking to protect himself because of his affair with Frau K. Dora's father accused his own daughter of fantasizing, thus protecting Herr K. This story stands as a parable for the Thomas–Hill hearings, and its theme can be traced to the mistrust of women in the witch burning days, when women were also accused of being vengeful—and burned for it, a most vengeful act.

Shainess goes on to give examples to illustrate her belief that men accuse women of seductiveness when in fact it is the man who should have the responsibility for observing the boundary. A gynecologist reports a hospitalized patient as "extremely seductive" for not wearing a robe, and then it emerges that he visits his patient between midnight and 1:00 A.M. The Group for Advancement of Psychiatry (GAP) report on "Sex and the College Student" in 1965 contains several examples of sexual involvements between male teachers and female students, and in all instances except one, the onus was placed upon the girl. The one instance where the teacher was held responsible was a case in which the teacher was a woman—and a lesbian. Shainess concludes as follows:

Most of the theoretical concepts relating to feminine psychology were evolved by men, who have tended to have a self-serving perspective on women, and have taken for granted the superior position they have occupied in most societies. Women also have tended to accept their allotted place. Freud's views also reflected a phallo-centric bias and have remained relatively unchallenged by women analysts. [p. 273]

PSYCHOANALYSIS, POLITICS, POWER, AND SEX

Juliet Mitchell

Three other important writers who influenced the women's liberation movement should also be mentioned: Juliet Mitchell, Shulamith Firestone, and Kate Millett. Mitchell published her first book, *Woman's Estate,* in 1971, and then *Psychoanalysis and Feminism: Freud, Reich, Laing and Women* in 1974. She was born in New Zealand in 1940, was educated at King Alfred School, London, did postgraduate work in English literature at Oxford, and lectured at Leeds and Reading University. In *Woman's Estate,* she situates the genesis of the woman's movement in the radicalism of the sixties, especially among educated young middle-class women. She describes the organization, concepts, and principles of women's liberation and then devotes a large section to the politics of women's liberation. She compares and contrasts radical feminism with Marxist feminism. The Marxist, or socialist, feminists believed that the system of capitalism is the basic source of the oppression of women, whereas the radical feminists focused on all men as oppressors no matter what the political system and believed the core problem to be male domination. Mitchell believes that "the oppression of women is intrinsic to the capitalist system—as it is not to the socialist," but that the weakness of socialism is that the "feminist consciousness has been inadequately represented in the formation of socialist ideology, as the oppression of women has, so far, been inadequately combatted in socialist revolutions" (pp. 95–96). In the second part of the book, she analyzes the position of women in the productive system and in the family and points out many contradictions in their roles in society.

In her final chapter, "Psychoanalysis and the Family," Mitchell is critical of the rejection of Freud by the American women's movement.

The mistake largely originates from the post-Freudian analysts themselves, and from a confusion between psychoanalysis and psychology and psychiatry. All three have reduced Freud's discovery of a science to

vulgar empiricism. . . . There is no doubt that the ideology that Freud's
followers picked up from Freud, and made into their "theory" is
pernicious to women and should be forcefully combated. It is also
pernicious to psychoanalysis. Psychoanalysis, exploring the unconscious and the constructs of mental life, works on the terrain of which
the dominant form is the family. In studying women we cannot neglect
the methods of a science of the mind, a theory that attempts to explain
how women become women and men, men. . . . That Freud, personally, had a reactionary ideological attitude to women in no way affects
his science—it wouldn't be a science if it did. . . . It is post-Freudian
empiricism that has trapped most of Freud's tentative analysis of sexual
differences into a crude and offensive rigidity. Notorious concepts such
as "penis envy" have come to suggest to most people a wish to seize the
object itself. But what underlies this concept is, in fact, Freud's much
more complex notion of the power of the image of the phallus within
human society. It is its social, ideological and psychic power, embodied
in the thing itself. It is this basic distinction and relationship between
the idea and its object (not in the Platonic sense) that is crucial to
psychoanalytic theory and that, missed, leads to all the absurdities of
empirical refutation. [pp. 164–167]

Mitchell refers to the work of Naomi Weisstein and is critical of her in
this regard. However, we must question her conviction that Freud's
"reactionary ideological attitude to women in no way affects his science."
At that time the issue of the objectivity of scientists and their work had not
been carefully explored, as we saw in Chapter 1 in the work of Keller
(1985), who shows that the personal, the emotional, and the sexual affect
scientists through gender-biased practices that determine, for example, the
priority of interests and the criteria for success.

In *Psychoanalysis and Feminism,* Mitchell (1974) explores Freud's
psychology of women in depth and then analyzes the work of Wilhelm
Reich and R. D. Laing. Finally, she analyzes the critiques of Freud by de
Beauvoir, Friedan, Eva Figes, Germaine Greer, Firestone, and Millett, and
also explores anthropological theory. She recognizes that Freud's critics
praise his observations of women but

condemn his analysis on the grounds of its biological determinism and
lament that he did not see the reality of social causation. . . . There is
justification for this attack only in so far as Freud often gave up on this
question when he reached the "biological bedrock" that underlay his
psychoanalytic investigation. But what Freud did was to give up
precisely because psychoanalysis has nothing to do with biology—
except in the sense that our mental life also reflects, in a transformed
way, what culture has already done with our biological needs and
constitutions. It was with this transformation that Freud was con-

cerned. What we could, and should, criticize him for is that he never makes his repeated statements to this effect forcefully enough in the context of his accounts of psychological sexual differences. To the contrary, disastrously as it turned out for the future of the psychoanalysis of femininity, it is just at these points that he most frequently turned back from the problem, leaving the reader with a nasty feeling that Freud's last word on the subject referred her to biology or anatomy. [p. 401]

The appearance of Mitchell's second book in 1974 was a relief to those of us practicing psychotherapy with a psychoanalytic perspective. Here was an established and respected English feminist who came to the defense of psychoanalysis. It is possible, she assured us, to be a feminist and to practice psychoanalytically without being a traitor to the cause, as much of the attack on us implied. Being a "Freudian" made one most unpopular in the American woman's movement in those years. However, she failed to search for any meaning to Freud's "turning back" from the problem. I suggest that perhaps this was the way in which his failure at objectivity was expressed. His own conflictual feelings about female autonomy may have inhibited him from pursuing these questions.

Shulamith Firestone

Shulamith Firestone's *The Dialectic of Sex* appeared in 1970. It is not surprising, since the women's liberation movement grew out of the political ferment of the 1960s, that political conflicts emerged among the leadership. The theories of Marx and Engels on the class nature of economic production and the resulting class antagonisms included reference to the oppression of women and claimed that the revolution in the economy would also liberate women. Mao was often quoted in his beloved statement that "Women hold up half the sky," and Engel's work on "The Family" was standard reading. However, the mistreatment of women in the socialist organizations quickly disabused many feminists of their faith in relying on socialist men to free them from male domination, as those very same men seemed committed to continuing that domination in political organizations and to reserving women as sexual objects. The quickest way for a woman to raise her status was to become the sexual partner of a male in leadership. With women relegated to sex, office work, and cooking, the Marxist concept of "surplus value" could be seen expressing itself in the labor of women in the movement.

Firestone articulated the position that the first division of labor was between man and woman, and thus a Marxist analysis is inadequate to an understanding of women's oppression. The natural division of labor that occurs because of the female's ability to bear children creates a situation of female dependency that has been exploited in the form of male domination. The only solution is to free women from childbearing through the scientific control of reproduction.

> Feminists have to question, not just all of Western culture, but the organization of culture itself, and further, even the very organization of nature. . . . For feminist revolution, we shall need an analysis of the dynamics of sex war as comprehensive as the Marx-Engels analysis of class antagonism was for the economic revolution. More comprehensive. For we are dealing with a larger problem, with an oppression that goes back beyond recorded history to the animal kingdom itself. [p. 2]

> We have attempted to take the class analysis one step further to its roots in the biological division of the sexes. We have not thrown out the insights of the socialists; on the contrary, radical feminism enlarges their analysis, granting it an even deeper basis in objective conditions thereby explaining many of its insolubles. [p. 13]

Firestone describes a feminist revolution that incorporates egological concerns, such as the population explosion, in her treatise against the oppressions of the biological family. She calls for a cultural revolution, an androgynous culture that she believes will be superior to the modes of either of the current male (technological) or female (aesthetic) cultures. For Firestone, "individualism goes along with a liberated sexuality and both are inherently opposed to motherhood" (Chodorow 1989, p. 84).

What Firestone clearly lacks is any appreciation of all the positive and satisfying aspects of motherhood and family life. As is so evident twenty years later, some women forego motherhood for other occupations, but the majority still choose to mother and to combine mothering with career. Jean Bethke Elshtain (1982) critiques the criticism of the nuclear family by the radicals within the women's movement for their failure to recognize that basic human needs for intimacy and security are met by the nuclear family, although she admits to weaknesses of the traditional family.

Kate Millett

Kate Millett's *Sexual Politics* was published in 1970 and was a major contribution to feminist theory. By politics, she is referring to concepts of power and domination in the social and sexual relationship between the sexes. Millett, a sculptor, had studied at the University of Minnesota and Oxford and had taught in literature and philosophy departments. She illustrates her thesis with lengthy examples from the literary works of D. H.

Lawrence, Henry Miller, Norman Mailer, and Jean Genet, although Genet, a homosexual, decries the power relationship in sex. Millett says that "he appears to be the only living male writer of first-class literary gifts to have transcended the sexual myths of our era" (p. 22). Millett traces the history of the sexual revolution from its first phase (between 1830 and 1930) through what she calls the "counterrevolution" of 1930 to 1960, in which she offers her criticism of Freud and post-Freudians. Mitchell (1974) critiques Millett on Freud as follows:

> Her [Millett's] work serves as a perfect illustration of my thesis that if you study Freud's writings on femininity outside the context of the main concepts of psychoanalysis they are doomed to sound absurd and/or reactionary. Millett shares with Friedan, Figes, and Firestone a wish that Freud had seen the social explanation staring him in the face. . . . It is not what Freud says about women and femininity that is the real stake in the battle, but the very objects of psychoanalysis themselves, sexuality and the unconscious, that offend. Of course without them Freud's theories of sexual differences become far easier to attack—for then, indeed, robbed of their entire significance, they are only prejudices. What all these writers share is quite simply a fundamental rejection of the two crucial discoveries of psychoanalysis: the unconscious and with it infantile sexuality. . . . Desire, phantasy, the laws of the unconscious or even unconsciousness are absent from the social realism of the feminist critiques. [pp. 351–354]

Millett's critique of the sexism in the writings of some of our male literary icons touched on some raw nerves, and the book was highly controversial. In the fall of 1970, Millett's face was on the cover of *Time* magazine. The book explores the pervasive influence of the patriarchal system and male supremacy in the family, education, the legal system, myth and religion, the economic world, psychology, and biology. Millett describes the ideology of sexual politics as follows:

> Hannah Arendt has observed that government is upheld by power supported either through consent or imposed through violence. Conditioning to an ideology amounts to the former. Sexual politics obtains consent through the "socialization" of both sexes to basic patriarchal politics with regard to temperament, role, and status. As to status, a pervasive assent to the prejudice of male superiority guarantees superior status in the male, inferior in the female. . . . Temperament involves the formation of human personality along stereotyped lines of sex category . . . based on the needs and values of the dominant group. . . . Sex role decrees a consonant and highly elaborate code of conduct, gesture and attitude for each sex. . . . The limited role allotted the female tends to arrest her at the level of biological experience.

Therefore, nearly all that can be described as distinctly human rather
than animal activity . . . is largely reserved for the male. [p. 26]

Two pieces of research that appeared during this period, though not
written by feminists, greatly contributed to the feminist cause and specifically to a psychoanalytic-feminist critique. The year 1966 saw the publication of Masters's and Johnson's *Human Sexual Response,* which proved
that there is only one kind of female orgasm and that it is centered in the
clitoris. Their research also discovered the capacity for the female to
achieve multiple orgasms. The study by Broverman and colleagues, "Sex
Role Stereotypes and Clinical Judgments of Mental Health," published in
1970, showed the influence of cultural gender stereotyping among practicing psychotherapists. In their work, behaviors and characteristics judged
by clinicians as healthy for an adult, sex unspecified, resembled behaviors
judged healthy for men but differed from behaviors judged healthy for
women. The implication was that, in the eyes of both male and female
therapists treating women at that time, a so-called healthy female would
not be regarded as a healthy adult. An "unhealthy" female who would
qualify as a healthy adult would be in the double bind of being judged as
unfeminine and exhibiting deviant behavior. It was shocking to learn that
to a majority of therapists, a healthy woman is more suggestible, less
competitive, more excitable in minor crises, more likely to have her
feelings easily hurt, more emotional, more conceited about appearance,
less objective, and more illogical than either a healthy man or a healthy
adult. This research was very helpful in drawing attention to the problems
for women in psychotherapy and the need to educate therapists with
feminist theory.

CONSCIOUSNESS RAISING

Feminism has never been a united movement. In addition to that between
the propsychoanalytic feminists and the antipsychoanalytic feminists,
other conflicts have existed: over a stress on equality versus a stress on
differences; revolution versus liberal reform; heterosexual solutions (such
as sharing housework and childcare) versus separatism and homosexual
solutions; and, for racial and ethnic minorities, the primacy of racism
versus sexism. One belief that has crossed all divisions is in the value of
consciousness-raising groups for individual women and to prepare women
for social action.

These groups illustrate two of the basic theories of feminism: (1) the
personal is political, and (2) that there are no individual solutions for

women's problems. It is in studying our own and other women's lives that we come to understand how the cultural devaluation of woman, and the diminishment of her intelligence and talents by focusing exclusively on her biological role, has affected the decisions women have made about their futures and led them to focus on their attractiveness to men and their mothering of children to the exclusion of developing their own abilities. When Friedan writes of her decision to drop out of graduate school, she does this because it illustrates her thesis. When I, in Chapter 1 of this book, describe how the girls took homemaking in junior high school while the boys took science, I illustrate and support my argument concerning exclusion of women from science. It is typical of women's writing in the past twenty-five years to include personal data along with other references. This seems inappropriate to those used to the "objective" style of academic writing. The consciousness-raising group process relied heavily on personal narratives in combination with generalizations drawn from society to foster the process of self examination and the perspective that the life of an individual woman reflects societal values and expectations. We struggled to understand how our sense of our self worth and the decisions we made reflected these values and expectations, which we ourselves had internalized.

The woman's movement actually grew out of the civil rights movement of the late 1950s and 1960s and the antiwar movement and "new left" of the '60s. Women workers in these movements to free oppressed people began to be conscious of their own oppression within those very movements. In 1966, women who demanded that a plank on woman's liberation be inserted in the Students for a Democratic Society (SDS) resolution that year were pelted with tomatoes and thrown out of the convention. Robin Morgan wrote a stirring piece called "Goodbye to All That" (1970b), indicting what she called the "counterfeit left" and urging women to fight for their own rights. She addresses men of the left-wing political groups, including the peace movement, hip culture, and publications such as *Rat,* and bids them "goodbye forever." In her moving conclusion, she addresses women:

> Women are the real Left. We are rising, powerful in our unclean bodies; bright glowing mad in our inferior brains; wild voices keening; undaunted by blood we who hemorrhage every twenty-eight days; laughing at our own beauty we who have lost our sense of humor; mourning for all each precious one of us might have been in this one living time-place had she not been born a woman; stuffing fingers into our mouths to stop the screams of fear and hate and pity for men we have loved and love still; tears in our eyes and bitterness in our mouths for children we couldn't have or couldn't not have, or didn't want, or

didn't want yet, or wanted and had in this place and this time of horror.
We are rising with a fury older and potentially greater than any force in
history, and this time we will be free or no one will survive. [p. 7]

The new-left women began forming small groups, to become known
as consciousness-raising (CR) groups. The National Organization for
Women (NOW), a group that allows men as members, formed in 1966, was
favored by more middle-class, professional, and middle-aged women and
was more in the liberal-reform tradition of American politics, but it also
organized CR groups for its members. By 1967 the small groups were
spreading to colleges and cities across the country, and by 1970 there were
over 200 in New York alone and they had begun spreading to other
countries (Morgan 1970a, p. xxviii).

In late 1969, I became aware of the women's liberation movement,
ironically by reading an article in *Life* magazine. I can still see the painting
of Eve on the cover with the heading "Eve was Framed" and remember my
astonishment. The article described CR groups forming around the country. I attended some large meetings in San Francisco and then formed a
group in Marin County in January 1970. It continued meeting until 1987.
Our group helped to form dozens of others and the word spread rapidly.
We met biweekly, and the membership was large and fluid for the first
year, then narrowed down to a group of four women who made a
commitment to regular attendance. One thing we learned that first year
was that mothers and nonmothers were not compatible in the same group.
The mothers wanted to talk about their children and the nonmothers did
not want to listen—they had different issues.

During the course of those years we shared our fears and triumphs,
joys, and sorrows. There was much criticism of the nuclear family in the
women's movement in the early years, but many women struggled to keep
their families together. We analyzed sexism in ourselves, in the media, in
the culture, in the Bible, and even in baboons. We struggled with it on all
fronts: in the office, the university, banks, mortgage companies, restrooms;
through hundreds of dinner parties; and, most painfully, in our marriages.
We told each other our tales and nourished each other with that fabulous
food, women's support. Our husbands were suspicious, felt threatened,
and were envious. They wished they could get that wonderful milk from
other men but they were all dry.

Over the years we earned one B.A., three master's degrees, and one
law degree (I already had my M.S.W.). Three of us divorced, our nine
children have gone to college, and at latest count we have eight grandchildren. We shared holidays with our families and felt like a big extended
family at those times. We took vacations with our children and once a year
a special weekend just for the four of us. We were all, at various times, in

individual psychotherapy, so it was possible to observe the way the individual work fed back into the group and how the issues the group was bringing up created the need for further individual exploration. Each complemented the other and deepened the psychological level of the group. One member became a psychotherapist during those years.

Other CR groups were shorter-lived, often lasting only one to three years. One major factor that connects all of them, however, is the exclusion of men. The theory behind this exclusion is that in the presence of men, women would not have the confidence to speak, men would dominate the discussion, and women would be told how they should think, feel, and behave. An important goal for the group was to encourage women to speak about their lives, their ambitions, their conflicts about independent achievement and success, their relationships, and their fear of social disapproval and loss of male love; and to get responses from other women. These conflicts were being reflected in the minds of women patients in those years as well, and what we learned about the needs of women in the groups was often transferrable to women in therapy.

Another important factor in all CR groups was dealing with competitive feelings between women. For so many years women had been raised to compare themselves—who is prettier, who has the better figure—and to compete for desirable males, that these competitive feelings had to be acknowledged, exposed, and dealt with in order for the honesty and intimacy of the group to develop. It was clear there could be no real trust among women as long as competitive feelings continued. Here too, there was crossover for women therapists in analyzing competitive factors in transference and countertransference work with women patients. This process took time and effort, as it does in psychotherapy. The concept of *sisterhood* implies this absence of competition, although it became clear this was a naive notion, since the existence of competition between actual sisters often was transferred from early family experience and became a basis for mistrust and competition in the group. Sisterhood can be a foundation for closeness, but only after competitive conflicts are acknowledged and dealt with.

We shared an awareness of how our lives had been constricted as women, how we had tried to live up to an ideal of femininity, and the price we had paid in personal development for social approval and romantic success. We became aware that the obstacles for change were as much internal as external, but that we were not alone—that this was a phenomenon among women all over the country—and that women could help each other because of profound historical and cultural similarities. Class and ethnic differences emerged but were secondary to the significance of gender stereotyping, around which we were able to form a bond.

The issue of male domination was often analyzed in the women's movement. We understood that this view of relationships effected the entire society, including women, and we were determined to free our-selves from this distorted view of human relationships. We recognized the distinction between content and process in discussions and were deter-mined that the process be cooperative, that each member have an equal voice in decision making, and that the process was as important as the result. The ideal of cooperation and consensus, as opposed to the author-itarian model of domination and submission, was easier to put into practice in the groups than it was in the family or the workplace, where centuries of tradition had established hierarchical forms of relationship. Marital tensions were high as women tried to institute the new cooperative form into long-standing marriages.

The contrast between the psychotherapeutic view of the individual problem and the CR view of a societal problem that is responsible for the problems of all women has often been stressed in the literature, but, in fact, the interaction of individual psychotherapy and the group was common for many of the women in the movement. This led to the development of *feminist therapy,* which will be explored in Chapter 4. The abandonment of anonymity and neutrality were major flaws in this approach.

The strength and encouragement provided by these groups have been a model for groups throughout the country that deal with a variety of issues. Although Alcoholics Anonymous (AA) groups had been meeting for years, the tremendous growth in self-help groups seen in the last decade has been a testimony to the value of group support for individuals in crisis and was given impetus by the success of CR groups. Psychotherapists have learned a lot from this model and have used issue-oriented groups in clinics and private practice for such problems as overeating; for assertiveness training; to help battered women, incest survivors, and male batterers; as well as in treating alcohol, chemical, and other dependencies. It is not always clear where a self-help group is appropriate and when a profession-ally led group is superior. What is clear is that the combination of individual psychotherapy and a group can be very successful for some patients and that in all these groups, professional or self-help, successful members serve as positive role models for the others. When money is in short supply, the ideal is professional individual psychotherapy combined with a self-help group.

During the course of the meetings of a CR group, individuals experi-enced rejections and disappointments in the outside world. Their growing anger at awareness of past injustices, combined with the legitimization of that anger provided by the group, led, in some cases, to angry confronta-tions with parents, friends, and husbands. Sometimes these confrontations resulted in severed relationships, and at those times the support of the group was especially vital. Depression at the realization of missed opportunities occurred, but often, with group encouragement, women divided housework, returned to school, and took up where they had left off ten or even twenty years earlier. Increased self-awareness, self-esteem, and consciousness of earlier needs to conform to the role of submissive and inferior wife enabled women to pursue higher academic goals than had been possible before the women's movement.

What is the secret ingredient of the group for women? What do we really mean by support? I have asked myself these questions in regard to the CR group I was in and the therapy group for women that I co-led for two years, in which I saw women make progress that they were unable to make in individual therapy alone. What makes change occur so quickly and so effectively? Women have a capacity for closeness, caring, and sharing that we bring to such groups from our earlier connections with our mothers, sisters, and girlfriends; but these voices have usually been a chorus of taboos: don't be too smart, protect your virginity, cater to the man, don't take a career seriously. Many inhibiting voices all reflect the mentality of the oppressed with instructions on how to withstand that oppression and find a safe niche within it. In a women's group those voices are defeated and a new voice emerges. As each woman tells her story or presents a current conflict, the group responds like a chorus, with a range of voices but blended in a harmony of anger at the oppression and rebellion against it. It urges each woman to throw off constraints, to take risks, to put herself on the line, to have the courage to become what she dreams of becoming by taking charge of her life in a self-affirming way that truly says "Goodbye to all that." The voice of the group says it's OK to be angry, to be ambitious, to give up the ideal of femininity we were taught by our mothers, teachers, aunts, and the media. It exchanges the old ideal of femininity as self-sacrificing with a new ideal of enlightened self-interest. Womanhood becomes proud where it had been self-abnegating, demands respect where it had been selfless, becomes strong and courageous where it had been suffering and timid. We become for each other the kinds of mothers and sisters we never had in order to become more like the men we had wanted to marry.

Consciousness implies inside and outside: awareness, integration, and working through. The CR groups are examples of a positive integration of feminist and psychoanalytic theory. An understanding of internal dynamics and resistances, combined with the intellectual challenge of a reevaluation of the past from a feminist/political point of view, plus some necessary analysis of group dynamics and individual projections in a therapeutic (for the most part) milieu, all combine to foster insight and change. To be able to express anger in an environment of safety, to feel release from the fear that "there is something wrong with me" as conflicts are shared, and to gain a sense of pride and dignity in being a strong woman without the fear of destructiveness and loss, is the successful outcome of the consciousness-raising experience.

RESISTANCE TO THE NEW FEMINISM

The backlash against the women's movement was widespread. Women faced scorn, ridicule, and hostility at demonstrations and in the media as well as from their families, friends, and community. The leaders were often targets for contempt and vicious attacks. The internal changes required by men showed powerful and irrational resistance. Christopher Lasch (1979) wrote:

> The reasons for the recent intensification of sexual conflict lie in the transformation of capitalism from its paternalistic and familial form to a managerial, corporate, bureaucratic system of almost total control: more specifically, in the collapse of "chivalry," the liberation of sex from many of its former constraints, the pursuit of sexual pleasure as an end in itself; the emotional overloading of personal relations; and most important of all, the irrational male response to the emergence of the liberated woman. [pp. 322–323]

Using a psychoanalytic framework, Lasch analyzes male resistance to feminism:

> Today, impotence typically seems to originate not in renunciation of the mother but in earlier experiences, often reactivated by the apparently aggressive overtures of sexually liberated women. Fear of the devouring mother of pre-Oedipal fantasy gives rise to a generalized fear of women . . . [which,] closely associated with a fear of the consuming desires within, reveals itself not only as impotence but as a boundless rage against the female sex. This blind and impotent rage, which seems so prevalent at the present time, only superficially represents a defensive male reaction against feminism. It is only because the recent revival of feminism stirs up such deeply rooted memories that it gives rise to such primitive emotions. Men's fear of women . . . appears deeply irrational, and for that reason not likely to be appeased by changes in feminist tactics designed to reassure men that liberated women threaten no one. [pp. 346–347]

Teresa Bernardez-Bonesatti, a psychiatrist, reported in 1976 on the reaction of male therapists to all-female groups. She decided to form therapeutic groups of women to find out if they could be more useful than mixed groups in helping women with their conflicts around aggression and autonomy, and was surprised at how skeptical and negative the reactions of many of her colleagues were to her plan. They viewed the women's therapy groups as dangerous and expressed fear of increasing alienation between the sexes and even the fear that such groups would encourage the paranoid projection of all women's inadequacies onto men, precluding self-exploration.

> The idea of women's groups appeared to bring to mind the spectre of women who would turn out domineering and angry and who would find it easier to turn to revenge upon men. My suggestion is that the therapists saw these dangers because they were supporting the idea (although repudiating it consciously) that women have been "kept down," relegated to devalued positions and restricted in their choices and that they live under this tyranny with resentment, that if "liberated" they would feel fully justified in imposing upon men similar treatment and in so doing they would be acting in identification with the aggressor. . . . The notion that the female is frail and vulnerable and requires the protection of the male has been born of the necessity to reverse the dreaded instance in which the vulnerable male is at the mercy of a powerfully destructive female. [p. 64]

"The Impotence Boom"—*Esquire*

In October 1972, *Esquire* magazine ran a cover story with the headline "The Impotence Boom (Has it hit you yet?)," with a front page picture of a shocked handsome nude male looking down at what we assume is a limp penis. The article, titled "What is the New Impotence, and Who's Got It?" by Philip Nobile, refers to an article in *Medical Aspects of Human Sexuality* (October 1971) reporting that four out of the five sexologists in a round table agree that "impotence is most definitely increasing." Nobile reports on a paper published in *Archives of General Psychiatry* of March 1971 by a psychoanalyst, Dr. George L. Ginsberg, in which Ginsberg states that the sexual expectations of the American middle-class woman have changed from the ideal of virginity to the ideal of multiple orgasms, and that this naturally has affected the "war between men and women" (Nobile's words). Nobile quotes Ginsberg, who believes there are cultural changes creating a disequilibrium between young men and women, and that this cultural trend constitutes a significant etiological factor in their anxiety-producing impotence:

> While impotence has always existed, it now takes on an additional form. . . . There is a reversal of former roles. . . . The role of the put-upon Victorian woman is that of the put-upon man of the 1970's. Unconscious transmissions of feminine revenge by an aggressive

manner and overassertiveness may enhance a man's castration anxiety with consequent fear of the vagina. [p. 95]

It would seem that Ginsberg is hypothesizing hostility when there may just be simple lust and desire for sexual pleasure and gratification, but, according to Nobile:

Although Ginsberg fingers liberated women for upsetting the sexual applecart, he really does not blame them for the new impotence. That would be like blaming Cesar Chavez for the rising price of lettuce. Women should expect a decent erection and a half-decent orgasm in congress. If men fail to provide the wherewithal, they can scarcely escape sanction. "This is not a question of women's lib," insists Ginsberg, "but rather the way a man perceives it, that social pressures were perceived by the man as his having to *perform* some demand that he was not ready to satisfy." [p. 96]

The article continues with some debate among psychiatric experts on whether or not the theory of a "new" impotence is valid. This is not my concern. I am citing this article to illustrate the fears that emerged in response to the women's movement and the resistances that followed those fears. An understanding of the psychoanalytic theory of resistance, as applied in psychoanalysis and psychotherapy, is a most useful approach for feminists in appreciating the opposition they encountered to ideas that seemed so just and rational to them. I found that an integration of the theory of resistance with the feminist analysis of sexual politics was most helpful in both public and private discussions.

Resistance in psychotherapy is the patient's defense against treatment because of what treatment forces the patient to recognize about his or her past and present behavior and relationships. It may take many forms, such as coming late to an appointment, not being able to remember a dream, or missing an appointment due to complicated circumstances that might appear to an untrained person to be legitimate. We understand that in recognizing facts about the past and bringing back the feelings associated with certain persons and events, the patient is going to be confronted with feelings so strong that it will take tremendous energy to handle his or her reactions, and that when this is done, it will be almost impossible to return to former ways of relating and behaving. The recognition will produce pressure to make changes, and these changes can be excruciatingly difficult to decide upon and to carry through. Thus we are sympathetic with resistance, rather than critical of it, because we know it serves a protective function for the patient and that these changes will go to the very core of his or her existence. We don't pressure or hurry our patient because of the seriousness of the consequences, not only for him- or herself, but for parents, children, spouses, business partners, and friends who will be affected. We also know that it is the patient who must bear the burden of facing the unknown with no real assurance that it will be easy or successful and, as important, that it will not seriously hurt others.

In my observations of people's reaction to the Women's Liberation Movement, I believe that the same set of factors is present. The movement is leading people to think about their relationships and their behavior and the resistance to self-examination is equally as strong when the confrontation comes through the media or at a lecture or dinner party as in psychotherapy because of the pressure to reevaluate and change that is involved. The subject of women's liberation arouses very strong feelings of distrust, fear, and anger and then defenses against these feelings. Common defenses are humor, minimization, rationalization, and the more serious mechanisms of distortion of reality through denial, externalization, and projection.

It is a commonly held belief that in any relationship one person must be dominant and the other submissive. This undemocratic doctrine is often followed with the assumption that men are more suitable for the dominating role. The popular French phrase *vive la difference* is one that men and women have chuckled over for years with the knowledge that this has something to do with sexual pleasure and excitement. The plot is played out with a script that each knowingly follows, with the inevitable result that they land in bed together. Implicit is the assumption that the male is the pursuer, the female is coy, and the male dominates through his successful seduction. The woman is overcome and submits to the skill and aggressiveness of his approach. If they marry, his dominance will pervade their decisions as well as the bedroom. It is common in discussions of women's liberation that a man will say "vive la difference," and that a woman will say, seductively, that she *likes* being a woman. My impression is that the woman who takes this point of view is pandering to the men in the audience. She has been "liking" this role for so long and is so dependent upon it she can't imagine any other way of relating to a man. She doesn't know of any qualities other than her passivity and eagerness to please that make her valuable or attractive to a man.

The man who has said "vive la difference" would have a great deal of difficulty knowing how to approach a woman on any but the standard terms: that he is strong, firm, protective, powerful, and superior. They are both frightened of the assertiveness and strength of women in the movement because they are afraid that their sexuality will dissolve with the loss of this dominant–submissive gesturing. Could it really be that if a woman lit her own cigarette her date wouldn't be able to get an erection?

What is the significance of the differences that clearly exist between men and women? Basically, men can only be fathers and women can only be mothers. Everything else is so mitigated by cultural factors that it is extremely difficult to separate biological givens from cultural cause and effect. Science has shown that there are definite hormonal differences between males and females that produce differences in sexual as well as nonsexual behavior. An oft-quoted study showed that women who were treated with male hormones during pregnancy bore female children who were markedly aggressive and "unfeminine" (Levine 1971). These findings may reflect biases of the investigators, but, apart from that, they must be balanced against findings underscoring the enormous cultural effects of identifying a child as male or female and relating to him or her with the prescribed cultural expectations. Patients who have, because of the ambiguity of external genitalia, been assigned a gender role by the family, and then are later discovered to possess genitalia of the opposite sex, are so heavily inculcated by age 3 with the mistaken gender role that their sexual identification is irreversible (Hampson 1965).

Some women and men in our society seem to be victims of cultural learning in just as fatal a degree as the misassigned patients above. For women who have been reared with a strong concept of femininity as being child-like—that is, weak, silly, dumb, incompetent, uncoordinated, dependent, fearful, and so on—the enormity of the task of changing this self-concept, of turning this "doll" or "chick" into an adult woman, is nearly as great as that of changing the sexual identification of one of those unfortunate misidentified males or females. With increasing control of conception, pregnancy, and childbirth, the quotation "anatomy is destiny" is best applied to the human brain. It is in the human brain where, to date, no differences between the male and female have been discovered, and it is the products of the brain that make man's superior physical strength less significant as technology replaces muscle power. Survival depends on controlling weapons of destruction and on limiting childbirth. Margaret Mead has compared the freeing of women from childbearing to the freeing of men from tilling the soil. It used to take the full labor of a man to produce food for his family. Improvements in agricultural and stock-raising methods freed some men to be artists, scientists, politicians, and so on. We are now at a threshold in history when women are being freed to pursue art, science, or politics; or, if they wish, to continue to bear and rear children, just as some men choose to remain on the land. The woman's liberation movement is a response to these historical changes. As in all periods of transition, we are faced with a cultural lag that causes stress and conflict for men and women, some of which is reflected in the rising rate of divorce.

The traditional lives of men and women have created within our society two separate cultures that have existed side by side in a state of mutual distrust and hostility. Just as the fall of Adam was blamed on Eve, we have continued to project our weaknesses onto the opposite sex. Because men have controlled the arts and the media, women have fared worse in their public image—witness, for example, the proliferation of mother-in-law jokes and stereotypes, while the father-in-law role has remained untouched by ridicule. However, we should not underestimate the power of each separate gender-culture to transmit its own images apart from the media. The word is passed down from mother to daughter and from father to son not to trust the opposite sex. Daughters are told that men are after "one thing," their bodies. Men are told to beware of women as they only want to trap and then enslave you with a "ball and chain" and spend your money. Marriage is somehow supposed to miraculously join the two enemy camps in peace, love, and harmony.

In the work world men and women have been separated as well, through the perceived distinction between "women's work" and "men's work." Now women are moving into previously male professions, such as medicine and law, and into other male occupations as well, and demanding equality. The woman telephone "repairman," the woman "mailman," the woman "chairman," and even the woman "congressman" who is aggressive and asserts her power; combined with the wife who can earn as much or more than her husband, the respectable single woman who has affairs with several men, wives "swinging" along with their husbands—it is examples such as these that are shaking the very foundation of our society, the traditional beliefs about "man's work" and "woman's place." It is extremely threatening to all, even the most secure and successful persons, to see these cultural lines crossed. A woman in an administrative position with men reporting to her, or a man doing housework, are loosening the lines we have all counted on to help us conform to society's expectations—to assure us that we are doing the right thing, that we belong. A lot of frightened men and women are watching these changes and are confused, resentful, and angry about them. They want things to remain the same, so they can feel comfortable with their old stereotypes and ways of behaving and relating. They often need help in facing these changes and in working through their conflicts to make constructive adaptations.

Feminists experienced much frustration and discouragement at times, when they felt misunderstood, misinterpreted, and victimized. Gloria Steinem, in her book *Outrageous Acts and Everyday Rebellions* (1983), tells us that she was called variously a lesbian, a communist, and, by Al Capp, the "Shirley Temple of the New Left." Capp also compared her to the mass murderer Richard Speck (p. 22). One of the most offensive attacks and most difficult to bear was

seeing displayed on newsstands all over New York a *Screw* magazine
centerfold of a woman with my face and glasses, a nude body drawn in
labial detail, a collection of carefully drawn penises bordering the page,
and a headline instruction to PIN THE COCK ON THE FEMINIST.
Feeling helpless and humiliated, I sent a lawyer's letter to *Screw*'s editor
Al Goldstein—and got back a box of candy with a note that said "Eat
It." Only Bella Abzug's humor rescued me from my depression. When
I explained to her about this nude centerfold in full labial detail with my
face and head, she deadpanned, "and my labia." [pp. 23–24]

Steinem talks about "learning not to read" hurtful articles, "occasional bomb threats," frustration at "not being able to retain the legal rights
to your own life," and "anger at seeing survival issues ridiculed or
misunderstood" (p. 24). Accusations of man-hating and lesbianism were
especially common experiences for feminists. As a professional therapist, I
was fascinated to observe the paranoid mechanism of projection on a mass
level. Attacks by other women in defense of their chosen lives as housewives were also common and easy to understand. Clearly there were many
instances of insensitivity on the part of women in the movement that made
housewives feel deprecated and attacked. However, the vituperation of the
outcry against feminists by other women had a lot to do with the fears of
women who were unprepared for competing in the marketplace and who
saw the women's movement as a danger to their financial security. Here the
issue of equality versus difference in gender roles became evident. Women
often were not trained to be self-supporting, and were in fact not treated as
equals in the pay scales. To speak of equality thus meant to ignore the
economic realities that would have to be struggled with in the courts and
that are still not fully resolved, such as "equal pay for equal work" and the
economic issues contained in the Equal Rights Amendment.

"Women Power"—*Ramparts*

Another example of hostility among intellectual men can be found in a
cover of *Ramparts* magazine in February 1968, titled "Women Power." It
showed a woman from her shoulders to her groin, wearing a tightly fitted,
very low-cut black dress revealing deep cleavage. This headless woman
shocked and angered *Ramparts*' women readers, causing an outcry of
letters and cancellations; it was even rumored to have contributed to the
divorce of the managing editor, Robert Sheer. However, if we follow the
line of reasoning developed by Christopher Lasch, quoted in the beginning
of this section, the cover is not hard to understand. Education and native
intelligence have no effect on the unconscious. The male editors were thus
left to act out, in the broad use of that psychoanalytic term, their "deeply

irrational . . . blind and impotent rage'' against women. The article itself, by the magazine's editor Warren Hinckle and his wife Marianne, is a good piece on the Jeanette Rankin Brigade, a women's march on Washington that was held in January 1968 to protest the war in Vietnam. Rankin, 87-years-old at the time and still active, had been the first woman ever elected to the House of Representatives. Other than its repeated references to the women organizers as the ''ladies,'' common in those days, the article's content presented no problem and it was nice to have the women's peace movement recognized.

Norman Mailer's ''The Prisoner of Sex''—*Harper's*

One of the most vitriolic attacks against the leadership was made by Norman Mailer, who was obviously enraged by Kate Millett's attack on the sexism in his writing. *Harper's* magazine of March 1971 devoted nearly the entire issue to Mailer's long essay ''The Prisoner of Sex,'' which comprised nearly fifty full pages of text interrupted by only a few ads and by a four-page insert of illustrations. This insert, called ''An Arcade for the Game of Love,'' consists of ''designs for a set of machines that artist Rene Schumacher is constructing down to the last wire spring, ball bearing, screw and socket,'' which he calls ''Girl Game'' (pp. 73–76). The insert is in itself deserving of commentary. It is so horribly sexist, so totally dehumanizing of women, that one would expect to see it in *Playboy* or *Hustler*. Robot-like images of women, their naked bodies pink, brown, or yellow, are displayed on games with prominent nipples and pubic triangles. Four large targets have as their bull's eyes a breast and nipple, buttocks and labia, genitals and labia (front view), and an open mouth with red painted lips. One set of drawings includes changing numbers for eyes; in another target, painted lollipops are shown in women's mouths. What could possibly have motivated the editor, Willie Morris, to publish something so insulting to his female readership in an intellectual magazine? It is even more perplexing that he chose this particular issue (for the insert) and that he placed it in the center of the Mailer piece, which is a diatribe against the women's movement. If this was intended as satire, I suppose the commonly heard accusation against women in those years, that we had no sense of humor, would have been his response to my objection.

But the baddest ''bad boy'' of them all, Norman Mailer, in his *Harper's* essay, gleefully spews forth his views on the proper place for the female sex with unconcealed bigotry, as in this description of Bella Abzug: ''Bella! the future Congresswoman with bosoms which spoke of butter, milk, carnal abundance, and the firepower of hard-prowed gunboats'' (p. 44). Mailer feigns dismay that the television audience attending an interview in which he declared, in reply to a question by Orson Welles, that "women should be kept in cages," did not appreciate his cuteness nor his sense of humor.

> He [Mailer is referring to himself] had grinned broadly as he said this, delighted with the gasp which came up from the audience. Television audiences always reminded him of the bathers at Acapulco. The temperature of the air was 90 degrees, the temperature of the water was 90 degrees—one passed from one medium to the other with a minimum of sensation. So, too, was the passage of comment on television. Therefore this last bright sentiment poured ice cubes down everyone's back. He could feel electrons shuddering. And was pleased with himself, pleased that he might be the last of the public entertainers to cut such an outsize hunk of remark in the teeth of growing piety over the treatment of women. Even Welles was solemn about the matter. . . . The trouble with television is that you had to give direct responses, and most of his ideas were paradoxes. . . . What romantic zeal to think an audience would seize the dialectical spring of the idea, would recognize that no man who thought women should be kept in cages would ever dare to declare such a sentiment. Think of the retribution! No, the machines were moving in to replace such humor. The flat reaction of the television audience reminded him of his most pessimistic belief— that the spirit of the twentieth century was to convert man to a machine. If that were so, then the liberation of women might be a trap. [p. 46]

The feminist analysis of his essay is clear. This is a man who hates women, needs to dominate them; and who is an example of the dangers to women of a patriarchal ideology that, in the hands of a prominent literary figure—and of the male-controlled media that publish him and others like him—becomes even more frightening. An analysis of this quotation from a psychoanalytic perspective contributes to its feminist analysis, and the integration completes our understanding of this extremely gifted but very emotionally disturbed man. Remember, the writer here is the same man who, in 1960, stabbed second wife, Adele Morales. (Would *Harper's* select a woman writer to expound on the men's movement if she had stabbed her husband? I rather think that fact would disqualify her.) Mailer's capacity to externalize is enormous: Welles is dismissed as "solemn"; the audience is ridiculed as dull and lifeless, in need of awakening with ice cubes; television is the enemy of a complex and creative artist such as himself, and would turn him into a machine; how stupid they all are not to recognize the "dialectical spring" of his ideas, but after all, how can he expect ordinary people to comprehend the profound nature of such contradictions. In addition, we see here examples of many defense mechanisms described by psychoanalytic theory besides externalization. There is, for example,

Mailer's severe denial of his hostility and sadism; intellectualization is used extensively; and a hint of paranoid ideation appears in the idea of a "trap" by unnamed forces who are attempting to control his "humor" and his "romantic zeal." One doubts that Mailer would find it humorous if a German appeared on television and, "grinning broadly," said that he thought Jews should be kept in cages. Mailer divulges on the first page that he and his fourth wife have just separated and that he is experiencing sorrow over this loss, but either the sorrow is not deep enough, due to his narcissistic pathology, for him to pause and reflect on his four failed marriages; or he cannot tolerate the pain; or both. He launches instead into a lengthy and clearly over-determined attack on the women's movement, describing himself, in the aftermath of Kate Millet's critique,

> chewed half to death by a squadron of enraged Amazons, an honor guard of revolutionary (if we could only see them) vaginas. . . . And there were the legions of Women's Liberation. He had a vision of thin college ladies with eyeglasses, no-nonsense features, mouths thin as bologna slicers, a babe in one arm, a hatchet in the other, gray eyes bright with balefire. It was hard to think of himself as one of their leading enemies. Four times beaten at wedlock, his respect for the power of women was so large that the way they would tear through him (in his mind's eye) would be reminiscent of old newsreels of German tanks crunching through straw huts on their way across a border. [pp. 43–44]

These passages reveal the projection of Mailer's enormous and violent rage against women. His visions of violence and, at the same time, the helpless, childlike dependency that, when frustrated, produces this impotent rage, show their primitive oral character in the two references to "thin" (as in dry). Contrast the passage on the heavy-bosomed Abzug, where he is lured by an abundance of milk, only to be violently destroyed by her "firepower." Mailer had earlier described himself as unable to live without a woman, a "prisoner of wedlock," and, in the title, a "Prisoner of Sex."

Mailer saves his most vicious attacks for Kate Millett, as he tears into her book *Sexual Politics.* He starts the essay by referring to her, appropriately, as Millett, but as his wrath builds he shifts to the insidiously demeaning personal form "Kate," who is referred to alternately as a "pug-nosed wit" (p. 60), "Kate-baby" (p. 62), a "mouthpiece for a corporate body of ideas" (p. 65), a "literary Molotov" (p. 70), and a "true species of literary Mafia" (p. 71), whose writings are a "scum of hypocrisy" (p. 65) and whose mind is "totalitarian to the core" (p. 68). Perhaps we are to imagine him as Petruchio, taming the shrew. He goes on for many pages

about menstruation and the female orgasm, and defends Henry Miller and
D. H. Lawrence against distorted and unfair criticism by "Kate," in which
she always, according to Mailer, misses the metaphor, misses the subtleties.
Mailer concludes: "Women must have their rights to a life which would
allow them to look for a mate. And there would be no free search until they
were liberated" (p. 92).

He is willing to "let her" do this and "let her" do that and "allow
her" the other. After what must have been weeks of reading and thinking,
after producing fifty pages on the results of his thinking, he still hasn't got
the point. The days of his deciding what to "let" women do are over.

LIVING IN TRUTH—VACLAV HAVEL

In his 1984 essay "The power of the powerless" (in Havel 1989), Havel, the
playwright and current president of Czechoslovakia, writes of life in a
dictatorship—a dictatorship enforced by an army and secret police. This
kind of dictatorship need not be concerned about controlling the minds of
its citizens, because it can control their behavior. Another kind of dictatorship is over the mind; and in a democracy, where behavior cannot be so
rigidly controlled, it is control over the minds of the citizenry that is
essential. The patriarchal system has permeated every aspect of life: every
institution, both private and public; every art form and medium of
communication. It therefore in effect has dictated the culture of male
superiority and control in our democracy, so that opposition has remained
meager and easily quashed since the country's inception (except for the
victory over women's right to vote). As demeaned and stereotyped as black
people—brought here in chains—have been in the United States, it is
noteworthy that a black man preceded a white woman to the U.S. Supreme
Court by fourteen years (Thurgood Marshall was appointed in 1967, Sandra
Day O'Connor in 1981).

The chains on the minds of women have been imposed externally, but
also abided by internally, for reasons Havel well understands. He refers to
the psychology of wanting to belong, to be a member of the group, which
keeps individuals from questioning and rebelling. The terrible loneliness
and isolation of being a dissident is too painful for most of us to bear. If we
view male supremacy as an ideology in the same sense that Marxist-
Leninism is an ideology, than Havel's characterization of the Communist
dictatorship can be applied to our analysis of the resistance to change in our
sexual roles. Havel explains that the Communist system then in power in
his country differs from a classical dictatorship, which takes power by
overthrowing a ruler and thus can itself be overthrown by a different ruler.
Also, classical dictatorships lack historical roots, whereas Communism has

the authenticity of having been established by a social movement with a "correct understanding" of social conflicts, the class struggle.

In place of "class struggle," the defenders of the patriarchal system offer us the slogan "family values" as an ideology. Havel describes the strong appeal of ideology:

> In an era when metaphysical and existential certainties are in a state of crisis, when people are being uprooted and alienated and are losing their sense of what this world means, this ideology inevitably has a certain hypnotic charm. To wandering humankind it offers an immediately available home: all one has to do is accept it, and suddenly everything becomes clear once more, life takes on new meaning, and all mysteries, unanswered questions, anxiety, and loneliness vanish. . . . The principle involved here is that the centre of power is identical with the centre of truth. [pp. 38–39]

Appreciating this "homelike" quality of accepting a higher authority helps us to understand the appeal of the patriarchal system for many women, and explains why even today many women embrace fundamentalist religions—Christianity, Orthodox Judaism, and Islam—that clearly invoke male authority and relegate the women to assigned traditional roles. In the system as it was practiced in the U.S.S.R. and Eastern Europe, the state owned and controlled all the means of production, making it the sole employer and able to manipulate its citizens through this economic hegemony. Not too many women in the United States have either the control of inherited wealth or a totally independent means of earning a living. They are usually hired by government—local, state, or federal—or by male-owned and controlled companies or businesses, and thus are dependent on pleasing a male father, husband, or employer for their financial security throughout their lives.

Havel gives as an example of this need for group acceptance the manager of a fruit and vegetable shop who places a poster containing the slogan "Workers of the world, unite!" in his shop window. He is certain the manager doesn't think about the slogan, but merely displays it because that's the way things have been done for years, in order to get along, because it "guarantees him a relatively tranquil life in 'harmony with society,' as they say" (p. 41). Havel discusses the functions of conformity:

> Ideology is a specious way of relating to the world. It offers human beings the illusion of an identity, of dignity, and of morality while making it easier for them to part with them . . . it enables people to deceive their conscience and conceal their true position and their inglorious *modus vivendi,* both from the world and from themselves. It is very pragmatic. . . . The primary excusatory function of ideology,

> therefore, is to provide people, both as victims and pillars of the post-totalitarian system, with the illusion that the system is in harmony with the human order and the order of the universe . . . the . . . system demands conformity, uniformity, and discipline. . . . Anything which leads people to overstep their predetermined roles is regarded by the system as an attack upon itself. . . . Ideology . . . pretends that the requirements of the system derive from the requirements of life. . . . This is why life in the system is so thoroughly permeated with hypocrisy and lies; . . . the complete degradation of the individual is presented as his or her ultimate liberation. [pp. 42–45]

Havel helps us to see how essential conformity is to a social system and the ideology by which it is maintained. By replacing *patriarchal* for his references to the Communist system, we can understand why *Harper's* hired Norman Mailer to attempt to demolish Kate Millett, why Gloria Steinem and Bella Abzug were the butt of jokes for years, and why the media referred to activists in the women's movement as *bra-burners* whose "shrill outcries" were ridiculed. The system must fight for its life and thus defend the ideology that perpetuates it. Women must be told that their true femininity rests upon their passive subservience to their husbands, surely a fitting example of "the degradation of the individual presented as her ultimate liberation." When women are needed in the workplace, day care is provided. When they are not, then their children require them to be at home. When they must work for their own survival, day care is not provided and the system pretends it is not a requirement. Even more important from a psychological perspective, women find it is in their best interest to conform to the system, just as the greengrocer does, because it provides them with an illusion of an identity, an accepted place in society, and the approval of their community. The examples of what happens to the women who rebel serve as a warning of the dire consequences of speaking truth to power.

Havel then asks us to imagine the reaction if the greengrocer one day "snaps" and stops putting up the slogans. The system must punish him because he has done something quite serious.

> He has shattered the world of appearances, the fundamental pillar of the system. He has upset the power structure. . . . Living within the lie can constitute the system only if it is universal. . . . There are no terms whatsoever on which it can coexist with living within the truth, and therefore everyone who steps out of line denies it in principle and threatens it in its entirety. [pp. 55–56]

Havel says the greengrocer's act would be a threat to the system because of its "illuminating" effects in exposing that system. The consequences of such an illumination are incalculable, and therefore very threatening.

I believe that Friedan's *The Feminine Mystique* served to illuminate a lie and that its power lay in that illumination. She spoke the truth. She gave a name to "the problem that had no name" (p. 11) and thereby allowed women to start speaking the truth to each other. The truth was that the "Emperor had no clothes," that is, women were unhappy having everything they were told they wanted and needed, and so something must have been missing. They must have been living a lie.

However, Havel also points the finger at the individual:

> Everyone in his or her own way is both a victim and a supporter of the system. . . . Human beings are compelled to live within a lie, but they can be compelled to do so only because they are in fact capable of living in this way. . . . Is it not true that the far-reaching adaptability to living a lie . . . has some connection with the general unwillingness of consumption-oriented people to sacrifice some material certainties for the sake of their own spiritual and moral integrity? [pp. 53–54]

This statement points again to the importance of strong group support, as found in the consciousness-raising groups, in providing a sense of belonging when the individual is feeling alienated from society—support that is necessary if the individual is to withstand external attacks, as well as the internal tendency to choose the easier path of conforming over that of sacrificing certainties. For psychotherapists working with patients who are dissidents, whether they are feminists or nonconformists in the arts or in some other social or political arena, it is important not to trivialize the patient with a reductionistic analysis of rebellion based upon childhood conflicts. Although that may be a contributing factor, it may be a small factor. Turning again to Havel for insight into these individuals:

> A "dissident," we are told in our press, means something like "renegade" or "backslider." But dissidents do not consider themselves renegades for the simple reason that they are not primarily denying or rejecting anything. On the contrary, they have tried to affirm their own human identity, and if they reject anything at all, then it is merely what was false and alienating in their lives. . . . The term "dissident" [or women's libber], frequently implies a special profession, as if, along with the more normal vocations, there were another special one— grumbling about the state of things. In fact, a "dissident" is simply a physicist, a sociologist, a worker, a poet, individuals who are merely doing what they feel they must and, consequently, who find themselves in open conflict with the regime. This conflict has not come about through any conscious intention on their part, but simply through the inner logic of their thinking, behaviour or work. . . . They have not, in other words, consciously decided to be professional malcontents. . . .

It is truly a cruel paradox that the more some citizens stand up in
defence of other citizens, the more they are labelled with a word that in
effect separates them from those "other citizens." [pp. 77–80]

Now, let us imagine that it is turn-of-the-century Vienna. Every shop
has a sign in the window with the slogan "children are innocent and
women do not desire or enjoy sex." Havel's understanding of the role of
the dissident can also be applied to Freud and the psychoanalytic circle
working with him. They too, like the feminists in the United States in the
1960s, questioned the ideology that supported the system and espoused
ideas that created chaos where there was order. Both feminism and
psychoanalysis represent revolutions in thought, because they changed our
ways of thinking; and both were powerful and therefore threatening
because of the social and political consequences of these changes. Psychoanalysis and feminism are individualistic philosophies, based on the value
of individual autonomy and the right of the individual to solve his or her
problems individually. They both lead us to think more critically about the
nuclear family. Freud's notion of the legitimacy of a private world and the
value of exploring it by analysis of the unconscious asserts the value of the
individual as opposed to the primacy of the family and the state. Feminists
too have been sharply criticized as being selfish for focusing on the needs
of the individual woman rather than the primacy of the family and the
state. Infantile sexuality was surely as shocking to Viennese and European
society as the notion that a wife need not be subservient to her husband and
children was sixty years later. The closeness of the psychoanalytic circle
drawn to Freud—and the difficulty in containing within that circle those
who were dissidents, such as Jung—can be understood in context of the
enormous pressures felt by psychoanalysts of the time from the medical,
scientific, and religious communities. They drew together in circles, as
feminists did, to be better able to cope with assaults from without and
doubts and fears from within.

3

MODERN PSYCHOANALYSTS TAKE A SECOND LOOK

I, as a woman, ask in amazement, and what about motherhood? And the blissful consciousness of bearing a new life within oneself? And the ineffable happiness of the increasing expectation of the appearance of this new being? And the joy when it finally makes its appearance and one holds it for the first time in one's arms? And the deep pleasurable feeling of satisfaction in suckling it and the happiness of the whole period when the infant needs her care?

—Karen Horney

As the 1960s and 1970s marked a turning point in the history of American women, a turning point for psychoanalytic views of women followed within a few years. Are the two connected directly, or coincidentally? Some of the same forces influencing the women's revolution—the birth control pill, legalized abortion, and the failure of the "happy housewife" role for middle class women—surely were reflected in the consulting rooms of psychoanalysts as their women patients spoke of the frustrations of domesticity as well as their fears and guilt about independence. My first visit to a psychoanalyst was in 1965. I told him I had everything a woman could want, yet I was unhappy and therefore felt terribly guilty. To my amazement and relief he appeared sympathetic and said it was bad enough being depressed, I shouldn't add to it with the additional burden of feeling guilty.

In the papers published by psychoanalysts in the 1970s, reference is regularly made to the critique of Freud and psychoanalysis coming from the feminists (e.g., Schafer 1974). I suspect that a combination of what their women patients were talking about, what their wives and daughters (in the case of male analysts) were telling them, and their awareness of the tremendous upheaval being created by the women's movement—especially the anger directed at themselves—caused some analysts to reevaluate traditional beliefs about women. Karen Horney's essays on women are quoted repeatedly in these papers. Why were they ignored for forty years? I believe it was the revival of Horney's work by the feminists that allowed her to rise from the ashes of her denunciation into a new recognition in psychoanalytic writing. This instance of the interrelationship between feminism and psychoanalysis illustrates my thesis that each has enriched the other when they are integrated, and, conversely, each has suffered when the valuable insights of the other have been rejected. In the case of women analysts, could it be that the women activists gave them both the stimulation and the courage to speak out?

Janine Chasseguet-Smirgel's book *New Psychoanalytic Research on Feminine Sexuality* was published in France in 1964, a year after Betty Friedan's *The Feminine Mystique* was published in the United States. It was not published in this country until 1970, when it appeared as *Female Sexuality: New Psychoanalytic Views*. In 1967, Harold Kelman's collection of Horney's previously uncollected essays on women, *Feminine Psychology,* was published. *Psychoanalysis and Women,* edited by Jean Baker Miller, an American psychoanalyst, was published in 1973. *Women and Analysis: Dialogues on Psychoanalytic Views of Femininity,* compiled by Jean Strouse, appeared in 1974. Harold Blum, a psychoanalyst, edited *Female Psychology: Contemporary Psychoanalytic Views,* published in 1977. Along with these books, perhaps hundreds of articles appeared in journals, and a similar number of papers were presented at conferences by psychoanalysts, psychiatrists, psychologists, and social workers. The 1970s thus ushered in a new era of ferment in the study of women, in which the earlier work of Freud and Deutsch was reassessed, modified, revised, and modernized with the help of research on children and sexuality. Thus, psychoanalysis was enabled to remain alive and relevant to modern women.

THE FIRST DISSIDENT—KAREN HORNEY

Karen Danielssen was born in Hamburg, Germany, in 1885. Her father was a Norwegian sea captain. In her middle teens she made sea voyages with him that stimulated her interest in foreign customs and widened her horizons. Her mother was Dutch and was "a dynamic, intelligent and imperious beauty" (Kelman 1971, p. 2) who encouraged her wishes to study medicine, unusual for a woman in the early twentieth century. She married Heinrich Horney, a lawyer, in 1909, had their first child in 1911, and by 1913 had completed her medical, psychiatric, and psychoanalytic training in Berlin. She joined the Berlin Psychoanalytic Society in 1911, where she had her training analysis with Karl Abraham and later a second analysis with Hanns Sachs, both loyal disciples of Freud. She became a lecturer and training analyst at the Berlin Psychoanalytic Institute when it was founded in 1920. Horney began publishing in 1917, with a paper on her concept of "blockages," which contrasts with Freud's mechanistic notion of resistance. According to Kelman (1967):

> What she formulated in these early years was bound to cause a confrontation with the psychoanalysts who supported the Freudian approach to the treatment of psychoneuroses. Although Horney recognized the significance of unconscious forces, she believed that their dimension and meaning were quite different. For instance, she did not consider the term "dynamic" to mean the interaction between instinct and counter instinct, but rather she viewed the conflict between the spontaneous forces of growth and the perversions of those healthy energies as sickness. [pp. 13–14]

Horney then focused her attention on the psychology of women, male–female differences, and marriage, publishing papers on these subjects from 1923 until 1935. Ernest Jones agreed with some of her work, but Freud was unwelcoming of her contributions. Gay (1988) writes of Horney's problems with Freud: "Dissenters like Karen Horney and Ernest Jones concentrated on woman's nature and refused to acquiesce in Freud's formula that femininity is essentially acquired by the successive renunciation of masculine traits. After all, in defining the clitoris as a residual penis, Freud was offering a dubious and highly tendentious analogy" (p. 519).

At an international congress of psychoanalysts in Berlin in 1922, Freud was the chairman. It took real courage for Horney to suggest her revision of the theory of penis envy. She proposed that it existed, but saw it as part of normal female development, not a creator of femininity but rather an expression of it. She did not accept Freud's notion that it leads women to a "repudiation of their womanhood," but rather, she stated, "we can see that penis envy by no means precludes a deep and wholly womanly attachment to the father" (Gay p. 519), suggesting that it was masculine narcissism that led psychoanalysts to the belief that women reject their femaleness.

Horney (1926b) wrote, "Psychoanalysis is the creation of a male genius, and almost all those who have developed his ideas have been men.

Hence it was only 'right and reasonable' that psychoanalysis 'should evolve more easily a masculine psychology' " (p. 54). Jones (1927) wrote: "There is a healthy suspicion growing that men analysts have been led to adopt an unduly phallo-centric view of the problems in question, the importance of the female organs being correspondingly underestimated" (p. 459).

Horney and Freud debated their views through their papers, but Freud (in Kelman 1967) dismissed her revisions of his theories on female sexuality: "We shall not be so very greatly surprised if a woman analyst who has not been sufficiently convinced of the intensity of her own desire for a penis also fails to assign an adequate importance to that factor in her patients" (p. 26).

There could have been truth to Freud's position, but there was a serious danger in it as well. If an opinion that disagrees with a prevailing view is not accepted as a possible and logical argument needing further investigation and clinical testing, but is rather seen as evidence of a personal failing, debate is closed off and psychoanalysts are prevented from pursuing the subject with the freedom necessary to seek the truth. Harkening back to Havel's *Living in Truth,* a totalitarian political system is similar to a totalitarian religious or other belief system in that if dissidents are refused recognition, or are even persecuted, there is created a fear and a closure that permeates all areas of inquiry that could meet with disapproval of the "authorities." This is the position children are frequently in in relation to their parents, and we hear from our patients of the fear and anger it causes and the lasting effect on their spontaneity, their self-confidence, and their free pursuit of knowledge and pleasure. Freud was surely the chief authority on psychoanalysis, and deservedly so, but his refusal to tolerate dissent did a major disservice to the history of psychoanalysis.

Undaunted, Horney continued to write the truth as she saw it (quoted in Kelman 1926).

> But from the biological point of view woman has in motherhood, or in the capacity for motherhood, a quite indisputable and by no means negligible physiological superiority. This is most clearly reflected in the unconscious of the male psyche in the boy's intense envy of motherhood. We are familiar with this envy as such, but it has hardly received due consideration as a dynamic factor. When one begins, as I did, to analyze men only after a fairly long experience of analyzing women, one receives a most surprising impression of the intensity of this envy of pregnancy, childbirth, and motherhood, as well as of the breasts and of the act of suckling.
>
> In the light of this impression derived from analysis, one must naturally inquire whether an unconscious masculine tendency to de-

preciation is not expressing itself intellectually in the above mentioned view of motherhood [as a burden]. This depreciation would run as follows: In reality women do simply desire the penis; when all is said and done motherhood is only a burden that makes the struggle for existence harder, and men may be glad that they have not to bear it. [pp. 60–61]

Horney's insights on masculine depreciation of the female functions as a reflection of envy were brilliant. It would take fifty years for other women writers (Miller 1976; Dinnerstein 1976) to appreciate the power of the mother, and to see that so omnipotent is she in the lives of her children that depreciation of women is an important defense to women as well as men, as a means to diminish the fear of maternal power.

The gap between Horney's work in the 1920s and early 1930s, and the period of revision beginning in the 1960s and continuing, spans forty to fifty years. This is half the life of psychoanalysis and coincides with Friedan's view of the period between 1930 and 1960 as representing a regressive period for feminism in the United States, which she links with the popularity of psychoanalytic theory and its dissemination in the mass media. Horney's disagreements with Freud and the theories she enunciated in the 1920s sounded as fresh when read in the 1970s as if they had been written at the time. How can we understand the antagonism of those intervening years, Horney's own dropping of the issue after 1935, and the absence of dissent on female psychology from 1935 to 1964?

Horney's arrival in the United States in 1932 and her involvement in struggles in the American psychoanalytic movement appear to have turned her attention away from feminine psychology. She began to focus on cultural factors in neurotic disorders affecting both men and women. When her book *The Neurotic Personality of our Time* appeared in 1937, it produced a "landslide of anger" (Kelman 1971, p. 16), and Horney was demoted by the New York Psychoanalytic Institute from training analyst to lecturer. Five members—Horney, Clara Thompson, Bernard S. Robbins, Harmon S. Ephron, and Sarah R. Kelman—resigned, along with fourteen of their students. Kelman states:

The night of Horney's demotion was a most dramatic one. Psychoanalysis as a movement was never the same thereafter. Its organizational aspects, its methods of training, and its influence on psychiatry and a host of ancillary disciplines was permanently altered. At that meeting faculty and students were outraged by the blatant violation of academic freedom. Almost fifty percent of those present refrained from voting. After the vote, Horney and the four others marched jubilantly away from the Institute, led by Clara singing one of her favorite hymns, "Go Down Moses." [p. 16]

In 1941, dissident analysts founded a national organization, the Association for the Advancement of Psychoanalysis (AAP), which included Erich Fromm. Another group of dissidents, including Abram Kardiner, Sandor Rado, and David Levy, organized the Association for Psychoanalytic Medicine. However, another split developed over the issue of lay analysis, and Thompson and Fromm left the AAP to form the Washington School of Psychiatry with Harry Stack Sullivan in 1943. According to Kelman, Horney was quite disturbed by the first break, but after the second she was in despair.

We see that, like the women's liberation movement, psychoanalysis has not been a united movement. The goals are usually not the problem, but rather the means for attaining the goals. Feminists all agree that they are working for the liberation of women, just as all psychoanalysts are working for the liberation of the human psyche. Splits over theoretical disagreement, and also, at times, over personality and power, have been divisive but are part of the process in all human endeavors, revolutionary and conservative alike. As the factions divide and pursue their work separately, there continue to be opportunities for those on the outside to shed light on the issues of controversy, to bring together ideas from different individuals, and to move knowledge forward. Unfortunately, Horney's early death from cancer in 1952 prevented her from seeing the revival of her work on women by psychoanalysts and feminists and its contribution to the revision of psychoanalytic theory on women and to feminist theory.

It is interesting to speculate on the two leading women theorists of female psychology in the psychoanalytic movement: Helene Deutsch, born in 1884, and Karen Horney, born in 1885. Both were Europeans and both pioneers in attending medical school and becoming psychiatrists and analysts. Both even had the same analyst, Karl Abraham. And yet their lives and theories diverged markedly. Though both, according to their biographers, were dissatisfied with their marriages, Deutsch remained married, while Horney separated from her husband in 1926 and was divorced in 1939. Deutsch remained wedded to Freud and his theories of women; Horney separated and then divorced herself from Freud's views. How may their lives have affected their theories and, concomitantly, their theories affected their lives? Deutsch stressed passivity and masochism and saw women as weak and impaired. Horney stressed pride in female functions and male envy of female generativity. What we do know is that Deutsch was very badly treated by her mother and apparently they hated each other. She was closer to her father and idealized him. Horney was closer to her mother and admired her. She was also close to her father, but he was absent for long sea voyages and was a stern and deeply religious man whom she feared. She accepted her mother's depreciation of his religious views. She was also hurt by her older brother's rejection of her when he was in his teens. Deutsch's mother tried to prevent her education; Horney's mother encouraged her education.

Current feminist psychoanalytic theory stresses the lasting importance of the girl's relationship with her mother. Deutsch and Horney are examples of this importance. Horney's identification as a woman appears much more positive than Deutsch's, whose not "good enough" mothering even prevented her from enjoying motherhood. Deutsch had one child, Horney three (Gordon 1978, p. 25). Deutsch's need for Freud's approval, as for her father's, was overdetermined by the fact that she had no introjects of an early female figure to turn to for love and approval. She never challenged Freud's authority or even allowed herself to feel anger toward him. Horney did challenge him and was able to tolerate his anger, disapproval, and eventual rejection. Horney's good relationship with her mother allowed her to question Freud's authority, whereas Deutsch's theories and her life were limited and controlled by her submission to Freud, even as regards her marriage. Horney may have had a problem with authority, whereas Deutsch was too weakened by the hostility of her mother to separate and differentiate.

In 1970, I read Kelman's collection of Horney's essays on women, *Feminine Psychology* (1967), and I was stimulated by her divergent views on women. This was the year my consciousness-raising group was started, and the Horney work offered a welcome validation of some of the ideas I was developing about women in my practice and in my personal life. Inspired by the Horney essays, I published "The Femininity Complex and Female Therapists" (Krause 1971). The article is one of the earliest feminist-psychoanalytic writings on clinical work with women. Because its ideas were so strongly influenced by Karen Horney, it is an example of how psychoanalytic theory (Horney) influenced feminist theory, which then fed back into the psychiatric community. I read this paper at local psychiatric clinics and it stimulated much intense discussion. The men at times reacted as if I was recommending that all women see women therapists and naturally got defensive, though that was not my intention.

THE ENGLISH SCHOOL—MELANIE KLEIN

Between 1927 and 1935, Klein and E. Jones published articles in which they expressed their disagreement with Freud in regard to his theories of female development and psychology. Chasseguet-Smirgel (1970a) compares Klein's theories to Freud's as follows:

> According to Freud the castration complex leads the girl to hate her mother for not having given her a penis. Melanie Klein believes the little

girl hates her mother for the same reasons, but whereas Freud thought the girl wanted a penis for herself (her aim being a narcissistic one), Klein believes that she desires the penis libidinally: "She is brought under the sway of her Oedipal impulses not indirectly, through her masculine tendencies and her penis-envy, but directly, as a result of her dominant feminine instinctual components." [pp. 33–34]

Klein disagrees with Freud in her view of the clitoris: "The clitoris . . . is immediately cathected in a feminine way; the fantasies which accompany clitoral masturbation show a desire to incorporate the paternal penis and also stimulate vaginal sensations" (p. 35).

FEMALE SEXUALITY: NEW PSYCHOANALYTIC VIEWS

Janine Chasseguet-Smirgel

Chasseguet-Smirgel's *Female Sexuality: New Psychoanalytic Views,* consists of six papers by psychoanalysts of the Kleinian school. It contains extensive clinical material, with interpretations focusing on the infant–mother relation during the first year of life and how it influences feminine personality and determines almost all future sexual development. The editor states:

> The authors of the present book are united in their desire to reexamine the theories of female sexuality, using the Freudian approach to the unconscious. . . . The present authors have attempted as far as possible to free their theoretical ideas and their clinical interpretations from the unconscious fantasies which distort scientific objectivity. [p. 3]

Topics include masculine mythology of femininity, narcissism in female sexuality, the change of object, feminine guilt, penis envy, and homosexuality in women. The idea of a primary femininity has been supported by the research of Robert Stoller (1975). However, in their review of the book, Barglow and Schaefer (1977) write: "The Kleinian analysts make the girl's 'femininity' dependent on an inexplicable ability to recognize the father as an 'authentic' and the mother as an 'inadequate' sexual object in the first year of life, which is hardly commensurate with what we know of infantile perceptual-cognitive capacity in this period" (p. 421).

> Most genetic reconstructions include good and bad objects and breasts, but the omnipresent penis reigns supreme. Jones's adjective "phallocentric," intended for Freud, applies much more aptly to these writers. Interpretations are directed almost exclusively toward the uncon-

scious. . . . The concepts of ego resistance, character formations, the adaptive point of view and the principle of multiple functioning are missing. [p. 425]

Yet the essays contain some fascinating insights into female sexual development and are well worth reading. In addition, the editor presents a review of the major work on women by psychoanalysts, including Freud and his followers as well as those opposed to Freud. The review is clear, concise, and objectively written, and it makes valuable reading for all those interested in the subject as well as serving as an introduction to the essays that follow. In her own essay (1970b), "Feminine Guilt and the Oedipus Complex," Chasseguet-Smirgel's view is that the normal unconscious structure at the time of the change of object from mother to father involves projection of the bad object onto the mother and the good onto the father. "When reality cannot correct this unconscious image, severe problems are bound to arise" (p. 132). Under such circumstances, there is a terrible fusion of the aggressive and erotic instincts, corresponding to men's terrifying fantasies about femininity. In regard to feminine guilt and dependency, Chasseguet-Smirgel refers to the Creation myth and makes this interpretation:

Man and woman are born of woman: before all else we are our mother's child. Yet all our desires seem designed to deny this fact, so full of conflicts and reminiscent of our primitive dependence. The myth of Genesis seems to express this desire to free ourselves from our mother: man is born of God, an idealized paternal figure, a projection of lost omnipotence. Woman is born from man's body. If this myth expresses the victory of man over his mother and over woman, who thereby becomes his own child, it also provides a certain solution for woman inasmuch as she also is her mother's daughter: she chooses to belong to man, to be created for him, and not for herself, to be a part of him— Adam's rib—rather than to prolong her "attachment" to her mother. I have tried to show the conflicts which oblige so many women to choose between mother and husband as the object of dependent attachment. [pp. 133–134]

In the past, women were described as going from the father to the husband. Here we have the woman going from dependence on the mother to dependence on the husband. The woman as an independent adult never seems to exist. It is clear that it takes financial independence from both the father and the husband, in combination with emotional independence from the mother, to enable a woman to experience genuine adult autonomy and to achieve mature sexuality and mastery in the world. In Chapter 4 we will see how these ideas are developed by American feminist psychoanalytic writers into a more complete understanding of the deeply embedded conflicts in the mother–daughter relationship and its effects on the female personality.

Female Masturbation—Maria Torok

One of the most interesting of the articles in this book is the essay "The Significance of Penis Envy in Women" by Maria Torok (1970). Torok says that all analyses of women reveal an envy of the penis and its symbolic equivalents. With some patients this envy is merely episodic, but with others it can be central. However, "the conviction that what they feel themselves deprived of is exactly what other people have is common to patients of both sexes and is found in all analyses. . . . only women relate this feeling of deficiency to the very nature of their sex" (p. 135). Torok sees the source of penis envy in the mother–infant relationship, as do the other Kleinians, but she connects it more specifically to the mother's prohibition of the girl's masturbation, and the problem this causes in the development of independence for the girl. Penis envy is a camouflage; the penis itself is not involved. It is associated with conscious or unconscious hatred toward the mother, is always envy of an idealized penis, and is the effect of a deprivation or a renunciation—the renunciation of those desires the mother disapproved of in the daughter. The girl lets herself be deprived of her desire because she needs her mother's love. The girl, in effect, is saying to her mother, "In short, idealizing the penis, in order to envy it more, is reassuring you by showing you that this will never come between us, and that consequently I shall never be reunified, I shall never fulfill myself." Penis envy makes this oath of fidelity. Her own sexual parts, and thus her own true sexuality, are forbidden and repressed (p. 141).

> To conclude, we are led to consider that not only the repression of anal-pregenital conflicts underlies penis envy, but also a specific, total or partial, inhibition of masturbation, of orgasm and of their concomitant fantasy activities. Penis envy appears now to be a disguised claim—not for the organ and the attributes of the other sex—but for one's *own desires for maturation and development by means of the encounter with oneself in conjunction with orgastic experience and sexual identification.* [p. 142]

Torok believes that discovery of the boy's penis is often associated with the repressed memory of orgasmic experiences. The achievement of orgasm for the child signals an opening up of the future, of becoming oneself, and preparing for genital sexuality with confirmation of sensual pleasure.

Any inhibition regarding such an encounter with herself leaves the patient with a blank in place of an identification, however vital it is for her. The result is an unfulfilled body-self (some would say body-image) and, correspondingly, a world of fragmented reality. . . . One must add that this duality, the "touching oneself," the experience of "I-myself" authenticated by the orgasm, also suggests: "As I can do it to myself alone, I am emancipated from those who have hitherto permitted or forbidden me this pleasure according to their whim." Masturbation, literally touching oneself, and reflective fantasy free the child from maternal dependence and at the same time establish an autonomous maternal imago, that is to say, one which can find its pleasure somewhere other than with the child, a possibility missing when the mother forbids masturbation. . . . The ban on masturbation has the effect of tying the child to his mother's body and interfering with his essential growth. [pp. 144–145]

"Penis envy," Torok states, "will disappear by itself the day the patient no longer has that painful feeling of deficiency which caused it" (p. 138). Torok states that when, in the course of analysis, the woman patient is free to masturbate, this is always accompanied by a feeling of power. Prior to that she has been arrested in the process of her genital fulfillment and has therefore felt frustrated, has projected her own longed-for but unconscious desires for sexual gratification onto the male, believing that only the penis entitled one to such forbidden pleasures. The boy, after all, can touch his sexual parts. The envy of the penis is a symptom of having lost hope for herself, of feeling empty and envious of the boy who she imagines has not had to renounce sexual pleasure.

The greatest desire of a woman who suffers from penis envy is to meet the male in full orgasmic union, and to realize herself in an authentic act, but this is what she has to avoid most. In short, whether to be autonomous and have pleasure with the penis or to be the appendage of the Mother—that is the dilemma. If I [describing her patient, Ida] have pleasure, my mother becomes empty, this is unbearable for me. [Ida reassures her mother:] "There is no question of my satisfying myself alone, there is no danger for you, you can keep me as an appendage." [pp. 149–150]

Torok concludes her essay with two questions: first, why do women acquiesce in their limitations and dependency; and second, why is man her accomplice? In her view, no institution is established and none survives unless it resolves some particular interpersonal problem with advantages for both men and women. "This age-old inequality of the sexes requires woman's complicity, in spite of her apparent protest shown by penis envy" (p. 167). Her answer to the first question lies in her earlier

description of the girl's conflicts about autonomy from her mother combined with the oedipal obstacle, the anxiety around supplanting the
mother. Torok sees the husband as the heir to the daughter's view of
herself as an appendage to her mother. This, she believes, explains the
woman's acceptance of dependence on her husband. She adds that this
dependence is the price paid by the woman for some of the disguised
genital achievements that women sometimes allow themselves. Through
this shift to the husband the woman avoids deeply felt anxiety at the idea
of separation from her mother's domination and superiority.

Turning to the question of men, Torok says that although at first it
may appear easy to understand man's acceptance of his mastery and of
female dependence created by feminine guilt, on closer examination it is
not to their advantage:

> The falsity, the ambivalence, and the refusal of identifications it
> conceals should appear to him as so many snags on which his own full
> and authentic achievement comes to grief. And yet . . . who could
> doubt that in order to achieve his own interests in superiority man is
> almost universally the accomplice of woman's state of dependence and
> that he thrives in elevating all this into religious, metaphysical, or
> anthropological principles. What interest has he in giving in to his need
> to dominate the being through whom he could understand himself and
> who could understand him? To discover oneself through the other sex
> would be a genuine fulfillment of one's humanity, yet this is exactly
> what escapes most of us. [pp. 168–169]

The little boy can free himself from maternal domination by identification
with the father, possessor of the "phallus" and his ally, yet there is anxiety
about rejecting her domination. Later, the anxiety of the oedipal triangle is
added, in which the boy is forced into the untenable position of identifying
with his genital rival as well as desiring his elimination.

> An impossible desire is crystallized into an envy, paralleling that of the
> girl, of the same illusory object, the "penis." It is obvious that these
> envies are beyond any real genital differentiation and refer to the non-
> integrated anal relationship. . . . From then on phallic deception leads
> the way for the institutionalized relation between the sexes. The whole
> problem of the failure in identification will by fetishistic means be con-
> cealed behind active or passive fascination. The possession of the "fe-
> tish" is intended to arouse envy, and envy in turn is intended to confirm
> the value of the fetish for the man. . . . Once it is conceded that the
> exclusive possessor of the fetish is man, is not this so-called privilege,
> sustained by covetousness alone, nothing but a variant of envy, pro-
> jected on to woman? The penis-emblem allows the man to be enviable

and, thus, logically avoid living a life of envy. Man cannot be other than envious as long as he needs to objectify as well as hide in a fetish what is missing in his genital fulfillment. Thanks to this subterfuge he will continue to ignore his dangerous desire to take the Mother's part in the anally conceived Primal Scene. The woman, envious and guilty, is the ideal support for the projection of this desire. She can thus become man's unacknowledged "feminine part," which he must then master and control. That is why man will be driven to prefer a mutilated, dependent and envious woman to a partner, successful in her creative fullness. [pp. 169–170]

These notions of the reciprocal nature of men's and women's needs for women to remain inferior can help explain the very strong resistances in both sexes to the emancipation of women. Currently, the intense conflict about abortion is the focus of much anxiety about the power of women. I am struck by the possibility that the frequently heard explanation for rape by the rapist, that the woman really wanted it, can be the result of the projection described above of the man's desire to "take the Mother's part." I quoted earlier from Virginia Woolf, who referred to women as serving as "looking glasses" for men, reflecting the figure of man at twice its natural size, which explains in part the necessity that women so often are to men. Woolf did not understand the psychological defenses for the woman in allowing herself to be used and remain powerless in this way. She saw the woman as victimized by the patriarchal culture. She accurately described the external components of the situation, and Torok fills in the psychoanalytic theory to round out the feminist description of the inequality. Woolf's "looking glass" image can now be enhanced by Torok's notion that what is "twice its natural size" is the boy's view of his father's phallus and the power it holds in the patriarchal family, including the power to prevent the boy from fulfilling his erotic desires toward his mother. The boy, who then becomes the husband, attempts to prevent his wife from fulfilling her own desires, which are to become the mistress of her own self and in control of her own destiny. It is as if the man is attempting to master his own frustration at having been inhibited by his father by identifying with his father as the master over others and denying freedom to women.

However, we must wonder about the daughters who have been raised in modern times, by mothers who followed current recommendations on child rearing and therefore did not suppress masturbation, as well as mothers who themselves have been in therapy, have been freed of crippling sexual inhibitions, and have felt the power of that autonomy from the forbidding mother. One would hope that these girls could develop without the crippling symptoms of "penis envy." It would take more than just the actual allowing of masturbation, but also a mother who is fulfilled in her own life, through work and love; who does not need to suppress her daughter's desires or to keep her an appendage. If Torok's theory is correct, we could expect to see in these daughters no more than mild instances of penis envy—such as trying to urinate standing up—in childhood, and certainly not a persistent and pathological condition in adulthood. We can hope that such daughters are out there and are increasing in number; but they need to find men to love who can offer them the reciprocal relationship of not needing to be envied, and thus can welcome a woman who does not experience herself as mutilated and dependent.

Female Narcissism—Bela Grunberger

On this point, the essay by Bela Grunberger, "Outline for a Study of Narcissism in Female Sexuality" (1970), refers to the need for women to be loved, to be chosen, to be specially valued. One reason for this especially strong need in women might be their need to free themselves from guilt. But Grunberger asks

> why women seek narcissistic gratification above all else, even to the detriment of their own strong sexual needs and why they offer themselves sexually in order to be loved; whereas men tend to seek sexual satisfaction primarily, giving their partners narcissistic gratification only in order to obtain their own sexual satisfaction. [p. 70]

This inordinate need for love, if based on a feeling of incompleteness as well as on guilt in relation to a powerful but damaged mother, would also be modified in the case of a girl who grows up with pride in her physical and mental attributes because she has a mother who values herself and has a life of her own apart from her children. Such a mother can allow her daughter to develop independent of herself. However, Grunberger describes another factor in female narcissism:

> Women feel a certain lack in narcissistic confirmation and look to men to give it to them. We also know that such confirmation must be achieved in a manner which is both erotic and endorses its subject. Each aspect strengthens the other when they are combined, and this is precisely what is missing in woman's normal development because the first object, the mother, is a homosexual one. Man provides woman with narcissistic confirmation and, in her need for recognition (that is, for being loved), this means love, since love is a narcissistic contribution. [p. 82]

But what of the father? A girl wanting of confirmation by her mother should be able to receive that confirmation from her father. If she does not it must be because for her father, too, she is incomplete, inferior, and not as worthwhile as a son. Langs's case of Miss F.T. (1973), described in Chapter 5, is an example of a father who failed to validate his daughter's specialness as a woman. Here again we hope that modern fathers can give this confirmation of worth to their daughters, so that the daughter as a woman is not left narcissistically wounded, desperately seeking healing from men.

PSYCHOANALYSIS AND WOMEN

Jean Baker Miller

Miller, a psychiatrist and psychoanalyst, compiled a book of essays by sixteen prominent psychoanalysts entitled *Psychoanalysis and Women*. Published in 1973, it includes two papers of Karen Horney, three of Clara Thompson, two of Robert Stoller, and three of Robert Seidenberg, as well as papers by Adler, Fromm-Reichmann, Zilboorg, Sherfy, Cohen, Chodoff, Salzman, Marmor, Moulton, Symonds, and Gelb. All the papers had been previously published, but it is interesting to note that none had appeared in the *Journal of the American Psychoanalytic Association*. The authors all stress cultural, historical, and anthropological material in understanding the female personality. Some, such as Clara Thompson and Ruth Moulton, are from the Sullivanian or Washington school, the "interpersonal" school of psychiatry. Barglow and Schaefer (1977) are critical of the collection in their review:

> The social analysts' attack on Freudian theory, particularly that of the most recent ones in the Miller book . . . is characterized by a social-reformist zeal that, while most admirable in itself, confuses the role of the analyst with that of the political or spiritual leader. . . . many of the papers reflect theoretical orientations that are not analytic in any sense of the word. The essays by Gelb and Seidenberg, in particular, are not based on analytic data and show a striking neglect of metapsychology, the technique and philosophy of psychoanalysis, and the development point of view. Gelb's is a moral argument. . . . All are much more concerned with social advocacy than they are with broadening our analytic thinking. . . . But are these really psychoanalytic problems? Psychoanalysis, after all, is not an ideology but professes to be a science. . . . The contributors to the Miller volume . . . and other social critics almost completely ignore the likelihood that female as well as male infantile needs might have shaped and still shape the structure of social and cultural institutions as well as female personality. . . . To exclude all biological, developmental, and intrapsychic clinical data

from consideration in such matters risks the danger of throwing out the
baby with the bath water. [pp. 409–411]

The authors are correct in characterizing the essays as culturally oriented
(although the Sherfy article is surely biologically focused), but I believe
they are too severe in their criticism. They fail to recognize that psychoanalysis, unlike the idealistic description of it in the quotation above, had
failed to take account of cultural biases in the analysts themselves, biases
that created a view of women as "servant of the species" and did a
disservice to some women patients. The essays are a necessary corrective
to that bias and, when integrated into the body of psychoanalytic literature, provide a valuable balance. A careful reading of case material by
psychoanalysts often does not display the broad view, the view of "multiple complex actions," that Barglow and Schaefer correctly describe.

Barglow and Schaefer denigrate Seidenberg's essay "The Trauma of
Eventlessness" (1972) as a set of "simplified social examples," yet I find
the case he describes of an unhappy housewife thoughtful and meaningful.
He shows empathy for the plight of an intelligent woman who was denied
an education or choice about any aspect of her life. He analyzes her
symptoms: agoraphobia, fear of losing her mind, and fear of harming her
3-year-old daughter, stating that "the theory that she was beset with
imaginary dangers stemming from drives and affects from within was only
part of the story." I believe Seidenberg is saying here that he sees the
patient's social milieu as another part of the story, in his analysis of this
patient, he is not abandoning an intrapsychic approach.

"The Trauma of Eventlessness"—Robert Seidenberg

This 28-year-old patient was referred by the family
physician after failing to respond to a variety of tranquilizers and
other "psychotropic" drugs. "She was a plain-looking woman,
uneducated, showing all the signs of social bewilderment and
ineptness" (p. 352). The parents were immigrants from Eastern
Europe of the Russian-Orthodox religion who worked hard and
gradually were able to rise from poverty into the middle class,
but always were concerned with issues of respectability. The
father feared that his daughter could "go wild" if she went away
to college—become a tramp, get pregnant, and bring shame and
disgrace to the family. An uneducated man, he painfully realized
it was necessary for his son to attend college, but his pride could
not allow his daughter to have more education than he did. She
was raised under strict discipline, and taught to show obedience
and respect for her parents. Her father controlled her life,

including her friends and activities. After her graduation from high school, he got her a job as a stenographer in the small company where he worked in a semimanagerial position, from which he could keep an eye on her. The father arranged for her to meet a young man who worked for the company during the summer, an engineering student. She married him, and then left her job when he finished college and returned to the company to work. They bought a home, she had a baby, and she seemingly had everything she could want.

Her anxiety attacks appeared to have been triggered by the course of her brother's life. He was five years younger, not as good a student in high school as she had been, yet he was sent to college and even given a car for transportation. He graduated and obtained a good job at a good salary.

Seidenberg believes that her brother's success was a precipitating factor in the patient's neurotic rebellion. She was confronted with and angered by the very real inequities in their education, and hence in their futures.

The patient's anxiety was expressed in her exclamation that "something is going to happen, but I don't know what it is." Seidenberg's interpretation is that this is a case of "existential agoraphobia"; the patient was "secretly lamenting the danger that the opposite would be true, that in her life nothing would happen" (p. 355). She felt trapped, without challenge, decision making, or problem solving. This is what her analyst is calling the "trauma of eventlessness," the *absence of stimuli*. Her daughter at age 3 seemed self-sufficient and did not require all her attention, yet she feared for her daughter's future. Seidenberg interprets this anxiety in a nontraditional manner:

> Her untoward thoughts about her daughter originated not so much from pent-up sexualized or deneutralized aggression, but as a component of the chagrin over the fate of the female. Was her daughter to be destroyed as she thought herself to be? Would destiny impel her to foist upon her daughter the inequities she herself felt?
>
> These are *real* dangers and they are *external* but may not be apparent except to the observer who has thought about them. One is not justified in declaring these dangers either unreal or internal because they are not universally perceived or acknowledged. Often the therapist is still listening with the "third" ear when the times call for a fourth. [p. 357]

His hypothesis is that her "breakdown" occurred when she painfully realized that without some change, her life would continue to be characterized by submission to authority, absence of choice, and a general exclusion and isolation from the significant stimuli of life. He believes that, in her case, these fears were not irrational. "When she finally became aware of her legitimate struggle against 'disappearance,' her physical symptoms largely abated and her energies were channeled into areas that might change her plight" (p. 358).

This case analysis is in sharp contrast to Torok's case of "Ida" described earlier in this chapter. Seidenberg focuses exclusively on his patient's relationship with her father and brother and practically ignores the mother, either the preoedipal, oedipal, or current relationship, at least in this essay. His only reference to the mother is to say that toward her she was solicitous but felt no affection. Her father was the "ultimate figure of authority who would determine her destiny" (p. 359). Seidenberg omits the whole issue of the patient's identification with the mother and the quality of maternal nurturance which, in my view, must be significant factors in her symptomatology. It is surely of great significance that she felt no affection for her mother, and we should want to know more about why that was so. Might she have been guilty and anxious about her marriage to an educated man and their good sexual relationship (reference is made to this), by which she thus surpassed her mother? Seidenberg does analyze her transference reactions, which he does not describe but only refers to in telling us of his patient's doubts about being in therapy and the truth of her "infatuation" with her doctor. He ignores any reference to penis envy, in stark contrast to Robert Langs in the case of Miss F.T. (see Chapter 5). One would expect Langs's analysis of Seidenberg's patient to focus on penis envy as the source of her symptoms. It is interesting that all three therapists report great improvement in their patients, and we can believe them. A traditional analyst, a Kleinian analyst, and an existential analyst, all approaching their women patients from their own viewpoints, can all be successful because of the likelihood that they all possess part of the truth. I am reminded of the famous story of the blind men and the elephant—we can guess what part of the elephant Langs is feeling. No matter what the particular theoretical orientation, the work with the transference is always the best means for understanding the patient. If all three analysts accurately focused on the transference interactions and got even only part of the historical reconstruction right, that would be a sound enough basis for the patient's improvement. It is also likely that the patients got better because of the emotional caring and attention of the therapist. The communication of the patient's importance and uniqueness by the therapist has much therapeutic value itself. Each of these patients was a "favorite" of the therapist and was chosen to be written up for publication because she illustrated the success of the therapist's ideological system and treatment approach.

An additional factor in the Seidenberg case is his focus on the class background of the patient, and how both her family's anxiety about the alien culture they lived in and their desire for upward mobility put special strains on their daughter. I find this material a particularly valuable aspect of his case discussion. In my experience, class factors have been very significant in some cases, especially when the patient belonged to the lower or upper class. If the therapist belongs to the middle class, as is most often the case, she or he may not be aware of the low self-esteem and angry feelings of poor or formerly poor patients, and of how these feelings figure into their history and the transference. Similarly, the analyst may be unaware of some of the significant money issues for the wealthy, such as who controls the money, which spouse has more money, and conflicts around inheritance. Class factors have often been ignored by psychoanalysis. It is the sociologists who have studied class and from whom we have much to learn. The classic study by Hollingshead and Redlich, *Social Class and Mental Illness* (1958), describes the effect of class on diagnosis. *Hidden Injuries of Class* by Sennett (1972) is a startling examination of our educational system and the psychological effects on poor and working class children of low expectations. *Worlds of Pain* by Lillian Rubin (1976) explores the differences between working-class and middle-class women in marriage and sexuality. These three books are invaluable for the education of middle class therapists.

"Phobias After Marriage"—Alexandra Symonds

Another essay in this collection, by Alexandra Symonds of the Karen Horney school, is "Phobias After Marriage: Women's Declaration of Dependence" (1971), which describes three patients with agoraphobia, like Seidenberg's patient. Symonds's theoretical approach is to focus on the internal dynamics of unmet dependency needs plus anger, frustration, fear of conflict, and a profound resignation. She puts all the onus for conflict on to the husbands, though she acknowledges family patterns as determining. She does not focus on the mother–daughter relationship, nor does she see the husband–wife interaction as a recapitulation of a hostile–dependent tie to the mother. She describes their defenses as isolation, intellectualization, and compartmentalization. Symonds acknowledges that dependency for women in marriage is socially acceptable, but references to cultural factors are minimized. Not surprisingly, Symonds makes no reference to penis envy. As we can see, there is no more unanimity among the revisionists than among the feminists, but they all share the conviction that Freud, Deutsch, and their followers were in error about women and that these errors must be corrected for psychoanalysis to progress. A weakness of all the articles, no doubt due to the years in which they were written, is that none of the authors make any reference to the sexual molestation of children. So many symptoms of women are now being understood as the result of incest and other forms of childhood rape and sexual exploitation.

"WOMANHOOD AND THE INNER SPACE"—ERIK ERIKSON

Jean Strouse's book *Women and Analysis* (1974) is organized differently from the Miller and Chasseguet-Smirgel collections. Subtitled, "Dialogues on Psychoanalytic Views of Femininity," it is composed of eleven classical essays on female psychology by Freud, Abraham, Deutsch, Horney, Emma Jung, Bonaparte, Thompson, and Erikson, each followed by a commentary by a contemporary scholar, some but not all of whom are psychoanalysts. One exception to her format is the paper of Erik Erikson (1974). Since he was the only living writer in her group, Strouse invited him to comment on his own work, "Womanhood and the Inner Space," published in 1968. This piece had been frequently quoted and criticized by feminists, and Erikson attempts to respond to the criticism in his paper, "Once More the Inner Space." He defends his work, stating that it had been distorted by taking lines out of context and by misunderstanding and misinterpretation of some of his comments. For example, the earlier article states that "children of both sexes sooner or later 'know' the penis to be missing in one sex, leaving in its place a woundlike aperture" (p. 338). He explains:

> The mere underscoring of the word *children* would emphasize that I am referring to infantile observations made at a stage of development when the inviolacy of the body is a matter of anxious concern, leading to the well-known phobic "theories" which (as I insist throughout) are counteracted in the growing child's eventual awareness of a "protective inner-bodily space safely set in the center of female form and carriage." [pp. 373–374]

However, feminists and others can hardly be blamed for failing to realize that psychoanalysts are talking about children's *misunderstanding,* because they rarely refer to these childhood beliefs as misunderstandings. In fact, Freud (1925) added to the general confusion by referring to the little girl's discovery of "the *fact* of being castrated" (Reiff, p. 188). When we combine the fantasies of children with the fantasies of psychoanalysts and the fantasies of feminists, we really have a lot of work to do to separate fact from fiction.

CULTURAL FACTORS IN FEMALE PSYCHOLOGY— CLARA THOMPSON

Essays by Clara Thompson appear in both the Miller and the Strouse anthologies. She wrote six papers on the psychology of women between 1941 and 1950, a period that was relatively quiescent on the topic.

Thompson had left the New York Psychoanalytic Institute with Horney in 1941. She then split with Horney, joining with Erich Fromm and Harry Stack Sullivan in 1943 to found the Washington School of psychiatry, which attempted to integrate psychoanalysis with anthropology, political science, and social psychology. Her work was not accepted in the mainstream psychoanalytic institutes until, like Horney, she was recognized by the women's movement and her work was revived. Her death in 1958 prevented her, also like Horney, from enjoying her new prominence. Her essays cover penis envy, female sexuality, and cultural factors in female psychology. She describes (1942) the girl in puberty in Freud's time:

> Her training was in the direction of insincerity about her sexual interests. She was taught to be ashamed of menstruation. It was something to be concealed and any accident leading to its discovery was especially humiliating. In short womanhood began with much unpleasantness. It was characterized by feelings of body shame, loss of freedom, loss of equality with boys, and loss of the right to be aggressive. The training in insincerity especially about her sexual being and sexual interests has undoubtedly contributed much to a woman's diminished sense of self. [p. 74]

In regard to penis envy, Thompson writes (1950):

> What a woman needs rather is a feeling of the importance of her own organs. I believe that much more important than penis envy in the psychology of woman is her reaction to the undervaluation of her own organs. I think we can concede that the acceptance of one's body and all its functions is a basic need in the establishment of self-respect and self-esteem. [p. 65]

Cultural factors, yes, but in my view, psychodynamic ones. This theory describes how societal attitudes become internalized by the girl and determine her basic psychological state, resulting in poor mental health. Later writers, such as Mildred Ash and Harriet Lerner, would take up and expand this theme of feelings of shame towards the female genitalia.

FEMALE SEXUALITY—ETHEL PERSON

Ethel Person, a contemporary psychoanalyst, agrees with Thompson's focus on the importance for women of sexual freedom and achievement for increased self-esteem. In her paper "The Influence of Values in Psychoanalysis: The Case of Female Psychology" (1983), she says the critical question for psychoanalysts is why the female erotic impulse is vulnerable to suppression across so many different historical and cultural circumstances. She cites current studies on core gender identity based on the assignment of sex by the parents at birth as well as the very early self-identification. These learning experiences have formed a core gender identity by the time a child is 18 months, and are firmly and irrevocably established by no later than 3 years. Person concludes:

> Most theorists now believe that the developmental lines of gender precede those of sexuality, a complete reversal of Freud's original formulation.
>
> This change in theoretical formulation has manifold implications for therapy, many of which have been achieved without being explicitly noted. It frees the concept of normative femininity from the stereotypes of passivity, masochism, dependency, and narcissism. The content of femininity is regarded as multidetermined, with significant input from cultural prescriptions. . . . A critical developmental and psychoanalytic question remains. This is the question of the universal polarity of gender roles that exists despite the plasticity of the content of those roles. One requires a theory that integrates object relations, the symbolic investment of the genitals, and sexual differences, as well as a cultural perspective. [pp. 634–635]

Person states that penis envy is no longer seen as central to female neurosis and believes the fear of loss of love and of excessive dependency are currently the chief conflicts women bring to therapy. She lists the following as a cluster of traits found particularly in women in Western cultures: "dependency needs, fear of independence, fear of abandonment, unreconstructed longing for love relationships with a man, and fear of being alone" (p. 636). She asks why it is that penis envy "retained its power as a monolithic explanation for so many years and why sexuality and femininity were essentially seen as meagre and distorted. . . . [There are] at least three reasons: misogyny, the lack of the requirement of verification in psychoanalytic theorizing, and the underlying biological assumptions in psychoanalysis" (pp. 636–637).

As long as psychoanalysis insisted on a framework of biologically unfolding psychosexual stages, the familial, social, or cultural context could not be integrated into theory or practice. In fact, this change has occurred throughout medicine as physicians appreciate more fully the effect of what is happening in the patient's family and work life on his or her overall physical health. We now take for granted the relationship between external stress and internal malfunctioning. This is another way to answer the earlier question I raised, as to why it was that the work of Horney, Jones, and Thompson was so flatly rejected by mainstream psychoanalysis in the '20s through the mid '60s. Two major historical changes had to occur. One was the revitalization of the woman's movement, which brought pressure to bear on therapists and patients alike. The other was the development of ego psychology and the object relations school within psychoanalysis, which found libido theory an inadequate explanation of human development and which created what Person calls a "paradigm shift."

> While all psychoanalytic theory acknowledges the internalization of external values and prohibitions in the formation of ego ideal and superego, there is more emphasis in object-relations theory on the way subjectivity (fantasies, wishes) and the formation of ego is influenced by the experiential. Even sexuality, so clearly grounded in biology, is embedded in meaning and cannot be understood without reference to culture. Individuals internalize aspects of their interpersonal world, albeit distorted by infantile mental processes and fantasies. This internalization shapes both their experience of desire and expression of sexuality. [p. 644]

One very important aspect of female sexuality and therefore of self-esteem is the female orgasm. The integration of biological, psychological, familial, and cultural factors all combine to make this a highly complex issue and an area of concern for many women who are not able to achieve orgasm in sexual intercourse, or, for some, even in manual or oral stimulation. In Chapter 7 I will discuss this from a theoretical and a clinical perspective with some case examples. Helene Deutsch wrote extensively on this topic, but, surprisingly, it is often ignored in psychoanalytic and in feminist writing, with the exception of Mary Jane Sherfy's article (1970), which has no clinical examples. It seems to have been brought "out of the closet" by the research of Kinsey (1953) and the laboratory work of Masters and Johnson (1970).

FEMALE PSYCHOLOGY: CONTEMPORARY
PSYCHOANALYTIC VIEWS

Harold Blum

The volume *Female Psychology: Contemporary Psychoanalytic Views,* edited by Harold Blum, appeared in 1977 and marks the beginning of the acceptance of a broader view of the psychology of women within the traditional American Psychoanalytic Association. Most of the articles in this book had been published in a supplementary issue of the *Journal of the American Psychoanalytic Association.* The authors, who express radically differing views from traditional psychoanalytic theory of female development and female psychology, include, among others, Gertrude R. Ticho (1977), Robert J. Stoller (1975), Harold P. Blum, Adrienne Applegarth (1977), Roy Schafer (1977), and Peter Barglow and Margaret Schaefer (1977).

We are told that girls do not want to become men, but rather to become independent, autonomous women—a rejection of the damaged female thesis. We also learn that a young girl's wish to have a baby is not necessarily related to a wish to have a penis.

The authors call for revision and repair of Freud's psychology of women, which is described as distorted, irrational, and reductionistic. Psychoanalysts are urged to be involved in the contemporary discussion of the warping and exploitation of women in our society, and are warned that interpretations of criticisms of the role of women as rationalizations of penis envy on the part of neurotic females is a sign of intellectual isolationism.

We are told that even if girls do not develop as strict a superego as boys, Freud may have drawn the wrong conclusion; girls might develop a more enlightened and realistic moral code. Furthermore, Schafer goes so far as to say that Freud's view of women's morality and objectivity are "logically and empirically indefensible" (p. 34), and suggests that Freud's views developed out of patriarchal values that were erroneously believed to be objective and scientific.

Yes, psychoanalysis had come a long way. This collection includes revisions of almost all the theories comprising the Freud–Deutsch approach, including early female sexuality, the Oedipus complex, masturbation in latency, adolescence, female autonomy, masochism, penis envy, pregnancy, women and work inhibitions, learning inhibitions, orgasm, and male envy of women. All seventeen articles are surprisingly open in their criticism of Freud and their clear rejection of most of his theories of female development. Some come from a perspective of direct child observation, but most come from rejection of drive-oriented theory in favor of ego psychology and object-relations theory, as well as a clearer understanding of narcissistic character disorders. Some are especially sensitive to the plight of women in a patriarchal society and the difficulties for modern women who attempt to change but are confronted with resistance from external reality.

"Female Autonomy and Young Adult Women"—Gertrude Ticho

Gertrude Ticho, in her article "Female Autonomy and Young Adult Women" (1970), cites one of her patients, a physician, whose main problem was her fear of her unconscious aggression. She worked very hard in medical school and to her amazement was the second best in her class.

When some of the male students made sarcastic remarks about competitive women, she became afraid of social rejection and isolation and deliberately kept her grades down. She also felt hostility from the faculty. Ticho comments that often men respond defensively to women's quests for independence, and that it doesn't help to see bright women being paid less than men in equal positions, or to find so few women in responsible leading positions who could serve as role models.

Penis Envy as Metaphor—William Grossman and Walter Stewart

Other examples document cases in which the patient had been previously treated by an analyst who misdiagnosed the symptoms, and the patient suffered due to the analyst's bias. An oversimplified and reductionistic interpretation of penis envy can actually lead to a lowering of self-esteem and intensify a woman's neurotic image of herself as deficient and damaged. William Grossman and Walter Stewart's article "Penis Envy: From Childhood Wish to Developmental Metaphor," describes two women who were seen in second analyses. In both first analyses, the women's symptoms were interpreted as penis envy; both patients accepted the interpretation, one with masochistic gratification; and the analyses became stalemated. In the second analysis, this view was not confirmed. The patients were seen to suffer from a central conflict involving a sense of identity, narcissistic sensitivity, and problems of aggression, expressed in terms of a general envy, a sense of worthlessness, inadequacy, damage, and deprivation. The authors believe that the interpretation of penis envy had an organizing effect, but not a therapeutic one, functioning like a delusion. The interpretation increased the patients' sense of despair and injustice, and thus resulted in a constant state of envy. One woman became so obsessively preoccupied by the interpretation that she considered going to Denmark for a sex change operation. Grossman and Stewart conclude that "penis envy" must be treated like the manifest content of a dream or a screen memory, and state that in many cases the envy of men actually hides a sense of deprivation and worthlessness and a fear of abandonment.

Penis Envy in Female Psychology—Shahla Chehrazi

In a paper by Shahla Chehrazi (1986), published in the *Journal of the American Psychoanalytic Association,* the author, a psychoanalyst, illustrates the change in the view of the centrality of penis envy. She describes the case of a 12-year-old girl with tomboyish characteristics and a conscious wish to be a boy. The young girl gives her analyst a gift, which he interprets as stemming from a wish on her part to get something from him, or from a hope that the analyst will grant her wish to become a boy or help her to change into a boy. She responds with depression to this interpretation, because it inadvertently confirms her neurotic perception that having a penis will solve her conflicts. An alternative interpretation, based on a view that penis envy could serve many defensive functions and meanings, and that it is symptomatic of other anxiety and conflict, is that the patient has many fears and anxieties about being a girl and somehow finds it safer to wish to be a boy. In illustration of the latter interpretation, the patient revealed her fears about wearing skirts, and material concerning her anxiety about menstruation and genital injury emerged.

The articles in the Blum book weave together the unconscious fantasy life and the external realities of past and present in a way that results in a broad approach to the problems of women on cultural, interpersonal, and intrapsychic levels. However, although at times reference is made to the transference, it is not explored as often or with the depth one would expect from psychoanalysts. An exploration of countertransference reactions is totally absent.

"Some Observations on Work Inhibitions in Women"—Adrienne Applegarth

Some authors in the Blum volume incorporate feminist theory into their analysis in a way that results in what I would call an integration of feminist and psychoanalytic theory. One such author is Ticho, in the article discussed above. Roy Schafer, in "Problems in Freud's Psychology of Women," offers an excellent analysis and critique of Freudian theory that has all the power and conviction of the best feminist writing, with the added bonus that it comes from a man. Schafer provides no clinical examples, unfortunately, but his appreciation of the feminist position, though never articulated directly, is most gratifying. His article is divided into three sections: "The Problem of Women's Morality and Objectivity," "The Problem of Neglected Prephallic Development," and "The Problem of Naming." This sample from Schafer will illustrate his approach:

> Differences between men and women in ego functioning are qualitative, corresponding to modes of functioning rather than amounts. Contrary to Freud, there can be no final authority on the question of whether one mode of functioning is superior to another, for the question makes sense only in a context of values. Modes may be described, and different modes may be contrasted, but only a taken-for-granted patriarchal value system could lead to Freud's unqualified statement about women's relative mental incompetence. [p. 340]

Another example is presented by Adrienne Applegarth in "Some Observations on Work Inhibitions in Women." This article is an excellent presentation of psychoanalytic theory of work inhibitions as the result of aggressive and libidinal conflicts and pathological narcissism. But Applegarth is especially concerned with aspects of work inhibitions in women. She quotes Karen Horney extensively, as do most of the contributors in the Blum volume (there are 25 references to Horney in the index). She cites many instances of work inhibitions related to penis envy as a result of low self-esteem, which she sees as more significant in women than in men. Women's fear of defectiveness keeps them from taking on challenging jobs outside of traditional female fields.

> Their feeling that their career activities are masculine arouses fears that they have lost or will lose their sexual identity as women, to say nothing of their conviction that they will no longer be attractive to men. There is enough reality in this to make resistances around it difficult to analyze, for many men do have problems with women who actively use their intelligence. [p. 259]

Applegarth says she has been struck by the difficulty with which the conviction of female inferiority is given up, and she describes a number of resistances that block progress, including the part played by the mother. However, she states that her interpretations do not result in resolution as readily as in other symptomatology. She then goes on to include a cultural interpretation of these resistances along with her earlier intrapsychic interpretations: "However, it is also true that few neurotic convictions receive as much outside support as does this one, since society continues to restrict certain freedoms and opportunities for women, who are devalued in many ways and from whom less is expected" [p. 260].

Applegarth presents another, most interesting revision of Freud's famous inferior superego theory of females. She believes that Freud failed to distinguish between superego content and basic superego structure or function. Women often have as superego content the value that they should be responsive to the wishes and opinions of others, which superficially could appear to reflect a less inexorable, independent superego. However, the focus should be on the structure or function, for example, the fact that women have stronger strictures against aggression and sexuality and place a higher value on maintaining relationships than men. Applegarth states that in her observation it is not true that women are less governed by guilt or show relative superego weakness. These ideas, published in 1977, predate the publication by Carol Gilligan (1982) of a similar analysis of differences between boys and girls, men and women, in what Gilligan calls moral reasoning, which also focuses on difference, not deficiency. I will discuss the Gilligan work in Chapter 4.

Applegarth's article is an example of a combining of psychoanalytic theory and feminist theory. The resulting psychoanalytic approach is referred to as "cultural" or "societal," but to my way of thinking actually incorporates the influence of a feminist analysis of women's oppression, restriction, and lowered value, with the ego crippling and unhappiness they cause. Some analysts are more comfortable calling this a "cultural" approach than a "feminist" one, but there is no significant difference.

Blum himself, in his chapter "Masochism, the Ego Ideal, and the Psychology of Women," states his view that masochism is not essentially feminine. It derives from unresolved infantile conflict in men and women and is not a valuable aspect of female functioning or personality. He believes that femininity is a result of both cultural and familial influences, unique in individual women, in addition to a "universal psychobiological core" (p. 189) that is connected to specific female functions. He believes that psychoanalysts should not idealize or devalue these female roles. He distinguishes between neurotic masochistic suffering and tolerance for current deprivation for a long-term goal or to meet an ego ideal. This is very similar to the theories of feminist psychologist Paula Caplan that are discussed in Chapter 4.

In another article in the Blum book, Harriet Lerner writes that children and teenagers are taught that boys have a penis and girls have a vagina without reference to the external genitalia of the girl. This inaccurate picture prevents the girl from achieving knowledge and pride in her feminine sexuality, may lead to anxiety and confusion, and can be a contributing factor to penis envy because her female anatomy is not validated (p. 282).

In this brief review of the Blum book I hope to have convinced the reader that genuine changes have occurred in the current thinking of psychoanalysts. One of the positive by-products of the women's movement has been that many more women attend medical school and receive Ph.D.s in psychology than ever before, and some of these women have entered psychoanalytic institutes as candidates. These women have been having an effect on theory building and have helped to integrate a feminist approach into what had been a male preserve. As long as women did not go to medical school and psychoanalytic institutes did not accept non-M.D.s in their programs, there was not much opportunity for the woman's point of view to be heard.

FEMALE CASTRATION ANXIETY—ELIZABETH MAYER

The psychologist and psychoanalyst Elizabeth Mayer, in her paper " 'Everybody Must Be Just Like Me': Observations on Female Castration Anxiety" (1985), adds a unique observation to the ever-growing revision of traditional theory. She makes a distinction between a "phallic castration complex" and "female castration anxiety," and suggests that castration anxiety, in men or in women, is anxiety over losing the genital that is actually possessed. Mayer's 20-month-old daughter stirred her interest in this when the little girl pronounced, "Mummy, Daddy has something funny in his vulva" (p. 331). The child had made the assumption that "everyone is and must be like me," which had led her to believe that everyone must have a vulva.

Mayer then describes a number of female patients who have a similar point of view about men, seeing them as emotionally closed, unable to be receptive or empathic, and without access to inner feelings or inner sensations. These women believe that men are lacking something crucial, something feminine; and they are deeply anxious about their own capacity to be genitally "open," a capacity that can be lost, as it has been lost by the male sex. Mayer comments that, traditionally, psychoanalysis has viewed the clitoris as the external female genital and the vagina as the internal female genital, but in fact the girl's external genitalia include several observable and touchable parts that offer pleasurable sensation: the mons, the labia, the parting between the labia and the introitus. Even when the girl is too young to conceptualize a vagina and the other internal female organs, the ovaries and uterus, she can experience her genitals as having an opening and potential inside space, as represented in the enclosed spaces that little girls build, commented upon by Erikson (1968). Mayer concludes that as the girl recognizes the forbidden nature of her oedipal wishes, she might fear retribution in the form of loss or damage to her genitals. A number of authors, including Melanie Klein and Karen Horney (Horney 1933b), have referred to the girl's fear of internal damage. Mayer's patients imagined men as sealed over genitally and thus as not receptive to a woman's needs for love—that is, men are seen as emotionally closed and uncaring, whereas women are believed to be open and receptive, a hallmark of their femininity. Mayer's descriptions of the working through of the transference reveal the defensive functions served by this conviction, and the paper is especially valuable because the analyst elaborates on the transference.

The feminist movement has effected psychoanalysis in a number of ways. It has brought about a recognition of the work of Horney and Thompson. It has helped to encourage change from within by women analysts who have written of their own views of their women patients. It has affected male analysts, who have contributed by criticizing earlier errors in women's psychology, and by bringing more women into psychoanalytic institutes, where they now comprise half of the candidates. The next step was to bring the strengths of psychoanalytic theory into feminism, and to integrate the best of both into a true psychoanalytic feminism.

4

PSYCHOANALYTIC FEMINISM

To have her walkin' funny we try to abuse it
A big stinking p——y can't do it all
So we try real hard just to bust the walls
I'll break ya down and d——k ya long
Bust your p——y then break your backbone.
                              —2 Live Crew, "Nasty As They Wanna Be," 1989

"Stand by Your Man."

                                        —Tammy Wynette

Many important women writers have contributed to the goal of creating a theory and a practice that incorporate values and knowledge from feminist studies into the venerable estate of psychoanalysis. I believe that many of these writers would like their voices to be heard within the halls of the psychoanalytic institutes; and some of them are indeed members of these institutes. But the real goal has been to correct the errors within psychoanalysis and to create a new psychology of women for the sake of those patients who continue to come for help to analysts and psychotherapists throughout the country, and whose symptoms and needs can be better treated by means of this integration. Many of these writers do not describe clinical examples, however, and so their books are limited to academic circles, feminists, and those clinicians who study them for a theoretical foundation for clinical practice informed by feminist thinking.

In a later volume I will illustrate how this integration can be applied in clinical practice, but I first want to present the ideas that have been most influential in this field and can be most usefully applied.

Early in the women's movement, the focus was on eradicating the barriers of the past and promoting equality between the sexes. Inspired to some degree by the Civil Rights movement, in which some of us had fought, women decried discrimination and urged acceptance of women into all aspects of society. Later, a new trend emerged that involved recognition of differences between men and women. Some seized on this trend to promote women as superior to men, but its primary goal lay in seeking to understand the sources of these differences. Debates about the relative importance of biological, cultural, and individual psychological influences often involved an exploration of the deep psychological roots of gender differences and gender arrangements. The theories of psychoanalysis were invaluable to those seeking the sources of difference in unconscious material and in the fantasies of boys and girls about sexual difference. On the political front, the battle for equality goes on over issues like the Equal Rights Amendment, abortion rights, and equal pay for equal work. Psychological understanding of men's fear of women helps us put these defeats into perspective, but it doesn't make us happy about it.

Many women writers found a lack of sufficient attention paid to mothers and mother–child relationships in the Freudian approach. Melanie Klein and Margaret Mahler focused on early mother–child interaction but did not relate their work to the political side of the issue, the degradation of adult women by adult men, and the problems for men and women in forming bonds of love and trust. Another common theme in these writers is that existing theories are rooted strongly in the male experience, as the experts have usually been men, with women understood in terms of what they are missing when compared to the male paradigm. As women have developed their own theory on female development, there has been a corresponding focus on what men are missing, usually in the areas of intimacy and empathy. The psychoanalytic feminist writers, beginning in 1976, took on these issues and successfully related a psychoanalytic understanding to the important questions of gender differences and arrangements and the deeply held prejudices against women held by men and women alike. Such questions as why women collude in their own depreciation and limitation, why boys and girls play differently, why men and women seem to have different needs in marriage, and why women appear to be more depressed than men and men more violent than women, have been addressed and answered in at times brilliant and always stimulating writing. In addition to the theoretical contributions offered by these women writers, their books left no doubt as to the intellectual achievements of which women are capable once they are given the opportunity for educational advancement and recognition, which the women's movement had done so much to achieve.

THE ONMIPOTENT MOTHER—DOROTHY DINNERSTEIN

The Mermaid and The Minotaur: Sexual Arrangements and Human Malaise, by Dorothy Dinnerstein (1976), was one of the first books in this genre. Only in 1974 had Juliet Mitchell written her pioneering work *Psychoanalysis and Feminism.* Dinnerstein, a psychologist at Rutgers University, was influential in turning our attention to the powerful position of the mother in the infancy and childhood of both men and women. Her critique of Freud, Deutsch, and others is in their underestimation of the mother's omnipotent role in the life of her baby and its powerful lifelong effects. Freud (1927) recognized the mother as the first love-object of the child and its first protection against the external world. But he then dismisses the mother by saying that her protective function is "soon replaced by the stronger father who retains that position for the rest of childhood" (p. 34). The irony is that Freud and Deutsch may have failed to recognize the true power of the mother because of their resistance to acknowledging the powerful influence of their own mothers in their personal lives. In addition, we now have in this country, and in much of the Western world, many millions of women raising children without fathers in the home, thus giving the mother even more power.

Dinnerstein draws much of her feminist approach from Simone de Beauvoir's *The Second Sex* (1952), and she quotes extensively from Norman O. Brown, but much of her work is original. She refers to Freud with admiration as well as criticism, and, calling him a "revolutionary," credits him with recognizing the importance of female mothering; though she describes him as "conservative" for assuming that this is a fixed condition that must be accepted as inevitable. Freud discovered that infantile sexuality grows out of the care that mothers give to the bodies of their babies, and he recognized the central importance of female child rearing in the oedipal complex. Dinnerstein is certain that the idea of male supremacy, the double standard, is an outgrowth of the fact that women are in charge of children, and believes that there can be no genuine change in the situation of women until we have full male participation in early child care. The mother of infancy is a "magically powerful goddess," the source of "ultimate distress as well as ultimate joy." We all feel extreme ambivalence toward women because:

> Like nature, she is both nourishing and disappointing, both alluring and threatening, both comforting and unreliable. The infant loves her

touch, warmth, shape, taste, sound, movement. . . . And it hates her because, like nature, she does not perfectly protect and provide for it. . . . The mother . . . is perceived as capricious, sometimes actively malevolent. [p. 95]

Dinnerstein quotes Melanie Klein's statement that there are fundamental lifelong consequences of the fact that the infant has such "happy experiences" and "unavoidable grievances," resulting in destructive rage or "envy" (p. 96). Dinnerstein continues:

The early mother's apparent omnipotence, then, her ambivalent role as ultimate source of good and evil, is a central source of human malaise: our species' uneasy, unstable stance toward nature, and its uneasy, unstable sexual arrangements. . . . Women, then, are both the most acceptable and the most accepting victims of the human need for a quasi-human source of richness and target of greedy rage. If this were not the case, if there did not exist a special category of human being who seems on an infant level of thought naturally fit to fulfill this infantile need, our species might be forced to outgrow it. Under present conditions, the availability of women as especially suitable victims encourages people to indulge the need. [pp. 100–102]

Most men, she says, believe in their right to rule the world and most women feel a willingness to let them. Why do women comply? Because the crucial psychological fact is that both men and women fear the will of woman.

Man's dominion over what we think of as the world rests on a terror that we all feel: the terror of sinking back wholly into the helplessness of infancy. . . . Female will is embedded in female power, which is under present conditions the earliest and profoundest prototype of absolute power. . . . Its reign is total, all-pervasive, throughout our most vulnerable, our most fatefully impressionable, years. Power of this kind, concentrated in one sex and exerted at the outset over both, is far too potent and dangerous a force to be allowed free sway in adult life. To contain it, to keep it under control and harness it to chosen purposes, is a vital need, a vital task, for every mother-raised human. [p. 161]

In addition to the mother's power to give and withhold care is her power to foster or forbid autonomy. Our awareness of her "separate intentionality" can result in humiliation, and her will can easily prevail over our own emerging will through force exerted upon the weak and small child. Woman is the first adversary. "In our first real contests of will, we find ourselves, more often than not, defeated. The defeat is always intimately carnal; and the victor is always female. . . . It may be a gentle or a harsh will, a sympathetic or an overbearing or a woundingly indifferent will, but it is in any case a uniquely potent will" (p. 167).

Yet Dinnerstein adds that woman is also "the audience who has acclaimed our first triumphs" (p. 168), who "nurtures, celebrates, and stimulates . . . the growth of the child's own will" (p. 169). She has the power to confer existence but is thus the target for unjust blame for misfortunes she has warned against. We must challenge mother's supremacy, and in this challenge there is a vindictiveness. Men may express it directly, through an arrogant attitude toward everything female. Women express it directly in distrust and disrespect toward other women and indirectly by allowing ourselves to be the targets for male vindictiveness, from which we experience vicarious satisfaction. She proposes that male authority is bound to look like a "reasonable refuge" (p. 175) from female authority, so we are enticed into the trap of male domination.

We can see in Dinnerstein's work the essential influence of Freud, because, before him, the rich nature of infancy and early childhood went unrecognized. Dinnerstein enhances the psychoanalytic understanding of the key importance of childhood with her feminist analysis of how the mother's power in childhood creates the need to diminish women—something Freud completely missed. She integrates cultural and psychological causation for what she calls "man's worldmaking monopoly," declaring that man's monopoly of history-making follows from the double sexual standard. Man is free to travel, to go to a war or to a laboratory, to spend all night writing or painting. He can withdraw erotic energy from love "with propriety" and invest it in worldly affairs, while she must be receptive and undemanding. Woman's exclusion from history is a result of her status as representative of the flesh, which disqualifies her to take part in our "communal defiance of the flesh, in our collective counter-assertion to carnality and mortality" (p. 210). This exclusion of women from history is buttressed by societal coercion, but it could not be maintained by force alone. It is supported from within by powerful emotional factors, the interdependence between men and women. The two female motives for compliance, she believes, have been "socially sanctioned existential cowardice" (p. 211) and motherhood.

Dinnerstein refers to Simone de Beauvoir's view that the "central bribe" to which woman succumbs is "the privilege of enjoying man's achievements and triumphs vicariously, honored and treasured by him as arbiter, witness, nurturant servant-goddess, while enjoying immunity from the risks he must take" (p. 211).

Man would like immunity from freedom and responsibility, but he has no choice in the matter. Woman has such immunity, with the liability that she must act as supportive "other" to him, his practical servant maintaining life while he pursues freedom and risk. I have been struck by the frequency with which, when the issue of woman's freedom is raised in conversation, men will, with much passion, confront the outspoken woman with the challenge, "But are you willing to go to war, to be drafted?" This comment expresses the awareness of the complementarity of the two roles, and the unfairness men fear will be the result of women's new-found freedom to achieve and explore, without the responsibilities and dangers. Dinnerstein refers to Margaret Mead's thesis that women consent to man's dominance in history-making because "his self-respect requires it to counterbalance her more impressive contribution as child-bearer. . . . She cherishes his self-respect because—if for no other reason—his male sexual vigor, which it is in her interest to foster, depends upon it" (p. 213).

She is not satisfied with this theory, and believes that man's exclusive right to aggressive actions and woman's exclusive reign over the world of intimacy allow each to express a part for the other, to experience their own needs vicariously through the other, in a reciprocal and mutually satisfactory way that deprives each of a part of themselves. He feels masculine, she feels feminine, and the basic interdependence is reinforced. Keller's work on gender and science (1985) expands this idea and shows how this separation weakens scientific inquiry.

Another result of woman's mothering is the blaming of mothers, and thus all women, and eventually the girl child's self-blame.

> Woman, who introduced us to the human situation and who at the beginning seemed to us responsible for every drawback of that situation, carries for all of us a pre-rational onus of ultimately culpable responsibility forever after. And this incomparable onus—so heavy and so unjust that one must keep it out of focal awareness if one is to stay sane . . . keeps a radical feeling of "No!" strong in every girl and woman whose core of self-affirmation is not wholly crushed by it. The feeling is usually buried, but it is buried alive. It exists as an inarticulate source—the most profound source, I believe—of that refusal to accept the way things are that keeps simmering close to the calmest-looking surfaces of our communal awareness. [p. 234]

Nowhere in this book does Dinnerstein ever mention penis envy, but I believe it is here that she gives her view on this issue. She tells us that the profound sense of unfairness that women have is related to the way in which they are blamed, are made the scapegoats for the ills of life. It is in this sense, I believe, that women—who in fact make up the majority of the population—are often linked with minorities in their sense of injustice and prejudice and exclusion from the sources of power. Just as African-

Americans, Jews, American Indians, or Mexicans bear the brunt of blame for a nation's ills, women in every land have had to bear the blame for individual ills, including the blame for schizophrenia (the schizophreno-getic mother), for male impotence, and for all forms of neurosis. Dinner-stein seems to be saying that this is the source of anger and bitterness, not any anatomical lack. She refers to Freud's question "What do women want?" and answers: "What women want is to stop serving as scapegoats (their own scapegoats as well as men's and children's scapegoats) for human resentment of the human condition" (p. 234).

In the relationship to the infant the mother actually has unilateral power, but this real power becomes a fantasy of everlasting power in the minds of her children as they grow to be men and women. Women must be tolerant of the infant's and child's difficult behavior, because the baby can do no wrong; but a woman's own misdeeds are unforgivable. In relations with man, Dinnerstein says, woman is expected to continue this "one-sidedly nurturant tolerance of the early parent" (p. 235), understandingly and forgivingly accepting his faults, while her own are unforgivable, as if the early power inequity still exists. But "she is without the mother's superior practical power and immunity from retaliation. Her transgres-sions, like the child's, are punishable; his, like the parent's are not" (p. 236). One of the great country music hits is a song by Tammy Wynette entitled "Stand by Your Man," which expresses this double standard. The woman indulges her man's unfaithfulness and forgives him because, after all, "he's just a man." This is the flip side of the more readily acknowl-edged depreciation of women: the man is a baby who needs holding and comforting, and the woman mothers him. Of course, the woman gets held and warmed in this reciprocal arrangement as well. Here Dinnerstein's thesis is confirmed in popular culture. Should the woman stay out all night, one shudders at the likely violent retaliation awaiting her.

> She thus carries the moral obligations of the parent while suffering the powerlessness of the child. . . . No wonder masochism and split-off fury are "truly feminine" traits. They are the underside of the "truly feminine" woman's monstrously overdeveloped talent for unrecipro-cated empathy. . . . [Man] vents against her the infant's boundless rage at the early parent. It is a situation that calls for masochism: since the helpless fury it evokes in her would destroy her if she let herself feel it, splitting some of it off and turning the rest of it inward—joining man against herself, lending her person to the project of getting back at mama—is the best that she can do. [pp. 236–237]

Something else she can do is to make the man pay for this unfair situation: pay literally by supporting her, and pay also by her withholding sex when he fails to treat her as she wishes to be treated. Dinnerstein rejects the traditional theory of female masochism as due to the biological givens of woman's anatomy, as described by Helene Deutsch. In seeing masochism as a result of woman's powerful mothering role and the resultant defenses against women's power created in both men and women, she offers a remedy against perpetuation of female masochism—the joint parenting of the young by both men and women.

> The trouble is that in the mother these negative qualities have their impact where it is most possible for them to do deep damage: on the vulnerable sensibility of the very young child. It is for this reason that certain real faults of women are felt as so much less tolerable than the same real faults in men: in women, these faults in fact inflicted worse wounds. . . . The mother's major human frailties are at bottom less humanly acceptable than the father's. His . . . are more bearable because later encountered. . . . Man is of course willful, tough, earthy, masterful. In her, these same shortcomings are those of a monster: a bitch, a slob, a ball-breaking battleax. . . . Woman does not share man's right to have such traits . . . and man does not share woman's obligation to work at mastering them. . . . Woman never will have this right, nor man this obligation, until male imperfection begins to impinge on all of us when we are tiny and helpless, so that it becomes as culpable as female imperfection. [pp. 237–238]

Dinnerstein has a theory that the tolerance of women for man's sexual infidelity has to do with the woman's vicarious satisfaction in the man's opportunity to act out directly the early wish to "own a woman" and enjoy sole access to her "erotic resources." She can enjoy through him access to another woman, to a body like the one she herself loved at the beginning. In this way the woman connects to the early loved mother and simultaneously punishes her through masochism. This theory relies on the psychoanalytic theory of projection as a defense against homosexuality. Ordinarily we come in contact with this defense in paranoid disorders, but Dinnerstein's understanding could offer less pathological interpretations of both masochism and projections: the anger towards the mother for the forced separation from her body, which men may continue to enjoy through access to other women, and which the wife enjoys vicariously and masochistically distorts. However, factors of economic dependency may be more important in this "tolerance."

A major omission in *The Mermaid and the Minotaur* is any reference to incest. This omission exists in almost all feminist and psychoanalytic writing before 1986, when, due to the insistence of women in the women's movement and some outstanding books by women therapists, attention finally began being paid to this profoundly traumatic experience, which is depressingly common among women (less so among men). When Dinner-stein says that the father's faults are more bearable than the mother's, she clearly is leaving out the issue of the physical and sexual abuse of children by men. This is a serious omission. Incest is commonly committed on children between the ages of 2 and 3 years, surely a most vulnerable time. The lasting traumatic effects of these abuses are now being exposed, showing how damaging and destructive the symptom picture is. Clinical experience is showing how long it takes to work through the effects. However, Dinnerstein's thesis can help to explain why the truth about this frequent father damage has been so long in emerging, since both men and women have protected fathers in order to rescue themselves from the feared maternal power and because of economic dependence. Initially, mothers were blamed for incest with theories that the mother "encour-aged" the father's acting out; but fortunately this error is also being corrected by those working in the field, who find the mother often feels as helpless as the child in the situation. The emergence of shelters for mothers proves to be the best protection for the children.

At the end of Dinnerstein's book there is a brief historical analysis of the women's movement and its relation to the period in the 1960s of intense political activity among young people. Dinnerstein believes that the absence of political activity among young people during the 1950s was due less to McCarthyism than to the events that had shaped the lives of their parents, and left that generation of the 1930s and 1940s in a state of "moral shock," stupefied and in retreat. The depression, World War II with the horrors of Nazism, and then the bombing of Hiroshima left those who were adults during those years frightened and in a state of bereave-ment, trying to assimilate the meaning of these horrendous events. In addition, the revelations following Stalin's death produced the loss of the Soviet Union as a possible source of moral leadership. People of that generation withdrew from history into intensely personalistic, inward-turning domestic life, as a result of a "deeply, fatefully altered view of the societal process" (p. 259). This turn to traditional paths and traditional roles from public life was an "endeavor to find some immediate new core of meaning" (p. 265). Betty Friedan's *The Feminine Mystique,* about the role of women in the 1950s, makes sense when seen from this perspective. I had focused on the lack of women's control over their bodies in the years prior to the birth control pill and legalized abortion as the determining factor, but I was impressed with Dinnerstein's analysis of the 1950s as a waiting period—a generation waiting for the next one to take up the torch that had been carried by the politically active generation of the 1930s. In locating the creation of the resurgent feminist movement in the New Left of the 1960s, Dinnerstein comments on this group of young men's redefini-tion of the traditional male role, as exhibited symbolically by long hair.

These men wanted freedom from traditional male responsibility but wanted to maintain traditional male privilege to subordinate women.

> What these men continued to want from women was maternal applause, menial services, and body contact. What they largely withdrew from women was the personal commitment that men in the traditional symbiotic arrangement have been able to offer them, the commitment one offers a deeply, centrally needed person. . . . The failure of the men in those circles . . . opened a fateful personal rift between the sexes. It insulted and disinherited, in personally intolerable ways, the women who could have worked with them as peers. [p. 273]

This is a psychological view that deepens Barbara Ehrenreich's thesis (1983) of the history behind the women's liberation movement described in Chapter 2. The sexual attachments of the 1960s, the "sexual freedom" for men and women, by eliminating the responsibilities of marriage, discredited the value to women and children of this mutually supportive union that meets basic needs for security, although in its traditional form it also often included the subservience of women. Dinnerstein's conclusion is a disquieting one: "It seems possible that now, for the first time in history, women in substantial numbers hate, fear and loathe men as profoundly as men have all along hated, feared and loathed women" (p. 276).

TOWARD A NEW PSYCHOLOGY OF WOMEN—JEAN BAKER MILLER

Toward a New Psychology of Women was published in 1976, three years after Jean Baker Miller edited *Psychoanalysis and Women* (1973). Miller, a Sullivanian analyst, writes from an interpersonal and cultural approach, attributing women's qualities to cultural proscription and suppression. Like Dinnerstein, she emphasizes the mother–daughter relationship. This book is an original work, and, like Dinnerstein's book, is quite unconventional in style, focusing on the subordination of women and the effects of this unequal relationship on the psychology of both men and women. Miller describes the situation for subordinates in general, whether in race, class, nationality, or gender, as one in which they are considered to be innately defective or deficient in mind or body and thus unable to perform the preferred roles in society. They are expected to be pleasing to the dominant group: passive, docile, lacking initiative and decisiveness, immature, weak, and helpless. If subordinates fit this picture they are considered well-adjusted; if not, they are deemed abnormal. The dominant group is the model for "normal." The subordinates learn to be highly attuned to the dominants in order to please them, because their fate depends upon it. Unfortunately, the subordinates internalize the belief in their inferiority advanced by the dominants, though some are able to see the truth and protest the injustice of their position, thus challenging the mythology of the dominant group. "Mutually enhancing interaction is not probable between unequals" (p. 12), and thus conflict inevitably results.

Traditionally, conflict has been kept covert, with women who don't accept the subordinate role using deception and manipulation to keep up the pretense of male superiority. If they are open about their dissatisfaction with an inferior role, and state that their needs have equal validity, they will be seen as creating conflict and accused of not being true women, that is, not fitting the male's image of what a woman should be in order to please him. Women are warned that if they try to attain their own goals and concentrate on their self-development, they will never attract a man and will suffer isolation. Miller states that this threat is "by no means imaginary" (p. 19). To avoid this fate, women are urged not to explore or express their needs and to transform those needs by seeing them as if they were identical to those of others: husbands, children, employers.

Miller then moves into the subject of what she sees as women's strengths. These are, first, and paradoxically, weakness, helplessness, and vulnerability; and also emotionality, an ability to foster the growth of others, a sense of cooperation, and creativity. With regard to the first, she describes the now well-recognized fact that men are encouraged to dread and deny any feelings of weakness or helplessness, whereas women are encouraged to "cultivate this state of being," in spite of the fact that such feelings are inevitable and natural for all of us (p. 29). Because, she says, women are able to admit to feelings of weakness or vulnerability, they are more able to tolerate such feelings, and so their apparent weakness is a strength. The problem is that women believe it is right for them to feel weak, are fearful of not being weak, and find it most difficult to admit their strengths and use their resources for fear of being "unfeminine." On the other hand, she points out, since men claim not to have feelings of insecurity, it has been the role of women to supply men's needs so that men can continue to deny these feelings. Shades of Virginia Woolf again. However, as long as women refrain from testing themselves, they retain the idea that men do have some special strength that enables them to function in the outside world, something magical that a woman cannot attain. Miller's explanation for this is that women are conditioned throughout their lives to believe that men have this special quality. Thus, she gives a cultural explanation for a quality that psychoanalysts would see as evidence of women's "penis envy." Miller says that women do not have to remain weak, that the only thing they lack is opportunity to practice in the real world and the "lifelong belief that one has the right to do so" (p. 35).

I would like to cite some personal examples on this point. My family used to enjoy telling the following story about me as a child. If I broke a plate, I was told that my father would fix it, and then my father would appear with another plate, unbroken. I would later say, after breaking another plate, "Daddy, fix," and he would produce a new plate again. It was not until I was in my thirties and asked my father to put up some drapery rods for me that I observed him struggling with the job and realized he was ordinary, not the super-human he and my mother had conspired to lead me to believe. I started trying to fix things myself after that, and struggled, but by getting advice from experienced friends I did become moderately competent. But why did my parents want me to believe that my father had magical powers? Perhaps it started innocently, as a means to ease my distress when I broke something, but we cannot help but observe that it was not my mother who took the credit for having such power.

Also in my thirties, I went for a bicycle ride with a male friend. As we were cycling up a long hill I said I had to stop, because my legs were hurting. He replied that was no reason to stop, and urged me to keep going, quoting "no pain, no gain," an expression I had never heard before. I was amazed, as it had never before occurred to me that physical discomfort was not grounds for stopping an activity. Now this may have been an example of male masochism, but I was challenged by what I saw as his strength, and made the effort to continue, with a whole new attitude about physical endurance. Several years later I completed a 15-mile run to raise funds for a women's building.

On the humorous side, in the early days of my women's group, a member told the story of how, after her divorce, she had to learn how to change the filter in her home furnace. She was amazed at how simple a procedure it was, taking only a minute. She described how for years, whenever her husband changed the filter, he would remain in the basement for a long time and then would come upstairs and lie down on the sofa. She had assumed it was a strenuous job.

My first story is an example of actual deception, which led me to believe my father had some superior qualities. The second is illustrative of the idea that there are two separate cultures in our society. In the male culture, strength is highly valued, and so boys learn to endure hardship in order to develop strength. Girls are not raised with this value, but with other values. And yet though women, due to biological differences, can never develop the muscle strength that men can, they certainly need not be physically weak. The third story is also one of deception, but it was effective because the woman never asked to watch the man so that she could learn how the job was done, presumably accepting filter changing as a masculine pursuit.

Now, can we integrate these three cultural examples with the psychoanalytic approach that sees women's sense of weakness and inadequacy as a symptom of penis envy? Only, I believe, in the very narrow sense that a little girl, surrounded by all these cultural dictates, cannot possibly appreciate their sociological implications and may naively believe that the possessor of a penis has special strengths that she, without one, can never attain.

But this is only part of a larger picture. The girl would observe the many domestic skills of her mother and perhaps an older sister, grand-mother, or aunt as well, and would wonder if she could ever possess *their* strength and knowledge. If, as an adult, she felt inferior, particularly to men, it would indicate that her mother and other females in her household never encouraged her to develop her strengths; and that they perhaps considered themselves inferior to men, deprecated female functions, and did not believe in their right to pursue challenging, untraditional goals. The adult woman's beliefs in male superiority, and hence her envy, could be corrected with experience and maturity if she had the opportunity to associate with women who had developed themselves and could serve as positive role models. Surely today such examples are numerous, but in the past they were hard to find.

I would like to offer another personal example, also from when I was in my thirties. Attending a conference on women and the law, I heard a woman attorney lecture on the issue of equal employment opportunity for women. I can still remember the impact on me, not so much of what she said, but the way she said it: her confidence, her expertise, the way she approached the blackboard and wrote things down, her overall sense of competence. Mary Dunlap changed my life that day. I realized that in my four years as an undergraduate at the University of California I had never had a female professor, and so had been denied the opportunity to have a role model of intellectual strength and competence. While attending graduate school in social work I had women professors (I learned years later that most of them were never tenured), but because social work was women's work, this somehow did not count as the "real world" for me. One may predict that the daughters of this new generation of capable working women, with ample role models, will not feel weak and deficient, so that their observations of anatomical difference will remain just that. Boys are different; they have some things girls don't have and might wish they could have; but that need not become the basis for a lifelong feeling of damage and inadequacy, so long as parents make it clear to their daughters that they too have some wonderful parts in their bodies that make them very special. Such a prediction, however, also posits the continuation of changes in society that challenge male supremacy and male privilege and the entry of women into positions of political power and economic responsibility; so that any earlier "temporary misunderstanding" of boys' better fortune in life is not continually confirmed by actual male advantage in the real adult world. For example, as long as a majority of college professors continue to be male, the argument for all-women colleges remains valid, as shown in the battle at Mills College in Oakland, California, in 1990. The Board of Trustees, in response to financial difficulties, voted to open the college to men. The outcry among the students was so great that the vote was rescinded. The most compelling argument against the vote was the higher achievement levels attained after graduation by women who had attended all women's colleges, compared to those of women who had studied at coeducational schools.

The next strength of women that Miller discusses is emotionality. Miller believes that women's greater sense of the emotional aspects of life is a result of their subordinate position, of their having learned to be attuned to the moods of the dominant group. However, women have concentrated so much on the emotions and reactions of others that they have often failed to recognize and give credence to their own emotions. The dominant male culture has viewed emotions as an impediment, an evil to be controlled, not a good to be valued as a potential source of strength. Women believe that "events are important and satisfying only if they occur within the context of emotional relatedness" (p. 39). The fear is that if they act and think rationally, they will lose this capacity for emotional connect-edness.

Another strength of women lies in their participation in the develop-ment of others, a quality not valued by the dominant society, as evidenced by the low status and low pay of child-care work and teaching. Women appreciate more than men the pleasure of this close connection with the growth of others, a pleasure central to the role of the psychotherapist. Fostering their own growth has been another matter, not encouraged because it is seen as a threat to the role of women as caretakers for men and children. "Women have now stated that helping in the growth of others without the equal opportunity and right to growth for themselves is a form of oppression" (p. 40).

Miller believes that women have a greater recognition of the "essen-tial cooperative nature of human existence," whereas men may experience cooperation as somehow detracting from themselves (p. 41). She does not deny that women too can be competitive, and have been so with other women for men, but she believes they are working more toward cooper-ation with women. The consciousness-raising groups are a good example of this trend. In addition to cooperation, Miller also sees creativity as a necessity for human beings—the creativity of not artistic productions, but rather a personal creativity that everyone must have throughout life.

Women, she says, have had to create an inner person with "different desires and ways of living than those recognized and rewarded by the dominate culture" (p. 47).

An interesting question about Miller's views on female strengths is whether she is proposing a separate-but-equal thesis, or whether in fact she is claiming female superiority. Although in several places she denies that she is saying women are better or more virtuous than men, in fact her language is the language of superiority. She says women are "ahead of psychological theory and practice—and of the culture that gave rise to present theory" (p. 47), that women are "in advance of the values of this society" (p. 44), and that the dominant male culture "holds up narrow and ultimately destructive goals and attempts to deny vast areas of life" (p. 47). This seems to me to come close to proposing a new feminine mystique that says the personal and emotional is superior. In my view, the ultimate goal should be an integration of the best of the male style and values with the best of the female. Such an integration would include the emotional strengths in which women excel, and the male strengths involved in taking risks, having courage, and challenging oneself to achieve goals for intellectual, physical, and social satisfaction. The bicycle story I told above represents an example of male courage that women would do well to emulate, as they should emulate men's willingness to take the risks and commit to the dedication involved in scientific pursuits.

Miller contrasts men and women in their attitude toward "giving." She observes that women in psychotherapy spend a great deal more time than men do talking about issues of giving, questioning whether they are giving enough, and that they often fear not being givers. Men rarely have this concern, and it is not part of their self-image. Men are concerned about "doing," and their identity revolves more around measuring up in their performance. The problem for women is feeling that other people demand too much from them and resenting it, yet being unable to say "no" except in indirect ways such as somatic symptoms.

> Women have traditionally built a sense of self-worth on activities that they can manage to define as taking care of and giving to others. . . . Women, more easily than men, can believe that any activity is more satisfying when it takes place in the context of relationships to other human beings—and even more so when it leads to the enhancement of others. [p. 53]

This is an accurate view of a common conflict for women in the past; it may be less true today, fifteen years later. Women are entering business and the professions in great numbers and dedicating years to their education, training, and achievement. I believe a more contemporary conflict lies around the dilemma of trying to have a career and a family and do justice to both.

Miller, discussing change, expresses the idea that "change and growth are intimate parts of women's lives in a way in which they are not for men" (p. 55). This does not seem accurate to me. Men do teach, both in schools and on the job in the journeyman-apprentice relationship. They do coach Little League and treat the sick and fight for justice in the courts and even make revolutions. If there is a difference, I believe it lies in the fact that men are more likely to do these things as part of a paid job with status and recognition, and not out of a sense of self-sacrifice. For women, however, doing for others can be an escape, an easy way out:

> One can divert oneself almost entirely from the difficult exploration of one's own needs and concentrate on serving other's needs. But when this happens, women often develop the belief—usually not explicitly articulated—that their own needs, even though unexamined, untested, and unexpressed, will somehow be fulfilled in return. To compound the situation, some women come to believe that others will love them (and become permanently devoted to them) because they are serving those others so much and so well. The tragedy here is that people do not usually love others for this reason. [pp. 64–65]

But what makes this a tragedy is that these women had been doing what they were told they must do, what nature determined women should do, and they had every right to expect they would be appreciated for it. Their daughters have had their consciousness raised, and most are determined not to repeat their mother's mistakes. Some fear marriage for this reason.

Miller keeps telling us that men are missing a lot, that "the dominant group is seriously deprived of knowing what it is like to fully integrate living for oneself and for others" (p. 69). Her rationale for this is vague, and she seems to me to make the error of a reaction-formation kind of praise of women with a "mother knows best" countering of male supremacy. Women have a lot to learn from men about pursuing their own self-interest, and the real dilemma is who will take care of the children. Women should not be patronized by telling them how strong they are.

Miller's next subject is woman's sense of failure, of being wrong, and of self-blame—an important topic and one that is a frequent area of work in psychotherapy.

> Since women have had to live by trying to please men, they have been conditioned to prevent men from feeling even uncomfortable. Moreover, when women suspect that they have caused men to feel unhappy or angry, they have a strong tendency to assume that they themselves are wrong. . . . One also becomes angry but has nowhere to go with this

> anger, no way to understand it. The anger adds further to the sense of
> being wrong. Now one builds up a store of angry negative emotions,
> feeling . . . bad and evil. [p. 57]

She raises a key question: How can women be caring without being
subservient?

Miller continues to develop her thesis that women's values are a
"more advanced approach to living and functioning" with her development of the idea that "affiliation is valued as highly as, or more highly than,
self-enhancement" (p. 83). She discusses some case examples and concludes:

> They all expressed a common theme: the lack of ability to really value
> and credit their own thoughts, feelings, and actions. . . . Unless there is
> another person present, the entire event—the thought, the feeling, the
> accomplishment, or whatever it may be—lacks pleasure and signifi-
> cance. It is not simply that she feels like half a person, lacking total
> satisfaction and wanting another person, but still able to take some
> satisfaction from her own half. It is like being no person at all—at least
> no person that matters. As soon as she can believe she is using herself
> *with* someone else and *for* someone else, her own self moves into
> action and seems satisfying and worthwhile. . . . When women act on
> the basis of this underlying psychological motive, they are usually led
> into subservience. [pp. 89–90]

Miller correctly points out that this mode of relating through attachment to
others includes the danger of depression when there is a loss of affiliation,
which is valued more highly than self-enhancement. From my point of
view, it is important, when working with a woman who complains of
depression due to a relational loss, to determine whether she is experiencing abandonment, a feeling stemming from actual loss plus anger at the
person for abandoning her—anger that she may have trouble feeling is
legitimate if she devalues herself and doesn't feel entitled to love and
attention; or, more seriously, if she is actually experiencing annihilation,
which would indicate that the problem is more in the direction of a
borderline condition. This, I believe, is a weakness in Miller's book: she
fails to make diagnostic distinctions between women who suffer from the
culture's failure to value their strengths and who thus feel less valuable than
men, and women who suffer from serious boundary problems due to the
failure in early object relations for validation of their separate and autonomous functioning. Such failure may result from parental needs for the
child's dependence, most likely because of boundary problems of the
parents themselves, or because a mother with boundary problems is the
primary caretaker and the father is not caring or involved enough to help
his daughter to develop in an independent way. Miller is so focused on

correcting the undervaluation of women that she ignores the very real pathological consequences for children that can result from their mother's crippling as a person of consequence in her own right. I have seen these consequences repeatedly in my women patients.

Yet Miller is not so enthusiastic about autonomy:

> We need a terminology that is not based on inappropriate carryovers from men's situation. Even a word like *autonomy,* which many of us have used and liked, may need revamping for women. It carries the implication—and for many women the threat—that one should be able to pay the price of giving up affiliations in order to become a separate and self-directed individual. In reality, when women have struggled through to develop themselves as strong, independent individuals they did, and do threaten many relationships, relationships in which the other person will not tolerate a self-directed woman. . . . Unlike other groups, women do not need to set affiliation and strength in opposition one against the other. We can readily integrate the two, search for more and better ways to use affiliation to enhance strength—and strength to enhance affiliation. [pp. 95–96]

In her discussion of the problem of authenticity for women, Miller points out that authenticity and subordination are totally incompatible, and that anger can be one of the first authentic reactions. The risk for women is that by pursuing authenticity there is a danger of displeasing others, which they fear will result in abandonment. The reason is, she believes, "because male–female relationships have been so effectively structured to deflect women away from their own reactions and fulfillment" (p. 110). "To achieve ways of living that will attend to all women's needs, the forms inevitably will have to include more mutuality, cooperation, and affiliation, on both a personal and a larger social scale" (p. 113).

Day care would surely be an example of meeting the needs of women and children, and therefore of families, on a social scale. The neglect of this important need in the United States cannot be attributed to male domination alone, because in socialist countries and throughout the Western European democracies day care is fully supported at the national level, with no evidence that the men in those countries have any less power in the society than in our own. There is a peculiar American mentality, which merges with the neglect of women's and children's needs in this case, that the individual should be able to solve his or her own problems and not rely or depend on the state—a fact reflected in our lack of national health insurance as well. This may be the result of our pioneer experience, but whatever the cause, it must be understood and resolved, because it is urgent that these needs be addressed.

In her discussion of power, Miller proposes defining power for women as "the capacity to implement." She divides the concept of power into "power *for* oneself and power *over* others," distinguishing between the "ability to influence others and the power to control and restrict them" (p. 116). She says that the background of women does not teach them that they need subordinates. Her thesis here seems invalid to me, partially because she either is not aware of or else discounts the common practice in other cultures of the mother-in-law having vital power over her daughter-in-law; for example, in Japan, India, and prerevolutionary China, where the young daughter-in-law is brought into her husband's home and is immediately placed in a position of subordination to his mother. There are instances of very cruel treatment to these young girls, who if they run away back to their own family home will be returned for reasons connected with dowry requirements, so that they have no recourse but to suffer or commit suicide. Miller also neglects the forms of subtle but significant power women have over men through the granting or withholding of sexual favors. There appears to me to be a need to deny many unappealing aspects of women's psychic structure in Miller's thesis. Dinnerstein seems more realistic. Miller would have to modify her work to include an appreciation of women's anger and its power to attempt a reformulation of female psychology.

In her discussion of masochism and power, Miller acknowledges that a woman, by remaining a victim, does not have to confront the anger she has accumulated over her position and can blame the other person, avoiding responsibility to change her situation. Of course, attempting to change brings up the fear of abandonment. It may be quite difficult to separate anger from assertiveness and easier to convince oneself that the anger is unjustified, thus "continuing the masochistic circle of self-condemnation" (p. 123). Miller reminds us that an understanding of conflict is at the core of psychoanalysis, and she distinguishes between productive and destructive conflict. Conflict between a dominant and a subordinate is a matter of winning and losing, whereas conflict between equals can, though painful, be a "respectful interaction" (p. 133). For women, the threat of isolation has been the greatest obstacle to feeling and expressing conflict. "Some of women's best impulses and sources of energy are thus nipped in the bud. The overwhelming pressure is for women to believe they must be wrong: they are to blame, there must be something very wrong with *them*" (p. 131).

THE STONE CENTER—JUDITH JORDAN, JANET SURREY, ALEXANDRA KAPLAN, IRENE STIVER

In 1979, inspired by Miller's work, a group of five women clinicians, including Miller, established the Stone Center for Developmental Services and Studies at Wellesley College in Massachusetts. Their "Work in Progress," papers on women's issues, explore the implications of the role of empathy in women's relationships and advance the notion of "self-in-relation" theory as a means of understanding the psychology of women and the high incidence of depression in women. The Stone Center group, which continues to develop Miller's thesis and create new hypotheses of women's functioning, is an affiliation of women therapists working in connection with each other in a cooperative setting where the works in progress are discussed among the members and at colloquia. They do not write collectively, but "relationally and collaboratively" (Surrey 1990, p. 2). One can assume that Miller's theory of conflict between equals as a productive process is put into practice. The other writers, all practicing clinicians, include Judith V. Jordan, Janet L. Surrey, Alexandra G. Kaplan, and Irene P. Stiver.

The most recent papers issued by the group include revisions of earlier work. Surrey (1990) writes that while she previously defined the basic core self-structure in women as "self-in-relation," originating in the mother–daughter relationship, she now sees empathy as a mutual, active, and interactive process involving a new concept, *mutual empathy*. Self-development has been replaced by the development of mutually empathic relationships as a goal of development.

> As *self* recedes as the primary object of study, we are trying to describe relational processes which enlarge and deepen connections that empower all participants. Thus, I have moved from self to self-in-relation to the *movement of relation. Connection* has replaced *self* as the core element or the locus of creative energy of development. [p. 3]

Psychological growth is described as a process; self–other differentiation is no longer the core feature of development. The process encourages healthy strengths arising from healthy connections based on flexibility, responsiveness, adaptation, receptivity, creativity, and activity. Relationships are described as moving forward in a movement of interaction. Change occurs through interaction, which results in a greater sense of power in the relationship, rather than in the separate self. Surrey wonders about the separation issues used in the diagnosis of borderline personality and suggests their replacement with connection issues.

Kaplan's "Empathy and its Vicissitudes" (1990) also describes the group's revised thinking on empathy as:

> relational flow, a mutual exchange in which each shares, absorbs, reflects upon and enhances her own and the other's experience, and the relationship itself. Participation in such a relational flow requires

affective attunement to the other, the ability to absorb the other's experience without losing your own, the balance of affective and cognitive components, and comfort within a relational context of mutual understanding . . . which transcends the experiences of the individuals involved and moves toward a shared sense of enhanced meaning, clarity and enrichment. [p. 6]

She questions Roy Schafer's (1983) notion that an analyst who appears quite unempathic in his or her personal relationships can be empathic as a therapist.

From the Stone Center perspective, Schafer has essentially turned empathy on its head, seeing it as emerging from relational constraints and distance, rather than arising from relational engagement. Whereas he posits that clients grow by becoming recipients of the therapist's empathy, we believe that clients *and* therapists grow through active participation in an empathic process which enhances their sense of themselves as relational beings, able to join with others in relational connection. [p. 8]

Jordan (1990) writes in "Relational Development Through Empathy: Therapeutic Applications" that a relationship is of the self but beyond the self and that growth occurs in becoming a part of relationship rather than apart from relationship.

Thus increasing the experience of connection through empathy in- volves some sense of "loss of self," if by "self" we mean the self- contained, self-sufficient, in-control self of Western psychology. This does not mean, however, a loss of clarity, purpose, feeling of well- being, or experience of wholeness . . . quite the contrary. And this is the paradox at the heart of all relating: In diminishing individual self-consciousness and moving into relational awareness, we experi- ence an expansion of our sense of integrity, realness, and freedom. [p. 11]

Being for the relationship can encompass being for the self and for the other, thus avoiding the dilemma of selfishness versus selflessness. Each party contributes to, grows in, and depends on the relationship in a way which Jordan believes is not "giving" and "taking" but rather "relational interdependence." She believes that our notion of self-sufficiency and separateness is exaggerated and distorted.

She describes a case example to illustrate the development of empathy in a woman patient, Sue, who was able to develop in therapy from a relational image of bad daughter/good-but-fleeing mother to the next stage of angry, victim daughter/selfish, bad mother to the final stage of limited, overburdened mother/empathic daughter, in which she experienced the problem as a relational failure rather than just a failure of self or other. In "developing empathy for her mother, Sue experienced increased empathy for herself, and her empathy for self enhanced her empathy for her mother and for others" (p. 13).

My difficulty with the Stone Center writers is their lack of differential diagnosis. Not all patients are alike, just as not all therapists are alike in their capacities for relatedness. The classic, white Anglo-Saxon Protestant may need help in allowing herself to depend on others and in reducing her conviction of the value of self-sufficiency, but patients from other cultures, Italian, Jewish, or Mexican, for example, may need help in differentiating from their families. The cultural factor is just one, of course, and the pathological problems some patients have in differentiation or closeness ultimately stem from their particular family relationships and the vicissitudes of their life experience. For example, a white Protestant patient of mine has been terribly tied to dependency on her mother because at the time of the death of her father, when she was 9, her mother used her to re-create the bond of security that she had just lost with her husband. Some women are in hostile-dependent relationships with mothers, husbands, and children; they need clearer boundaries before they can begin to work on true empathy. There are women who attempt to control their families with manipulation, retaliation, and even suicide threats because they feel so helpless without the merging connection.

A focus on the value of connection needs further refining. People can only come together in connection after they have established some self-sufficiency and have a true self to offer to a relationship. This discussion cannot take place outside a discussion of values, which I will attempt in Chapter 8, because it is the values we place on marriage, the family, and friendships that determine how much we stress autonomy or connection.

I understand that the Stone Center group stresses that connection does not need to be regressive, that people can grow within a relationship, but I do not think it is possible to deny that compromise of one's own desires are a necessary aspect of relationship. This issue is avoided and relationship is extolled in the Stone Center approach. It appears to me that there is a denial of the genuine conflicts for individuals in close relationships and these conflicts are the very essence of much of the work we do in psychotherapy. For the Stone Center writers, the conflicts seem to melt away in some wonderful togetherness. What about the genuine differences between a husband and wife that can lead to differing priorities in terms of money, time, and values such as social life, family visiting, and leisure time pursuits. And more importantly, how is the conflict between career and parenting resolved without some sacrifice? Greater empathy and awareness of the other may result in a recognition of differences that cannot be resolved, but merely tolerated. As true recognition grows of the other's values and limitations, no amount of empathic connection will change certain features of another's personhood that may be distasteful, disagreeable, or weak, and being able to bear it may be the best resolution for maintaining the marital bond in order to preserve the positive components in the relationship for each partner.

I would say that life for a woman or a man is very different within a marriage than it is as a single person, and that each has advantages and disadvantages. People choose which losses they are willing to sustain when they choose to marry or not (or live in a marriage-like union). Divorce is always tragic, but it is especially so when either party is so dependent and lacking in self-sufficiency that they can barely survive the break-up of the relationship. With divorce a reality, one needs to be cautious in building too much of one's life around a love relationship. A good approach may be to have many good connections to others in one's life so as to avoid the pitfalls of devastating loss if a marriage fails or a child needs to break away from home and family. In his play *No Exit,* Jean-Paul Sartre writes about hell. The key line is, "Hell is other people," yet each character constructs his or her own hell with dependency on the praise and approval of others.

An interesting example of the importance of connection in women's lives is in the person of First Lady Barbara Bush. She has built her life around loving and caring for her children and grandchildren while her husband, the president, makes decisions about war and the economy. On a news program (MacNeil-Lehrer) I heard a speaker say that today's women college students have a lot to learn from Mrs. Bush's unselfishness, implying that these young women are selfish. Another news report I heard said that Mrs. Bush speaks to each of her five children by telephone every day. We also hear of her intense involvement with her dog and the puppies the dog gave birth to in the White House. What are we to make of this contrast in the lives of a husband and wife? Reports indicate that most Americans are very comfortable with it, and she is a very popular first lady. Is her speaking to each child each day a positive means of remaining in connection? Is it due to anxiety resulting from the traumatic loss of one of her children? Do her children grow in this relationship with their mother or are they stifled by it? How we view this daily involvement with grown, married children is surely going to say a lot about how each of us feels about family ties and independent needs. She is surely undaunted by the stereotypical mother-in-law jokes.

An illustration of Miller's thesis of the connectedness between women has come to my attention in reading the acknowledgments at the beginning of the books I have been reading in preparation for writing this book. Many of the women authors go on at some length thanking lists of people for their helpful ideas and advice, for reading the whole or portions of the manuscript, and express the idea that the book has really been possible only with this supportive help from others, men and women. Dinnerstein thanks twenty-six people, Chodorow, in her preface (1978) thanks thirty-five people, Jessica Benjamin (1988) thanks thirty-two people, Carol Gilligan thanks thirty-nine people. I could go on but that is sufficient to make the point that even for women authors, and writing is surely a solitary job, affiliation with others is viewed as valuable and even essential for their development and productivity, and appreciation for others' help is a positive form of connection, rather than a detraction from one's independent achievement. Thanks are extended to libraries, foundations, children, husbands, a generosity of appreciation which values relationship and diminishes autonomy. However, we might wonder whether there is too much of this sharing of the credit and whether it is possibly an unnecessary detraction from the author's own creative achievement, which could have some components of fear of envy, fear of standing out away from others, with the resultant isolation that is so painful for women to bear. I believe it can represent both, the genuine appreciation of closeness to others and the fear of the loss of that closeness if one asserts oneself and separates oneself from others by an independent project.

The work of Miller and the Stone Center group has been very valuable in contributing toward a new psychology of women and in stimulating our thoughts on the dialectic of autonomy and connection. How to balance the two in one's life, whether male or female, is an ongoing challenge. Psychoanalysis and feminism have both asserted the needs of the individual and have both focused on autonomy. Erik Erikson's (1950) eight stages of development contrast autonomy with self-doubt, initiative with guilt, and industry with inferiority until he moves into the intimacy and generativity stages in adulthood. Feminism has been pulled in two directions: one based on "sisterhood," focusing on women developing and maintaining closeness with one another, and the other representing the pull to the masculine world of achievement and independence with demands for equality in that world.

Miller and colleagues are correct to keep reminding us that the valuing of relatedness is our best hope for a cooperative family life and a cooperative world. It is my belief that in the course of a woman's life, connections to others can be maintained in a healthier style, if she develops an authentic self during adolescence and young adulthood and then brings this to her relationships. Girls need to develop their separate identity, values, goals, talents, interests, and opinions. This requires time to be alone; to read, to walk, to think about herself and her relationship to the world. Young women need to value their independent selves enough to take that time alone, alternating with time with others. Erikson suggested a psychosocial moratorium and said that for men, military service often served this function. Women need such a moratorium for their identity formation before marriage and child bearing in order to grow into *self-contained* but not self-centered human beings. This might be time to work and support themselves and, if possible, to travel, but it should be a time of transition between dependence on family and formation of coupling. In this way she can learn the distinction between self-sacrifice in order to please others and *self-knowledge* so that she can be self-caring in her relationship with others. The self-in-relationship theme, which has recently been altered to a stronger connection theme, represents a fundamental difference in the way one can see the development of autonomy. It presupposes that all of life's questions, conflicts, joys, and pain are embedded in relationship and can only develop in relationship. It leaves out the woman as reader, observer, and thinker and therefore, in my view, cannot be a full new psychology of women. This is often a large part of what women in psychotherapy are in need of, and although the therapist is another, and is in a relationship to the woman patient, the therapist's neutrality is what allows the woman to think through the meaning of her life until that point, and evolve the direction that she wishes to go in the future. This may be the first opportunity she has had in her life to think through her needs, values, and goals without having to be concerned about someone else's opinion. If the analyst can truly give her the privacy and freedom to do this without imposing his or her own values, this opportunity can lead to some of the most significant gains of treatment.

SOCIOLOGY AND PSYCHOANALYSIS—NANCY CHODOROW

There is a delightful film that was popular in 1989 called *When Harry Met Sally,* written by Nora Ephron. I don't know if Ms. Ephron is familiar with the work of Nancy Chodorow, but her male and female characters are so in keeping with Chodorow's descriptions of male–female differences in relationships that I almost think she must be. Either way, her characters are the fictionalized version of Chodorow's theory. The film is basically a love story set in New York City in the 1980s, with Sally, a career woman who has trouble admitting she wants to marry and so pretends to be happy and independent, and Harry, who finds his masculine independence empty and lonely but has trouble getting past his facade of Don Juanism and admitting his needs for love, that is, his dependence on a woman. Harry is afraid of the close connection of marriage and Sally is yearning for it.

Harry and Sally keep meeting every few years. When Sally is 31, they meet after she has ended a two-year relationship with "Joe" and Harry is devastated because his wife of five years has left him. Harry asks why her relationship ended and she tells him the following story. She was taking a friend's daughter out for the afternoon. They were driving in a cab on the way to the circus and playing the game "I spy," as in "I spy a mailbox, I spy a lamppost," when the little girl looked out the window and saw a man and a woman with two little kids, the man carrying one of the kids on his shoulders. The little girl said "I spy a family" and, Sally relates, she started to cry. She went home and said to Joe, "This is what I want." Joe said, "Well, I don't," so he moved out. Sally could no longer deny that she wanted to be a mother and recapitulate the earlier oedipal triangle by creating a family of her own, something Chodorow calls the reproduction of mothering. Being an American movie, *When Harry Met Sally* has a happy ending.

Chodorow, a full professor in the Department of Sociology at the University of California, Berkeley campus, and a candidate at The San Francisco Psychoanalytic Institute, wrote *The Reproduction of Mothering,* published in 1978, and thus established herself as the leading theoretician in the field of reformulation of psychoanalytic theory from a feminist perspective. Chodorow integrates theory from anthropology, sociology, Marxism, feminism, and psychoanalysis in a brilliant formulation that focuses on the importance of mothering, the differences in the psychological development of boys and girls as a result of having been mothered exclusively by women, and the effects on the adult personality that then make men and women emotionally incompatible in marriage. She calls these different relational needs "asymmetrical" and refers to "contradictions" in heterosexual relationships as a result. Lillian Rubin's book *Intimate Strangers* (1983) relies on Chodorow's thesis to analyze marital problems in the couples who come to her for help.

Chodorow acknowledges two contributions to feminist theory that have significantly influenced her work. One is Gayle Rubin's essay "The Traffic in Women: Notes on the 'Political Economy' of Sex" (1975). This anthropological/feminist work points out that, as anthropologists have recognized, all kinship systems rest at least partly on marriage, and on the sexual division of labor in which rules are established regulating whom one can and cannot marry. That is, all are based on the assumption of heterosexuality. Thus, heterosexuality is a fundamental organizational principle of the family and the sex/gender system. Rubin tries to construct a theory of women's oppression and focuses on the "exchange of women" which she views as a concept both powerful and seductive.

> It places the oppression of women within social systems, rather than in biology. Moreover, it suggests that we look for the ultimate locus of women's oppression within the traffic in women, rather than within

the traffic in merchandise. . . . Kinship systems do not merely exchange women. They exchange sexual access, genealogical statuses, lineage names and ancestors, rights and people . . . in concrete systems of social relationships. . . . The exchange of women is a profound perception of a system in which women do not have full rights to themselves. [pp. 175–177]

Rubin finds Marxist theory of class oppression very useful in understanding the oppression of women, but says it cannot explain that oppression because "women are oppressed in societies which can by no stretch of the imagination be described as capitalist" (p. 163). She adds, "The division of labor by sex can therefore be seen as a 'taboo': a taboo against the sameness of men and women, a taboo dividing the sexes into two mutually exclusive categories, a taboo which exacerbates the biological differences between the sexes and thereby creates gender" (p. 178). Another function of the division of labor, she points out, is as a taboo to reenforce heterosexual marriage.

The second important influence on Chodorow from feminist theory is that "women's mothering is a central and defining feature of the social organization of gender and is implicated in the construction and reproduction of male dominance itself" (1978, p. 9), for which she recognizes Michelle Rosaldo and Sherry Ortner. All societies contain both domestic and public aspects of social organization. Women's primary social location is domestic, whereas men's is in the public sphere.

Men's location in the public sphere, then, defines society itself as masculine. It gives men power to create and enforce institutions of social and political control, important among these to control marriage as an institution that both expresses men's rights in women's sexual and reproductive capacities and reinforces these rights. . . . Women's mothering determines women's primary location in the domestic sphere and creates a basis for the structural differentiation of domestic and public spheres. . . . Culturally and politically, the public sphere dominates the domestic, and hence men dominate women. [pp. 9–10]

Chodorow's unique contribution was actually spelled out in her essay "Oedipal Asymmetries and Heterosexual Knots," first published in 1976, in which "she addresses a central issue in the social sciences—the dialectical relationship between individual selves and social structures. . . . She explicitly recognizes that selves are both female and male and that they occupy different locations in the social structure" (Parlee 1982, p. 152).

What is most strikingly new and original about *The Reproduction of Mothering* arises from Chodorow's perspective as a feminist scholar.

That is, she takes the experience of females as the central focus of an inquiry dealing with experiences of both females and males. . . . This conceptual shift to a focus on the female experience and actions as meaningful *per se* rather than significant only in the ways they differ from the male's is the hallmark of feminist scholarship and the source of its potentially immense creativity. Not that a feminist focus yields up the truth any more readily than its male-focused counterpart, but it does usually describe a substantial aspect of social reality that has been distorted or ignored by theories fashioned from and for a male perspective. [p. 153]

In both the essay and the book, Chodorow continues the focus on gender difference in the tradition of Karen Horney, and refutes the psychoanalytic thesis of female deficiency, as do Horney, Thompson, Dinnerstein, and Miller, and later, Carol Gilligan. Her central questions are "how do women today come to mother?" and "how we might change things to transform the sexual division of labor in which women mother" (1978, p. 4). She argues that:

the contemporary reproduction of mothering occurs through social structurally induced psychological processes. It is neither a product of biology nor of intentional role-training. I draw on the psychoanalytic account of female and male personality development to demonstrate that women's mothering reproduces itself cyclically. Women, as mothers, produce daughters with mothering capacities and the desire to mother. These capacities and needs are built into and grow out of the mother-daughter relationship itself. By contrast, women as mothers (and men as not-mothers) produce sons whose nurturant capacities and needs have been systematically curtailed and repressed. This prepares men for their less affective later family role, and for primary participation in the impersonal extra-familial world of work and public life. The sexual and familial division of labor in which women mother and are more involved in interpersonal, affective relationships than men produces in daughters and sons a division of psychological capacities which leads them to reproduce this sexual and familial division of labor. [p. 7]

Chodorow sees the Oedipus complex quite differently than Freud. All infants, both boys and girls, are totally dependent upon and intimately attached to their mothers. Boys, in order to become men, must extricate themselves from this close involvement with the mother in order to identify with their fathers and other men and to enter into the male culture. This is a major emotional loss that girls need not sustain. Girls do not need to detach themselves from their mothers in order to become women. In fact, they learn how to become women by remaining in close connection with their mothers. Thus, women can tolerate dependency and men are threatened by it. Men have trouble with intimacy and women have trouble with separation. Male psychology and masculine values are based on independence and autonomy. Women have more permeable ego boundaries but have a greater capacity for empathy than men do. They place a higher value on connection, self-in-relation, and therefore have closer personal ties. It is harder for them to individuate than it is for men, and hard for women to hold this ability as a value or goal. These differences, or asymmetries, produce several results. Mothers of girls do not experience themselves as separate from their daughters as they do from their sons. Therefore, identification and symbiosis with daughters is stronger, and it is more likely that mothers experience daughters as extensions of themselves, which may lead to boundary diffusion.

For the daughter, an oedipal attachment to her father does not preclude her ongoing intense preoedipal tie to her mother. Chodorow (1978) challenges the classic psychoanalytic theory of a "change of object" for the girl as a result of her erotic turning toward her father. When a girl's father does become an important primary person it is in the context of a "bisexual relational triangle" (p. 192), as compared to the "primacy and exclusivity of an oedipal boy's emotional tie to his mother and women" (p. 193). The girl maintains her strong emotional attachment to her mother, and her father remains relatively emotionally and physically distant. The girl needs to separate from her mother but needs her mother's love and emotional connectedness as well. She also relies on her mother for her identification as a woman, using her mother as her role model. Love for her father is part of the girl's effort to loosen her dependence on her mother, but the father is more idealized and the attachment less intense.

Chodorow states further that "girls and boys expect and assume women's unique capacities for sacrifice, caring, and mothering, and associate women with their own fears of regression and powerlessness. They fantasize more about men, and associate them with idealized virtues and growth" (p. 83). The father, Chodorow says, "becomes an object of ambivalence" for the boy as a result of his oedipal attachment to his mother, but the girl's "intense ambivalent attachment remains with her mother" (p. 97).

An important contribution of Chodorow toward understanding the difficulties in male–female relationships is her conclusion that because men grow up having to reject their need for love, they find it threatening to meet women's emotional needs, and thus maintain emotional distance from women. Men both want and fear intimacy with women, want the return to the preoedipal exclusivity of the infant–mother symbiosis, and fear the regression and loss of masculinity in that closeness. "The relationship to the mother thus builds itself directly into contradictions in masculine heterosexual commitment" (1976, p. 244).

Chodorow believes that women are more important to both men and other women on a basic emotional level than men are, and that men fall in love more romantically and become more depressed after a death or breakup of a relationship than women do.

Having a child completes the relational triangle for a woman as well as re-creating the exclusive mother–child relationship of her own infancy. But the new baby interrupts the husband–wife intimacy for the man, just as his own father intruded into his exclusive relationship to his mother in infancy. Chodorow's thesis is that for a woman, having a child re-creates for herself the exclusive mother–infant bond of her own past, which is re-created for men by a heterosexual relationship. Chodorow calls this the re-creation of the woman's "internalized asymmetrical triangle" (1978, p. 202). Thus, she says, men's lack of emotional availability and women's less exclusive heterosexual commitment help ensure women's mothering.

Chodorow further sees economic implications in the different relational needs of men and women. Male denial of dependence and of attachment to women helps to guarantee both masculinity and performance in the world of work and fits appropriately with participation in capitalist relations of production. This view of work, as a means to separate from the regressive pull of women, helps us to understand the anger and hostility of men when women integrate the work force and enter previously all-male domains. She integrates her work in anthropology, sociology, and psychoanalysis as follows (1978):

> That women mother is a fundamental organizational feature of the sex-gender system: It is basic to the sexual division of labor and generates a psychology and ideology of male dominance as well as an ideology about women's capacities and nature. . . . Social reproduction is thus asymmetrical. Women in their domestic role reproduce men and children physically, psychologically and emotionally. Women in their domestic role as houseworkers reconstitute themselves physically on a daily basis and reproduce themselves as mothers, emotionally and psychologically, in the next generation. They thus contribute to the perpetuation of their own social roles and position in the hierarchy of gender. [pp. 208–209]

Chodorow concludes by stating that the sexual division of labor cannot be separated from sexual inequality. She proposes a "fundamental reorganization of parenting" in which men and women share the role of mother as her solution to inequality between the sexes (1978, p. 215). Such a solution would also alleviate many of the contradictions and unfortunate by-products of women's overinvolvement with their children because of the failure of marriage to meet women's needs for intimacy. Chodorow thus shares with Dinnerstein a focus on reducing the power of the mother as a means to diminish the discrimination against women.

In her review of *Reproduction of Mothering,* Jessica Benjamin (1982), referring to the polarity between male and female, relatedness and autonomy, writes that there is a paradox between the desire for recognition and the desire for independence. She asks, must the price of achieving selfhood be the loss of closeness, or conversely, is the price of maintaining attachment to be the inhibition of autonomy?

> The insistence on gender polarity is really a foreclosure of the differentiation struggle, a supercession of paradox ambivalence. This insistence seems to grow, if we accept Chodorow's analysis, above all from the incompatibility of maternal identification, nurturance and empathy with male identity. The repudiation of femininity, the psychic correlate of the social fact of male domination, results in a consistent distortion of human individuation. . . . The paradox of differentiation returns with a vengeance, as increasingly fluid familial institutions confront individuals with the task of reconciling intimacy and autonomy in their adult lives. [pp. 160–161]

Chodorow's second book, *Feminism and Psychoanalytic Theory,* appeared in 1989. It is a compilation of ten essays written over the previous twenty years, many since the publication of her first book. In her introduction she gives us a glimpse into the intellectual and emotional struggles of a very intelligent woman whose academic growth as a social scientist occurs in the same period of history as the growth of the woman's movement. She tries to be a bridge builder between sociologists, psychoanalysts, and feminists, and calls for dialogue: "The essays argue for the necessity to include psychoanalytic understanding, broadly construed, in feminist theory and also feminist understanding, broadly construed, in psychoanalysis" (pp. 13–14). Not surprisingly she is at times left feeling "in the middle, and as a result there is often a sense, in the concluding chapters, of someone feeling buffeted around the disciplines, reacting rather than creating" (p. 18). The reader becomes acquainted with the intensity of the academic debate on this issue—a debate that can span a range from respectful disagreement to ugly denunciations in the highly competitive academic world—and with the difficulties for a writer who tries to integrate psychoanalytic and feminist theories.

Chodorow places herself squarely in the object relations camp within psychoanalysis and critiques both drive theory and Lacanian theory. She is clear that role learning and cultural theories are inadequate to explain behavior, and argues forcefully for the inclusion of unconscious mental factors to understand gender psychology and behavior.

> As I now see feminist theory as a more multiplex account of relations in many domains, I care less to justify my interests by arguing that psychoanalysis is *the* feminist theory. I am more convinced even than I was during an earlier period that psychoanalysis describes a significant level of reality that is not reducible to, or in the last instance caused by, social or cultural organization. I would not, as I believe I do in *Reproduction,* give a determinist primacy to social relations that generate certain psychological patterns or processes, but would argue that psychology itself is equally important to, constitutive and determinative of, human life. If I were to discover that the 'central dynamic' or 'cause' of women's oppression were located outside of the personal, interiorized, subjective, and intersubjective realm of psychic life and primary relationships that psychoanalysis describes, I would still be concerned with this realm and its relation to gender, sexuality and self. [p. 7]

In spite of her "love affair" with psychoanalysis, Chodorow can be quite critical of Freud. She states (1978) that "the account he provides moves from sexist bias into the distortion of reality" (p. 146). Again, "his cavalier dismissal [of women] is appalling" (p. 153); and again, "the Freudian edifice stands on shaky ground" (p. 157).

Chodorow offers an excellent history of the work done to date about psychoanalysis and women, both by psychoanalysts of different schools and by psychoanalytic feminist scholars, whom she divides into object relations feminists, interpersonal or cultural feminists, and Lacanian feminists. In the first group she places herself, Dinnerstein, Jessica Benjamin, Jane Flax, and Evylyn Fox Keller. In the second group, which she describes as similar to the first, are Jean Baker Miller, the Stone Center group, and Carol Gilligan. Object relations feminists pay more attention to the complexities of the inner object world; to internalizations, unconscious defenses, and conflicts; and to the unconscious structuring of self. Interpersonal theorists pay more attention to cultural and personal evaluations of different qualities and capacities (p. 186). Juliet Mitchell, now a psychoanalyst, is a proponent of the Lacanian school, which opposes the notion of primary femininity and the Kleinian and object relations account of the importance of the preoedipal mother–child experience.

> Lacanian feminism makes radical psychoanalytic and feminist claims. It argues that there are no other aspects to gender division, identity, or personality than sexuality and symbolized genital difference and that

there is no subjectivity outside of sexuality: any speaking being must locate him or herself in relation to the phallus. Such a theory locates every action firmly in an unequal sexual world and never loses sight of our developmentally inevitable placement in a phallocentric culture. It speaks to women's lack of self and sense of being the Other, other fundamental alienation from and objectification in culture. [p. 189]

A final concept introduced by Chodorow is that of *gender salience,* which she discovered in her interviews of woman analysts trained in the 1920s, 1930s, and early 1940s. The analysts were not gender blind, but their gender consciousness was different from her own, and they experienced a different salience of gender as a social category and aspect of professional identity. Chodorow concludes that gender consciousness is differentially salient at different times and places. She concludes her review of psychoanalytic feminism as follows:

A melding of object-relations feminism and recent psychoanalysis might take us further in the right direction. Against the essentialism of psychoanalytic gender theory, object relations feminism enables an understanding of variability and fluidity in gender salience, because it sees development as contingently determined by experience and what one makes of this experience, and because it incorporates an understanding of gender characteristics like the self-in-relationship that are not necessarily available as gender conceptions. At the same time, as a feminist theory it remains continuously cognizant of gender hierarchy and relations of inequality, even as it also sees these as multiplex and situationally variable. Like clinical psychoanalysis, object-relations theory enables many developmental and psychological stories and leads to a recognition of variation, of ways that identities may or may not be invoked or experienced in different contexts and interpersonal or intrapsychic situations. [p. 197]

One idea I found striking in Lacanian theory that Chodorow does not mention is the notion that when the young child is able to understand that its name is the name of the father [*nom du père*], in that one moment of recognition, the entire patriarchal system is transmitted to that child. This idea struck a chord of truth within me, bringing me back to a very early awareness of the fact that my last name was my father's and therefore of my father's superior position in the family and society.

In spite of differences among themselves, Chodorow points out, psychoanalytic feminists are all in agreement in their opposition to overly biological psychoanalytic interpretations and their claims to a value-free "scientific" study of gender difference. They also see masculine and feminine personality, development, and identity as interrelated and connected to social, cultural, and psychological relations. A distinction that I make is between what I call the academic psychoanalytic feminists and the clinical psychoanalytic feminists. This distinction is based on those who develop theory and whose writing remains at the theoretical level, and those who develop theory and put it into practice, providing case examples in their writing to illustrate how the developmental revisions they are proposing affect their clinical perspective and can be applied to work with patients. Dinnerstein's and Chodorow's books are theoretical only. Jean Baker Miller offers both theory and case illustrations. Surrey, Kaplan, Jordan, and Stiver of the Stone Center also combine theory and practice. Carol Gilligan illustrates her theory with many examples from her research interviews, but she is not a clinician and thus gives no examples from psychotherapy. Jessica Benjamin's writing is primarily theoretical, and Harriet Lerner illustrates her ideas with case examples. All these writers except Gilligan are clinicians, but, curiously, not all chose to describe their clinical work to show us how theory can be applied in practice.

Chodorow recognizes some changes in attitudes towards women by psychoanalysts, but is not satisfied at the lack of challenge to the division of gender and parental roles and to normative notions of sexuality, and at the lack of recognition that "masculinity is problematic" (p. 195). Psychoanalytic feminism, she says, challenges psychoanalysis in all these arenas. "In the case of rape and incest, for instance, psychoanalysts have found it hard to give up the view that unconscious desires on the part of the female victim are involved" (pp. 195–196).

Yet it is in the area of incest that Chodorow is weakest. In discussing Freud's seduction theory (1978), she refers to his theory of "parental innocence" and states that he sees fathers, in particular, as "victims of childhood fantasy," but that "he ignores the reciprocal possibility—that absence of actual paternal seduction is not the same thing as absence of seductive fantasies toward a daughter or behavior which expresses such fantasy" (p. 160). Chodorow quotes from Therese Benedek and Gregory Zilboorg to support her thesis that Freud neglected the role of the parents in the oedipal experience. Incestuous fantasies may, in fact, originate in the mind of the parents. Benedek (1959) suggests that the parents' own feelings are communicated to the child and are the source of the child's own emotions. These sexual drives toward one's child must be repressed, but, as we know, the repression is often weak and, more often than we want to think, fails altogether. Chodorow writes, "Thus, the reawakened, guilt-laden, and conflicted oedipus situation in parents helps to reproduce a similar oedipus situation in their child" (p. 161). Zilboorg (1944) states, "The unconscious hostility against one's own children is well nigh a universal clinical finding among men" (p. 162).

Chodorow (1978) concludes that "the implication of these accounts is that members of both generations come to have significant conscious and unconscious conflicts about libidinal and aggressive feelings and fantasies, and about the inevitable coming to sexual maturity of the younger generation and its replacement of the elder" (p. 163). But she stops there, making her point about parental fantasy, and never goes on to discuss the reality of incest and the effects on the child.

There are a few other weaknesses in Chodorow's work, but nothing serious enough to detract from the value of her overall project. As others have pointed out, she is describing a family that is limited to the narrow version of family in a particular time and place and that to some extent is a middle-class version of reality. The upper class uses hired help for the greater part of child rearing. Especially from the vantage point of 1990, twelve years later, it is clear that the family Chodorow describes is the typical configuration of the 1960s and earlier, with the father going out to work every day and the mother staying home isolated with the children. It is not an extended family; it is not a rural family, with the father working the land on which the family lives; it is not a divorced family. We are all well aware now that the number of such typical nuclear families has dwindled dramatically, and that a majority of children are no longer raised under these conditions, but rather in single-mother homes, homes with two working parents, and stepfamilies. In San Francisco, one in four children is born to an unmarried mother. How these variations affect the oedipal drama and its outcome is of great interest and importance. Children who spend most of their waking hours in day care are forming attachments to teachers and other children at an early age, which reduces the intensity of the attachment to the mother, though not to female figures in general. The mother's power may be reduced as she shares power with the day-care providers, and then with the father during evenings and weekends.

Yet in many families there have been other significant members, such as grandparents and siblings, and in Chodorow as well as other feminist psychoanalytic writers these family members are completely missing. I believe that grandparents, siblings, and in some cases aunts, uncles, cousins, and nursemaids can be very significant figures, even to the extent of being a factor in the oedipal configuration. In clinical work, these figures need to be asked about and attended to.

Diane Ehrensaft (1985) has studied families in which the parents have agreed to co-parent the child or children, and has found some surprising results. "The phenomenon involves the blossoming of intimacy between father and child, a less tension-laden relationship between a child and a mother freed from the burdens of full-time mothering, but a new gender-related tension between men and women as to who is getting the father's intimacy—mother or child" (p. 323). Inspired by the work of Dinnerstein and Chodorow, Ehrensaft interviewed in depth five couples and had extensive discussions with many more. These were middle-class professionals in their thirties or forties who, because of their feminist beliefs, made a commitment to co-parent. The results were that the father's emotional involvement with his child was much greater than either he or his wife ever anticipated. The fathers "worry about their child's development, encourage close physical contact with their child, often find it difficult to separate from him or her. They form a permanent and intimate primary relationship" (p. 326).

Ehrensaft's thesis is that these men enter their fathering role with a hunger for intimacy because they have had to relinquish their early intimacy with their own mother and, following Dinnerstein's and Chodorow's thesis, have then developed ambivalent relationships with women because of a desire for the intimacy of the mother–son bond but a countervailing fear of regressive engulfment. This longing for intimacy can be safely achieved and gratified with the child. It may be true, as Chodorow and Dinnerstein state, that men do not have the same internalized relational capacities as women, but Ehrensaft believes they have an intense desire for relationship. They fall totally in love with the child, which creates in the mother, especially if the child is a girl, jealousy and resentment as she sees the child receiving a quality of intimacy from her husband that she longs for but that he does not give to her. This is a reversal of the often-commented-upon phenomenon of the young father's jealousy as he sees his wife's love and attention devoted to the baby and withdrawn from him. Thus, Ehrensaft's work indicates that a man does have the emotional capacity for mothering, based on his early relationship with his own mother, but which he has defended against in his quest for his masculine identity.

In posing the question of what happens to the children, Ehrensaft (1980) states:

> The infant's sense of self is developed in relationship to two people, a man and a woman. This means that later individuation of self will also be from two people, both a mother and a father. . . . Fathers are no longer abstractions or once-in-a-while idealized figures. . . . Both boys and girls will have parallel struggles of individuation from like- and opposite-sex parents, albeit in different combination. They will have a parental interpersonal environment that is not gender-linked. [p. 61]

However, Ehrensaft cautions that elements of the larger culture are also influential, such as schools and television. It is still too early to study the long term effects of co-parenting on children's gender identity, but it surely is a fascinating question. One wonders what conflicts will arise in a marriage where one spouse has been co-parented and the other has not.

There is another point made by Chodorow that needs comment. Chodorow sees a woman's love relationships as an extension of her erotic attachment to her father—but this attachment is not as powerful as a man's, because of the bisexual triangle that leaves a woman with a strong attachment to her mother and other women. Chodorow concludes that men do not become as emotionally important to women as women do to men. I find this conclusion doubtful and not consistent with my clinical experience. Of course patients in psychotherapy may not serve as good examples for the general population, since they are people with acknowledged emotional problems. Nevertheless, I tend to agree with Freud's (1931) observation, which she cites, that women seek to recapture their relationship with their mother in heterosexual relationships and that they often impose on their relation to their father, and later to other men, the feelings and desires from the earlier relationship with the mother. Separation problems rooted in a woman's failure to attain autonomy from her attachment to her mother can re-create themselves in projections onto her husband or other male lovers, and she may experience herself as an extension of the man, seek his approval, and fear losing him. This can badly inhibit her capacity to express feelings of anger, or even to acknowledge such feelings, because of the fear of abandonment if she does. If her mother could not tolerate the independence that anger requires, she fears her husband will not either. Certainly cultural aspects and practical considerations are important here, especially if the woman is financially dependent on the man. The taking of the man's name is a traditional and still common practice that merges the woman's identity with the man's and negates her separate background and individuality, thus supporting her dependency.

Because of the combination of these factors—a woman's projection of dependency onto the man from her own parental dependency and the merging of her needs with his; her erotic attachment determined by her love, first for her mother, then for her father; the infantalizing imposed by financial dependency, often a consequence of childbearing; plus the internalization of cultural stereotypes of male superiority and female weakness—I find it hard to accept Chodorow's characterization of women's dependency on men as less than men's on women. It may be that the research showing men's response to loss, once dependency is established, to be greater than women's—for example in the response to loss through death—is accurate, but I do not believe that there is overall a lesser dependency in women. Yes, we have all observed the phenomenon of female friendship and appreciate the value of it, but it is still true that women will cancel plans with a woman friend if an opportunity for a date with a man occurs. In addition, some women fear the regressive pull of relating to women when there is no male in their life, which may be due to homosexual fears or simply to issues of boundary maintenance. This pull may be lessened among older widows who enjoy travel and leisure with other widows, but reports still indicate that widowers or recently divorced men are at a premium. In this regard, financial or social factors may be of equal importance to deeply held psychological needs. But I tend to think that men and women have equal needs for intimacy with each other because, for the majority of women as for men, heterosexual bonding is still the primary source of both sexual satisfaction and emotional security, as well as the most acceptable way of being in the world, where people socialize in pairs.

What may be true is that a man's marriage or love affair will satisfy his need for intimacy so that he does not need male friendship, whereas women need female friendship to satisfy the emotional completeness of the bisexual triangle. This would leave a man more isolated and depressed at a time of divorce or death. But the imbalance in the ratio of men to women assures that a man will not be alone very long. It is difficult to determine how much men's faster remarriage rate can be attributed to a man's greater need for a woman, and how much to the simple fact that more women—especially younger women—are available for the divorced or widowed man. But it is a well-documented fact of life, and one that causes women much anger and sorrow.

Women's closer relationship with children may leave women in a stronger emotional position after divorce or death than men, especially when, in the case of a divorce, the children continue to live with the mother. But social isolation, financial hardship, and the need to feel loved by a man usually find the woman seeking a man as soon as she has weathered the psychological crisis. The phenomenon of age difference between husbands and wives—the male tending to be older, especially in remarriage—serves the function of maintaining male superiority but serves women's dependency needs as well. A father transference may be erotic and dependent, with the woman wanting to be taken care of both economically and emotionally; although some women insist that men their own age are simply too immature. The security and protection of an older man can meet transference needs from both a woman's mother and her father.

How can we separate the economic advantages often offered by an older man from psychological dependency? This would need to be ana-lyzed in each individual case. On the individual level it comes down to resources, internal, and external. Women may have stronger internal resources for psychological connections, but men are likely to have stronger external resources. What is clear is that when a woman is economically independent, she is often less dependent on a man and more likely to initiate divorce. When a man is "care" independent, when he can shop, cook, do laundry, and keep house for himself, he is less dependent on a woman. If you want to assess a man's independence, look in his refrigerator. If you find nothing but beer, mustard, and ketchup, he won't be single long. The reciprocally reinforced dependency roles that are based on gender and prescribed by the culture foster dependency in both men and women and support the institution of marriage. Gayle Rubin (1975) shows how this has worked to subordinate women and support heterosexuality, but it also creates male dependency. Also, women have needed men in order to have children, but now even this anatomical dependency is being minimized, as single women adopt babies or are fertilized artificially. This new world is exciting but confusing. The family has been a basic source of meaning, as well as security and companionship, for adults, in addition to its child-rearing functions. Without a family, both men and women must find meaning in other places. For, in spite of their autonomy, men don't do very well psychologically or physically without the nurturing care of a woman, often sinking into alcoholism or drug addiction, and all but the most unusual woman needs a man's companionship in her life to feel contentment and meaning.

The psychoanalytic feminists agree with the psychoanalysts as to the significance of love relationships in the lives of women, but disagree as to the *terms* of those relationships. The role of a woman in marriage must include self-determination and self-fulfillment, as well as a serving of others.

IN A DIFFERENT VOICE—CAROL FRIEDMAN GILLIGAN

Nancy Chodorow's brilliant feminist revision of Freud's oedipal theory presents the differences between boys and girls, men and women in a light that no longer shows women as damaged, envious, and weakened. In like manner, Carol Gilligan—a psychologist and a full professor in the School of Education at Harvard University, one of Harvard's few tenured women— gives us a brilliant feminist revision of Freud's theory of an inferior superego in girls and women that no longer slanders women as morally inferior. Her well-publicized and highly controversial book *In A Different Voice: Psychological Theory and Women's Development* appeared in 1982, proposing her thesis that in moral reasoning women are different, but not deficient. Because her writing has fewer highly complex theoretical formulations, is less abstract, and includes many interesting examples from her research, it has crossed over into a nonacademic reading audience (over 425,000 copies sold to date) and led to her picture appearing on the cover of *Ms.* magazine. (In January 1990, Gilligan's picture was on the cover of *The New York Times Magazine,* which featured a story on the publication of her latest book [Prose 1990].)

Chodorow's and Gilligan's work together comprise, in my view, a true revolution in the reformulation of the psychoanalytic theory of female development and female–male differences, which makes current feminist psychoanalytic thinking about women both theoretically viable and clinically useful. Additionally, the two gain for women a respect, a dignity, and a recognition that we have not held before in Western culture. Not that this respect is universal by a long shot; but I believe it is contributory to a new sense of self-esteem in women and to some acknowledgment by men in the mental health professions, perhaps grudging, that women have gotten a bad deal in psychology and psychoanalysis. I have written Table 4–1 to show some concepts of Gilligan and Chodorow.

Gilligan's thesis can be presented in condensed form as her discovery that for boys and men, not playing fair is the worst sin, and for girls and women, hurting people is: two different moral ideologies. Because she claims a different kind of morality for women, some feminists have been critical of her work and fear that her results could be used to discriminate against women. The concern is that Gilligan's apparent reinforcement of the stereotypical view of women as more nurturant, more caring, less harsh than men is the old-fashioned sentimental view, which has limited women to caring, maternal roles such as mother, nurse, social worker, and primary school teacher, and excluded them from "thinking" roles in government, business, law, and science, where "tough decisions" are made. Gilligan has also been attacked for her criticism of the classical truisms of psychology by those representing the "establishment." So we can say, in political terms, they came at her from both the left and the right.

I do not read Gilligan's work in this manner. I understand her as

TABLE 4–1

Masculinity		Femininity
Separation	< Is defined through >	Attachment
Intimacy, Entrapment	< Sees danger in >	Separation, Success
Close relationships	< Has a problem with >	Individuation, Ego boundaries
Individualism, Independence	< Primary value is >	Connection, Caring
Individual rights, Justice	< Ethical value is >	Responsibility for others' feelings
Cowboy, Warrior, Self-made millionaire	< Hollywood hero/heroine is >	Woman who gives up career for love and marriage

viewing the two values dialectically, calling for integration, not polarity. She has a vision of a mature adult that would include the best of the male values with the best of the female values. Such an integration would require the inclusion of women at all levels of society.

> To understand how the tension between responsibilities and rights sustains the dialectic of human development is to see the integrity of two disparate modes of experience that are in the end connected. While an ethic of justice proceeds from the premise of equality—that everyone should be treated the same—an ethic of care rests on the premise of nonviolence—that no one should be hurt. In the representation of maturity, both perspectives converge. . . . Through this expansion in perspective, we can begin to envision how a marriage between adult development as it is currently portrayed and women's development as it begins to be seen could lead to a changed understanding of human development and a more generative view of human life. [1982, p. 174]

Like Chodorow, Gilligan has had to withstand attack from members of her own profession, men and women alike, but has endured. She quotes Chodorow and Jean Baker Miller and acknowledges the influences of their theories on her work. For Gilligan, Chodorow, Miller, and Dinnerstein the cliché "She thinks like a man" is no compliment. Gilligan is careful to state that the different voice she hears is not related absolutely to women, that there is an "interplay of these voices within each sex"; and she suggests that their "convergence marks times of crisis and change" (p. 2). Her complaint against psychologists is that they have neither listened to nor valued the voice of caring, which is associated with women. Psychological theorists, starting with Freud, have been biased in their observations by assuming that the male life is the norm and that women's differences are deviations from that norm and therefore inferior. The flaw in the theory became cast as a flaw in women.

It is not only Freud who views female morality as inferior. Gilligan quotes Piaget as believing that the legal sense "is far less developed in little girls than in boys" (1932, p. 77), because he observed that in children's play, girls have a less strict, more "pragmatic" attitude toward rules than boys. Janet Lever (1976) also reports her observations of sex differences in children's play.

> When disputes arose in the course of a game, boys were able to resolve the disputes more effectively than girls: "During the course of this study, boys were seen quarreling all the time, but not once was a game terminated because of a quarrel". . . . In contrast, the eruption of disputes among girls tended to end the game. . . . Rather than elabo-

rating a system of rules for resolving disputes, girls subordinated the continuation of the game to the continuation of relationships. [pp. 9–10]

Lever, in agreement with Piaget, assumes the male model is better. Gilligan's contribution to feminist psychology is her reinterpretation of these differences. Boys are better able to be competitive, but girls are better able to be cooperative. Boys are more developed in following rules, but girls are more developed in qualities of empathy and sensitivity to others. Gilligan refers to the Broverman study (1972), saying in reference to Broverman, that the "discrepancy between womanhood and adulthood is nowhere more evident" than as reported in this study, where capacities for love and work are stereotyped (p. 17).

In the mid-1970s Gilligan was a section leader at Harvard University for Erik Erikson's course on the life cycle. Erikson too, she claims, in his eight stages of psychosocial development, is basing his theories on the male child. She points out, for example, that in adolescence, Stage V, when building an identity is the major task, identity precedes intimacy. Although Erikson anchors his developmental theory in the first stage in the crisis in "trust vs. mistrust," he then shifts the goal in the succeeding stages to individuation, culminating in his view of adolescence as "the celebration of the autonomous, initiating, industrious self" (p. 12). But according to Erikson, the sequence is different for the female. Her identity cannot be resolved until marriage, when it is defined by and fused with her husband's identity, intimacy thus preceding identity. Attachments, in Erikson's schema, are impediments to development, echoing the male fear of regression to maternal closeness elaborated by Chodorow.

A very important study elucidating the effects of women's high valuing of connections is that of Matina Horner (1972). Horner shows, through analysis of Thematic Apperception Test scores (TAT), that women fear success and have problems with competitive achievement because of a fear of social rejection due to a conflict between femininity and success. This "success anxiety" is present, however, only when one person's success comes at the expense of another's failure, thus bringing us back to the discovery that connection, affiliation, and intimacy are, for women, values that can create conflict in a situation of competition.

Referring to Virginia Woolf's criticism of the deference to male values and the confusion shown by women writers, Gilligan states:

Women's deference is rooted not only in their social subordination but also in the substance of their moral concern. Sensitivity to the needs of others and the assumption of responsibility for taking care lead women to attend to voices other than their own and to include in their judgment other points of view. Women's moral weakness, manifest in an apparent diffusion and confusion of judgment, is thus inseparable from women's moral strength, an overriding concern with relationships and responsibilities. [pp. 16–17]

Gilligan's most significant critique in *In a Different Voice* is reserved for Lawrence Kohlberg, with whom she studied at Harvard. In Kohlberg's research, she writes, "females simply do not exist" (p. 18). His six stages of moral development are based on a study of eighty-four boys whose development Kohlberg followed for over twenty years. The following quotations are from the *International Encyclopedia of Social Sciences* (1968).

Level I. Premoral:

Stage 1. Punishment and obedience orientation.

Stage 2. Naive instrumental hedonism.

Level II. Morality of conventional role conformity:

Stage 3. Good-boy morality of maintaining good relations, approval by others.

Stage 4. Authority maintaining morality.

Level III. Morality of self-accepted moral principles:

Stage 5. Morality of contract, of individual rights, and of democratically accepted law.

Stage 6. Morality of individual principles of conscience. [p. 489]

Each of these six general stages of moral orientation can be defined in terms of its specific stance on some thirty-two aspects of morality, such as "motivation for rule obedience or moral action," in which the stages are defined as follows:

Stage 1. Obey rules to avoid punishment.

Stage 2. Conform to obtain rewards, have favors returned, and so on.

Stage 3. Conform to avoid disapproval, dislike by others.

Stage 4. Conform to avoid censure by legitimate authorities and resultant guilt.

Stage 5. Conform to maintain the respect of the impartial spectator judging in terms of community welfare.

Stage 6. Conform to avoid self-condemnation. [p. 489]

Women, not included in Kohlberg's sample, rarely reach his higher stages, five and six. Yet herein lies a paradox, says Gilligan,

> for the very traits that traditionally have defined the 'goodness' of women, their care for and sensitivity to the needs of others, are those that mark them as deficient in moral development. . . . The conception of maturity is derived from the study of men's lives and reflects the importance of individuation in their development. . . . When one begins with the study of women . . . *the moral problem arises from conflicting responsibilities rather than from competing rights* and requires for its resolution a mode of thinking that is contextual and narrative rather than formal and abstract. . . . This different construction of the moral problem by women may be seen as the critical reason for their failure to develop within the constraints of Kohlberg's system. . . . *The morality of rights differs from the morality of responsibility in its emphasis on separation rather than connection, in its consideration of the individual rather than the relationship as primary.* . . . The moral dilemma changes from how to exercise one's rights without interfering with the rights of others to how "to lead a moral life which includes obligations to myself and my family and people in general." [pp. 18–21, italics added]

Gilligan distinguishes among three levels without defining structural stages: a preconventional level that is primarily egocentric, a conventional level that is primarily concerned with caring for others, and a postconventional level that balances care for self and care for others. She then compares responses from a 25-year-old male participant in Kohlberg's study to those from a female, also 25, in her own study. She concludes that a morality of rights and noninterference may appear frightening to women in its potential justification of indifference and unconcern, whereas a morality of responsibility appears inconclusive and diffuse, given its insistent contextual relativism, from a male perspective. She believes that women's moral development needs to be judged on a different scale from Kohlberg's, because Kohlberg's scale ignores women's values, women's "different voice" (p. 22).

Gilligan's reformulations are based on three studies. All involved interviews, because of her assumption that the way people talk, the language they use, and the connections they make reveal their conceptions of self and morality and help us to understand their experiences of conflict and choice. The first study, which examines attitudes toward rights and responsibilities, involves males and females in matching pairs at nine points in the life cycle: 6–9, 11, 15, 19, 22, 25–27, 35, 45, and 60. The second, a study of college students, includes twenty-five students, male and female, interviewed as seniors and then five years after graduation. The third, which deals with the decision to have an abortion, involves interviews with twenty-nine women, aged 15 through 33, of varying ethnicity and class. They were interviewed in the first trimester while they were making a decision about abortion, and again one year later.

Two key characters in the emergence of Gilligan's thesis are to be found in the first study. They are 11-year-old "Amy" and "Jake," matched for high intelligence, education, and social class. Amy and Jake express their opinions on a moral question from the Kohlberg research, and are both endearing in their earnestness, thoughtfulness, and sense of justice. But the important point is that each child sees the same dilemma as a very different moral problem, and, "while current theory brightly illuminates the line and the logic of the boy's thought, it casts scant light on that of the girl" (p. 25). In Gilligan's view we can consider these male–female differences without scaling them from better to worse. Another difference we may be dealing with here involves the known propensity for men to measure everything.

The dilemma the children are asked to resolve is as follows. A man named Heinz must decide whether or not to steal a drug he cannot afford to buy for his wife in order to save her life. The druggist has refused to lower the price. The child is asked, "Should Heinz steal the drug?" and is questioned to reveal the structuring of his or her moral thought. Jake is certain that Heinz should steal the drug, constructing the dilemma as Kohlberg did as a conflict between the values of property and life:

> For one thing, a human life is worth more than money, and if the druggist only makes $1,000, he is still going to live, but if Heinz doesn't steal the drug, his wife is going to die. [Why is life worth more than money?] Because the druggist can get a thousand dollars later from rich people with cancer, but Heinz can't get his wife again. [Why not?] Because people are all different and so you couldn't get Heinz's wife again. [p. 26]

Jake is sure the judge will recognize the logic of his reasoning and give Heinz a light sentence. His response would score a mixture of stages three and four on Kohlberg's scale and points toward the principled conception of justice equated with moral maturity. In contrast, Amy considers neither property nor law, but rather what effect the theft could have on the relationship between Heinz and his wife:

> Well, I don't think so. I think there might be other ways besides stealing it, like if he could borrow the money or make a loan or something, but he really shouldn't steal the drug—but his wife shouldn't die either. [Why not?] If he stole the drug, he might save his wife then, but if he

did, he might have to go to jail, and then his wife might get sicker again, and he couldn't get more of the drug, and it might not be good. So, they should really just talk it out and find some other way to make the money. [p. 28]

Amy's response appears to be a failure in logic and an inability to think for herself. She tries to resolve the dilemma in a way in which all the relationships would be sustained. "Seeing a world comprised of relationships rather than of people standing alone, a world that coheres through human connection rather than through systems of rules, she finds the puzzle in the dilemma to lie in the failure of the druggist to respond to the wife" (p. 29).

According to Kohlberg's definitions, Amy scores a full stage lower than Jake. Gilligan defends Amy's position and interprets it in a more positive light.

Amy's judgments contain the insights central to an ethic of care, just as Jake's judgments reflect the logic of the justice approach. Her incipient awareness of the "method of truth," the central tenet of nonviolent conflict resolution, and her belief in the restorative activity of care, lead her to see the actors in the dilemma arrayed not as opponents in a contest of right but as members of a network of relationships on whose continuation they all depend. . . . These two children see two very different moral problems—Jake a conflict between life and property that can be resolved by logical deduction, Amy a fracture of human relationship that must be mended with its own thread. [pp. 30–31]

Amy's approach is nonconfrontational and nonadversarial. The children are also asked: "When responsibility to oneself and responsibility to others conflict, how should one choose?" Jake divides the responsibility into one-fourth for others and three-fourths for oneself, stating that one needs to take other people into consideration, but one's self is more important. He gives a strikingly violent example. A person who intends to kill himself should blow himself up with a hand grenade rather than with an atomic bomb so as not to kill his neighbors.

Amy responds contextually rather than categorically, answering that it depends on the situation whether one's needs or the other person's needs are seen as more important. She mentions as contributory factors how close one is to the other person and how one feels about the person or persons involved. Her example involves not putting a job ahead of someone one loves.

For Jake, responsibility means *not doing* what he wants because he is thinking of others; for Amy, it means *doing* what others are counting on her to do regardless of what she herself wants, "he seeing hurt to arise from the expression of aggression, she from a failure of response" (p. 38). There are several surprising images of violence in Jake's responses. Such images occur as well in Gilligan's study of college students' responses to TAT pictures, in which there is "seemingly bizarre imagery of violence in men's stories about a picture of what appeared to be a tranquil scene" (p. 39). In a Thematic Apperception Test, the subject is asked to tell a story about a picture. By encouraging fantasy, the test causes the respondent to project her or his own internal thoughts and feelings onto the characters in the picture. In the picture referred to by Gilligan, a couple is sitting on a bench by a river next to a low bridge. More than 21 percent of the eighty-eight men in the class wrote stories containing violence—homicide, suicide, stabbing, kidnapping, or rape. None of the fifty women projected violence in their stories (p. 40). However, women were more likely than men to project violence in impersonal situations of achievement. The case example offered by Ticho in Chapter 3, of a woman medical student who deliberately kept her grades down when her top grades resulted in hostile remarks from men students and faculty, indicates there is reality to these fears of success. Ticho and Applegarth in the Blum volume, *Feminine Psychology* (1977a), and Horner (1972), all confirm Gilligan's findings that women have a fear of achievement and experience conflicts about success. All four recognize that a combination of (1) internalized prohibitions, and (2) the real dangers of rejection in real-life situations for women who successfully compete against both other women and, especially, men, account for these fears. As I typed this sentence I made an error and wrote "complete" rather than compete. This is a telling point. It is not only doing the work, but, most importantly, *completing* the work, that exposes women to these internal fears and external dangers. I realize that I can work on this book endlessly, but it is only by my completing the book that these competitive factors, and thus dangers, come into play. Gilligan concludes that "men and women may perceive danger in different social situations . . . men seeing danger more often in close personal affiliation than in achievement and constructing danger to arise from intimacy, women perceiving danger in impersonal achievement situations and constructing danger to result from competitive success" (p. 42).

An illustration of the dilemma between ambition and caring in women's lives occurred in my consciousness-raising group during the 1970s, when one of our members—who had returned to school in her forties, gotten a graduate degree, and begun her professional career—used the word "calculating" in describing her career plans. I was stunned and told the group I couldn't bear the idea of being calculating, that this meant to me using other people and climbing over them for one's own selfish purposes. *In a Different Voice* places the ensuing discussion, which continued at our meetings for a number of months, in the now-familiar context of how women's moral imperatives can interfere with their success in the broader world outside the family and friendship, much as we believe there is a need for the values of caring in that world. As we talked in the group and as I thought the question through on my own, I began to see that it could be possible to be calculating on your own behalf without necessarily harming anyone else. I realized that the expression "calculating woman" had always been a very negative image for me—a woman self-centered, immoral, and deplorable. I gradually came to see this as another example of sexism, as the same word applied to a man did not conjure up for me such a negative image. A "calculating man" was a man who was clever and wanted to succeed. I realized that my ex-husband had been calculating in pursuing his career in much the same way my friend was proposing, and that I had never been shocked by it or disapproving. I was then able to consider the possibility of being calculating on my own behalf and came to feel empowered by this new attitude.

Elizabeth Cady Stanton, at the Seneca Falls conference in 1848, recognized this dilemma for women and said clearly, "self-development is a higher duty than self-sacrifice"—a statement very similar to that made to "Sarah" in the women's magazine story Friedan tells us about. "The thing which most retards and militates against women's self-development is self-sacrifice," says Gilligan (p. 129). Selfishness is the cardinal sin in the ladder of feminine virtue, whose ideal is perfect devotion and self-abnegation. Gilligan correctly connects this issue to the debate, current at the time of her writing, over the Equal Rights Amendment, stating that "women's self-development continues to raise the specter of selfishness, the fear that freedom for women will lead to an abandonment of responsibility in relationships" (p. 130). Here again we see the valuation of women's morality and the fear of its loss at the same time that it is devalued and made to seem inferior. A wonderful story to this effect was once told to me by a patient. She was an attorney in Washington, D.C., working for the Civil Rights Commission. Her job was to lobby in Congress for passage of the ERA, and in this capacity she had spent an hour with a Congressman putting forth her position. She thought the meeting had gone well, and she called his secretary the next day to find out how he would be voting. The secretary told her that the Congressman would be voting against the ERA and had stated as his reason: "Now my son doesn't listen to anything I say. If this passes my daughter won't listen to anything I say either." Gilligan states:

> The notion that virtue for women lies in self-sacrifice has complicated the course of women's development by pitting the moral issue of goodness against the adult questions of responsibility and choice. In addition the ethic of self-sacrifice is directly in conflict with the

concept of rights that has, in this past century, supported women's
claim to a fair share of social justice. [p. 132]

The threat in the ERA is men's fear that women will lose their focus on the
care of others, with all the self-sacrifice this entails, and become just as
concerned with their self-development and individual rights as men are.
This, it is further feared, will bring down the entire system on which the
traditional family is based and on which the entire economic structure
functions. Woman's fulfillment of her "femininity" has served male
society by keeping her as servant to the species, whether that service is
provided free as a housewife and mother or at fifty-nine cents on the dollar
in factories and offices.

A demand for equality is clearly a rejection of self-sacrifice. This
connection can be seen as follows: femininity = self-sacrifice = low self-
esteem = vulnerability = dependency = suppression of anger = depression = masochism = self-sacrifice. I believe this is the equation for
understanding the greater prevalence of depression and masochism in
women. What is lacking in Gilligan's work is a recognition of how
women's morality can lead to a dependency on others, which has a
pathological consequence for many women. Chodorow recognizes this,
with her description of more permeable ego boundaries in women, but
neither writer carries the idea into the clinical picture we so often see of
women who must have someone dependent on their caring in order to feel
valued, and in some cases, even to have a feeling of existing. Much female
self-satisfaction is obtained from these intimate relationships; but when a
dependent relationship is lost, as when a child plans to go to college or a
boyfriend leaves, many women experience significant depression. In order
to avoid loss, some women placate others and suppress anger. Whether the
fear of loss stems primarily from economic or from emotional dependence,
many women's lives need more autonomous functioning that will provide
independent sources of self-satisfaction and leave them less vulnerable to
depression at the times of withdrawal from close relationships, and thus
less vulnerable to emotional and economic exploitation. The real challenge
is to find a comfortable balance between self-development on the one hand
and caring relationships on the other. It is through this challenge that
modern women may achieve their highest levels of functioning in both
arenas and the greatest self-esteem. Men too, face this challenge, but their
internal voices are not as demanding of them to care for others. The
dilemma has often been that women have sought dependency on men in
marriage to protect them from the risks of sexual and economic exploitation in the work world. This has resulted in their trading one vulnerable
position for another. Women need, as do all adults, to find a proper balance

between self-sacrifice at one extreme and self-centeredness at the other extreme, resulting in a *healthy self-caring.*

Kernberg (1975) refers to "normal narcissism" as opposed to "pathological narcissism." This concept is a valuable one to keep in mind when working with women patients. Kernberg defines normal narcissism as "the libidinal investment of the self" (p. 315).

> The regulation of normal narcissism can be understood only in terms of the relative predominance of libidinal over aggressive investment by these same intrapsychic structures. . . . the intrapsychic structures and the external factors influencing the libidinal investment of the self, that is, normal narcissism, [include] the ideal self and ego goals, object representations, superego factors and instinctual and organic factors. . . . External factors . . . may be classified as: 1) libidinal gratifications stemming from external objects; 2) gratification of ego goals and aspirations in social effectiveness or success; and 3) gratification of intellectual or cultural aspirations realized in the environment . . . [which] reflect superego and ego demands as well as reality factors. . . . there is an increase of libidinal investment of the self with love or gratification from external objects, success in reality, increase of harmony between the self and superego structures, reconfirmation of love from internal objects, and direct instinctual gratification and physical health. [pp. 318–320]

Kernberg makes no distinction here between men and women. Thus, we can assume he does not support the idea that women need not have independent sources of narcissistic success. Surely "gratification of intellectual or cultural aspirations realized in the environment" in no way limits women to the family environment. Remember that the adult goals of love and work are combined for women who are homemakers, so that their achievement of success in both areas depends upon their attracting and holding onto a man. In individual psychotherapy, many women are now receiving encouragement to pursue their independent interests and advanced education. While the women patients of an earlier generation of analysts and therapists were told to stay home and fulfill themselves as homemakers, the woman's movement has brought patients and therapists alike to recognize the need for healthy autonomous functioning in women. A superficial glance at the wives and daughters of psychoanalysts today reveals many professional women, and such discouragement as that of Anna Freud's desire to attend medical school is no longer evident in my observation.

Gilligan's book represented a breakthrough in the understanding of male–female differences. It helped me to understand frustrating, apparently irresolvable disagreements I had for years with men in my own family but had never placed in the framework of gender difference. Conflicting opinions would emerge around certain legal issues, such as those related to pornography or drunk driving. I was finally able to see that the source of these disagreements lay in my placing a greater value on protecting and caring for the feelings of others, while the men gave greater value to individual rights. Civil liberties, a time-honored liberal-intellectual cause, is based on individual rights and freedoms. The freedom for neo-Nazis to march in the streets of Skokie, Illinois, in uniform and carrying flags with swastikas is—by this thinking—a higher value than protection of the feelings of Jews and others who are deeply distressed by the sight. The freedom of men to view pornography, even that showing terrible violence toward women (I make a distinction between pornography and erotica, as does Gloria Steinem [1983]), is valued more highly than the feelings of women, who are all degraded by such pictures and words. The belief in the right of a man or woman to drink and drive and make his or her own independent decision about that capacity, and to be entitled to be proven incompetent by a court, created opposition to any law setting a blood alcohol level above which one is presumed incompetent. Recently, the flag burning issue has pitted civil libertarians against those who believe that the feelings of those who have lost sons and husbands in wars—sons and husbands whose bodies were buried draped in the American flag—are more important than someone's right to use the flag for a political protest. My concern about individual freedom in each case was tempered by my concern for the feelings of those who are hurt.

In the case of drunk driving, my pleas of "but what if your daughter or son were killed by a drunk driver?" were never able to penetrate the others' conviction of the rightness of the principle. Is it any wonder that it was a group of women—the Mothers Against Drunk Driving—who finally forced attention to this issue and won? The battle around pornography has resulted in the creation of strange bedfellows, with civil-liberties feminists and the giant porno industry on one side, and the antiviolence-in-pornography feminists aligned with religious fundamentalists on the other. Gilligan's work on gender differences helps put these issues in a perspective in which we can see that neither side is wrong, but rather each side is emphasizing a different truth about the issue. A balancing of values is necessary to help resolve these dilemmas, which may reflect gender differences as well as the distinction between individual rights and the general good of the community.

A clinical example of men's and women's different moral reasoning leading to differing solutions occurred in my practice. It enabled me to see an argument between a husband and wife in a clearer light and, I believe, to portray it to them in a way that presented the value in each of their positions.

> Tom and Angela had been married a short time and had one child. The two were out for the evening in Chinatown when they passed two men fighting. According to Tom, one man was clearly stronger and was in the process of hurting the other. Tom—an ex-Marine—felt morally compelled to intervene to protect the weaker man. Angela, very distressed, yelled at him not to get involved, but Tom ignored her pleas and entered the fray, breaking up the fight. In my office, Angela expressed her worry that by getting involved, Tom could have been injured and would then not have been able to provide for her and their child. She felt the men should have been left to deal with their own problems. Tom, on the other hand, saw a clear duty to prevent an injustice and acted on that principle. I immediately thought of "Amy" and her concern that if Heinz stole the drug he could be sent to jail and not be able to care for his sick wife in the future. Tom's ethic of justice was in direct conflict with Angela's ethic of care—how Tom's possible injury would affect the family relationships, the caring connection between husband, wife, and child. I presented the conflict to them in these terms, stating that they each had a valid point and it was hard to reconcile the two. They each felt affirmed and each could then respect the other's position. There was no right or wrong, no scale on which they were being scored.

Critique—Martha Mednick

The Gilligan work met with a mixed reaction by feminists and psychologists. Some feared that the work could be used as an argument against the goal of equality for women in the workplace. Faludi (1991) states "difference became the new magic word uttered to defuse the feminist campaign for equality" (p. 327). Faludi misconstrues the focus on the value of relatedness in the Gilligan work with a "cult of domesticity. . . . In the end, legislators would not be influenced to enact 'special' rights for women. Instead, in the wider backlash era in which relational feminists were writing, their words would be used and misused—by antifeminist authors and, worse, corporate lawyers battling sex discrimination suits" (p. 327).

If Gilligan's thesis were used to prove that "independence was an unnatural and unhealthy state for women" (p. 331), that is surely a distortion of its meaning and further evidence of the power of the backlash against feminist efforts at gaining political and economic equality while recognizing that cultural and social pressures have created a special psychology of women.

In an article critical of Gilligan's work, Martha Mednick (1989) refers to those who have joined in a view of women's differences from men as having jumped on the "bandwagon." I believe that Mednick and Faludi, as well as other critics, miss the point because they do not place Gilligan's work in the conceptual framework provided by Freud and psychoanalysis—that the female superego is weak, deficient, and inferior. It is only when viewing Gilligan's work in this context and in the context of the Piaget and Kohlberg theories, that the enormous advances of her thinking become clear. *Different* is so far superior to *deficient* as to have revolutionary implications in the progress of feminist theory.

Although Mednick claims she is not dismissing the work of Gilligan, to link her with right-wing antifeminists, thus confusing the author's work with its distortions by some for political expediency, is unfair. Different is not synonymous with inferior. Differences can be seen as stimulating and broadening, and thus highly valued. We study other cultures and travel abroad because we are interested in differences. In our current economic slump, we continually read of comparisons to Japanese models of business as possible sources of new methods that can be applied in the United States. Mednick also describes Gilligan's work as "simplistic," which in my mind is a dismissal. "Such models of behavior (the social and historical context of gender) are complex and thus less easily reduced, as is Gilligans's view and other women's nature models, to a simplistic, dichotomously presented, intuitively appealing, bandwagon construct" (p. 1120).

Gilligan's work can be interpreted to mean that women have a point of view that has something special and valuable to contribute to the world of business and government, and that is the light in which I use her work and find it of value. Mednick's discussion of class differences in moral reasoning is also valuable and more work on this aspect of differences would be welcomed. But Mednick's reference to bandwagon is demeaning and insulting to women who have found true value in these concepts. Mednick is wrong when she implies that Gilligan and Chodorow's work is about women's "special nature" (p. 1122). This is not their approach at all. Rather they view women's personalities as a result of highly complex psychosocial interactions combined with intrapsychic responses.

Mednick's criticism that Gilligan's work adds to the female stereotype assumes there is one female stereotype. In fact there are many, and they are often contradictory. There is the stereotype of women as "empty-headed," the "dumb blond," silly, childlike, jealous, and narcissistic. Then there is the stereotype of women as demanding, domineering, overprotective and overinvolved as mothers, the cause of all their children's problems. Another female stereotype is the "femme fatale," the sexually powerful, conniving, duplicitous, dangerous woman whose motives can't be trusted. Gilligan's woman is caring, thoughtful and rational, careful about hurting others' feelings; she prefers to preserve relationships rather than compete. This is surely far superior to any of the traditional stereotypes.

There is also an elitist bias in this article. If an idea is popular, that is, of the people, it must be suspect. The people can only react intuitively. In addition, it certainly can't be "scientific," because popular ideas are so simplistic. The hard truth can only be known to a select few, the academic elite, who do the only "correct" research. "In sum, the simplicity of such ideas is appealing; such gender dichotomy confirms stereotypes and provides strong intuitive resonance" (p. 1122). I sense a masculine bias about knowledge here.

Eleanor E. Maccoby

By contrast, Eleanor E. Maccoby, professor emeritus of psychology at Stanford University, continues to write about gender differences. In a recent article (1990), she describes at some length observed differences in the relational styles of girls and boys that lead them to prefer playing with same-sex playmates.

> I want to suggest that it is because women and girls use more enabling styles that they are able to form more intimate and more integrated relationships. Also I think it likely that it is the male concern for turf and dominance—that is, with not showing weakness to other men and boys—that underlies their restrictive interaction style and their lack of self-disclosure. . . . Groups of women have more success on tasks that require discussion and negotiation, whereas male groups do better on tasks where success depends on the volume of ideas being generated. Overall, it appears that *both* styles are productive, though in different ways. [pp. 517–518]

Maccoby can talk about difference without falling into the trap of superior–inferior judgments. In reference to Gilligan and Chodorow she states:

> In my view, processes within the nuclear family have been given too much credit—or too much blame—for this aspect [interactional styles] of sex-typing. I doubt that the development of distinctive interactive styles has much to do with the fact that children are parented primarily by women, as some have claimed (Chodorow, 1978; Gilligan, 1982), and it seems likely to me that children's "identification" with the same-sex parent is more a consequence than a cause of children's

acquisition of sex-typed interaction styles. I would place most of the emphasis on the peer group as the setting in which children first discover the compatibility of same-sex others. [p. 519]

One biological difference between the sexes that is often neglected in discussions of male–female differences in relational style is that a male can rape a female, a male can rape a male, but a female cannot be raped by another female. The only exception to this is the sexual abuse of girls by their mothers or older girls by the insertion of objects into the vagina. But compared to the incidence of male attack, the likelihood of such abuse is minimal. I believe that this biological fact accounts, on an unconscious level, for the comfort women take in intimacy with other women and men's lack of intimacy, their restrictive interactional style, with other men. Men fear sexual attack from more powerful men. This is well known in prisons but exists in other situations as well, such as male groups, where a weaker member will be selected as a target by a bully, or older boys will attack a younger boy.

An example of this fear came to light in my work with a male patient who described his discomfort when he attended a photography exhibit that included a nude photograph of the male photographer. There had been nude photos of women in the show, which didn't bother him, so I questioned his response. At first he insisted that it was clearly unseemly for a man to photograph himself nude. But as we explored the issue the idea emerged that he would never want to pose nude for a male photographer, that that would feel threatening to him, that he would be putting himself in a vulnerable position where he could be sexually assaulted. This difference in the potential for violence helps explain women's greater ability to tolerate close relationships. Traditionally, men have been taught that they are never to hit a woman, which has provided protection for women in close relationships with men. Unfortunately, this protection is frequently violated.

The Relational Worlds of Adolescent Girls

Gilligan's latest book, *Making Connections: The Relational Worlds of Adolescent Girls at Emma Willard School,* is the work of the Project on the Psychology of Women and the Development of Girls, established at Harvard in 1983, which performed a five-year study funded by the Dodge Foundation. The book is a collection of essays written individually and collectively by study team members. Like Jean Baker Miller at the Stone Center, Gilligan puts her principles into practice by taking the focus off her individual achievement and joining in a cooperative effort with other women working in connection, in an affiliation, to discover new components in the psychology of women. The study involved extensive interviews and tests to determine girls' attitudes towards friendship, leadership, sexual morality, politics, and violence. Gilligan (quoted in Prose 1990) describes the team members' "common intention to listen for the ways in which girls orchestrate themes of connection and separation and concerns about care and justice in speaking about themselves, about their relationships, and about their experiences of conflict" (pp. 23–25).

What the interviewers heard was that many girls of around age 11 have a "moment of resistance," "that is, a sharp and particular clarity of vision, an almost perfect confidence in what they know and see, a belief in their integrity and in their highly complex responsibilities toward the world. 'Eleven-year-olds are not for sale,' says Gilligan" (p. 23). According to Lyn Mikel Brown, also quoted by Prose, a co-researcher with Gilligan,

> As they get older the girls seem to undergo a kind of crisis in response to adolescence and to the strictures of demands of the culture which, in Gilligan's view, sends a particular message to women: "Keep quiet and notice the absence of women and say nothing." [p. 23]

Prose, summarizing the findings of Gilligan and her team, finds "disbelief and dismay at repeatedly seeing a morally articulate preadolescent transformed into an apologetic, hesitant teen-ager who prefaces every opinion with 'this may sound mediocre but . . .' " (p. 40). According to Gilligan, during adolescence girls come up against "the wall of Western culture." They fear that their "clearsightedness may be dangerous and seditious; in consequence they learn to hide and protect what they know—not only to censor themselves but 'to think in ways that differ from what they really think' " (p. 45).

Following Gilligan's challenge to the hallmark of psychological development based on the study of men—individuation—plus her emphasis on the different value of collectivity for women, the teachers and administrators at Emma Willard initiated the practice of collaborative work among their students. A dramatic rise in quiz scores in a geography class occurred when students were placed in groups and told their grades would be the average of all the group members' scores. Almost everyone got a perfect score.

Of course, one wonders how this can be translated to the highly competitive "real world" in a capitalist economy. The experience is reminiscent of stories of classroom work from the People's Republic of China, where the collective approach in school is congruent with the economic realities. However, even in China, admission to college and training schools is highly competitive. Thus, it is a beautiful example of the benefits of collaboration, but likely to be incongruent with later academic and employment realities. It can, however, serve to show girls how capable they can be when the competitive factor is removed, and in that sense might help them to break through that impediment when they need to. I believe that, ideally, men and women should be able to function collectively whenever possible for the enhancement of the group, as in a family, a neighborhood, or a nation. But it is also important to be able to compete freely when one finds oneself in a competitive situation—for example, in admission to college or graduate school; or, sometimes, in a dating situation, when one is well aware that the man or woman is dating others. Being "calculating" in these situations cannot help but mean competing at someone else's expense, yet this choice needs to be weighed against not trying, which can be self-defeating. Here lies the essence of the problem for many women, and for some men. Self-assertion in such circumstances does require a healthy self-caring, which can only be attained with the recognition that "if I am not for myself, who will be for me, but if I am only for myself, what am I."

The strengths and growth enjoyed in the collective project of girls working together in their geography class is consistent with the experience seen in consciousness-raising groups and other support groups. It shows the value of group morale and encouragement, which has also proven its value in study groups used, for example, by law students studying for the Bar. The group can act as a kind of Greek Chorus for the individual, lending commentary and community approval in a way that individual therapy cannot. This may be especially important for groups such as women and minorities, who are belittled and denied success in the larger society except in certain traditional roles. The success of all the group members reduces anxiety about independent success, and the competitive world can seem less frightening for men and women if we have some help and encouragement.

Summary

Gilligan's work has been a major contributing force toward a feminist revision of psychoanalytic theory about women. The view that women, due to their anatomical difference from men, suffered from lifelong mental and emotional deficiencies has been alienating to women and has contributed to angry feelings toward psychoanalysis. Gilligan's proposal that women's moral development is different, but not deficient, recognizes the differences but allows us to see them in terms of positive qualities that women have in relationships, and of how these qualities can help to sustain connections among people. It is not that women are never competitive, but rather that competition does not play as crucial a part in women's relationships as it does among men, for whom independence is a higher value than connection. The paradox is that the very traits that have defined women as "good" and "feminine" are those that have marked them deficient in moral development, according to male psychologists and psychoanalysts.

The value men have assigned to individuation has led to a definition of maturity founded on the primacy of independence and individual rights, in a hierarchy of values that they claim is objective. For women, the moral problem centers on conflicting responsibilities, such as in the abortion decision, or career versus homemaker choices, rather than competing rights. The danger is that concerns about not hurting others can lead women into an attitude of self-sacrifice that can impede their success and lead to dependency and depression.

For women, self-development has been equated with selfishness and has been viewed as unfeminine. However, women's concern for the effect of their success upon others, because of the value of connection to others, has been used to demean their intelligence and competence. A demand for equality is a rejection of the feminine virtue of self-sacrifice, but need not lead to a loss of concern for the feelings of others.

Critics of Gilligan's thesis are fearful that viewing women as different will be used to disqualify them from certain jobs, jobs that require "tough" decisions. For this reason her book has created controversy among feminist scholars. In my view, healthy self-caring strikes a balance between self-sacrifice at one extreme and self-centeredness at the other. The general good of the community on issues of social concern, such as drinking and driving, must be balanced with the value of individual rights. Women have a clearer vision of this need for balance. Women can contribute the balancing view when they are integrated into the workforce in jobs of responsibility in law, medicine, business, and government.

WOMEN AND ANGER—TERESA BERNARDEZ-BONESATTI

One of the best early articles on female anger was written by psychiatrist Bernardez-Bonesatti (1978): "Women and Anger: Conflicts with Aggression in Contemporary Women." Bernardez-Bonesatti believes that the inhibition of anger in women results in difficulties in creative and active pursuits. Using Miller's notion of the fear of women's omnipotence shared by men and women alike, Bernardez-Bonesatti believes that the demythologizing of women's destructive power must precede the effort to free women to become aware of their anger, its sources and its aims, in order to focus creative energy toward change. This article contains no reference to psychoanalytic theory and is not an effort to reformulate or revise that theory. It has a clinical focus and is based on Bernardez-Bonesatti's experience treating women patients, combining her recognition of the anger over injustice voiced by the women's movement with her experience of how the expression of anger has been thwarted by adherence to the stereotype of femininity.

The fear of women's anger by men and women has one source in women's nurturant role and the wish to protect the infants in their care, and another source in the unconscious belief in the "excessive vulnerability of the male to critical, disapproving, rejecting or directly attacking" female behavior. As long as women can be kept "submissive, dependent, noncompetitive and unaggressive," men and children will be protected from their magical danger. Women have cooperated in inhibiting their anger for fear of losing their sexual identity and attractiveness to men, and to avoid the danger of falling into the stereotype of the "ferocious, envious, vengeful or castrating" woman—in other words, of being a "witch" or "bitch" (p. 216).

Bernardez-Bonesatti believes that the fear of her own anger is related to women's need to feel connected to others and to be of service to them, whereas in anger "the person establishes automatic aloneness and makes herself temporarily separate from the object of the anger" (p. 216). She observes that very often when women do express anger it is contaminated or nullified by tears and expressions of guilt and sorrow.

> In this complex response the woman appears to be expressing her anger, her conflict and fear about it, her sorrow at the loss of a relationship, the sadness at her own self-betrayal and her impotence in making herself clear, all at the same time. . . . Such a response tends primarily to preserve a threatened loss of bonding with the other. [p. 216]

It is only when women can reduce their dependence on men that they can risk the loss they fear from directly expressing their anger. Bernardez-Bonesatti recognizes that this dependence has been transferred from old individuation struggles with the mother in which dependency wishes were not resolved, and that therefore women experience anger as quite a dangerous threat to their dependence on important figures in their current life—husbands, bosses, even children. The situation is further complicated by projections of disapproval, and often results in her turning the anger against herself, perceiving herself as hateful, so that the differentiation between legitimate and irrational anger is then made more difficult. Additionally, Bernardez-Bonesatti proposes that women's awareness of their approval-seeking behavior, and their fraudulent efforts to keep that approval, lead to self-contempt. Their self-betrayal decreases their self-esteem as they become aware of their dishonesty and lack of courage.

Bernardez-Bonesatti stresses the crucial importance of clear expression of anger in goal-directed behavior, separation, and self-definition. We are all aware of the "terrible two's" as the stage when children must say "no" in order to develop autonomy and separate from their parents. For many women, learning to say "no" to figures of authority and those upon whom they feel dependent is a developmental task that often goes awry and cripples them in their adult lives. Therapy can correct this if the therapist can encourage and tolerate a woman patient's anger. The fear of disapproval and abandonment must be dealt with in therapy, and its rational component must be faced, for it may in fact be dangerous for a woman to risk open expression of anger. She may destroy her marriage if her husband, partially because of his irrational fear, cannot tolerate such expression.

Women have developed covert ways of showing anger that Bernardez-Bonesatti enumerates. 1) Resentment: The woman never identifies the source of the anger or ventilates it, but appears disgruntled and bitter and shows passive-aggressive behavior. 2) Outbursts of irrational complaints: These may seem like temper-tantrums and thus may be dismissed as infantile. 3) The raving maniac: She conforms to the frightening female stereotype. All of these distorted expressions of anger may result in a further sense of powerlessness, guilt, and lowered self-esteem, because they appear as disturbed behavior to the woman and others. The goal in therapy with these women is to help them to assert legitimate anger in a manner that is self-respectful and that enhances personal dignity.

Bernardez-Bonesatti does not use the term "hysterical," a common accusation against women. In my experience, behavior described by men and even women as "hysterical" can vary from true grief expressed by sobbing to genuine anger expressed by yelling and perhaps even throwing things. The peculiarity in this situation is that in the latter case, the woman may be feeling and expressing genuine anger, a clear, honest emotion, but it is not identified as anger. It is called "hysterical," and so its righteousness is denied and the woman herself is labeled "hysterical" or even "crazy." The woman needs to be clear in her own mind that she is angry, not crazy, in order to assert her point that what she is feeling is anger, not hysteria. Certainly, it is best not to throw things or yell. But the amazing thing is that when men yell, pound tables with their fists, throw things, slam doors, storm out of the house, kick in a door, put a fist through the wall, and so on in arguments, they are not called hysterical; it is very clear to them and to those around them that they are very angry and that the violent behavior is a way to intimidate others in order to gain control of the situation. A woman's expression of anger involving yelling and throwing results in her further loss of respect and esteem, whereas the very same behavior in a man will bring about fear and compliance. What we are dealing with here is the recognized but rarely mentioned factor of physical strength, and the physical threat that goes with it, that men have and women lack except in relation to young children. Women are sometimes battered by their teenaged sons. The ever-present knowledge of the male's superior physical strength is a constant in all male–female relationships and is a significant factor in women's suppression of anger. Bernardez-Bonesatti fails to recognize this element, which must be dealt with in therapy. All women should be questioned about whether they have been struck. It is often a forbidden topic, like rape and incest, and therapists need to overcome their own anxiety about the subject so that they can be comfortable questioning their patients.

There are of course hundreds of examples of male rage expressed in violence in films, whether through cowboy, detective, or gang fights, or in the many war movies. The men in these films are not characterized as hysterical, but rather as powerful. A recent (1987) film, *Moonstruck,* is typical of a film that is not basically violent, but a romance. In the film, we see Nicolas Cage talking to Cher at a kitchen table. He is suddenly filled with strong emotion and knocks over the table, letting the bottle of liquor and glasses go crashing to the floor—at which point he grabs Cher in his arms, kisses her passionately, and carries her off to the bedroom. I tried to imagine a role reversal of this scene, with Cher turning over the table and demanding sex from Cage. It seemed impossible. If a woman turned over a table and dishes came crashing down, someone would try to calm this hysterical woman and she would probably end up sobbing. Women, according to our feminist analysis, are both too dangerous and too fearful to be powerful.

Women frequently have conflicts with aggression that inhibit creativity, imagination, and zest. Obedience to dependency figures limits the freedom to "explore, investigate and invent. The energy bound in suppressing, inhibiting and redirecting anger makes it unavailable to creative pursuits" (p. 218). Bernardez-Bonesatti observes, as did Gilligan, that:

> The dread of social isolation and disapproval leads women to suppress and avoid competitive behavior. . . . The sources of guilt that have to do with early feelings of competition with maternal authority or with other rivals for mother's attention are further reinforced by standards of femininity that negate the possibility of women doing better than men and diagnose such possibility as indicative of the woman's hostility toward the male. . . . The dread of defeating men and awareness of envy toward competent women is defended against by withdrawal and/or claims of incompetence. [p. 218]

She reminds us that therapists too may share the same fear and disapproval of women's anger, and thus a successful outcome to psychotherapy cannot be expected unless the therapist has worked through this irrational fear.

In my practice I find that the most common way of covering up anger is to use the word "upset." Women, and sometimes men, are always saying that an experience has resulted in their being "upset." I tell them that the word "upset" tells neither them or me what they are really feeling and that I want them to try to describe the actual feelings they had. I even at times have said that I have a rule against using the word "upset" in my office and they remember that, correcting themselves in the future. Yes, this can be seen as an effort to please me, but it is the most effective way I have found of cutting through the vagueness, denial, and self-deception so character-istic of women's fear of exposing—to me and at times even themselves—the strong feelings of anger they carry.

This leads to the issue of suicide among women. The frequency of suicidal thoughts among women is well known to psychotherapists, and learning to distinguish when there is a real danger is part of our training. What I have been surprised to discover, in working with male patients and from other sources of observation, is how common it is for the threat of suicide to be used by women in relationships with their husbands and even their children. This is an omission in Bernardez-Bonesatti's list of covert ways of expressing anger. Depression in women is a serious concern, and one that I will address later with clinical examples, but—as in the formula I described above—surely one significant and dangerous component in the ideal of feminine virtue as self-abnegating is the suppression of anger, its conversion to depression, and the resulting danger of suicide. However, as sympathetic as we may be to a depressed woman, the controlling and manipulative benefits she receives from the availability of this threat can at times constitute emotional blackmail, and must—for her own sake as well as that of her family—be confronted directly by the therapist. This is one reason I do not allow the camouflaging of anger with such vague and watered down expressions as "I'm upset." Some women say more directly that they are "hurt," but this too is insufficient. The state of mind must be identified more precisely by the addition of: "You are hurt *and angry*," so that the masochistic alternative of suppressing anger toward others and turning it inward with suicidal ideation—and sometimes attempts—can be forestalled. The blackmail manipulation may work, temporarily, but it demeans the woman in the judgment of others, and destroys her self-respect as well.

MASOCHISM, DOMINATION, AND PORNOGRAPHY

In *The Bonds of Love: Psychoanalysis, Feminism and the Problem of Domination* (1988), Jessica Benjamin, a psychoanalyst, builds on the foundation developed by Dinnerstein, Chodorow, Keller, and Gilligan. Benjamin acknowledges her indebtedness to their contributions. She is critical of the work of Chasseguet-Smirgel on the oedipal complex, because Chasseguet-Smirgel continues to promote the idea that the father represents separation from the mother and thus protects the child from regression. Like Gilligan and the others, Benjamin believes that psychoanalysis overvalues separation, creating a strong bias in psychoanalytic theory. Benjamin's unique contribution is to take Dinnerstein's discussion of the subordination of women into the realm of female masochism and to explore this area with a thoughtful and at times remarkably perceptive new understanding, adding her reformulation of psychoanalytic theory to Chodorow's work on the oedipal complex and Gilligan's on the female superego.

Psychoanalytic Views of Masochism

Helene Deutsch and Marie Bonaparte expanded on Freud's theory that female masochism was founded in biological and constitutional facts of life, and was therefore part of female nature. Their ideas took hold in much psychoanalytic literature, and in the popularized versions of this literature, to the point where women were held responsible for their own suffering, whether this be due to rape, wife beating, or simply a characterological state of mind. This view led to the feminist critique of the 1960s and beyond, that psychoanalysis is responsible for "blaming the victim." The Freudian theory does appear to be quite unsympathetic, and anger by women at the lack of recognition of their vulnerability is understandable. One of my most regretted memories is of an incident that occurred when I was a young therapist, after I had read the two-volume Deutsch work but prior to the appearance of the feminist critique of Deutsch. I saw a woman who had been raped on a college campus and attempted to explore with her why she had been walking alone at night. Fortunately, she never returned, but I still cringe at my lack of appreciation of the trauma that she had suffered.

Karen Horney took issue with the Freud and Deutsch approach in her 1933 paper, "The Problem of Feminine Masochism." Horney lists the cultural conditions that predispose women to masochism, such as blocking of outlets for expansiveness and sexuality, restriction in the number of children, belief in the inferiority of women, economic dependence on men, fostering emotional dependence, restriction of women to spheres of life built upon emotional bonds, and a surplus of marriageable women. She concludes. "The problem of feminine masochism cannot be related to factors inherent in the anatomical-physiological-psychic characteristics of woman alone, but must be considered as importantly conditioned by the culture-complex or social organization in which the particular masochistic woman has developed" (pp. 232–233).

Clara Thompson (1942) wrote that masochism is often an adaptation to an unsatisfactory and circumscribed life. Harold P. Blum (1977b) also departed from the traditional view in his article "Masochism, the Ego Ideal, and the Psychology of Women," referred to in Chapter 3.

However, in 1985, some psychoanalysts, such as Robert L. Spitzer, chairman of the American Psychiatric Association (APA) panel in charge of revising the *DSM (Diagnostic and Statistical Manual)*, decided to reintroduce the diagnosis of masochism in the forthcoming *DSM-III-R* (1987). Subverting the agreed upon process, they failed to notify Teresa Bernardez, chair of the APA's Committee on Women, and the other committee members. The APA panel planned to add three diagnoses affecting women: "Premenstrual Dysphoric Disorder," "Paraphiliac Rapism Disorder," as well as the "Masochistic Personality Disorder" diagnosis.

Under much pressure from Dr. Bernardez and other women, and finally a threatened lawsuit by The Feminist Therapy Institute, Spitzer granted a hearing to the women by the nearly all-male body. The only woman on the panel was Spitzer's wife, a social worker. At the hearing in November 1985, Spitzer revealed that his evidence for the inclusion of the "masochism" diagnosis was his study involving eight patients. Six women opposing inclusion of the diagnosis were allowed to testify but were cut off at noon after having been promised a day-long hearing. Spitzer claimed that their evidence was "irrelevant." The women protested and were allowed to return for the afternoon's proceedings but not allowed to speak (Faludi 1991).

After the hearing many critical letters, a formal protest by the Committee on Women of the American Psychological Association, and petitions signed by thousands of mental health practitioners resulted in a compromise. The names were changed but the definitions remained the same. Premenstrual syndrome is described as "Late Luteal Phase Dysphoric Disorder," and masochism became "Self-defeating Personality Disorder." Bernardez and other feminists continued to lodge protests, but, in the end, the APA's trustees approved both the masochism and PMS diagnoses and shelved the rapism disorder. The compromise was that they were listed in the appendix, rather than the main body, with the following explanation: "This appendix presents three diagnoses that were proposed for inclusion in *DSM-III-R*. They are included here to facilitate further systematic clinical study and research" (APA 1987, p. 213). Also included in the appendix is the diagnosis "Sadistic Personality Disorder." Ordinarily, disorders in the appendix do not have code numbers, to discourage their use for medical insurance purposes, but in this case code numbers are assigned to these supposedly provisional diagnoses, encouraging their use.

According to Faludi in her book *Backlash* (1991), Dr. Bernardez's outspokeness was punished by the APA. When her term on the women's committee came up for renewal, she was not invited back, and within a year all the women who had spoken out against these new diagnoses had been purged from the committee.

Paula J. Caplan

Paula J. Caplan, an assistant professor of psychology at the University of Toronto, published a paper based on a study of juvenile female prostitutes (Newman and Caplan 1982) that she then expanded into a book (1985). Caplan, quoted in the *New York Times* (Collins 1985), stated that she believes that women's behavior that has been diagnosed as masochistic is actually due to the following traits:

> the ability to delay gratification and wait for rewards through effort; the capacity to put other people's needs ahead of one's own; the belief, based on past experience, that one should have limited expectations, and the effort to avoid punishment, rejection or guilt. The same behaviors that are defined as masochistic in women . . . would be defined quite healthily as sacrificial, or courageous or facing realities, or hard work, in men. [p. 12]

In the same issue of the *New York Times,* Eleanor Galenson, a psychoanalyst, defends the Freudian approach. Arnold M. Cooper, another analyst, disagrees, stating that "Masochism is present in men as well as women. Its cause is not biological, but rather, an aspect of development" (p. 12). Natalie Shainess tells the newspaper:

> Paula and a number of other women insist quite rightly that masochism is not instinctual, and I agree with that. But where I part company is that there is a whole group of personality traits that go together, that may be described as masochistic. In my clinical experience many women have this masochistic problem. There is no sense in denying it. [p. 12]

Caplan, who is critical of Shainess's 1984 book, replies, "I'm not denying therapists' clinical experience that they have seen unhappy women but the reason is not masochism" (p. 12).

Caplan's thesis is that the recognized complex of female self-sacrifice is learned behavior that goes along with low self-esteem and the view all women learn that only through serving others can they attain any value. Caplan takes exception to the use of the term *masochism* to describe what she considers to be culturally sanctioned, nurturant, altruistic qualities in women, and points out the irony of raising women to be subservient as a means of survival and then labeling them as pathological for it. She sees two aspects of female functioning: "the willingness to make do with less because one has never had more, and the willingness to endure the bad in order to get the good" (1984, p. 131). These aspects of functioning are quite different from masochism, and more accurately described the juvenile female prostitutes in her study.

Benjamin agrees with Caplan's assessment that the association of femininity with masochism persists in the culture, but she disagrees with the idea that, once the biological explanation is repudiated, a cultural explanation can suffice. Benjamin believes the basis for masochism can be found in the interaction of culture and psychological processes. "To begin to explain it, we must start with the way in which the mother's lack of subjectivity, as perceived by both male and female children, creates an internal propensity toward feminine masochism and male sadism" (1988, p. 81).

Some of the argument seems to stem from the failure to find a consistent definition of the problem. There is a confusion between masochism as a specific sexual perversion, with pain, humiliation, and subjugation needed for sexual satisfaction, and pain inflicted upon oneself through cutting or other forms of self-mutilation unconnected with any immediate sexual act. There are also the depressive-masochistic character structures as described by Kernberg (1975) and seen in the depressive personality and the sadomasochistic character (pp. 18–19). These diagnoses apply both to men and to women, but because of the cultural support for women's self-sacrificial behavior for the sake of others (as opposed to self-sacrifice to meet one's own goals, such as graduation from medical school), the appearance of masochistic traits in men can actually indicate more serious pathology, particularly paranoia. I have seen a combination of depression, masochism, and narcissism in a number of patients who need extensive treatment, but because of their deeply injured egos, change is slow and difficult. I don't think a distinction of "female masochism" is helpful, because I believe the pathology appears in both men and women and can be best understood by an analysis of their development and their identifications and interactions with significant others who carry the pathology. The most pervasive misunderstanding lies in the notion that women "enjoy" pain and therefore invite it upon themselves. This, I believe, is a distortion of the theory of reenaction; that is, that there can be a neurotic repetition of earlier traumatic events, in which the man or woman unconsciously engages in behavior that will result in confirmation of the earlier event, in a thwarted attempt at mastery.

Jessica Benjamin

Benjamin opens her book with a quotation from Freud's *Civilization and Its Discontents* (1930) describing "men" as aggressive, exploitative, and capable of inflicting pain, humiliation, and sexual and physical abuse on their neighbors. It is unclear whether Freud is referring to men only or all people. "Who, in the face of all his experience of life and of history, will have the courage to dispute this assertion?" (p. 3). Yet how tempting and inspiring it is to read Anne Frank's belief that people are really good at heart. If we cast our lot with Freud, as Benjamin does, we must accept that domination is inevitable, the strong dominating the weak: stronger men dominating weaker men, men dominating women, and women dominating children.

> This book is an analysis of the interplay between love and domination. It conceives domination as a two-way process, a system involving the participation of those who submit to power as well as those who exercise it. Above all, this book seeks to understand how domination is anchored in the hearts of the dominated. [p. 5]

Benjamin's book is a critique of psychoanalytic thinking about individual development, gender difference, and authority. Freud saw the primal struggle between father and son as the origin of civilization, the establishment of law and authority, as the son overthrows the father and then restores his authority in his image. Thus, every revolution is betrayed by the establishment of a new center of authority. The problem with this formulation is that it leaves out women because, according to Benjamin, psychoanalysts simply assumed the subordination of women to men. Benjamin offers a feminist criticism and reinterpretation of the problem of domination. She takes de Beauvoir's starting point of viewing gender domination as a complementarity of subject and object, and shows how gender polarity underlies the dualism of autonomy and dependency, and thus of master and slave. She asks how it is that these polarities persist in spite of our society's commitment to equality. However, she is concerned that a feminist critique not simply reverse the polarity by devaluing men and overvaluing women, thus maintaining a dualism.

> A major tendency in feminism has constructed the problem of domination as a drama of female vulnerability victimized by male aggression. Even the more sophisticated feminist thinkers frequently shy away from the analysis of submission, for fear that in admitting woman's participation in the relationship of domination, the onus of responsibility will appear to shift from men to women, and the moral victory from women to men. More generally, this has been a weakness of radical politics: to idealize the oppressed, as if their politics and culture were untouched by the system of domination, as if people did not participate in their own submission. . . . A theory or a politics that cannot cope with contradiction, that denies the irrational, that tries to

sanitize the erotic, fantastic components of human life cannot visualize
an authentic end to domination but only vacate the field. [pp. 9–10]

Benjamin is critical of feminists who joined the movement against
pornography, forgetting that the actual title of the organization was
"Women Against *Violence* in Pornography and the Media." She believes
there is a wish to see domination in personal terms, viewing all women as
victims or potential victims of male violence, when in fact male domination works through impersonal organization, formal rules, autonomous
individuals, control of the object world, accumulation of profit—all impersonal. But for an individual woman, male violence can be very personal.
Benjamin fails to distinguish between erotica and pornography; or between
feminists—mainly lesbians—who have irrationally distorted reality, de-
picting men as the enemy out to get women, and who have distorted
heterosexual sex into female masochistic submission to male sadistic
gratification, and feminists—both lesbians and heterosexuals—who have
maintained positive relationships with men but are deeply concerned
about the amount of violence against women and believe that pornography
may be a contributing factor.

Unfortunately, there is a similarity between Deutsch's view of the
female position in heterosexual sex and the radical lesbian view. Neither
Deutsch nor these feminists can imagine that the majority of women get at
least some pleasure from intercourse, and that many seek out sexual
contact and find it extremely pleasurable. By "radical lesbian" I refer to the
small percentage of lesbians who are what I consider paranoid about men,
but who call themselves "radical." This is another topic, untouched by
Benjamin and others, that needs to be addressed: that is, the feminists who
are completely hostile to all men and speak as if their view represents a
general feminist view, perhaps even the only "true" feminist view. I
believe there is a justification for concern about violence against women in
pornography, just as there is a reason to be concerned about the proliferation of violence of men on men and men on women in film and on TV. But
this need not entail, as Benjamin has it, a puritanical rejection of sexuality.
We can easily discern the difference between sexuality and sexism, although I agree that for some feminists that difference is blurred. The debate
still goes on as to whether the depiction of violence can actually stimulate
violence. My concern is that it can, as many psychological experiments
show that a percentage of children and adults become more violent after
viewing violence. The fact that a small group of women irrationally
associate all men with rape should not nullify the real danger of the
proliferation of violence against women in the many forms it takes, both in
the media and in the real world.

Benjamin does accurately point out the error of some feminists who deny the difference between "voluntary, ritual acts of submission that are subjectively considered pleasurable and acts of battery or violation that are terrifying and involuntary" (p. 260). The best resource on this subject is a book that appeared in 1980, *Take Back the Night: Women on Pornography,* edited by Laura Lederer and containing essays by many leading feminist writers, including Gloria Steinem, Susan Brownmiller, Diana Russell, Alice Walker, Robin Morgan, Andrea Dworkin, Susan Griffin, and Audre Lorde. It is a powerful collection, one that leaves the reader horrified and angry at the atrocities against women depicted in pornography. It is definitely not easy reading. The First Amendment dilemma continues to make the suppression of pornography a complex and controversial issue, but surely its existence and mass circulation informs us, painfully, of men's strong need to have control and feel powerful in relation to women, perhaps as a means of reversing the roles from the days when little boys were fearful of their powerful mothers. They could identify with their powerful fathers, and thereby benefit from their power, but the graphic depiction of slave-like women as sexual objects being tortured may for some men be the only coping method to contain their old rage and anxiety at their former helplessness. The real question is, does the viewing of pornography contain this hostility, or does it unleash it, making it more likely that violence will be acted out against women?

Elizabeth Fox-Genovese and the Paradox of Pornography for Feminism

Elizabeth Fox-Genovese, in a new and important book, *Feminism Without Illusions* (1991), sees the debate over pornography as divided into four camps: two opposers and two tolerators. The opposers consist of conservatives, for whom the issue is public morals and decency, and radical feminists, who see pornography as a support for men's brutalization and oppression of women and who are willing to turn to the states to help enforce its curtailment. Those who oppose any government interference are either radical individualists or libertarians from either the left or the right, and what she calls "uneasy liberals," who fear censorship and believe we must protect the First Amendment. The conservatives may be aligned with the feminists, but for different reasons. The conservatives would like to restore women to men's protection, whereas the radical feminists would like to free women from the control of men. Thus, for one group pornography is a crime against public decency, and for the other it is a crime against women.

　　Fox-Genovese points out the contradiction for feminist theory in arguing for the freedom of abortion on the basis of a right to privacy, and then opposing pornography, which could also be claimed to be a private relationship between an individual and what he or she reads, on which the government should not be free to impose restrictions. But Fox-Genovese correctly points out that there is a difference between the imagination and the commodity it uses or produces. Government could never censor the imagination; that is, fantasy. But it may censor a commodity, pornography.

> But if we agree that it is not the business of the state to reform imaginations, we may nonetheless recognize that the forms in which imaginations are expressed is indeed a matter for public concern. . . . The Supreme Court's decision notwithstanding, neither flag burning nor pornography has anything to do with free speech, at least not with the free speech intended by the Founding Fathers. . . .
>
> In striking some balance between freedom and order, societies have always had to distinguish between liberty and license. By attaching the idea of liberty exclusively to the right of the individual, we have effectively destroyed the possibility for the distinction. . . . Only by grounding the idea of liberty in the collectivity—in the recognition that there has never been and cannot be any individual freedom unrooted in community discipline—can we hope to enact laws that recognize liberties as interdependent and as inseparable from social responsibility. [pp. 110–111]

Fox-Genovese's discussion of the paradox of pornography for feminists lends a valuable perspective to the debate about female masochism among psychotherapists. The role of the state in our personal lives is at times welcomed by feminists, such as in the case of incest or wife beating, and rejected when it comes to abortion and, for some, pornography.

The Bonds of Love—Domination and Submission

Benjamin's major thesis (1988) is a psychological one, that "domination and submission result from a breakdown of the necessary tension between self-assertion and mutual recognition that allows self and other to meet as sovereign equals" (p. 12). Based on her studies of D. W. Winnicott (1956) and Heinz Kohut (1977) pointing to disturbances in the sense of self, the feeling of acute loneliness and emptiness and the self's need to find cohesion and mirroring in the other, plus the new infancy research of Daniel Stern (1985), showing that the infant is never totally undifferentiated from the mother but from the beginning can distinguish him- or herself from others, Benjamin states the shift in the issue as "not only how we separate from oneness, but also how we connect to and recognize others; the issue is not how we become free of the other, but how we

actively engage and make ourselves known in relationship to the other''
(p. 18). She calls this the *intersubjective view*.

> The individual grows in and through the relationship to other subjects.
> Most important, this perspective observes that the other whom the self
> meets is also a self, a subject in his or her own right. It assumes that we
> are able and need to recognize that other subject as different and yet
> alike, as an other who is capable of sharing similar mental experience.
> The idea of intersubjectivity reorients the conception of the psychic
> world from a subject's relation to its object toward a subject meeting
> another subject. (pp. 19–20)

Thus, she distinguishes the intersubjective view, in which the self has
"capacities that emerge in the interaction between self and others" from
the intrapsychic view, in which the self is a "discrete unit with a complex
internal structure. . . . The crucial area we uncover with intrapsychic
theory is the unconscious; the crucial element we explore with intersubjective theory is the representation of self and other as distinct but
interrelated beings" (p. 20).

Benjamin believes that the two views need not be seen in opposition
to each other, but rather as complementary ways of understanding the
psyche. We need not deny the importance of the inner world of fantasy,
wish, anxiety, and defense, where the other is a mental object, not a real
being. Benjamin urges that we grasp both realities, because without the
intrapsychic concept of the unconscious the intersubjective theory becomes one-dimensional. The concept that unifies intersubjective theories
of self-development is the need for recognition. "Recognition is the
essential response, the constant companion of assertion" (p. 21).

This leads to the key role of the mother in Benjamin's theory of
domination. In psychoanalytic theory, there has not been sufficient recognition of the mother as a subject in her own right. The recent feminist
analysis of the mother–child relationship allows us to see that the mother
cannot be simply an extension of the child's needs, a servant to the child's
desire. "The recognition a child seeks is something the mother is able to
give only by virtue of her independent identity" (p. 24). Benjamin rejects
the notion of self psychologists that what the mother does is "mirror" the
child, but rather claims that the mother is an independent other with her
own separate subjectivity.

> Recognition must be mutual and allow for the assertion of each self.
> Thus I stress that mutual recognition, including the child's ability to
> recognize the mother as a person in her own right, is as significant a
> developmental goal as separation. Hence the need for a theory that
> understands how the capacity for mutuality evolves, a theory based on

the premise that from the beginning there are always (at least) two subjects. . . . the reciprocity of self and other, the balance of assertion and recognition. [pp. 24–25]

Benjamin critiques Mahler's theory of differentiation because it is unilinear, going from oneness to separateness, rather than "a continual dynamic, evolving balance of the two" (p. 25). She points out that in erotic union there is mutual recognition without loss of self. Attunement, or pleasure in being with the other, is the essence of erotic bonding. The conflict for the child is between the wish to fulfill his own desire and the wish to please his or her parent's desire. Thus, "the desire to remain attuned can be converted into submission to the other's will" (p. 31).

> The paradox of recognition, the need for acknowledgement that turns us back to dependence on the other, brings about a struggle for control. This struggle can result in the realization that if we fully negate the other, that is, if we assume complete control over him and destroy his identity and will, then we have negated ourselves as well. For then there is no one there to recognize us, no one there for us to desire. [p. 39]

Object relations theory modifies drive theory by defining the other, not as merely the source of satisfaction of a drive, such as hunger or sex, but rather as a significant object for the development of relatedness. However, both view differentiation and merging as opposites, and relaxation of the boundary between self and other as regressive and dangerous. Benjamin stresses that "being with" the other in a state of mutuality and compassion can be a continuum, not a complementarity of active–passive or doer–done-to, which is the basic structure of domination. Domination begins with the attempt to deny dependency.

> True independence means sustaining the essential tension of these contradictory impulses; that is, both asserting the self and recognizing the other. Domination is the consequence of refusing this condition. In mutual recognition the subject accepts the premise that others are separate but nonetheless share like feelings and intentions. The subject is compensated for his loss of sovereignty by the pleasure of sharing, the communion with another subject. . . . The primary consequence of the inability to reconcile dependence with independence, then, is the transformation of need for the other into domination of him. [pp. 53–54]

But what of the submissive member of this duality? Benjamin asks what satisfaction is sought and found in submission and seeks an explanation in Reagé's novel *The Story of O* (1965). There, she sees the desire for submission as representing a "peculiar transposition of the desire for recognition." O's masochism is a "search for recognition through an other who is powerful enough to bestow this recognition. This other has the power for which the self longs and through his recognition she gains it, though vicariously" (p. 56).

Benjamin disagrees with the assertion of Freud that the masochist takes pleasure in pain. She states that "the masochist's pleasure cannot be understood as a direct, unmediated enjoyment of pain" (p. 61). The deepest fears of the submissive person are abandonment and separation. Through submission to an idealized figure, even when this is painful, the masochist is assured of connection, of psychic survival and safety. She actually protects herself from the feared abandonment through maintaining the submissive connection, and only in this sense is there pleasure, as freedom from fear. It is the dominator who receives pleasure from the other's pain. In the child's development, having to internalize aggression and experience pain becomes the desire to hurt and humiliate the other as one has been hurt oneself. "Aggression, internalized as masochism, reappears as sadism" (p. 69).

This brings us to the vital question of how sadism and masochism have come to be associated with masculinity and femininity. Using Robert Stoller's 1975 work on the disruption of gender identity for the male, we see that male identity is a secondary phenomenon, achieved only after overcoming a primary identification with the mother. Through this process of disidentification, the mother is repudiated in order for the son to achieve individuation.

> The tendency of erotic love to become erotic domination can be seen as a casualty of this characteristically male form of establishing separation. . . . the boy is in danger of losing his capacity for mutual recognition altogether. . . . the other, especially the female other, is related to as object. Erotic domination represents an intensification of male anxiety and defense in relation to the mother. [pp. 76–77]

The other side of the coin is the woman's identification with her self-sacrificing mother, who offers recognition but *does not expect recognition in return*. The ideal of motherhood is the denial of the self. Borrowing from Chodorow, Benjamin asserts that the fact of women's mothering not only explains masculine sadism, but in the case of female development leads to masochism. "The girl's sense of self is shaped by the realization that her mother's source of power resides in her self-sacrifice" (p. 79). Yet Western culture contains another model of supreme self-sacrifice by a man, Jesus, who sacrificed himself to save us from our sins. The key to understanding this apparent contradiction may lie in the story of Abraham, who was prepared to sacrifice his son Isaac. The sacrifice is demanded by God and Abraham submits to the "Almighty." In the story of Jesus we also learn that "God gave his only Son," so it is not in fact that the male figure voluntarily sacrifices himself, but rather that he submits to the demand of an all powerful male God in a continuation of the dominant–submissive polarity, man over man over woman over child. The little child is sometimes idealized as the holder of truth in Christianity and in folklore, as in the tale of the Emperor who had no clothes, thus completing the circle of power.

Independence for the girl is experienced as dangerous. Her mother is her source of love and identity, and her fear that her independence will destroy her mother forces her to protect the mother by being compliant, at the price of suppressing the pleasures of autonomy. When the girl's compliance is transposed into erotic submission to a male authority, she vicariously enjoys his assertion of subjectivity and difference "like a breath of the inaccessible outdoors."

> The vicarious quality of her enjoyment recapitulates the vicarious pleasure of the self-sacrificing mother with whom she identifies. Thus submission for women allows a reenactment of their early identificatory relationship to the mother; it is a replication of the maternal attitude itself. [p. 79]

The all-powerful mother may also be the all-submissive mother and the dependent, depressed mother—a contradiction that goes to the heart of the dilemma for us all. This fact points to the importance to the male and female child alike of having a mother who can hold her own, who has a sense of self that enables her to be nurturing and caring, but not at the price of denial of her separate selfhood. Can a modern mother attain this delicate balance? Only if she does not fear her destructive power and attempt to mask it with weakness. Masochism need not be inevitable in female sexuality and motherhood as long as the woman values herself and expects recognition for her value, not just as a servant to others, but in her own right, for whatever her separate needs and desires may be. Just as this is a tough balancing act for a mother, it is hard for a child to accept that his or her mother has independent interests. But we can see that this is a necessary loss for the child, a narcissistic injury that must be sustained in order for sons to grow into husbands who respect their wives' own desires, and for daughters to identify with a mother who is a whole person in her own right. Ultimately, all benefit. The mother no longer needs to fulfill her desires vicariously through her husband and children's success, while at the same time resenting them for it and attempting to control their independence. She can rather allow them the freedom to find their own way, while she finds hers. It is no wonder that envy appears frequently in women—not envy for the penis itself, but for the penis as a symbol of that freedom to pursue one's desires, to assert one's wishes and needs, to fulfill one's potential, that being male represents.

Benjamin then looks at the girl's relationship with her father in terms of the idealization of male power and autonomous individuality. If the father allows the girl to identify with some of his desirable qualities, she can avoid envy. If not, the "missing father," that is, the father who fails to nurture his daughter and encourage her desire, will return in the form of her masochistic submission to a powerful male and her vicarious pleasure through connection to him. This is the "lack" that women feel, the lack of the strength and power that come from autonomy. The father who fails to respond to his daughter's need for recognition of her independent desires—in the absence of positive identification with and permission to separate from the mother—prevents her self-realization. Idealization of the father leads to displacement of the fear of the father's power onto the mother, so that she bears the burden of badness for both.

Benjamin is critical of oedipal theory because the notions that, first, the mother's love is regressive, and second, the father is needed to intervene and free the child, create the "paradox that the only liberation is paternal domination. Oedipal theory thus denies the necessity of mutual recognition between man and woman" and focuses on father–son rivalry (p. 181).

> The psychic repudiation of femininity, which includes the negation of dependency and mutual recognition, is homologous with the social banishment of nurturance and intersubjective relatedness to the private domestic world of women and children. The social separation of private and public spheres—long noted by feminists as the crucial form of the sexual division of labor and thus the social vehicle of gender domination—is patently linked to the split between the father of autonomy and the mother of dependency. . . . The destruction of maternal values is not the result of women's liberation; it is the consequence of the ascendance of male rationality. [p. 185] The psychosocial core of this unfettered individuality is the subjugation of woman by man. [p. 188]

Here we see the ideas of Keller, Chodorow, and Gilligan as they have been integrated into Benjamin's feminist-psychoanalytic approach to the problem of domination. Benjamin agrees that the idealization of motherhood stems from a belief in maternal omnipotence, and points out that this polarity reinforces the split between the nurturant female and the rational male. "On the social level, male rationality sabotages maternal recognition, while on the psychic level, the oedipal repudiation of the mother splits her into the debased and the idealized objects. The reparation for debasing her takes the form of sentimentalizing and idealizing the mother" (pp. 214–215). Benjamin is doubtful of Chodorow's and Dinnerstein's solution to this dilemma, that of shared parenting, because she does not believe this personal solution will change the core gender system that splits gender into polar opposites common in both the psyche and in cultural representations.

Table 4–2 shows aspects of male–female splitting based on Benjamin's work. By contrast, the intersubjective approach would contain these opposites in a dialectical tension resulting in mutual recognition. Feminist theory questions the logic or necessity of such splitting, and—when it can avoid role reversal, which reinforces splitting—can, according to Benjamin, lead to personal and social change. The political/philosophical/psychological problem with the different-not-deficient position, and with the idealizing aspects of the focus on early mother–child interaction, is that it can reinforce stereotyping and polarity, keeping men and women in their separate-but-equal worlds, though these are an improvement over separate and unequal. The same issue was raised as in race relations, where separate-but-equal was found to be unconstitutional in the 1954 case of Brown versus the Board of Education—because separate, when one group is dominant and in all positions of power, can never be equal.

Benjamin describes her conclusion as both "modest and utopian" (p. 223) in her call for a renewal of mutual recognition between men and women. I agree with her belief that feminism has created an opportunity for this new form of male–female relationship, but I find that there is a tendency for the feminist writers I have been reviewing to seek a happy ending: a peaceful world, equality, freer children, marriages of mutual recognition. I fear that our old fairy-tale mentality continues to creep in,

TABLE 4–2

Male		Female
the subject		the object
idealization		repudiation
public world		private world
objective		subjective
rationality		emotionality
neutrality		empathy
domination	SPLITTING	submission
assertion		recognition
autonomy		dependency
impersonal		personal

and that they, as well as I, feel the urge to end a book with "and they lived happily ever after." This is a myth, a very appealing myth, for which there is no substantial evidence. Yes, there are isolated examples of couples who share childcare and whose partners work in positions of equal status and respect. But some couples also lived in loving respect prior to the women's movement. Reality keeps showing us that, for the majority of women, there is no equality and no happy ending. Divorce is epidemic, children are emotionally abandoned, and wonderful women are living alone and growing old alone as men still select younger women who are easier to feel superior to. I cannot really see what feminism can offer men that will make up for the loss of the position of power, control, and superiority that they have held. True mutual recognition in a love relationship involves much struggle, and some form of recognition can be found in business and professional life or athletics without the struggle and without giving up anything. I know this sounds cynical, but I wish to be realistic. A woman who has much to offer in terms of professional or academic success can also offer a man the reward of the stimulation and recognition he can receive through her. But the vast majority of women cannot offer these compensations for the loss of power that the man must experience in a relationship of equals. In the business and political worlds, domination and submission continue to be the order of the day, as the weak are gobbled up by the powerful. Nevertheless, progress is worth working for, even if the victories are small.

FAMILY SYSTEMS—HARRIET GOLDHOR LERNER

Harriet Lerner, a psychologist on the staff of the Menninger Foundation, has been publishing papers on the psychology of women from a clinical perspective since 1974. Her *Women in Therapy* (1988) is a collection of her previous publications, with the addition of a chapter that reviews and critiques other contributions to feminist-psychoanalytic theory. Lerner has both contributed to theory and presented clinical examples from her practice as a psychotherapist. In the forward to the book, she defines her goal as to "revise psychoanalytic assumptions about femininity and to reformulate phallocentric views of women which pathologize female functioning and perpetuate a narrow intrapsychic focus that obscures the larger context" (p. xix). Lerner criticizes what she considers the narrow feminist focus on the mother–child relationship, and proposes a family-systems perspective to include the father–daughter dyad, the marital relationship, and other family relationships, including siblings, grandparents, and earlier generations. Her approach is to study the "complex, circular interconnectedness between the individual, family and culture"

(p. xx). She views women in Miller's terms, as a subordinate group in a patriarchal society, and she believes the impact of patriarchal bias is profound and pervasive. Using a family-systems approach allows her to see the symptoms and behavior of a woman patient in the context of the role she plays in her family. This is a valuable addition to a feminist psychoanalytic analysis. I too have wondered where the siblings, grandparents, and other family members are in the writings of many feminists as well as psychoanalysts. I believe the extended family has been missing in feminist theory because it has been missing in psychoanalytic theory, and so much feminist-psychological writing is based on a reworking of that theory. Lerner brings back the family, though she too does not give to siblings the significance I am convinced they deserve. I believe that in some cases, an older sibling can actually be as important as a parent in the development of a younger sibling.

Lerner does value autonomy and differentiation for women, and many of her case examples are illustrations of work that leads to greater separation from family as a condition for progress. She differs from the Stone Center writers in this regard. She is also critical of them for their focus on the mother–daughter dyad. The papers in Lerner's book concern such issues as anger, sex-role stereotypes, the hysterical personality, dependency, work inhibitions, and depression. Lerner's work draws heavily on the writing of Murray Bowen and Teresa Bernardez-Bonesatti, and she has been influenced by the work of Dinnerstein and Miller, but she minimizes Chodorow's contributions because of the lack in her work of family-systems theory. This is true; but I believe Lerner comes close to dismissing the valuable revisions made by Chodorow and Gilligan because of what they *didn't* write about. Chodorow talks about much more than motherhood, and Gilligan can be credited with finally ridding us of the tremendous scourge of the "inferior superego" insult.

In her essay "The Hysterical Personality," Lerner offers the beginning of a reevaluation of the hysterical component in the functioning of some women—which has been used in a decidedly insulting fashion against women—as she develops her ideas on the importance of social and cultural factors influencing female development, the learned behavior approach. She states that "many of the diagnostic indicators of hysteria are related to essential aspects of femininity and female attractiveness" (p. 109). Lerner challenges the explanation for hysteria offered by psychoanalytic theory— that repression against the awareness or expression of instinctual impulses and their derivatives accounts for a nonintellectual, highly emotional style that is shallow and naively romantic. She contends that women suppress, rather than repress, intellectual skills in order to achieve social success. I agree. I have observed women who could be characterized as having a hysterical style in relating to men, but who are hard and competent workers in their chosen fields and who have achieved academic, business, and professional success. The most significant omission in this paper is the connection between so-called hysterical symptoms and a history of actual sexual molestation in childhood. This omission may be due to the fact that this and other essays in the book were written ten or fifteen years before its publication. (Lerner does attach a note to this essay in which she borrows from Marcie Kaplan's article "A Woman's View of DSM-III" (1983) to question her own "devaluing of traditional feminine traits" at the time she wrote this paper [p. 117].)

Kaplan's paper is a must-read for an infusion of humor into this serious subject. She critiques the *DSM-III* diagnosis of "Histrionic Personality Disorder" and "Dependent Personality Disorder," and proposes two fictitious diagnostic categories to illustrate her point of the sexist bias in these diagnoses: Independent Personality Disorder and Restricted Personality Disorder. As a sample, here are the three characteristics of Independent Personality Disorder:

A. Puts work (career) above relationships with loved ones (e.g., travels a lot on business, works late at night and on weekends).

B. Is reluctant to take into account the others' needs when making decisions, especially concerning the individual's career or use of leisure time (e.g., expects spouse and children to relocate to another city because of individual's career plans).

C. Passively allows others to assume responsibility for major areas of social life because of inability to express necessary emotion (e.g., lets spouse assume most child-care responsibilities). [p. 790]

In a later essay on depression in women originally published in 1987, Lerner gives us a good example of her work on family of origin as she incorporates this approach into her work on internal dynamics. She uses Murray Bowen's concepts of differentiation of self, identifying in her patient the problem of the negotiable self, or "pseudo self." Lerner analyzes Ms. R.'s depression as the result of a sacrifice of self, related to a fear of object loss. She challenges the traditional view, which would see Ms. R as masochistic, and views her resistance to change as due instead to her conviction that she had to choose between "having a marriage and having a self" (p. 230). Lerner's questioning led to her conclusion that her patient remained depressed, dependent, and resistant to change because her depression served the systems-maintaining function of preserving the marriage. Her anxiety about challenging the status quo in her marriage was related to her problems achieving separation and autonomy from her family of origin, which stemmed from her conviction that she must maintain a special bond with her mother, who could not tolerate separation. A fear of guilt and disloyalty to her mother had prevented her from becoming close to her father, and later to her husband. It is interesting to note that Ms. R has selected a "feminist" therapist because she has the idea that she can form a bond with the therapist against her husband just as her mother had formed a bond with her against her father. It is important to explore the projections of each patient as to what a "feminist therapist" means to her as this can produce valuable material. Clearly, to Ms. R., a "feminist therapist"—like her mother—could be close to women but resented men and blamed them for women's problems.

However, Lerner does not present in this book any critical evaluation of the family therapy or systems approach to psychotherapy as it has affected women. In fact, much criticism was heard in the mid-1980s, from women within the family therapy movement itself, of the failure of family therapists to consider the family within the context of a patriarchal society, and the ensuing neglect of issues of power in the marriage, including the power of money when the husband is the sole provider. The November/ December 1985 issue of *The Family Therapy Networker,* subtitled "Feminism: Shedding New Light on the Family," contains many excellent articles on this issue, including one by Lerner. An early critic on this topic was Michele Bograd (1986). In September 1984, almost fifty women family therapy clinicians met at a colloquium to address the role of women in families and in family therapy, in order to focus attention on an examination of gender issues in theory, practice, and research. Their statement, published in *Networker,* concludes:

> We are resolved to challenge sexist theory and practice within family therapy in our work settings, workshops, and conferences—wherever it appears. We are committed to supporting women's professional development in our field. We offer the suggestion that colleagues form study groups to develop non-sexist theory and clinical interventions, and then share this work in public forums in our field. [p. 17]

The fact that this assemblage was necessary as late as 1984 is quite amazing considering that family therapy is a relatively young field. Compare this case to that of psychoanalysis, the usual target for complaints of sexism. The Blum volume *Female Psychology* appeared in 1977, and most of the chapters in it were originally published in a special edition of the *Journal of the American Psychoanalytic Association* in 1976, a full eight years before the *Networker* issue on feminism. I believe this tells us that the problems of sexism in the mental health profession are not limited to psychoanalysis, but are endemic among all the various groups of practitioners in our field, because sexism is such a deeply ingrained part of all of our psyches, stemming from our families and the larger society.

The importance of women's economic dependence is given considerable attention by these family therapists. Lerner (1988), too, tells us of her conviction that women need a life plan that is independent of marriage, but that may include marriage. I heartily agree, and made this point (Krause 1971) in regard to a 25-year-old patient who suffered a depression after a divorce, in spite of the fact that she had a successful career. However, the career was not sufficient to protect my patient from depression, because she had seen her career as temporary, to last until she had children (as did most women before the 1970s). Her life plan still involved marriage and motherhood until therapy helped her to see alternatives.

The case of Ms. R. fits my picture of the circular nature of women's symptoms, cited earlier in this chapter: femininity = self-sacrifice = low self-esteem = vulnerability = dependency = suppression of anger = depression = masochism = self-sacrifice.

The case is described in much interesting detail, especially the inclusion of historical family material that lends a depth and richness to our appreciation of the patient's background. But there is something missing— something I find missing in most cases written up in the feminist psycho-analytic literature, including the Stone Center work: that is, a text of what the therapist and the patient actually said, so that we can see the work of the therapist and its effect on the patient's state of mind and emotional development in the course of the treatment. A recent example of this flaw is found in a new book by Joan Robbins, *Knowing Herself* (1990), which presents narrative descriptions of cases of women in treatment with Robbins, with frequent quotations of what the patient says but hardly a word about what the therapist has said. Could it be that many therapists are unwilling to expose their own work in this revealing manner? Their silence keeps the therapy process a mystery and the therapist mythical. An example that does reveal the therapist's work is the newly revised (1990) book of Steven T. Levy, *Principles of Interpretation* (first published 1984), in which actual samples of therapist–patient interaction are included. In training, this is called process recording, and it is the best way to learn how a student is actually doing in her or his work. I think it is the best way for a skilled therapist to convey to the reader what she or he actually *says* that makes the exchange therapeutic. Lerner's "Special Issues for Women in Psychotherapy" (in 1988, first published in 1982), is especially interesting, because it deals with the issue of the psychotherapist's attitude toward women and its effect on therapeutic work with a woman patient. This raises the issues of values affecting therapeutic practice, with its attendant danger that what has traditionally been seen as normal for women will not be questioned by a therapist who has not himself or herself questioned patriarchal values in regard to female roles and feminine qualities. Lerner divides therapists into two categories, "traditional" and "feminist." This is not an adequate differentiation in my experience. I wonder if, practicing in Topeka, Kansas, she may see fewer kinds of feminist practice of psychotherapy than I do in the San Francisco Bay area. It has become clear to me that there are feminist-oriented psychoanalytic psychotherapists, in which category I place myself and many of the women whose work I know well; and then there are feminist therapists, who are decidedly antipsychoanalytic in their practice, and who fail to conform to the basic principles of traditional practice around issues such as neutrality, fees, the fifty-minute hour, and so on, due to their belief that these principles are patriarchal and set therapist and patient in a superior–inferior position. Some of these therapists may even consider my group of practitioners traitors and part of the enemy. Other therapists are feminists and adhere to Jungian, self psychology, and other nontraditional positions.

Using Lerner's illustration of how Therapist A., a traditional therapist, approaches a woman patient's symptoms, contrasted with how Therapist B., a feminist therapist, would understand the same patient, presents an interesting clash of beliefs and values. The case is hypothetical, but it is not so different from that of Ms. R. described previously. "Janet" is a 34-year-old homemaker with two children who has become depressed and angry. She seeks help in being a better wife and mother and wants to be more satisfied with her life. Ms. R. is a 35-year-old homemaker with three children, also complaining of depression and blaming her husband for it. This kind of woman patient is much less common now than in the 1970s, and the kinds of problems presented by today's 34-year-old in an urban center are unlikely to have to do with satisfaction at being a wife and mother. The problems of women patients today are an indication of the tremendous changes brought about by the women's movement and the difficulty of living on one income, but they certainly do not herald an end to women's depression. In Lerner's example, Therapist A. would see "Janet" as having unconscious conflicts, making her role of wife and mother difficult, and might advise her to take up a hobby. Therapist B. would see Janet's problem as trying to suppress her hopes and aspirations and live vicariously through her husband and children. Therapist B. would analyze her unconscious anxiety and guilt about autonomous functioning, mastery, and success, while viewing her difficulties as a result of the patriarchal institutions of marriage and the family. Therapist B. sounds very much like Therapist Lerner in the Ms. R. case.

A further example, which illustrates a Therapist A.-type problem, is of Dr. B., a male therapist who fails to question any of the traditional assumptions about woman's place, and who believes that if he did raise questions in his work with a married couple about the wife's financial dependency, he would be "imposing values" on his clients. He believes that accepting the traditional role of the woman in marriage is being "neutral" and "objective." Lerner correctly points out that these errors of omission, by not raising such questions, do a disservice to the female patient. She gets no help from the therapist in clarifying the legitimate basis of her anger, which is expressed in the form of an "unconscious wildcat strike"—that is, depression and useless complaining.

The woman patient in this third case example is similar to the first two, a dissatisfied housewife with three children who is suffering from depression and dependency. Actually, all three of these women are good examples of the women of the 1950s and 1960s that Betty Friedan wrote about as suffering from the "problem that has no name." By now, I believe, we have a new generation of male therapists, whose wives most likely have independent careers and who are more conscious of these issues of autonomy and dependency in women. It may be harder for some of the older male analysts and therapists to incorporate this modern reality into their values, but even they now have daughters who are psychiatrists and other professionals. In an area like San Francisco, the housewife syndrome belongs in the history books. I have seen women in their forties in the last ten years who were still struggling with the issue of family versus career, but I doubt that there are many married women in their thirties today who are housewives and who struggle with the kinds of profound identity issues we saw in women in years past. The younger women have different problems. They already have careers, they may be divorced, and they may wonder if they can add children to their lives without damaging their careers or themselves. Young women may choose to take time out for child rearing when their children are young, but very few could even afford not to work throughout their adulthood even if they might wish not to.

Summary

Lerner's essays, spanning the years from 1974 to 1988, are, in my view, a part of the feminist psychoanalytic literature. Yet in her final chapter, "A Critique of the Feminist Psychoanalytic Contribution," she appears to distance herself from this group of writers. Her point, that much of feminist psychoanalytic theory is too narrowly mother-focused at the expense of recognizing family processes, is well taken. But she fails to credit the outstanding contributions of writers such as Chodorow, Gilligan, Benjamin, and scores of others to a revision of psychoanalytic theory that frees us from the erroneous view of women as suffering from penis envy, inferior superegos, and a general mental and emotional deprivation. Lerner also never mentions numerous original contributions on a variety of issues affecting women's lives and women in therapy, such as special features of the transference and countertransference when women work with women. The problem is she never defines her territory. Who is she calling a psychoanalytic feminist writer, and by what criteria does she include the few she critiques and omit so many others? Her critique of Kim Chernin (1986) and Jordan and Surrey (1986) of the Stone Center repeats her point of the absence of fathers and siblings, a point well taken but not adequate to dismiss the valuable contributions of these writers and many others. Lerner claims that feminist writers polarize views of masculine and feminine development. She reinforces a distorted misinterpretation of Gilligan's thesis, and contributes to the outcry that by recognizing and describing gender differences we do women a disservice in the job market. If Gilligan's work has been misinterpreted, it seems to me that there is a need in society to misinterpret it, that the misinterpretation itself should be analyzed as resistence to the expanding roles of women. Lerner, unfortunately, blames the author for the fact that her work is misinterpreted.

Lerner's review of only a handful of feminist psychoanalytic writers is inadequate and not inclusive of the valuable contributions of dozens of women who have published papers on this subject: psychoanalysts, psychologists, and social workers. Many of these writers are reviewed in this chapter. In addition, a thorough analysis of this subject can be found in Nancy Chodorow (1989), in a chapter titled "Psychoanalytic Feminism and the Psychoanalytic Psychology of Women."

FEMINIST PSYCHOTHERAPY

The writers I have reviewed thus far have been primarily women academics. Although some are also clinicians, their writing is definitely focused on theory and not on practice. The practice of psychotherapy by feminists is complicated by the variety of approaches among the women who call themselves *therapists* and *feminists*. Some are not professionally trained at all, and consider themselves therapists based on their work with women in such women's agencies as battered women's shelters, rape crisis centers, or health centers. Others may be behaviorists, gestalt therapists, or radical therapists, or belong to one of the variety of psychoanalytic schools, such as those of Jung, Horney, Sullivan, Lacan, Freud, or object relations. Some are psychiatrists, psychologists, social workers, or, more recently, marriage and family counselors. Putting the issue in its historical perspective is a good way to understand this field.

As I stated earlier, the woman's movement grew out of the radical student movement of the 1960s, when women began to realize that they were an oppressed group and were being oppressed by the men in the "movement." This led in two separate but related directions: to social action on the one hand, and consciousness-raising groups on the other.

Feminist therapy began as an outgrowth of the theory and philosophy behind the CR groups, which was designed to help women stop blaming themselves, stop feeling isolated, and see what in the external world is responsible for their unhappiness as women.

Hannah Lerman

Lerman, in her article "What Happens in Feminist Therapy" (1976), sees feminist therapy as an outgrowth of humanistic thought as well as of the 1960s student movement. All feminist therapists have in common a recognition of the effects of the patriarchal system on female development and female lack of self-esteem, and of the importance for individual women to be able to break out of constricted roles, to allow themselves autonomy and personal development, and to stop believing that their only role is to serve men and children. The differences among feminist therapists have to do with major disagreements about the technique of psychotherapy. As I stated in the Introduction, I do not call myself a feminist therapist, because that can imply a rejection of basic principles of practice that I believe are essential to my professional ethics.

According to Lerman's description, the feminist therapist does not take the position of expert about her client, does not presume to tell the client about herself, and does not diagnose the client, prescribe treatment, or assume that her opinions have any greater weight than those of the client. Lerman calls this stance nonauthoritarian. She believes that in this way, the woman patient will develop a sense of her own competence and of power rather than self-doubt.

Lerman's second position is that the usual therapeutic goal of introspection is not good for women. Women, she says, need to look outward as well as inward, in order to differentiate what belongs to the society and is being imposed from what is internal. Most women believe, deep down, that they are crazy, and so it is important for the therapist to validate her client's feelings, especially her feelings of anger. "Owning one's own anger is, I think, for women, an important, perhaps even an essential, step toward personal power" (p. 381).

A third aspect of feminist therapy for Lerman is encouraging self-nurturance. Since women have been trained to nurture others, they have nurtured everybody but themselves. "We encourage them to turn this nurturance around and give some of it to themselves: Be selfish. Be self loving. Choose themselves over others. Allow themselves to do things that make them feel good" (p. 382). This will enhance their sense of self-esteem and worth. In my CR group, women often brought sewing or knitting to the meetings. We became aware that we were always knitting or sewing for someone else and began to make things for ourselves.

However, Lerman states that it is not her goal to change her women patients by making them feminists. "The goal is to help them become the best person they can be, within the limits of their personal circumstances and the patterns of society in general" (p. 383).

Ellyn Kaschak

Kaschak (1981) writes that feminist therapy has been identified with one specific technique, the feminist analysis of the societal forms of oppression that affect all women.

> This analysis allows the individual woman client to understand the ways in which her problems are the problems of all women and to become aware of forces of which she was previously unaware. . . . this author considers the feminist analysis of women's status in society and its concomitant intrapsychic and interpersonal effects to be the hallmark technique of feminist therapy, much as the analysis of the unconscious is associated with psychoanalysis. [p. 391]

Just as a personal analysis is considered essential for a psychoanalytically-oriented therapist, so is a feminist analysis of her own life, such as that available through a CR group, essential for a feminist therapist. Also, a feminist therapist "strives to live in a manner congruent with feminist principles, and is familiar with current psychology of women and feminist therapy literature" (p. 391). Feminist therapy believes that a woman should be free to transcend traditional sex roles, and that the power between therapist and client should either be equal or continually approach equality. There is a serious concern that the relationship between therapist and patient not reinforce the woman's feeling of inferiority or incompetence and her self-demeaning attitudes, so the issue of expertise in the therapist is connected with the issue of power. The feminist therapist tries to eliminate exploitive power differentials in the relationship. The fee is negotiable and flexible, depending on the ability to pay. Kaschak identifies five stages in feminist therapy, individual or group:

1. The woman believes there is something wrong with her, that her unhappiness represents a personal failure.

2. She becomes aware that her problems are both individual and social in nature.

3. A tremendous amount of anger emerges at others, at society, and at herself for having "been blind" for so long.

4. Her anger is channeled constructively into action and change.

5. She gives up "self-deprecatory and helpless behavior in favor of personal power and self-esteem" (p. 397), and learns to nurture herself and other women and to value herself and other women. She reclaims and reintegrates lost parts of herself as a woman.

Kaschak places feminist therapists in three categories 1) Those who are politically radical and have not been professionally trained and who practice in collectives within the alternative culture. 2) Those who are politically radical but who do have academic degrees and professional training (some began as grass roots feminist therapists and returned to school in the 1970s for formal training). 3) A group she calls "liberal professional feminist therapists" (p. 400), who believe in a liberal reform approach to the problems of sexism rather than the complete reorganization of our social structure.

Much good work has been done by all three of these groups of therapists, but there are certain flaws in the approach of feminist therapists that I want to describe. I believe that many of these women have a problem with power and authority, and confuse authority—that is, knowledge—with being authoritarian—a manner of relating in which the dominant person, usually male, suppresses the weak, usually female or working class. Claude Steiner (1971) of the Radical Therapy Collective in Berkeley made this distinction when he described hierarchies that are voluntary, self-dissolving, and based on differences of skill, in which one person who wishes to learn a craft seeks out another who can teach it.

Women's problems with differentiation and separation have led to their attempt to deny that there is a difference between the therapist and the patient. This in my mind is an error. How can you charge money for your time if you are not a specialist? They have failed to differentiate between friendship and the patient–therapist relationship. Psychotherapists are not paid for love and friendship, but for their expertise. I used to explain to my new patients, if they brought up this issue, that I was an expert in mental health just as they were experts in their fields—teaching, music, law—and that they were consulting me just as I might consult an architect if I wanted to build a house. It didn't mean that the architect was superior and I was inferior, but only that he or she had a special skill that I needed to help me build my house.

The so-called "medical model" came under much attack in the 1970s, as the distrust feminists felt for male physicians and psychoanalysts spread to any woman who practiced psychotherapy. Women were hostile about the power differential in the therapist–patient relationship and did not want to be "one-down." Unfortunately, some therapists capitulated to the pressures and abandoned the neutral stance, thereby failing to analyze the dependency conflicts or the patient's projections of irrational authority, as well as adding to her problems of boundary differentiation. Observing the boundary in the therapeutic relationship provides an excellent opportunity to analyze and work through earlier boundary diffusion problems from the maternal relationship, and to clarify issues of exploitation in male–female relationships.

This reaction was a classic case of throwing out the baby with the bath water. I knew of cases in which therapists left on vacation without leaving anyone to cover for them, a basic tenet of the medical model. Some therapists socialized with their patients, and some fell in love with their patients and proposed sexual relationships to them. I saw some of the casualties. (Of course, I have seen casualties in traditional psychotherapy as well, where a male therapist's countertransference produced errors in treatment and resulted in the woman failing to receive the help she deserved.) In addition, there was no well-grounded understanding of the importance of boundaries in the setting and collecting of fees, contact outside the hour, the setting of time limits, and such conduct as not revealing personal data and personal opinions. The merging that resulted at times resulted in further damage to the patient, as the therapist tried to meet her own needs and rationalized her actions as eliminating the power factor.

I believe that women in the 1970s had a hard time respecting other women. This was expressed in the demeaning of the woman therapist and the cooperation with this belittlement by some women therapists. How could a woman be an expert? By demeaning yourself as a woman therapist, you don't allow your patient to identify with your pride and competence in your work and with your sense of yourself as a complete person who has something of value to offer. Your fee is the way you communicate your value, and this sense of value can be internalized by a woman patient. The fee is also often an arena in which the patient's envy is expressed and can be analyzed. During the 1970s, feelings of envy and competition between women were minimized by feminist therapists, who feared the anger of the patient just as they feared their own and other people's anger. Women patients were inadvertently denied the opportunity for positive identification with a woman working independently who values herself and her work.

In *Knowing Herself* (1990), Joan Robbins candidly acknowledges her mistakes:

> After many years I have come to value something I did not originally subscribe to, the importance of the therapist's neutrality. In the sisterhood of the 1970's I participated in the sharing that sometimes went on

between some feminist therapists and their clients. Then, I believed that discussing my own experience communicated the range and diversity of options available to women and also demystified the therapist and the therapy process. We were two women working together, one of whom was in need of the services and skills the other had to offer. However, over the years I have come to appreciate other, more complex reasons for generally not stating my experience or opinion. . . . By my not interjecting my experience, the focus remains with the clients. [p. 22]

Luise Eichenbaum and Susie Orbach

One of the best clinical books written on psychotherapy from a feminist perspective is *Understanding Women: A Feminist Psychoanalytic Approach* (1983), by Luise Eichenbaum and Susie Orbach, who practiced in London, England. They identify themselves as object relations psychoanalytically oriented therapists, relying on the work of Fairbairn, Winnicott, and especially Harry Guntrip, who emphasized the importance of nurturance within the therapy relationship. Eichenbaum and Orbach call this idea the cornerstone of their feminist psychotherapy. They differ from these theorists in their belief that the mother is not an object, but is a person, a social and psychological being. Thus, what becomes internalized is not the object, but the different aspects of mother. "What the object relations theorists have failed to take into account is the psychology of the mother and the effect of the social position of women on the mother's psychology" (p. 34).

Eichenbaum's and Orbach's therapy involves attention to both the internal and the external world of the woman. Their thesis involves the concept of a neglected "little girl" within each woman who can emerge in the therapy relationship.

A daughter hides the little-girl part of herself because she has picked up a painful and powerful message from mother that tells her she should not have expectations of being looked after emotionally, or of having her desires met, either by mother or by anyone else. Mother encourages her daughter to look to a man to be emotionally involved with; she teaches her daughter to direct her energies toward men and to someday depend on a man. . . . Mother simultaneously transmits a message that men are disappointments. They may convey disdain and contempt for them. Mother's messages about men are then more than a little ambivalent. [p. 51]

The girl is left with feelings of deprivation, unworthiness, and rejection from her mother, whose maternal nurturance is denied her, as the mother herself feels bereft and is unable to nourish her daughter emotionally. Women then look to men for mothering and are disappointed. Also, since the mother never felt nurtured herself, she may have trouble letting go of her daughter, in hopes of getting some of that longed-for nurturance from her, for her own hungry "little girl."

Eichenbaum and Orbach see both men and women as afraid of women's dependency needs. This is quite a different approach than that viewing both men and women as fearful of the mother's power. "Women carry with them the feeling that their needs are overwhelming, unending, insatiable, bad, shameful. They feel their needs will drive other people away" (p. 88). They believe that when women enter therapy, they are hoping to find nurturance, yet they expect to be disappointed. They are entrapped by yearnings for nurturance, acceptance, love, and autonomy against which they have erected defenses. Depression and phobic symptoms are seen as the result of these unmet needs and the anger generated by them.

Eichenbaum's and Orbach's book gives a very perceptive view of the emotional problems that women present in therapy. Unfortunately, like other clinical writers, they offer ample clinical material to illustrate their thesis, but fail to tell us what they say to the patient, so the process of healing and change remains a mystery. We can assume that their understanding of women gets translated into helpful interpretations, but we don't really know what these are. The view of mothers as dependent, and the fear of women's dependence, in many ways seems more sensible than the view of women as powerful. Yet both are true and can be integrated as follows.

The early mother of infancy and childhood is experienced as all-powerful by both boys and girls. As the child grows and its world expands to include fathers, siblings, grandparents, neighbors, teachers, and friends, the realization of the mother's diminished status becomes apparent to the child, who starts to incorporate the realities of the patriarchal culture. The child experiences guilt at adapting to the culture's depreciation of the mother, and a gradual recognition of the mother's powerlessness outside the confines of the kitchen, and perhaps the bedroom, if the mother is a sexual person. As the child becomes independent and moves away from mother, he or she experiences the mother's sadness and longing and realizes that the mother is alone, unless the mother is active and accomplished. The child senses that he or she is betraying the mother by his or her autonomy, and is caught in a conflict of guilt over leaving the mother lonely, or of self-denial if the child stays to take care of the mother. Various compromises are tried. Often a son is better able to work out a compromise, developing an independent life and still being caring of the mother, because so much less is expected of him. If the father is competent and caring, the child feels confident that the mother is being left in good hands. If the mother does not love or respect the father, or is divorced or widowed, the burden on the child is greater. Daughters often take more of the burden of meeting the mother's needs, thereby denying and depleting themselves, leaving themselves needy. As the unconscious still retains the mother as all-powerful, any neglect of the mother can fill the child with fear of retaliation. The original potent mother can, in fantasy, become angry and punish the child (now adult). Thus, the relationship with the mother, filled with unconscious dependency and fear and conscious guilt and shame at abandonment and betrayal, is always a powerful force. The mother-in-law stereotype conveys this image of the powerful yet demeaned woman who has no life of her own and who therefore intrudes on the life of her married children, but who cannot be ignored.

Psychoanalytic feminism covers a wide span of writers, including both academicians and clinicians. Eichenbaum and Orbach make an important contribution in their theories on the needs of women who come to therapy, how these needs relate to weaknesses in the mother–daughter relationship, and how a feminist-informed psychotherapist—through her awareness of the way society's demeaning of women affects the mother-daughter relationship, depriving both of adequate recognition—can address the issue of the "little girl" within, hungry for love, care, and attention. Their clinical examples are good illustrations of their developmental theory, failing only by not providing us with actual comments and interpretations from the therapists.

5

PSYCHOANALYSIS UNDER THE INFLUENCE OF THE FREUDIAN VIEW OF WOMEN

Many women tell horror stories of psychoanalytic treatment that occurred before the advent of feminist influence. Some of these stories involve a male analyst protecting a male who had mistreated the woman patient. One friend, a psychotherapist, tells of the time she told her analyst of having been raped by her brother when she was 9. The analyst responded, "You can imagine how hard that was on your brother." Another friend, also a psychotherapist, tells of her several years in therapy working on her incestuous relationship with her father, which had lasted from her ninth to her fourteenth year. When she became strong enough to confront her parents with the facts, she decided she would also visit her father's psychoanalyst, who had treated her father for twenty years. She confronted the analyst and asked if he had known that her father was having intercourse with her for so many years. The analyst replied that he had suspected it, but was waiting for her father to bring it up.

Probably the most frequent complaints come from women who claim that they were urged to stay home and adjust to being housewives and mothers rather than to seek independent satisfactions. Some of them may well have entered analysis with the goal of becoming content to remain at home. They complained of depression and frustration, but their symptoms were considered representative of a masculinity complex or penis envy rather than of legitimate needs for intellectual stimulation and an autonomous existence.

"MARRIAGE TOO ABHORS A POWER VACUUM"—
HENRY V. DICKS

The following quotation appears in a book assigned to members of an extension division seminar on the treatment of marital couples at the Psychoanalytic Institute in San Francisco in the late 1960s. The author, Henry V. Dicks, a psychiatrist at the Tavistock Clinic in London, writes (1967) that things have not changed much since the Bible: "It is in the nature of the world that females shall bear and cherish offspring as their primary task, while males having been impelled by that nature to fertilize them, will feel the urge to be protective to the nest and feeding ground, and hunt for the sustenance to keep the mother and young alive and safe." He quotes the sociologists T. Parsons and R. F. Bales: "The father role is relative to the others . . . in the family—high on power and *instrumentality,* and mother's high on power and *expressiveness.*"

> The man's sexual identity is linked as a rule to his implicit readiness for action, by which he achieves economic security and social-occupational status. . . . The woman's identity is typically linked with cherishing, nourishing, maternal functions towards *his* children *for* him. . . . Marriage too abhors a power vacuum. . . . A woman can best fulfil her rôle as a woman when she can be the wife to a man "who is somebody" . . . who can show achievement. Then she is prepared to surrender her self-containment, her own masculine instrumentality and detachment. It is highly unlikely that a woman can achieve full sexuality if she does not feel this condition to be present. [pp. 32–33]

This psychoanalyst believes he has the inside track on the nature of the world and presents it as scientific truth, while at the same time quoting from the Bible. Would that fathers were as protective and caring toward their children as his belief system describes them to be. This illustration shows the unfortunate application of biased and dated views of women to clinical practice. Dicks clearly follows Freud's "anatomy is destiny" view of gender relationships, and the prevailing view—as influenced by Helene Deutsch—of the proper and destined role of husband and wife: the husband to be aggressive and the wife passive. The notion that this is all for the wife's good is also apparent. But why, we can ask, cannot both partners be "somebody," and why cannot both be instrumental *and* expressive? Why a woman should have to "surrender" self-containment in order to be married is never explained, but it is clear that the author believes she will be punished by not being able to enjoy sex is she does not. Is self-containment masculine?

THE FEAR OF WOMEN—WOLFGANG LEDERER

The persistence of irrational ideas about women is indicative of the strong defensive needs they serve, as described by the psychoanalytic feminist writers in the 1970s. The belief in the intellectual limitations of women is another area where male prejudice has distorted the thinking of male psychoanalysts. The following quotation from *The Fear of Women* (Lederer 1968) is especially remarkable because the book in which it appears is quite outstanding for its time. Lederer offers a valuable historical analysis and is noteworthy in his disagreement with aspects of traditional psychoanalytic theory. Thus, it is especially surprising and illustrative to read:

> I think, perhaps, that in so far as insight—the seeing into, the throwing of light into darkness, the intellectual illumination—aims at greater self-awareness and a more conscious functioning, it belongs into the *mode or sphere of male development.* The eternal feminine, static, perfect in itself, does not and need not develop. What any woman does not know about it, insight therapy cannot ever teach her. Insight therapy, even in women, can only address itself to the *masculine aspect.* A given woman, through insight, can become more aware and more conscious, but not more feminine. . . . Therapeutic theories stressing insight deal primarily with men because only men—and the masculine aspects of women—can be approached by and can utilize insight. [p. 270, italics added]

This seems like complete nonsense, and the writer provides no scientific basis for his statements. I wonder how he reached these conclusions and how he validates them in his own mind. The passage seems to be paying women a great compliment at the same time that it depreciates them, a paradox common in much male writing about women and illustrative of the strong ambivalence many men feel toward women. It speaks to the unconscious, irrational, defensive needs of the author. It is the basis of chivalry.

Many of the errors of psychoanalysts and other psychotherapists no doubt were quite personal in origin—that is, due to unexamined countertransference, rather than theory. This lack of examination of male bias, reinforced by the lack of training in awareness of such bias, further illustrates the problems inherent for women in treatment prior to the feminist movement of the 1970s, and, to a lesser extent, even today.

In Chapter 3, I referred to an article by Grossman and Stewart (1977), in which the authors describe the second analysis of female patients for whom the interpretation of ''penis envy'' was offered for the patient's symptoms in the first analysis and had resulted in treatment failure. In the authors' view, penis envy was not the central conflict of these two women. Rather, this envy of men actually hid a sense of deprivation and worthlessness and a fear of abandonment. This view would certainly be compatible with a feminist orientation.

I believe that the best way to examine clinical work is to look at the actual process that takes place within a therapy session. It is in the back-and-forth dialogue between therapist and patient that we can observe how the therapist's theoretical foundation is translated into the interpretations he or she offers the patient.

A FEMINIST PSYCHOANALYTIC INTERPRETATION— ROBERT LANGS

In 1973 and 1974 Robert Langs published a two-volume work, *The Technique of Psychoanalytic Psychotherapy,* which has remained a standard learning text and has been an excellent source for experienced psychotherapists as well. Reading some of his case vignettes today, we can note examples of both the best of Freud's contributions and unfortunate errors that have hindered psychotherapists, which, I believe, unfairly affected the chances of women patients to receive accurate treatment.

I will attempt, on the basis of the case material available, to show how a feminist analysis of these patients would differ from Langs's traditional approach. Although the focus of the book is on technique, it is readily apparent how the developmental theory Langs ascribes to influences his conceptualization of each case and determines the content of his interpretations. I will illustrate how the technique—analyzing dreams, analyzing the transference, eliciting memories and fantasies, and drawing the material together to formulate interpretations—is valid and can be preserved, if the erroneous attitudes about women's psychology are corrected and updated. What is needed is a more sensitive understanding of the needs and fears of women and, in some cases, of their real victimization as members of a less powerful and demeaned group, and the defensive reactions resulting from this depreciated status.

First, let us look at three brief vignettes, each followed by Langs's commentary (1973).

Mrs. E.K.

Mrs. E.K. was in therapy because of depressive episodes caused, on the surface, largely by her husband's several affairs. In one session, she described how she had read a note from her husband's mistress that had been left on his dresser, and she went on to rage against the two of them. It became clear as she continued, and the therapist eventually pointed this out to her, that she had ignored the existence of the note and had never mentioned it to her husband, even though it was left in a place where she would inevitably find it. The patient responded immediately to this intervention by realizing that she had unwittingly promoted the continuation of the affair by her failure to confront her husband with the note, and went on to explore the implications of this sudden insight.

In a subsequent session, Mrs. E.K. described how her husband was telephoned at home by a girlfriend who was in acute distress with an emergency. The patient agreed to her husband's going to see this other woman and proceeded to rationalize: she feared that harm would come to the woman; this was an exceptional situation; and so on. The therapist repeated these latter excuses back to the patient in a questioning tone and this led her again to recognize at once her own participation in, and promotion of, her husbands's affairs. [pp. 419–420]

Langs's commentary:

The first intervention was a confrontation, while the second was actually more in the form of a clarification with confrontational aspects. Both related to the behavior of the patient and the surface implications, albeit unconscious ones, which the patient had failed to recognize. Confrontations of this kind enabled this patient to recognize her own unconscious motivation and the specific fantasies and genetic experiences on which it was based. This is, however, the first step toward such discoveries.

Confrontations of this kind also foster improved ego functioning. Here, the patient was helped to observe and consider her own behavior, something she was not especially prone to do. Acting out, of which this behavior is one form, is most often accompanied by defensive denial of the true implications of the behavior and by a related failure in self-scrutiny, which is an important aid to the development of impulse controls and the curtailment of destructive acting out.

These particular confrontations also inherently demonstrated to the patient her defenses of denial, avoidance, and rationalization. They also alluded to aspects of her failure to resolve her real conflicts with her husband, and pointed toward the basis for this in her own intrapsychic conflicts and unconscious fantasies. Thus, we see that confrontations may serve to bring into awareness repressed aspects of surface behavior that the patient has failed to recognize, but not unconscious fantasy systems, to which they can, however, prepare the way. Unfortunately, many therapists confine their work to this confrontational level, and fail to go beyond it; effective inner change can occur only if the underlying specific unconscious fantasies are reached and resolved. [pp. 419–420]

A nonanalytically oriented feminist reading this case would likely consider Langs's commentary a classic example of "blaming the victim." After all, the husband is breaking the bonds of matrimony by having affairs, the wife feels angry but helpless, and the therapist is blaming the wife by accusing her of participating in and even promoting her husband's adultery. However, a feminist who believes in the theory of the unconscious, in repression, and in the use of dream interpretation to reach unconscious motives for behavior, could accept Langs's approach. I believe with Langs that the wife's denial, avoidance, and rationalizations are issues for her to work on through traditional analytic methods. Langs goes on to stress the need for the wife to examine the unconscious motivation behind her behavior, and her unconscious fantasies. This is, of course, important—but I cannot agree that the wife's problems all revolve around her "acting out." Clearly, it is the husband who is acting out and the wife who is very frightened. I see no mention of fear in Langs's discussion.

My questions to Mrs. E.K. would concern her fears of abandonment by her husband were she to confront him. Langs correctly, I believe, encourages confrontation (he does not remain neutral in the face of self-destructive behavior). But there is surely a chance the husband will leave Mrs. E.K. for a life of open sexual freedom, or for his current mistress, if she gets in his way. What are her financial resources? Can she support herself? Will she lose her home? Are there children to be supported? Will Mr. K. be a dependable provider and father following a divorce? The statistics on this last point are abysmal. Such an exploration of the wife's fears and, thus, her resistance to change, would partially involve unconscious fantasies and intrapsychic conflicts. But it would also entail facing the hard realities of women's financial dependence on men (remember, the case predates the book's publication in 1973) fostered by the traditional patriarchal family system.

Additionally, does Mrs. E.K. fear being alone, unable to remarry? Is she feeling too old and unattractive to enter the dating world, where— divorced men typically marrying women ten years younger than themselves—younger women have a distinct advantage? Of course, how Mrs. E.K. approached these fears would be influenced by intrapsychic conflicts. We would want to know about her parents' marriage, her father's trustworthiness, her mother's degree of dependence, and Mrs. E.K.'s conclusions (partly unconscious) about all these things, as we explored the internal and external forces creating her fear and, thus, her denial and avoidance of confrontation.

In sum, I would not see the patient's denial and avoidance as unconscious "encouragement" based on internal conflicts alone. I would rather wonder whether Mrs. E.K. might be consciously protecting her own and her children's security, out of a fear that she could not manage on her own—a belief she may have been raised to accept as true and internalized as a fact. Between the job market and the "meat market," Mrs. E.K. may have a lot of realistic fears.

Miss F.D.

> Miss F.D. was a very resistant patient who had sought treatment because her fiancé had left her for another girl and then returned to her. She blamed him for her suffering and focused on the reality issues involved, rather than her inner fantasies and conflicts. After the therapist confronted her with the indication that she had actually encouraged the relationship between her fiancé and the other girl, she missed a session. In the next hour, after ruminating and rationalizing about her absence, which was without realistic cause, she spoke of a girlfriend who had run out of her dentist's office in a panic when a tooth was being drilled. [pp. 473–474]

Langs's commentary:

> Since Miss F.D. further ruminated, and since the acting out through the absence from the session was a clear indication (therapeutic context), the therapist elected to intervene at this point, and to do so in two steps: a confrontation and superficial interpretation, and an interpretation of a specific unconscious fantasy. Thus, he interpreted first Miss F.D.'s absence as a flight from the therapy and suggested that the motive for it was her fear of her own inappropriate (neurotic) participation in creating her suffering. To help to motivate her toward therapeutic work, he also pointed out her fear of the implication of this behavior—that she herself had emotional problems. Secondly, he interpreted a specific fantasy on which the resistance was based: her unconscious view of treatment as a dangerous and painful penetration and attack upon her integrity. While this latter intervention was based on a minimum of clinical material, it was offered because the therapist had confronted the patient with her general fears of therapy on many occasions, with little result. This interpretation actually led the patient to report phobic symptoms and bodily anxieties not previously described. [p. 474]

Here we have another instance that could be critiqued as an example of "blaming the victim." The fiancé has left and then returned. Clearly he is acting out some unconscious conflict in a rather cruel way toward the patient. Langs sees the situation as one in which the patient has actually encouraged this cruelty toward herself. In other words, she has brought about her own suffering, an example of unconsciously masochistic behavior à la Helene Deutsch. But we are not given any data to support this interpretation. Perhaps the patient encouraged a friendship, trusting both the fiancé and the "other girl" (a friend of hers?) to be loyal and not to betray her own friendship and openness. (Most likely we would think of the other as a woman, not a "girl.")

Langs is correct in approaching the missed session with transference interpretations of the patient's fear of the therapeutic uncovering that could occur with a "penetrating" analysis. A penetrating analysis by a male analyst would clearly involve sexual danger; by a woman analyst it would more likely have to do with fears of boundary invasion based on the powerful mother–daughter relationship. However, Langs makes no mention of the patient's anger. She may have felt angered by the accusation of having "encouraged" the affair, because she believed it was unfair to blame her for her fiancé's disloyal and hurtful behavior. If she felt misunderstood and her feelings unappreciated, she could have "acted out" her anger against her therapist because, like many women, she lacked the courage to express her anger directly and confront him with her feelings. Following an interpretation of angry retaliation as the basis for the missed session, the patient and analyst could have worked together to see if he had missed an important factor, whether or not his initial interpretation was valid. The story of the friend fleeing her dentist's office in a panic speaks of pain and fear and powerlessness. The only power lay in escape. We cannot speculate on what that situation meant to the friend. But it can be interpreted in terms of Miss F.D. as representing the pain of feeling betrayed by her analyst, who blames her for her suffering when she longs for his understanding. Langs describes her in the first sentence as a "very resistant patient." What does this really mean? It may mean that she does not accept the analyst's interpretations, perhaps because his ideas are insufficient or just plain wrong.

The issues of disloyalty and betrayal could be key here, perhaps in terms of the patient's earlier dependent relationships. She may not feel entitled to loyalty, and thus is not able to demand it of her fiancé or her analyst. On the other hand, she may have been unconsciously testing her fiancé to see if he would betray her, reenacting an old trauma.

It is wise to be most cautious in masochistic interpretations of a woman patient's suffering. The logical extreme could result, as it often has in the past, in a rape victim being held responsible for her perpetrator's violence, because of her dress or because she was in a bar or on the street alone. Rape victims and battered women have too often been seen by the psychiatric profession as having "encouraged" their own suffering, as the male establishment—the courts, lawyers, law enforcement agents, and physicians—protected the males who committed the crimes. I have often wondered how much this rationalization of male hostility to women has served to protect the protectors themselves, from their own ambivalence toward women and their own hostile fantasies of sadistic power over women.

Mrs. E.X.

Mrs. E.X. had been in therapy for over two years when considerable material slowly and very painfully emerged, conveying an image of her self and body as deformed and mutilated. She responded to this by activating her long-considered plans to seek out a plastic surgeon for a number of cosmetic procedures, and with thoughts of terminating her psychotherapy. The therapist interpreted this as an attempt to concretely repair her damaged image of herself by external measures rather than through anxiety-provoking inner change, and to flee these emerging awarenesses by leaving her treatment. She responded over several subsequent sessions with two dreams: in the first, she is in her session with a cousin who had (in fact and in the dream) muscular dystrophy and leaves with her. In the second, she sees her mother's vulva; it is ugly and repulsive. Her associations related to her upset over having discussed in treatment her feelings about her body, and to memories of seeing her mother nude and feeling repulsed. The therapist interpreted one unconscious meaning of therapy for her through this last dream and her associations; it was experienced as a confrontation with her body, which she found ugly and defective, much as she had responded to the sight of her mother's genitals. Further genetic material related to frightening primal scene memories, and expressions of her negative feelings about therapy and her body followed. [pp. 453–454]

Langs's commentary:

The therapeutic problem and context for this material was the patient's desire to terminate treatment, a crucial resistance and rupture in the therapeutic alliance. The adaptive context for the resistance was the patient's growing awareness of her defective body-image and the consequent anxieties, intrapsychic conflicts, and fantasies, evoked, in part, by hurtful remarks from Mrs. E.X.'s husband. In fact, the flight from the therapist was to some extent displaced from her husband. This interpretation was not made at the time, but may serve to remind us of the overdetermination of symptoms and acting out, and the need to make many different specific interpretations to resolve a symptom or piece of disturbed behavior. [p. 454]

I have found the dissatisfaction of women with their bodies to be ubiquitous, and external changes—from make-up and bleaching or dyeing of hair to nose jobs, breast enhancement or reduction, hip surgery (lipo-suction), and "face lifts"—very common among patients and nonpatients alike. The number of mature women who color their hair to cover the gray is very high. The nation was shocked in 1989 that our new president's wife, Barbara Bush, refused to dye her white hair. I have myself been surprised at how often these measures are truly helpful to a woman's self-confidence and success, because, in reality, women are judged so much on their appearance. I once asked a successful, married woman therapist why she colored her graying hair and her response was that when her hair was gray, men didn't look at her.

In the case of Mrs. E.X., the pathology sounds severe, as she is described as believing her self and body to be deformed and mutilated. Yet her solution is the common one of cosmetic surgery. Langs takes the position that the problem is all internal. We cannot judge, as we lack specifics on the patient's actual appearance; though we do know that her husband had made "hurtful remarks." However, the interpretation of the dream and of memories in which she is repulsed at seeing her mother nude seems very narrow to me. Disgust, after all, can be a defense against sexual curiosity and excitement. How many thousands of paintings of nude women have drawn admiration for centuries, and how many millions of photographs of nude women have been sold in magazines and, now, home videos, apparently to satisfy a curiosity about and desire for the female body: breasts, hips, and genitalia. Mrs. E.X.'s disgust may have been a defense against anxiety triggered by yearnings for her mother's body—an attachment that must be repressed but that remains unconscious in the form of a bisexual triangle.

No interpretation is offered for the patient's negative feelings about therapy and about her body following frightening primal scene memories, but we are left with the impression that this too is a result of disgust at the female genitalia. I am concerned about Langs's reference, in the case history, to an interpretation that the patient sought to "concretely repair her damaged image of herself" (p. 453). Does Langs believe that the patient is in fact damaged as a woman? Nowhere is there any reference to fantasy here. Is the term *image* her word or his? Are we to believe that "damaged image" implies fantasy, as in imagination? Are the "emerging awarenesses" being interpreted as awarenesses of damage or as awarenesses of *fantasies* of damage? I wonder whether Mrs. E.X. may be getting the impression from her analyst that he too believes the female body is defective and inferior, and that being a woman is not an honorable identity. If so, she may wish to flee therapy because her yearnings for pride are not being acknowledged or understood. A male analyst cannot comment favorably about women's bodies without risking a seductive implication, so he walks a tightrope in this arena. But he can certainly focus on the patient's notion of the female body as being deformed as a *misunderstanding* on the part of a young girl. The concepts of penis envy and castration anxiety are apparent throughout this discussion, though they are never openly stated in the vignette.

As a final example of an integration of feminist and psychoanalytic theory, I will examine a lengthy case discussion.

Miss F.T.

Miss F.T. was a young woman in psychotherapy because of tendencies to act out and a moderate character disorder. During the first six months of her treatment, she had worked effectively and developed new controls and insights leading to notable improvement in her problems. At the turn of the year, her therapist informed her of a vacation he planned for the end of February. She became depressed and angry, thought of stopping treatment, and dreamt of sleeping with an old boyfriend. When this was interpretively related to the pending separation, as reflecting a sexualized way of holding on to the therapist, she remembered that the dream had an additional part; she and her sister were having an affair with an older man, someone the age of her therapist.

Over the next few sessions, she went on to speak of feeling slighted by the therapist's leaving and of how her father favored one of her two sisters over herself. Her mother's neglect—because she had worked when the patient was a child—was also described. Other, specific memories from her early childhood followed: an accidental fall in which she bloodies her head and a vaginal infection that a woman doctor painfully probed—it was like being impregnated with a bullet (both from about age eight); trips with her parents throughout her childhood during summer vacation; and being accident-prone—catching her leg in the spokes of a bike when her parents were away, and often being bruised from falls. She did not recall masturbating at that time, she added, in discussing the vaginal infection.

She then reported this dream: she is in a shoe store, waiting. Two of her friends get pointed shoes; she herself does not get what she wants. There is a saleslady—then she is a salesman—and he had three pairs of shoes, two brown and one blue. In the session, she went on to ruminate about one of her sisters who had recently been a bridesmaid, about waiting to hear from her father (the patient did not live at home), reading a book about sex and wanting to have intercourse with someone, and that her girlfriend's psychiatrist had said that a sock in a shoe represented intercourse. She then remembered that she had masturbated before going to sleep the night of the dream, and wondered if masturbating had actually caused the vaginal infection she had as a child; she felt guilty about it.

The therapist in turn wondered aloud to the patient about the wish in her dream. The patient said: maybe it was to have a penis. The therapist agreed; he suggested that as a child she had probably seen her father's penis—possibly when they had traveled and shared a room—and that she had wanted to have a penis herself, and to be a boy.

The patient was uncertain, though somehow she knew that she did not feel fully feminine. Her father had always wanted a son (he had instead three daughters) and she was the one who had most shared his activities and worked with him on his job. One of her greatest wishes as a child was to own toy guns.

In subsequent sessions, she related this wish for a penis to her promiscuity and added other confirmations to the reconstruction. A dream in which she had two highballs while in a bedroom with an older man was notable among these; she wanted her own set of balls. After some flight which was analyzed as a resistance, she then reported a recurrent fantasy of being a popular male singer. Further, a dream of her aged, senile grandmother led to an exploration of her view of women as helpless and endangered. When this was interpreted to her, she recalled seeing her mother's bloody menstrual pads as a child, and her fantasies that her mother had been damaged and penetrated by her father. She now remembered fantasies of wishing she could get pregnant without ever menstruating. In later sessions, her wish to bear her parents—especially her father—the son they wanted also emerged.

During these few months after the reconstruction, nothing more was said regarding possible primal scene experiences and seeing her father nude. Her functioning was so much improved and her acting out so well controlled that she began to plan to terminate her therapy with the end of her college year in June. Soon after, her mother took ill and required a cholecystectomy.

At this point, Miss F.T. dreamt of being in a movie theater and seeing *Love Story*. She went on to recall past hospitalizations of various family members. She had had sexual relations with an old boyfriend and dreamt that she was "balling" (having relations with) a famous male performer. She was anxious about her own bodily integrity; associations also focused on the past illnesses of her mother and father, particularly a near-fatal illness of the latter.

She then dreamt of a movie theater in which a monkey was clawing at her head. Associations were to her mother's then-pending surgery, and to an older man she knew who owned a monkey. She then ruminated a good deal. Here, the therapist again offered a reconstruction. He had not forgotten the patient's missing allusions to observing parental intercourse. He also felt that an element needed to account for the fantasies evoked in Miss F.T. by her mother's pending surgery was missing, and detected hints of its nature in the material. The reconstruction seemed necessary to help the patient work through her anxieties about her mother's surgery and the termination of her treatment.

In the material were references to movies (and observing, looking, and death), to movie stars (and admiring), to intercourse, and to her head being attacked (often this is a displacement upwards from below and from the genitals). It suggested two interrelated fantasies and sets of memories to the therapist: experiences of observing parental intercourse, and accompanying unconscious fantasies that it represented a powerful, handsome, man—father—attacking and harming the woman—mother; related to this were unconscious fantasies of her mother's need for surgery—and possibly the surgery itself—as a result of, and comparable to, the sexual attack.

Thus, when the patient spoke again of the clawing and then related it to the planned surgery, the therapist suggested that it also seemed to refer to some ideas about intercourse that were based on earlier observations of her parents having relations.

At first, Miss F.T. denied any such memory, though she reviewed again the occasions where she had shared motel rooms with her parents. One of her sisters had had her first menstrual period on one of these trips and was afraid that her father would notice it. Then the patient suddenly, but vaguely, recalled waking up herself one time—she was already a freshman in college and still shared a room while away with her parents—and hearing movement of some kind. To a direct inquiry, based on a hunch of the therapist's that used previous material (this was a reconstruction of a later sequence of events), the patient recalled that just three weeks later she had first had intercourse; it had indeed followed that experience in the motel, as the therapist's question had suggested.

In subsequent sessions, a great deal emerged. First, memories of overhearing and seeing her sisters in bed with boyfriends, one of whom was very hairy, like a monkey. Then she recalled for the first time in therapy that she would consciously fantasize about her parents in intercourse; it was quite upsetting and she linked it to their many daily quarrels. Dreams of being unattractive followed, as did acting out (including stealing) calculated to anger her father with whom she was now living at home while her mother was in the hospital.

Then, a dream of a cold, gray forest with felled trees led to memories from early childhood when Miss F.T. shared a room in a cabin with her parents; she had awakened during the night to noises there too. Other even earlier similar experiences were then recalled, as were the nightmares that accompanied them—of tidal waves and drowning. Masturbatory fantasies, including conscious sexual wishes for her father, also emerged, and further material related to her view of intercourse in terms of her mother being attacked, damaged, and bloodied. While all of this was analyzed, her mother's surgery was successful and the patient handled it well.

Then, in the final session of her therapy, Miss F.T. remembered for the first time in many years an early childhood fantasy: she would imagine an alligator under her bed and feared that it would bite off her foot if she stepped on the floor. She also recalled a frightening image she had had at age six or so while in the first motel room that she could recall having shared with her parents: something small was getting large. She thought of a penis, of her mistrust of men, and of her fantasies that her father had done something to her mother. Fantasies of having had a penis, of her father having bitten it (and her mother's) off, and impulses of revenge-in-kind against her father, were all in evidence. [pp. 524–529]

In the first paragraph, Langs correctly interprets a dream as a sexualized transference response to his announcement of a vacation. In the second paragraph we are told that Miss F.T.'s mother worked and therefore neglected her. Since Langs surely would not conclude that a father's working constituted "neglect," we are dealing here with a bias against the mother for working. The patient may have felt neglected by her mother, but we would need to examine the quality of the mother–child relationship to determine the source of the neglect in the mother's character. The fact of her working, as long as she provided warm and competent child care, would not, from a feminist perspective, constitute neglect.

We learn that the patient is one of three sisters (we are not told the birth order), that her father had always wanted a son, and that he had favored one of her two sisters over herself. The therapy is progressing well as the announcement of the analyst's vacation brings up the issues of favoritism and neglect. It is in Langs's analysis of the next dream that I believe he gets off track.

Miss F.T. is from a "tilted" family, three girls, no boys. This means that there were four women competing for the attention of one man. Miss F.T. learned that a way to get attention from her father was by sexualizing her relationship with him. In the dream, she and her two friends (likely the two sisters) are in a shoe store and she doesn't get what she wants, first from a woman and then from a man, making the family of five. Associations include one sister recently being a bridesmaid. I would comment to the patient here that the sister had just gotten special attention, most likely involving a special dress and shoes along with all the wedding planning, and that she herself may be feeling neglected. The patient again associates to sex as a means for getting her emotional needs met, and she provides for her own pleasure through masturbation, thus asserting her independence from her mother as the sole provider of her needs (as described by Maria Torok). She suggests that perhaps she did masturbate as a young girl. This could be interpreted in terms of her not being anyone's favorite and consequent withdrawal into fantasy. However, no questioning is reported about the content of her current masturbation fantasy, or about what makes her feel guilty. I would suggest to the patient that, because her mother shared a bed with her father, in fact the patient believed that the mother was the favorite of the father and the father the favorite of the mother.

However, we read that the patient herself suggests the interpretation that the dream represents a wish for a penis. Where did this idea come from? I suggest that it came earlier in the therapeutic work from her analyst. The patient also may have picked up the idea from magazines, books about sex, and her friend's psychiatrist—the "sock in the shoe" type of shallow interpretation. But remember, this young woman wants and needs to feel special and valuable, to be somebody's favorite. How better to please her Freudian analyst than to comply with his wish that she confirm his ideas about her problems. So she gives him what he wants to hear to get what she needs—his acceptance and approval. And she continues to try to hold on to him through sex, as he accurately interpreted.

Both the patient and analyst agree that her wanting to own toy guns as a child means she wanted a penis. An alternate feminist interpretation could be that she did not feel close to her mother, wanted to be close to her father, and shared his activities to get a special closeness with him. She fantasized that if she were a boy she would be special to both of them. The patient's wish for a penis is symbolic of her wanting recognition in her family from her neglectful mother, and of a way for her to compete with her two sisters. I believe that such an interpretation would encourage memories of loneliness and sadness that could be therapeutic, whereas the former would add to the patient's depression by encouraging feelings of hopelessness and confirming feelings of deprivation. Langs's interpretation of the highball dream, "She wanted her own set of balls," again, I believe, misses the point, and doesn't make sense. My reconstruction would be that Miss F.T. felt neglected by her mother, turned to her father for love and appreciation, and hoped to get his attention through sexuality as her mother did. What would be the point for a woman of being in a bedroom and having drinks with an older man, surely a setting for seduction, if she wanted a penis on her own body? As a patient of mine once said, "Sure I want a penis, but on the inside, not on the outside." Moreover, even if this or other dreams did indicate a wish for a penis, the correct interpretation might be that in this way she imagined she could get more attention from her mother, who slept in bed with her father.

The fantasy of being a popular male singer could be interpreted as the patient's longing for attention and appreciation from women and men, and as representing her belief that she would have gotten more admiration from both parents had she been born a son, rather than as a wish for a penis. The patient imagines that, rather than being neglected, she would have been privileged in the family, a star—and she could be right. I would be curious to know whether the mother admired some male singer—Frank Sinatra perhaps, or Elvis Presley.

In the grandmother dream we learn that the patient has a view of women as helpless and endangered. She clearly never was given a positive view of menstruation as a sign of health and fecundity. Yet she does have fantasies of pregnancy, so her feelings about being a woman are ambivalent. There is something special and valuable that only women have. Here Langs makes the first reference to the mother's wishes for a son. Might the patient have been the third daughter, the one who should have been the longed-for son of both parents?

Langs returns to his interpretation of Miss F.T.'s view of intercourse as attacking and damaging to women. Yet how could such an interpretation explain her desire for intercourse with men? It shows significant conflict: the patient wants sexual attention and the pleasure of sexuality with men, and yet fears it. Perhaps Langs is relying on Deutsch's theory, though he does not state this explicitly, that sex for a woman is a passive, masochistic submission, or receiving. However, her masturbation as a child and as a young woman has informed the patient that genital stimulation is extremely pleasurable; in fact, it is such a secret and forbidden independent pleasure that she feels guilty about it. Langs may be projecting onto his woman patient a pathological view held by some males of intercourse as a sadistic, defiling attack on a woman. However, the patient may have felt threatened as a child by the size of her father's penis, and therefore fears that penetration would be damaging to her. This unconscious fear could be alleviated through therapy by her conscious recognition as an adult of the adult-to-adult fit. Therapy could also help her to see her mother as less helpless and injured, possibly even as an active, enjoying participant in sex.

The case material then takes a significant turn to the times throughout her life when the patient and her sisters shared a motel room with her parents, when she was exposed to both hearing and seeing her parents in intercourse; and to the times when she was exposed to her sisters' intercourse with boyfriends. For centuries past—and in much of the world today—whole families have shared a single room, and thus most humans have been raised with the awareness of parental intercourse. However, in a modern, sexually shamed, American middle-class family, it is worth remarking on the possible meaning of the parents sharing a motel room with three young or adolescent daughters, with the parents having sexual relations under these conditions; and the peculiar circumstance of the sisters exposing their sexuality to the patient, which seems to confirm my hunch that she is the youngest. What is going on in this family?

I suggest that the sisters are reenacting in relation to the patient what the parents did to all three of them—an act of exhibitionism and perhaps a cruel, rivalrous act as well, as a way of handling the trauma all three sisters experienced. These exposures may have had the unconscious meaning for the parents of the daughters' inclusion in the sexual act, first on their own part, and then, for the patient, in the reenactment by her sisters. The patient's father may have been enjoying a harem fantasy, and her mother may have unconsciously been triumphing over her daughters, acting out her own old oedipal rivalries.

The fact that the patient acts out to anger her father is analyzed as the result of her anger toward him for her not having a penis, and her fantasies of his having damaged her mother and herself. The two are alone together in the house while the mother is in the hospital. Is she called home to take the mother's place? I believe she deals with her anxiety about this intimacy by creating distance through anger-provoking behavior. In fact, this is the opportunity she has longed for in her fantasies. The father's seductive behavior in exposing her to his sexuality not surprisingly created frustrated sexual excitement, and her feelings of anger and of being unattractive followed. I see no basis for a penis envy/anger interpretation here.

In the final paragraph, we learn of the patient's childhood fear of an alligator under her bed and the fantasy that her father had bitten off her mother's penis and her own. What are we to make of this? Helene Deutsch has written that the girl blames her mother for her lack of a penis and resents her for it. Langs's patient blames her father. I believe that the daughter is likely to blame whichever parent is more powerful and/or more angry. This is another illustration of how Deutsch's personal trauma with her own mother affected her theorizing. Could the alligator have been a projection of Miss F.T.'s angry feelings toward her mother? Or, might she have felt angry at her mother for not protecting her from her father's seductiveness and his anger? She had been exposed to their daily angry fighting. The oral attack of the alligator could have its source in these verbal battles, which surely were frightening to her. In any event, the patient and her analyst agree on penis envy as the correct interpretation, reinforcing their therapeutic alliance.

An Interpretation of the Symptoms as Possible
Evidence of Sexual Molestation

Now I may surprise the reader by offering another interpretation of Miss
F.T.'s reconstructions, one that Langs doesn't mention, although I do so
with the realization that this is speculative. I propose the possibility that
Miss F.T. was sexually molested as a child, possibly by her father, and that
this is repressed and has not come up in treatment because her analyst
never thought of it and never asked the proper questions. The clues are all
in the material.

1. A childhood vaginal infection. This is not normally caused by
masturbation, Langs's explanation for it.

2. The abundance of dreams and fantasies repeating the theme of sex
being a dangerous attack on a woman and damaging her.

3. The visual image at age 6 of something small getting larger. There
is no way a girl of 6 would know of penile engorgement by hearing or even
seeing her parents having intercourse (likely under covers) in a dark motel
room.

4. The crocodile terror, combined with the fantasy of the father
biting off her penis. This could be the result of forced oral copulation in a
sexual assault on her.

5. The clawing monkey causing bleeding on her head could represent
displacement from the vagina and a concealment of the perpetrator,
possibly a hairy man or even the man with the monkey, by giving him the
form of an animal. It is common in dreams of molested girls that the danger
takes the form of an animal, as anthropomorphic animals are so common in
children's stories.

6. Promiscuity, also common in molested girls.

7. The occurrence of older men in her dreams and primal scene
memories and derivatives might actually be screen memories for her own
sexual assault.

8. The wish to own a toy gun. This could reflect anger at her
molester, and an attempt at mastery of her fear and mistrust of men, as well
as her fantasy of revenge.

In 1973 and before, analysts were looking for penis envy. In 1990, we are looking for sexual abuse. It is true that, now as then, we are more likely to find what we are looking for—the subjective component of our scientific investigation. It is common for therapists today to see a great number of women patients reporting sexual abuse, because that is what they are reading about and hearing about on radio and television. Women in the 1950s read and heard about happy housewives; they came to therapists distressed because they were unhappy and had concluded there must be something wrong with them. The analysts' answer was that they envied their husbands. Patient and analyst are living in the same culture, and are being formed by similar trends. They may collude in what they believe is an accurate diagnosis of the patient's problems. But because they are both culture-bound, the truth may elude them both.

Summary

It is clear that Miss F.T. was unhappy and conflicted as a child for a number of reasons. She felt neglected by her mother; she understood that she had disappointed both her parents by not having been born a boy; she had to compete for both parents' attention with two sisters and possibly a sickly grandmother, and apparently had no special beauty or talent to help her stand out; and she was exposed to her parents' sexual acts, which she mistakenly interpreted as violence against her mother. Her response to these conflicts was not passive, but rather the active one of seeking attention from other men, including her analyst. This was a healthy reaction unless she was self-destructive, which we are given no data that she was, although Langs refers to her as "promiscuous." Remembering her childhood misconceptions and fantasies should be very helpful to her in reevaluating her internalized view of herself as damaged and undesirable, and could reduce her anger toward her father, who she now realizes is not to blame for her lack of a penis. My concern is with her analyst's ability to help her feel pride in and satisfaction with her female body and its creative power, if he too believes she is defective and cannot ever be satisfied without a penis.

Traditional psychoanalytic theory focuses on penis envy as the key to women's unhappiness. There is surely truth to this specific jealousy for some girls, just as some boys envy girls' capacity to bear children, and it needs to be understood in the context of each individual patient's history and fantasies. But not all anxiety is based on fantasy. I believe errors have been made by overemphasizing this component and not recognizing the more basic human needs of boys and girls for recognition, appreciation, and loving acceptance. The case of Miss F.T. illustrates this overemphasis, as well as exemplifying the compliance of the woman patient with her

analyst's interpretations in order to win recognition, approval, and acceptance from him. Her wish for a toy gun, her "promiscuity" (would a
sexually active male of college age be labeled promiscuous?), her wanting
pointed shoes (fashionable at the time), are all interpreted concretely rather
than symbolically as her wish for the love, respect, and admiration she
believed she would receive if she were a boy. Her wish to bear a son also
illustrates this conviction. But she does learn that she can get male
attention through sexuality, and proceeds to act on that recognition—not
such an unhealthy response, as it is, in fact, quite realistic.

Miss F.T.'s improvement in therapy is due to some very good work,
but may also be because she has finally been able to please a parental figure
by giving her analyst what he wants, a patient who conforms to his
diagnosis of penis-envy. Clearly she felt she was special to him and pleased
him. We know that she did please him, because she was chosen for a
lengthy vignette in his book.

RESPECT FOR INDEPENDENT WOMEN—JEROME OREMLAND

In his recent book, *Interpretation and Interaction—Psychoanalysis or
Psychotherapy?* (1991), which distinguishes between psychoanalysis, psychoanalytically oriented psychotherapy, and interactive psychotherapy,
Oremland gives two case examples of his work with women patients that
serve as illustrations of enlightened psychoanalytic work with women. As
an example of a psychotherapeutic interactive interchange, Oremland tells
of a 28-year-old unmarried woman artist whom he saw for only one visit.
She had developed the symptom of a swelling of her tongue and lips that
made it difficult for her to speak. This symptom first occurred when she
went to purchase her airline ticket for a trip to Europe to join a woman
friend, and it recurred later whenever she spoke about the trip. She had
attended private school in Europe and knew it very well, and the trip came
at an ideal time for her, as she had just ended a long-term relationship with
an artist thirty years older than herself. The patient's story is as follows. She
had remained in Europe after school, studying art, and had become an
ardent skier and ski instructor. She described her skiing as having become
"more and more aggressive," including racing with male skiers. She had
suffered a bad fall, severely fractured her leg, and spent some time in a large
cast. When she returned home she enrolled at an art institute and became
involved with her teacher, an esteemed artist. She devoted herself to caring
for him, and spent less and less time on her own painting. Oremland
describes the relationship as "an eight-year bondage." Here is how he
interprets her symptom:

I told her that I felt that her symptom represented her fear of speaking for herself. I told her that for many years, apparently, she could allow herself to develop only vicariously. I indicated that she had helped her artist boyfriend do what she could not allow herself to do—develop, assert, and achieve. I suggested that the skiing accident had frightened her, that perhaps it had seemed a "deserved" punishment for being competent and assertive and that subsequently she was fearful of such strivings. [p. 25]

The patient listened and then asked if Oremland thought she should proceed with her trip, or delay it in order to continue seeing him. He answered that, though she could continue to see him, she could take the trip and could easily return if her difficulties continued. She left on her trip and sent a postcard several months later saying she was enjoying the trip and had had no more problems. In a later chance meeting, he learned that her work was progressing well. His analysis goes as follows:

The skiing injury became a symbolic punishment for assertive, exhibitionistic, competitive success with men. The injury resulted in her inhibiting and defending against phallic strivings by devoting herself to an older, already accomplished man. Vicariously she participated in his achievement without having to continue her own. . . .

The "swelling tongue," with its interference with speech, became in the classical hysterical sense a compromise formation symbolizing the phallic wishes and the punishment for them. . . .

My *selective interpretation of the psychodynamics* enabled her to gain insight into the meaning of the symptom. I indicated that the symptom protected her from asserting herself, just as the relationship with the older man had. By encouraging her to continue with her plans, I at once endorsed her asserting herself and discouraged her from involving herself, potentially endlessly, once again with an older man (me).

I was fully on the side of mastering assertion conflicts *using* the transference and selective insight toward that specific goal. . . . [pp. 27–28]

This case, first published in 1976, serves as an example of interactive interpretation, but also as an example of a male analyst who sees independence and assertion in women as a positive goal and helps his patient toward independence and success in her chosen field. His choice of the phrase "phallic strivings" is unfortunate. I would say assertive or independent strivings, because I don't link assertion or independence directly with masculinity, but rather with healthy, normal development for both sexes.

Nevertheless, Oremland's approach to the case is a good example of an integration of feminist and psychoanalytic theory and values.

In a later discussion of how the psychotherapist or analyst handles cancellations, Oremland again shows his recognition of the differences between men and women and the special interpretations that are sometimes necessary to help women overcome the burdens of the cultural expectations that they have internalized.

> It is striking how many female patients assume that they will interrupt their psychotherapy at the time of their husbands' vacation. Even more startling are the female patients who assume that they will interrupt their own psychotherapy when their husbands' psychoanalysts, particularly those in training psychoanalyses, take their vacation. Discussion of these expectations is remarkably revealing of the multiple, subtle ways a woman may subordinate her self-interest to the needs of her husband. Sometimes revealed are fears, imagined and real, of her husband's anger should she assert her desires. Sometimes her inner disorganization and need to use her husband's life to structure her own become clear. [pp. 100–101]

In another example, Oremland again illustrates his sensitivity to the position of a career woman. In his discussion of the initial phase of psychoanalytically oriented psychotherapy, he says that "the initial phase is characterized by identification and interpretation of the transference–resistance manifestations in multiple contexts" (p. 70). He describes a woman who called for an appointment, stating that she was depressed because she had received a major promotion at work and was concerned that she could not "handle it." When she was greeted in the waiting room, she indicated the two keys on the table, which carried oversized tags marked MEN'S and WOMEN'S, and asked, "Are these the keys for the restroom?" Oremland replied, "I am struck that you begin by asking such an obvious question that makes you appear stupid." In the office, the woman attacked Oremland for calling her stupid. He emphasized that he did not call her stupid, but was pointing out the way that she was relating to him. As the session continued, she became aware of her discomfort at being assertive and positive with men. At the end of the session Oremland offered her a follow-up session for Tuesday at 2:30. She asked, "A.M. or P.M.?" Realizing the connection, she said "I think I'm being stupid with you again." Another significant exchange occurred in the following session. The patient asked if they should discuss her tendency to try to get men to do things by being "silly or flirtatious." Oremland pointed out to her that "she was asking for my direction to cover her own good idea" (p. 72).

As the patient's psychoanalytically oriented psychotherapy progressed, her self-confidence and inner serenity increased, and she rose rapidly to a high-level managerial position. She was able to work with and lead men well at work, but her personal relationships with men outside work were not succeeding. Oremland recognized the realistic problems she faced and respected her resentment, rather than dismissing it as penis envy.

> Her physical appearance, increasing age, and high-level work position made it hard to find suitable men. Younger men were not interested in her except as a "mother" or as "income." Older men who were interested in her were generally passive or boring. She deplored the fact that her male cohorts could date and marry women from a broader range of ages and professional experience than the men she could consider. She realized that envy of men and their "easy" situation did not help her. She began constructing a life as a single woman, regretfully resigning herself to not having a family of her own. [p. 81]

This patient completed psychotherapy after four and a half years and then called five years later. She was nearly 40, still unmarried, but wanted to have a baby. After extensive discussion she decided that she was ready and asked to be seen in "supportive psychotherapy." She was seen "interactively," according to Oremland's criteria, until a month prior to the birth of her son. Oremland adds, "Since that time, I see her periodically. I admire her skill as a mother, skillful and organized homemaker, and highly paid executive" (p. 82).

This case is surely a long cry from the earlier view of women as suitable only for the role of wife and mother. The analyst respects women as individuals with brains and talent as well as wombs, and his high regard for his women patients comes through in the case descriptions very clearly. Although never describing himself as a feminist, and perhaps not considering himself one, Oremland shows that he has been positively moved to separate himself from the earlier attitudes of psychoanalysis about women's roles, and the interpretation of strivings for career success and independence as pathological signs of "penis envy." It is interesting that in the preface to the book, he expresses appreciation to his two daughters for their help, identifying one as a lawyer and the other as an editor. As I suggested earlier, the woman's movement cannot help but have had some effect on psychoanalysts, who are surely aware of the great debates going on in society on these issues, and who hear from women patients, from wives, and from daughters of their frustration with women's traditional roles.

6

THE FEMALE ORGASM

"Hello, this is Dr. Ruth Westheimer. You're on the air."

"Dr. Ruth, I think you're the greatest, and I hope you can help me with my problem."

"Well, I'll try."

"Okay. It started about a year ago, when I was having some problems with my sexual encounters—you know, in the sack. So I went out and bought some pornographic magazines and looked at them just before and during intercourse. And then my wife started buying these magazines. Well, we have an eight-millimeter film projector, and she bought some porno films that she now shows while we're in bed having sex. She turns on the projector and watches movies while we're going through our routine."

"Do you have orgasm?"

"Oh, yeah."

"And she has good orgasms?"

"Yeah."

"Nothing to worry about then. You've found a way that's right for the two of you. And you both enjoy it. So everything is fine. Bye-bye."

—Dr. Ruth Westheimer, *Dr. Ruth's Guide to Good Sex*

Female sexuality has been a subject of fascination for centuries. During the Middle Ages, as I described in Chapter 1, European women were seen as very powerful and sexually aggressive. In an attempt to control them, severe punitive measures were taken against their sexual freedom, as well as their economic and social freedom, for example in the witch trials and burnings. This culminated in the severe repression of the Victorian era, when it was unthinkable that any decent woman should derive pleasure from sex, and it was firmly believed that the majority of women had neither the desire nor the capacity for sexual gratification. A woman merely submitted to her husband to please him. Women who did enjoy sex were seen as immoral and depraved; their enjoyment was considered a sign of their low moral character.

When research proved in the 1960s that women could enjoy sex— surely something many women already knew—it created a revolution in the relationship between men and women. This revolution joined with social and legal challenges to male supremacy to change marriage in profound ways. For example, in California, it was not until 1974 that a married woman had the right to conduct credit transactions in her own name without her husband's consent, or had the right to manage community property on an equal basis with her husband. It was 1975 before the husband was no longer legally the head of the household. I believe that sexual freedom and economic independence have always gone hand in hand. Money is power and power corrupts, thereby corrupting the relationship between men and women.

In the Eastern world, unlike the Western, female sexuality was celebrated, although individual women were suppressed in the roles of wives and courtesans, and powerful men had harems of many wives. The *Kama Sutra,* the classic study of the art of lovemaking, appeared in the third century A.D., written by the mysterious sage Vatsyayana. It was not translated into English until the nineteenth century, by Sir Richard Burton. More than a love manual, the *Kama Sutra* attempts to define the whole relationship between a man and a woman. Kama, the name of the Hindu god of love, means pleasure—not only sexual pleasure, but any pleasure that can be experienced through the senses. A translation of the title would be "Aphorisms on Pleasure."

Psychoanalysis emerged during the Victorian era, and therefore was biased by the period's severe sexual repression of women. This repression continued (except for small pockets of resistance, such as the Bohemian communities) until the 1960s, when a combination of the sex research of the 1950s and 1960s, the sexual liberation movement that grew out of this research, and then the women's liberation movement, caused a revolution in sexual attitudes and practices among women in this country. One of the issues to receive considerable attention was the female orgasm. Many women and married couples had remained ignorant about the women's potential for orgasm. The most common way for a woman to discover her orgasmic potential is in masturbation. If a woman had been coerced into suppressing her natural impulse to masturbate, she might have married and stayed married for years to an equally sexually naive man without even knowing what she was missing, until the reports of the sex researchers reached the media and knowledge became available to the general public. One of the functions of the consciousness-raising groups in the '70s was to give women their first chance to talk to other women about sex. As teenagers they had talked to friends about boys and dating, but they then had no sexual experience beyond "necking" and "petting" to talk about. Once married, a loyalty to and protection of the husband, and the desire to maintain a social facade of marital success, kept most women from talking to each other about sexual intercourse. Besides, in the '50s that topic was not openly talked about, even between friends.

CASE EXAMPLES—ORGASMIC DISORDERS

An integration of psychoanalytic theory and feminist theory, combined with the results of sex researchers and sex therapists, gives us a complete picture of the problem of orgasmic disorders in women. In the 1970s I had two patients, a woman and a man, who shed light on the subject for me.

Control of Feelings—Tammy

Tammy was in her mid-twenties and came for therapy because of depression and dissatisfaction with her relationships with men. I saw her twice a week for two and a half years, until her political group assigned her to another city and she moved. She was one of three children, the only girl, in a working class family. When she was 5, her father abandoned the family. She had one or two memories of his returning for a brief visit, but for the most part she had no contact with him. It seemed, from her few memories of the time her father did live with the family, that she was close to him and that he was affectionate with her. Her mother struggled to support the family, and Tammy had bad memories of bill collectors calling and coming to the house.

Tammy went to her local university, and was there during the height of the anti-Vietnam war protests. She became politically involved and joined a small but very active Communist party, which appealed to her because of its sensitivity to the issues of poverty that were so significant in her life. She dropped out of college to do political work, and supported herself in a skilled trade. She was tough—for example, she prided herself on being a very good pool player—but she was in fact quite pretty and feminine looking. She often attracted men she met in politics, but she had problems in intimate relationships with them.

One issue we worked on was her smoking. She knew that smoking was dangerous for her, as she had severe asthma, yet she couldn't give it up. It was a discovery to us both when the function that smoking served for her was revealed through an incident that occurred when she did stop. After about ten days of not smoking, she was looking through a family photo album and saw pictures of her two brothers. She became so overwhelmed with love for them and with feelings of missing them that she went for a cigarette and resumed smoking. She said she couldn't bear such strong feelings.

This incident sheds light on our work on the issue of her inability to have an orgasm. Tammy wanted very much to be orgasmic and devoted a great deal of time and attention to the matter in our therapy. One of the first aspects of the problem that we explored was her extreme fear and shame at being seen naked by a man. I had the idea that her shame was related to an unconscious idea that her body was damaged, since she had grown up with two brothers, all close in age and probably in close quarters. I suspected that she had had the irrational idea as a child, when she compared herself to her brothers, that she had either had a penis and been castrated, and/or that she had an inferior body because of her lack of a penis. I explored this with her by asking probing questions about this fear, for example: "What do you think you're missing?" "What is the secret that you think your clothes conceal?" "You do have breasts and female genitals. What would be disappointing about that to a man?"

I never mentioned the word penis in this exploration, as it was not necessary. As the irrationality of her feelings became evident to her, Tammy was able to relax with men and started to enjoy sex more. She began to develop a close relationship with a particular man and found herself getting closer to orgasm. We continued to talk about her aborted relationship with her father. She was surprised at the fond memories of him that came to the surface, but she retained her long-held anger toward him for abandoning her and the family, and some of her resentment toward men, including her current boyfriend.

Why do they always pull the covers off you at night? I always wake up cold because he's pulled all the covers around him. It makes me so mad at how selfish they are. They get the bed wet and then they make you sleep on the wet spot, why shouldn't they have to sleep on the wet spot?

In general, there is no need for a therapist to respond to such complaints. In Tammy's case as well, I just listened and neither disputed the comments nor agreed. Although ordinarily silence means consent, in psychotherapy just listening with interest and attention is enough, and the patient interprets the silence in the way her transference dictates. This patient did not demand my agreement. If a patient did make such a demand, the response could be: "You wonder whether I share the resentment toward men that you have." "What do you imagine about that?"

In some cases a patient may not inquire directly, but hints at her curiosity about the female therapist's attitudes and relationships with men. ("You know what I mean, you know how men are" [merging] or "You probably can't understand. You never have these problems." [angry, envious, and distancing the therapist through idealization.]) In such cases it is best to move right in with the same question as above. In this way the therapist can elicit projections that can help illuminate her role in the process. Is the patient identifying with her therapist as a woman who she imagines resents men, as her mother probably did? Is she hoping she is in a loving, trusting relationship with a man so that she can provide a positive model?

The important interpretation that I made to Tammy, in various forms and as often as necessary, was as follows:

> You were so hurt by your father's abandoning you, it is not surprising that you have anger and resentment toward men. But is it fair to take this anger out on men who aren't your father, and who have never harmed you? By keeping them at a distance, you protect yourself from being hurt and disappointed and angry again, but you also prevent yourself from having a close and caring relationship with a man, which you have missed for so long. By not giving the man a chance, you don't give yourself a chance.

This interpretation can be altered to fit a particular woman's relationship with her father and other significant men:

because you felt your father rejected you

because you felt your father preferred your brother (or sister)

because you knew your father was having an affair

because your family sent your brother to college and not you because you trusted and loved your grandfather and he molested you

because your husband left you for another woman.

One day Tammy arrived for her session looking very distressed. She announced that she had had an orgasm in intercourse the previous night, and it was so powerful she had burst into tears and sobbed. She was very shocked and disturbed by the experience, and she stated that she never wanted to have an orgasm with a man again because she never wanted to let a man have that much power over her. I was surprised, but did not dispute her conclusion.

Tammy moved not too long afterward, so I don't know whether she continued in therapy or whether she was able to resolve her distress and pursue an orgasmic relationship with another man. The point to be learned is how significant the issue of control of feelings was for Tammy, and perhaps is for other women like her. Whether these feelings involved her deep love and longing for her brothers, which she suppressed with nicotine, or the powerful sensation of orgasm, which she decided she would continue to suppress after her sobbing experience, Tammy needed to be in control of her emotions and therefore felt unsafe when her feelings got out of her control. Ideally, we could have continued to work on her fear of strong feelings, and she could have learned that she could expose herself and still be safe, but she moved away. How much choice she had in regard to this move is unclear to me. The political party she was active in was quite authoritarian and did make assignments, but I wonder if she could have persuaded them to let her remain had she not wanted to escape the exposure resulting from her therapy. The move happened so fast that I never had a chance to explore this issue with her. Interpretations could have been:

> You are still so afraid of a man's power because your father had so much power over the family: the power to leave you poor and missing him.

> You react as if a man today has as much power as your father did when you were a little girl.

> You need to be in control because you are so afraid of strong feelings, as if they could damage you.

> Are you afraid of losing your mind?

The Male Orgasm—An Unusual Case

Another case in which I learned about the meaning of orgasm was that of a male patient of 26, who came for help with career decisions. He also revealed that he suffered from ejaculatory impotence, which is comparable to a woman's being inorgasmic. He was flippant about it, declaring that it wasn't really a problem, that his long staying power was enjoyed by women and made him more desirable. I questioned this, because I suspected that it was a source of frustration for him. What I learned was that he had had epilepsy since childhood; it was controlled by medication but was serious enough to leave him with some anxiety about the possibility of seizures. I suggested that having an orgasm (ejaculating) was terrifying for him because it reminded him of a seizure. I also told him that the French term for orgasm is *petit mort,* little death, because of the sensation like a loss of consciousness that occurs during orgasm; I said I imagined he was frightened of losing consciousness. When he realized the connection, and that that fear was the source of his problem, he was able to begin ejaculating in intercourse and found he could tolerate the sensation without fearing a seizure.

This experience, along with the example of Tammy, added to the development of my idea that orgasmic problems are related to the fear of loss of control. A review of the literature on this subject reveals some surprising results. The sex researchers put to rest many myths about female sexuality that came from psychoanalytic theory and from historical distortions.

PSYCHOANALYSIS AND THE FEMALE ORGASM

"Frigidity" is the term used in the psychoanalytic literature for the condition of a woman who does not experience orgasm. This term implies coldness and rigidity in the woman, and essentially labels her as the problem. In the fields of sex research and sex therapy, the label "frigid" has been abandoned. Instead, the term "inorgasmic" is used to describe women who do not reach orgasm except in masturbation, and "pre-orgasmic" is used for women who have never learned how to masturbate properly or to reach orgasm with a partner. Another current term is "situationally orgasmic" (or "situationally inorgasmic"), to distinguish women who, for example, are orgasmic with a man through manual or oral stimulation but not in intercourse, or to refer to other situations that make a difference in a woman's orgasmic potential. Unfortunately for many women, the term "frigidity" was used in psychoanalysis to cover all women who did not achieve orgasm through vaginal penetration. In reviewing the psychoanalytic theory, I will use the term frigidity, to conform to the texts.

Freud on Frigidity

In Chapter 1, I reviewed Freud's and Deutsch's theories on female development and sexuality. Focusing now on Freud's theory of frigidity in women, we see that his view of the sexual act is clearly from the point of view of the male. In 1905 he writes: "The penultimate stage of that act is once again appropriate stimulation of an erotogenic zone (the genital zone itself, in the glans penis) by the appropriate object (the mucous membrane of the vagina). . . . [The] last pleasure is the highest in intensity . . . brought about entirely by discharge" (in Young-Bruehl, p. 130). In 1927, "The vagina is . . . valued as the place of shelter for the penis; it enters into the heritage of the womb" (in Schafer 1974, p. 357).

In 1908, he spells out his views on frigidity in women:

> Anatomy has recognized the clitoris within the female pudenda as being an organ that is homologous to the penis . . . it becomes the seat of excitations which lead to its being touched, that its excitability gives the little girl's sexual activity a masculine character and that a wave of repression in the years of puberty is needed in order for this masculine sexuality to be discarded and the woman to emerge. Since the sexual function of many women is crippled, whether by their obstinate clinging on to this excitability of the clitoris so that they remain anaesthetic in intercourse, or by such excessive repression occurring that its operation is partly replaced by hysterical compensatory formations—all this seems to show that there is some truth in the infantile sexual theory that women, like men, possess a penis. [in Young-Bruehl, p. 158]

In 1905, he presents the girl's attachment to her parents as another source of frigidity:

> At the same time that these plainly incestuous phantasies are overcome and repudiated, one of the most significant, but also one of the most painful, psychical achievements of the pubertal period is completed: detachment from parental authority. . . . There are some who have never got over their parents' authority and have withdrawn their affection from them either very incompletely or not at all. They are mostly girls, who, to the delight of their parents, have persisted in all their childish love far beyond puberty. It is most instructive to find that it is precisely these girls who in their later marriage lack the capacity to give their husbands what is due to them; they make cold wives and remain sexually anaesthetic. [in Young-Bruehl, p. 142]

In 1918, Freud adds another component. He asks why in primitive societies the defloration of a virgin is a role given to another man, never to the husband, whereas in our society:

> The demand that a girl shall not bring to her marriage with a particular man any memory of sexual relations with another is, indeed, nothing other than a logical continuation of the right to exclusive possession of a woman, which forms the essence of monogamy, the extension of this monopoly to cover the past. . . . Whoever is the first to satisfy a virgin's desire for love, long and laboriously held in check, and who in doing so overcomes the resistances which have been built up in her through the influences of her milieu and education, that is the man she will take into a lasting relationship, the possibility of which will never again be open to any other man. This experience creates a state of bondage in the woman which guarantees that possession of her shall continue undisturbed and makes her able to resist new impressions and enticements from outside. [in Young-Bruehl, p. 205]

Freud refers to the term chosen by R. Krafft-Ebing in 1892, *sexual bondage,* to describe a high degree of dependence and loss of self-reliance toward a sexual partner: "This bondage can on occasion extend very far, as far as the loss of all independent will and as far as causing a person to suffer the greatest sacrifices of his own interests. . . . Some such measure of sexual bondage is, indeed, indispensable to the maintenance of civilized marriage and to holding at bay the polygamous tendencies which threaten it" (p. 206). Freud then proposes that some married women "take vengeance" against the husband for their defloration and for the state of bondage that it imposes through frigidity, which may then become "established as a neurotic inhibition or provide the foundation for the development of other neuroses" (pp. 209–210).

> We may say, then, in conclusion that defloration has not only the one, civilized consequence of binding the woman lastingly to the man; it also unleashes an archaic reaction of hostility towards him, which can assume pathological forms that are frequently enough expressed in the appearance of inhibitions in the erotic side of married life, and to which we may ascribe the fact that second marriages so often turn out better than first. The taboo of virginity, which seems so strange to us, the horror with which, among primitive peoples, the husband avoids the act of defloration, are fully justified by this hostile reaction. [p. 213]

If there were truth to Freud's theories, the decrease in the number of women who marry as virgins today would have a paradoxical result. On the one hand, there would be no hostility toward the new husband for defloration. On the other hand, neither would there be the "bondage" Freud and Krafft-Ebing propose, created by the woman's relinquishment of her virginity to her husband, with the resultant dependency that then enforces monogamy. This might contribute to the increasing number of divorces initiated by women.

In his most important work on this subject, "Femininity," written in 1932, Freud states:

> There is only one libido, which serves both the masculine and the feminine sexual functions. To it itself we cannot assign any sex; if following the conventional equation of activity and masculinity, we are inclined to describe it as masculine, we must not forget that it also covers trends with a passive aim. Nevertheless, the juxtaposition "feminine libido" is without any justification. Furthermore, it is our impression that more constraint has been applied to the libido when it is pressed into the service of the feminine function, and that—to speak teleologically—Nature takes less careful account of its [that function's] demands than in the case of masculinity. And the reason for this may lie—thinking once again teleologically—in the fact that the accomplishment of the aim of biology has been entrusted to the aggressiveness of men and has been made to some extent independent of women's consent.
>
> The sexual frigidity of women, the frequency of which appears to confirm this disregard, is a phenomenon that is still insufficiently understood. Sometimes it is psychogenic and in that case accessible to influence; but in other cases it suggests the hypothesis of its being constitutionally determined and even of there being a contributory anatomical factor. [p. 359]

Also in his essays on sexuality of 1905, Freud expresses his belief that masturbation in girls could be harmful, because they might get used to clitoral stimulation and then not be able to make the necessary switch to vaginal sensitivity, which he considered the only true mature sexuality. In 1908, he claims that women who have preserved their virginity by resorting to perverse practices and masturbation "show themselves anaesthetic to normal intercourse in marriage" (p. 179). On the other hand, the woman who refrains from masturbation is headed for a serious fate as well: "I think that the undoubted intellectual inferiority of so many women can rather be traced back to the inhibition of thought necessitated by sexual suppression" (p. 177).

However, Freud sees a similar problem for men who remain virgins until marriage, and believes men also develop diminished potency in marriage due to masturbation and other "abnormal" practices. "A marriage begun with a reduced capacity to love on both sides succumbs to the process of dissolution even more quickly than others. As a result of the man's weak potency, the woman is not satisfied, and she remains anaesthetic even in cases where her disposition to frigidity, derived from her education, could have been overcome by a powerful sexual experience" (p. 179).

Freud certainly saw the dangers of sexual repression, yet he was convinced sexual repression was necessary—another paradox, and part of his rather gloomy vision of man and womankind. Although Freud made many serious errors in his theory of female sexuality, his exposure of these problems contributed greatly to an understanding of sexuality and of woman's need for sexual satisfaction in order to avoid neurotic disturbance. Thus, he helped move the Western world away from Victorian severity and toward the years of sexual enlightenment that culminated in the sexual research of the 1950s and 1960s.

Helene Deutsch

Some controversy existed among Freud and his followers, particularly around the issues of female masturbation in latency and the awareness of and sensitivity in the vagina in prepubertal girls. As I described in Chapter 1, Helene Deutsch differed from Freud on the issue of female sexuality. She viewed women as basically masochistic; in her view, sex and reproduction in women were fundamentally linked and were primarily masochistic experiences. Frigidity was due to masochism. But since she saw masochism as normal, Deutsch believed that inorgasmic women were psychologically perfectly healthy, and that, in fact, a truly feminine woman is inorgasmic. According to Chasseguet-Smirgel (1970a), as late as 1960, Deutsch, chair of a symposium on frigidity in New York, stated: "In the vast majority of women, if they are not disturbed, the sexual act does not culminate in a sphincter-like activity of the vagina, but is brought to a happy end in a mild, slow relaxation." She says that this is the "most typical and the most feminine of female orgasms" (p. 23), confirming her belief in passive-receptivity, through which she defines her view of normality for women.

She stresses (1944) her psychological view of the problem:

> What is in question here is not at all the so frequently over stressed and even ridiculous demand made upon men by several sexologists, that they heighten the woman's erotic excitability (in the physical sense) by their dexterity. The road to the feminine woman as a sexual object leads through the psyche, and all the four fundamental factors noted above must be taken into account if her conditions are to be met. Her inhibition can be strengthened as a result of her narcissism, masochism, tie to former objects, and motherliness; and each of these four factors,

if present to an excessive degree, can become a source of frigidity. Especially in favor of the last-named component does the feminine woman often renounce orgastic gratification, without in the least suffering in her psychic health. But even if motherliness is not involved, she often tolerates her own sexual inhibition without losing her all-embracing warmth and harmony. [p. 218]

On the issue of the awareness of the vagina and the function of the clitoris she writes:

The awakening of the vagina to full sexual functioning is entirely dependent upon the man's activity; and this absence of spontaneous vaginal activity constitutes the physiologic background of feminine passivity. The competition of the clitoris, which intercepts the excitations unable to reach the vagina, and the genital trauma then create the dispositional basis of a permanent sexual inhibition, i.e., frigidity. It is this disposition acquired in childhood that is responsible for the very large number of frigid women. [p. 233]

Deutsch thus reasserts her conviction in female passivity: "Feminine love, the core of the 'feminine woman,' is naturally passive-narcissistic" (p. 190). Her view is that in the problem of female frigidity, social influences play a subsidiary role to constitutional factors of inhibition in female sexuality that have no parallel in men. Thus, the woman is at a biological disadvantage, combined with psychological inhibitions, and there seems to be no hope from her learning about sex. Deutsch's negative view of a woman's potential for orgasm is in keeping with her negativism about women's lives in general. Clearly she also suffered, like all writers in those years, from a lack of accurate anatomical information about women's sexual physiology, which led her to confuse myths and biases with scientific knowledge.

FEMALE FRIGIDITY AND PSYCHOANALYTIC ADVICE BOOKS

Some experts of the pre-Masters and Johnson period wrote advice books for women to help them overcome "frigidity." Marie N. Robinson, a psychiatrist and psychoanalyst, wrote *The Power of Sexual Surrender,* which appeared in 1959. She writes in her preface:

I believe that the problem of sexual frigidity in women is one of the gravest problems of our times. Over 40 per cent of married women suffer from it in one or another of its degrees or forms. And their suffering, emotionally and physically, is very real indeed.

Those who are most closely related to the frigid woman—husband and children—suffer too. This is so because frigidity is an expression of neurosis, a disturbance of the unconscious life of the individual destructive to personal relationships. No matter how much she may consciously wish to, the frigid woman cannot protect her loved ones from the effects of her problem. Thus frigidity constitutes a major danger of the stability of marriage and to the health and happiness of every member of the family. [p. v]

This is a total reversal of Deutsch's theory of just fifteen years earlier that there was no relationship between frigidity in women and mental ill health, that in fact it was perfectly normal for women to be inorgasmic, and that the best mothers often were inorgasmic. What was Robinson seeing in her patients that Deutsch was missing in hers? Or was it pure personal bias? Perhaps Robinson found orgasms very important to her own mental health, and Deutsch did not.

Robinson's view of the mature woman is one in whom, as prescribed by Freud, clitoral excitement has diminished, giving way to the vagina as the primary source of the greatest sexual pleasure. She modifies this somewhat: "However, many women who become fully mature sexually maintain much of the original sexual responsiveness of the clitoris" (p. 21). Yet a clitoral orgasm would not be a "full orgasm," the kind of orgasm she must have to be "mature," that "starts deep within her vagina" (p. 33).

Careers are quite secondary for the mature woman:

Our mature woman cannot get terribly excited about the subject. . . . She may be a career woman herself. . . . But now, happily married and with children . . . she can't feel that it's of central importance. . . . Any drive she had after high school or college to go far in it is sacrificed, if necessary, to her love-making and home-making instincts. [p. 37]

What are we to think of Robinson, then? Is she not a mature woman because she is pursuing her career? Maybe she is unmarried and pursuing only a career. Or perhaps she is unhappily married. This question goes back to the dreadful time when women were led to believe they had to choose between career and family. The mature woman who gives up her career to "embrace her true destiny" is Dr. Robinson's ideal (p. 40). That poor creature, the "clitoridal woman," is suffering from a form of frigidity. Only orgasms through penal penetration qualify her for maturity. With absolute certainty, Robinson has judged and categorized all women according to her views as if they are scientific fact. Feminists are the enemy of true femininity because "as we know, in sexual intercourse, as in life, man is the actor, woman the passive one, the receiver, the acted upon. [She gives herself] up in this passive manner to another human being" (p. 157).

From here, Robinson leads naturally into her basic thesis of sex as surrender, which involves giving up clitoral gratification and taking the path towards womanhood. I wonder how she felt when she read the results of Masters and Johnson's research, that there is only one orgasm and it is located in the clitoris? Did she feel foolish? Did she offer her patients an apology?

Women would have to wait for the American sex researchers to rescue them from such pronouncements and provide the first real factual information on both the nature of the female orgasm and the sources of its dysfunction. Then, psychoanalysts could write sensible articles, like that of Richard C. Robertiello (1970). Robertiello argues that there is only one orgasm physiologically, but not psychologically. Women, he says, report a subjective difference in orgasms that accompany intercourse: the clitoral is short and intense; the vaginal rises more slowly, does not reach such a sharp peak, and lasts much longer, giving a deeper and fuller feeling of satisfaction.

> The vaginal one is usually preferred although there is considerable satisfaction in the clitoral orgasm as well. . . . So though having orgasms might certainly be desirable it should not be equated either with the level of mental health or the degree of pleasure and satisfaction in sex. That is based on many complex personal and emotional variables. [pp. 308–309]

Robertiello recommends sexual experimentation and a variety of sexual experiences for women before marriage, so that they might learn what sort of satisfaction is available for them and which specific partner can best provide it. Schafer (1974) offers a critique of the Freudian view:

> There is a Victorian precept that in sexual relations "a lady doesn't move." The modern psychoanalyst has to recognize this role, not as passivity, but as a desperate form of activity—a drastic inhibition required to play this inactivated part. The inhibiting may be carried out unconsciously and supplemented by conscious aversion. . . . Yet, although Freud the clinician was ever alert to the many forms unconscious activity takes in the lives of women, Freud the theoretician . . . named this inhibition passivity and made it the crux of femininity. [p. 358]

SEXUAL BEHAVIOR IN THE HUMAN FEMALE—ALFRED KINSEY

The new woman has a freedom for open premarital sex that has taken her into a new realm of sexual experience. Entry into a teen-age girl's bedroom exposes one to giant posters of the current male sex symbols in very sexual poses, bare chested with belts undone and tight jeans unbuttoned. Going into the dressing room of a small women's clothing shop one might find oneself surrounded with photos of male playmates in suggestive poses. *Playgirl* magazine was the counter to *Playboy,* with a monthly centerfold. This does not mean, according to Epp (1991), that all young women are sexually sophisticated. They are often inhibited in being able to express their needs and desires and may still take the traditional passive role.

The cliché "times have changed" is certainly true. Regarding women born before 1940, most Americans had the impression that they married as virgins and never had sex with anyone other than their husbands, or in any other than the "missionary" position. In the post-pill, pre-AIDS paradise of 1960 to 1985, affairs before marriage, during marriage, and after divorce amounted to the likelihood of numerous sexual relationships, with the greatest risk being herpes, a serious but nonfatal consequence. "Reputation" was no longer a great concern, nor the threat of a woman's future being ruined by the judgment that she was "loose." Judged by European standards, Americans had been notoriously puritanical about sex.

When, in 1948, Alfred Kinsey and colleagues published *Sexual Behavior in the Human Male,* involving 7,000 interviews, the revelation that 90 percent of the men interviewed had masturbated and that at least one-third of them had had an orgasm with another male shocked the country. When their study on female sexuality, *Sexual Behavior in the Human Female,* appeared in 1953, it revealed that half of the 6,000 women surveyed admitted they were not virgins when they married; 24 percent said they had had extramarital affairs; 43 percent had performed fellatio; more than half had masturbated; and 13 percent had engaged in sexual relations with other women. The lid was off, and the awareness of a range of sexual activity by women was so shocking as to create a furor from which neither Kinsey nor his Institute could recover. The idea that women liked sex was considered absolutely subversive. The Chicago *Tribune* called Kinsey "a menace to society," little more than a pornographer. He was attacked by religious groups and his books were banned in some communities. According to Paul Gebhard, Kinsey's successor at the Kinsey Institute,

> The House Un-American Activities Committee and Joe McCarthy felt that large funding agencies like Guggenheim, Carnegie and Rockefeller

were supporting so-called "pink" professors, "com-symps" who were too liberal. And a special committee set up in Congress to investigate these agencies came to Rockefeller (the major source of the Institute's funding) and used the Kinsey Institute as a club to beat the foundation. As proof, it used the volume on female sexuality, saying it was an insult to American womanhood, that it would destroy the nuclear family, weaken American morality and make it easier for a communist take-over. [Robins 1991, p. 13]

The Kinsey Institute lost its funding in 1954. Since Kinsey's death in 1956 at the age of 62, it has continued to function modestly at Indiana University, the victim of politics and the fact that sex research is not as fashionable as it was in the 1950s and 1960s. According to Robins, "many in the field believe that Alfred Kinsey was hounded to his death for his work" (p. 12).

The problem with the Kinsey report's statistics is that we have no way of knowing, in individual cases, whether the premarital sex was a result of pressure from the male, or was engaged in freely, by the choice of the woman. Some women find it hard to know the difference. Remember, premarital in those years most likely meant ages 15 to 22, when women are most vulnerable to pressure. On the other hand, the fear of pregnancy, the shame of pregnancy before marriage, and the fear of being found out may have stopped some girls who truly wanted to try sex. I can remember a girl in my high school who got pregnant and was "sent away" to a home for unwed mothers. Her life was ruined, a warning to the rest of us.

Kinsey's study of orgasm in women produced important statistics. Prior to the Kinsey research there had been a total neglect of the topic after the work of Van de Velde (1930). Van de Velde had reported that a failure to have orgasm had harmful effects on women, due to unrelieved tension. Wilhelm Reich (1942) believed that failure to achieve orgasm was responsible for somatic symptoms and psychological disturbances, but his work was not considered reliable. One difficulty in comparing statistics on this topic is the different ways the dysfunction can be defined. At one end of the scale are women who have never experienced any orgasm, and this figure seems to regularly be reported at 10 percent. Women in the next group occasionally reach orgasm; in Kinsey's work this group numbered 75 percent after one year of marriage, increasing to 83 percent after five years of marriage and to 89 percent by twenty years of marriage. Another way to break down the figures is that used by Morton Hunt (1974). Hunt reported that in 1972, 53 percent of women reached orgasm 90–100 percent of the time, compared to the period from 1938 to 1949, when 45 percent did. In 1972, 30 percent of single women reported being consistently orgasmic with a partner, while 15 percent never had an orgasm. Kinsey, who studied 5,940 women in the 1940s, and Hunt, who studied 1,044 women in the early 1970s, both reported that only half of all married women in the United States experience orgasm with any consistency, leading Hunt to conclude that in spite of the sexual revolution, there had not been much progress for women in orgasmic responsivity in the twenty-odd years between the two surveys.

A complication of these statistics is that they do not tell us whether the orgasm includes clitoral stimulation before, during, or after vaginal penetration, an issue that continues to be of significance to some women who are concerned if they do not climax in intercourse. Another way to analyze statistics on orgasm is to break them down by groups who reach orgasm through masturbation, through manual or oral stimulation by a partner, through clitoral stimulation followed by intercourse, through intercourse combined with clitoral stimulation, and through vaginal intercourse alone. Several surveys indicate that, of the 90 percent of women who are orgasmic, about 50 percent or fewer can reach orgasm during intercourse, but that 50–75 percent of orgasmic women do not reach orgasm from intercourse alone.

Seymour Fisher, in his analysis (1973) of Kinsey's results, finds the Kinsey figures show poor results on the effect of "practice" on orgasmic consistency. In the span between one year and twenty years of marriage, there is only a 14 percent decrease in the number of women who never attain orgasm. From another perspective, there were only 8 percent more women who attained orgasm in "nearly all" of their coitus after twenty years of marriage than after one year (p. 406).

One difference between men and women is that men are fully aware of sexual arousal, which their bodies make obvious to them, whereas women's anatomy does not give them a clear physical sign, and they may be quite unaware of sexual arousal. Girls are taught to restrict knowledge of their genitals and their sexual response; and they have been given the message that it is desirable to be sexually responsive with one's partner, but not to be interested in sex for self-gratification. According to Patricia Morokoff of the University of Rhode Island (Goleman 1988) one way out of this double bind is physiological response without awareness of arousal. In a study, women reported no awareness of sexual arousal, although measurements of vaginal temperature showed that they were responding physiologically to erotic stories, erotic films, and sex fantasies. Ignorance about female sexuality was profound in the 1950s, and acknowledgment or awareness of the female orgasm or female sexual arousal was limited. Some college women were not even sure about how they could get pregnant, and worried about contact with sperm without intercourse. I can remember one patient in the 1960s who was about 28 and had had a number of sexual partners. She asked me one day what could be the source of the discharge she often found in her underpants, not recognizing that it was due to sexual arousal.

HUMAN SEXUAL RESPONSE—WILLIAM MASTERS AND VIRGINIA JOHNSON

Two aspects of the sexual liberation movement in the '70s were the development of "human sexuality" as a field of specialization, and the encouragement of women to discover their potential for orgasm through masturbation and with partners in extended foreplay, as illustrated by the Masters and Johnson experiments. Their books, *Human Sexual Response* (1966) and *Human Sexual Inadequacy* (1970), introduced major changes in our knowledge of the female orgasm, including the rejection of the psychoanalytic idea of two orgasms. Masters and Johnson's research showed there was only one source of the orgasm, and that was in the clitoris. In the meantime, there was a rush to publish books on female sexuality in the period following publication of the Kinsey report, and the topic became one of public interest and open discussion. However, a dramatic change in the level of education and discussion did not necessarily translate into a comparable change in orgasmic rates. Here are a few of the books published in the 1960s and 1970s:

1962. Helen Gurley Brown, *Sex and the Single Girl*

1964. Phyllis and Eberhard Kronhausen, *The Sexually Responsive Woman*

1965. Alexander Lowen, *Love and Orgasm*

1966. Frank Caprio, *The Sexually Adequate Female*

1966. Ruth and Edward Brecher, eds., *An Analysis of Human Sexual Response*

1969. David Reuben, *Everything You Always Wanted to Know About Sex But Were Afraid to Ask*

1971. Rachel Copeland, *The Sexually Fulfilled Woman*

1972. Mary Jane Sherfy, *The Nature and Evolution of Female Sexuality*

1973. Seymour Fisher, *The Female Orgasm*

1974. Helen Singer Kaplan, *The New Sex Therapy*

1974. Morton Hunt, *Sexual Behavior in the 1970's*

1975. G. Kline-Gruber, *Woman's Orgasm: Guide to Sexual Satisfaction*

1976. Shere Hite, *The Hite Report*

1976. Lonnie Barbach, *For Yourself: The Fulfillment of Female Sexuality*

1976. Rosemarie Santini, *The Secret Fire: A New View of Women and Passion*

1977. Alex Comfort, *The Joy of Sex*

These books vary in theory and approach, from the psychological approach of David Reuben, whose popular book proposes psychotherapy as the only treatment for orgasmic problems (in Reuben's view a psychiatric condition and symptomatic of deeper emotional dysfunction), to the educational approach of Masters and Johnson and Lonnie Barbach. The experts grapple with the questions of whether orgasm is necessary to sexual satisfaction and marital happiness in women, whether failure to reach orgasm is related to neurotic symptoms, and whether clitoral stimulation is a more significant component of the orgasm than vaginal stimulation. Regarding this last point, many believe the two are complementary.

Ruth Herschberger (1970) claims a central and primary role for the clitoris, with the vagina secondary. As early as 1953, Albert Ellis was a proponent of the idea that a clitoral orgasm is all that is necessary and that the "vaginal orgasm" is a myth.

Erwin J. Haeberle, in his 1982 book *The Sex Atlas,* reviews the publications on the subject and concludes that the consensus is that psychological and cultural conditioning, rather than biological differences, are responsible for women's inorgasmic problems, and that "psychological inhibitions" characterize the inorgasmic woman. He concludes that the most important reason for the absence of orgasm is the negative attitude toward sexual pleasure that women in our society internalize early in their lives. Haeberle lists the following causes for such an attitude; religious views, dislike of the partner, the partner is inadequate, or the woman has homosexual tendencies or simply is not interested in sex.

The psychological factors fall into three categories: 1) fear and anxiety, 2) hostility and aggression, and 3) conflict and guilt. These factors are further elaborated into six areas:

1. Fear of loss of ego-control or self-identity
2. Parental attachments and incestuous fixations

3. Envy of men, masculine identification, rejection of femininity

4. Specific conditioning against sexuality (often by mother)

5. Situational or temporary

6. Husband is inadequate or inhibited.

Yet Masters and Johnson's approach, focusing on technique, produced some impressive results. Their step-by-step formula for treating inorgasmic women is through couple therapy by male and female co-therapists, combined with daily homework sessions as follows:

1. Just touching and stroking each other's bodies for a few days with no effort to achieve orgasm, or touching of genitals.

2. Stroking, fondling of genitals and breasts with no striving for orgasm.

3. Coitus in the female superior position, just for pleasure and stimulation.

4. Coitus in the side by side position.

Using this approach, Masters and Johnson claim to have helped 80 percent of the women they treated.

The weakness in this approach is that it leaves out women who want help but are not married or coupled. Lonnie Barbach (1976), a psychologist and sex therapist at the University of California Medical Center in San Francisco, designed a five-week program of group treatment for preorgasmic women that included group discussions twice a week and daily homework of prescribed exercises for masturbation. The program's goal was to start by achieving orgasm through masturbation, and, when that was successful, to include a partner in the homework. The group discussion included provision of physiological information about anatomy and sexuality, and there was also individual instruction. The women in the program had a 93 percent success rate with masturbation by the end of the five weeks. A three month follow-up showed a 50 percent orgasmic success rate with partners, and an eight month follow-up showed a higher rate. Of seventeen women followed, twelve were consistently orgasmic, and three were orgasmic 25 percent of the time. The women also had general feelings of improved self-worth and confidence. They took more responsibility for communicating to their partners, and took more initiative. This assertiveness spread to other areas of their lives as well.

Leslie Farber—"I'm Sorry Dear"

Not surprisingly, the Masters and Johnson work produced some critical reactions. One noteworthy example is an essay by Leslie H. Farber, a psychoanalyst with the Washington School of Psychiatry, and an existentialist. The essay, "I'm Sorry, Dear" (1966), originally appeared in *Commentary* magazine in November 1964 and was much talked about at the time. The title refers to the apology made by a husband to his wife when the wife does not reach orgasm. Farber's beautifully written piece is an attack on the whole concept of sex research in the laboratory. Farber had become convinced that sex had "lost its viability as a human experience" (p. 294). He is both saddened by and contemptuous of the Masters and Johnson work; and is troubled by the nature of the relationship between the researchers and the subjects, which he compares unfavorably to the relationship between the analyst and the patient: the analyst is a listener, as opposed to the sex researcher, who merely watches. Farber asks, "Where did the sexologists find it [the female orgasm]? Did they discover it or invent it or both?" (p. 310). Referring to what he idealizes as the pre-female-orgasm days, he appears to believe a woman really had it better in the good old days.

> Her orgasm had not yet been abstracted and isolated from the totality of her pleasures and enshrined as a mean and measure of her erotic life. She was content with the mystery and variety of her difference from man, and in fact would not have had it otherwise. . . . So, with the abstraction, objectification and idealization of the female orgasm we have come to the last and perhaps most important clause of the contract that binds our lovers to their laboratory home, there to will the perfection on earth that cannot be willed, there to suffer the pathos that follows all such strivings toward heaven on earth. [pp. 310–311]

Who is this woman whom Farber idealizes, this all-accepting woman who has no desire for her own sexual satisfaction? She sounds very much like the Freudian woman, the Deutsch woman, for whom, we are to believe, ignorance was bliss. The poor creature was better off just pleasing her husband.

   Farber is deeply troubled by the methods of the laboratory experimenters, and that is understandable. But he carries it too far when he declares we are all better off never asking any questions or seeking the truth—hardly an admirable position for a psychoanalyst. Farber doesn't tell us whence his conclusions are drawn. Is it from his female patients? From his wife? What is his evidence that "she" is "content," and by what standard does he judge her contentment? Who has he been listening to? And since when do scientists elevate "mystery"? Or perhaps Farber is antiscientific when it comes to women, preferring to keep things as they were.

THE WOMAN'S RELATIONSHIP WITH HER FATHER—
SEYMOUR FISHER

The outstanding writer on women's orgasm is Seymour Fisher, whose book *The Female Orgasm* (1973) is the most comprehensive review of the research on this topic; it also includes his own research and conclusions. Fisher seeks to understand the psychological aspects of the various kinds of sexual behavior studied by Kinsey and by Masters and Johnson—that is, how a woman's personality influences her sexual responsiveness, as well as her experiences with menstruation and pregnancy.

Fisher acknowledges that his own sample is limited, but he believes his results are generalizable to middle-class women in the United States. His research group consisted of almost 300 married women between the ages of 21 and 45, living in the university community in Syracuse, New York, who had at least a high school education, were married primarily to students, had volunteered to be subjects, and were willing to have measuring devices attached to and even inserted into their bodies. They were primarily white and Protestant. About 39 percent reported that they orgasmed always or nearly always during intercourse, but that included clitoral stimulation by hand. Only 20 percent said they never required a final push to orgasm from manual stimulation.

Fisher introduces his book by noting that, in his analysis of previous studies, "it became evident that there are many widely accepted ideas about the nature of feminine sexuality that are erroneous. These erroneous ideas exist not only in the popular mind but also in the theories and procedures of professional disciplines" (p. 4). He later specifically holds psychoanalysis responsible for errors: "One can, for example, only lament the number of women in psychoanalytic treatment who have been given to understand that they cannot join the ranks of the 'normal' until they learn to attain orgasm primarily through vaginal stimulation" (p. 390).

The majority of the women in Fisher's study regarded clitoral stimulation as contributing more than vaginal stimulation to their sexual arousal. No support could be found for the psychoanalytic theory that clitorally oriented women are more immature or psychologically disturbed than vaginally oriented women. There was some evidence that the former were less anxious than the latter, and that the vaginally oriented women experienced their bodies as more alienated and depersonalized than did the clitorally oriented women. Fisher's findings also contradicted Kinsey's and Masters and Johnson's in that his subjects distinguished between two kinds of orgasm: that based upon direct clitoral manipulation, versus that primarily induced by direct penile intromission, with the clitoral type producing a greater "ecstatic" feeling. Fisher concludes that the female orgasm is probably a blend of vaginal and clitoral elements that cannot be clearly distinguished.

Another erroneous idea of psychoanalysis, according to Fisher, is that the average woman perceives her body as sexually inferior to that of a man, and consequently finds it a source of discomfort and anxiety.

> The scientific findings overwhelmingly contradict this concept. . . .
> One can, on the contrary, make out a good case for the assertion that
> men are more insecure and anxious about their bodies than are
> women. . . . She not only feels less body threat but can more clearly see
> a relationship between her body and her primary life roles. [p. 392]

A review of Fisher's book allows one to conclude that orgasmic capacity in women is *not* related to the following factors:

1. The mental health of the woman. No evidence could be found that women with neurotic or even schizophrenic symptomatology are any less orgasmic than normal women. Thus, her sexual responsiveness cannot be used to classify her as a psychologically adequate or inadequate person.
2. Femininity. No relationship to appearance, dress, makeup.
3. Being a friendly or a hostile person.
4. Her level of anger or her ability to cope with anger.
5. Her degree of aggressiveness or dominance.
6. Whether she is active and achievement oriented versus passive and dependent.
7. Being sociable, helpful and cheerful.
8. Being free, impulsive, emotional, adventurous, liking excitement.
9. Being conventional versus unconventional.
10. Being religious and church-going.
11. Her beliefs about sexual freedom.
12. Whether her parents were permissive and liberal or puritanical.
13. Whether she is extroverted or introverted.
14. Whether she is a smoker or a drinker.
15. Her degree of guilt.
16. Her degree of narcissism.
17. The manner in which she received her early sex education; from books, her mother, friends, or formal class.
18. The characteristics of her sex partner.
19. Her level of male–female competitiveness. No relation to "penis envy."

20. The amount and character of her sexual experience.
21. Her degree of menstrual discomfort.
22. Incidents of sexual trauma such as childhood rape, traumatic first intercourse, or abortion.
23. Her dating history and early sexual experiences.

Only four factors correlated positively with low orgasmic response:

1. Low level of education.
2. Low social class. Both points 1 and 2 lower sense of trust in stability of the world.
3. Low self-esteem and lack of optimism. This may relate to level of education and class, as well as point 4 below.
4. Her concern about the lack of dependability of love objects, her anxiety about "object loss," especially the dependability of her father. Actual loss of the father through death or separation in childhood, or his psychological absence through lack of caring.

Fisher speculates that the class and education factors may actually be a reflection of the dependability of the father, and since the third factor may also relate to the reliability of the father, point 4 seems to be the primary and perhaps the only significant factor corresponding directly with orgasmic success. It therefore seems important to focus on its meaning.

As indicated above, Fisher's studies found that the greater a woman's difficulty in reaching orgasm, the more likely she is to be concerned about the lack of dependability of love objects. She is concerned about how transitory relationships are and how easily loved ones can be lost, as revealed in the fantasies produced in response to inkblot and pictorial stimuli. Yet she has probably developed adequate defenses to cope with such anxiety and to "keep its influence from intruding significantly into most situations." Only in specialized contexts, such as in sexual relations, does the anxiety about object loss affect her functioning (p. 281). The example of Tammy at the beginning of this chapter confirms Fisher's research results.

A woman's attitudes toward her father are more related to her sexual responsiveness than are her attitudes toward her mother. Fisher constructs a model conceptualizing the impact of this fear of object loss on the orgasm process.

> Sexual excitement, by diminishing a woman's sensory awareness of the outer world, creates in her a feeling that objects "out there" are

"fading" and less real; this, in turn, elicits exaggerated concern about object loss in those who already feel that objects are undependable. The perceptual fading process set off by sexual excitement presumably alarms the woman who is doubtful about object stability, and this reaction in turn prevents sexual arousal from continuing to build up to orgasmic levels. [p. 7]

Fried (1960) proposes a similar theory of the significance of the fear of loss of control. Fisher summarizes this theory as follows:

The intensity of sexual passion is determined partly, though not altogether, by the individual's capacity for enduring and enjoying regressive processes. Nearly all acquisitions the ego has made are temporarily and partially given up. . . . Certain ego defenses which have been built up and used since childhood are shed and so the organism is in a rather vulnerable position. . . . If the regressive processes are experienced as too pronounced, the temporarily dissolved ego functions, defenses and boundaries are resurrected. . . . The individual man and woman, sensing that the ego, which is usually in the driver's seat, is about to dissolve, even though only partially, anticipates a permanent loss of ego, or, to put it differently, insanity. [p. 58]

Research findings do show that a woman's early interactions with her father are positively correlated with orgasm consistency. The child has experiences with her father in which she learns how interested he is in her as a person and how much energy he is willing to expend in guiding her and helping her to structure her life. Even if she resents her father's authoritarianism and intrusiveness, she feels that he is *dependably* invested in her. Fisher is especially disturbed by the fact that later sexual experiences with men in dating do not seem to affect a woman's orgasm potential.

One is reluctant to accept the message that a girl's history of sexual experience and her apparent capability of attracting and pleasing males count for nought in her later ability to achieve orgasm during regular intercourse. The crucial question must then be asked whether sexual practice does materially affect orgasm consistency. This is the pivot on which wavers the decision about how modifiable orgasm capacity is once a girl's basic socialization experiences have occurred. [p. 406]

Fisher is also troubled by the lack of correlation between a woman's orgasmic potential and her relationship with her mother.

It remains a mystery why the mother's attitudes have not been implicated. . . . Despite an earlier attempt to cope with this puzzle by suggesting that it is, after all, logical that a mode of response to a current male love object should be particularly linked to experiences with the original prime male love object (father), it still seems strange that feelings about the original female model (mother) should not also be implicated. Of course, the present studies have dealt only with a woman's *recall* of her mother's qualities and it is possible that, if more direct study of the mothers themselves had been possible some significant correlations . . . would have been obtained. One can also speculate that the difficulty in detecting the influence of the mother may stem from the fact that those of her attributes that are important involve not so much specific traits or qualities as her attitude toward her husband. Illustratively, if the mother relates to the father in a way that suggests that the mother thinks the father to be a dependable person and that his love can be counted upon, this might convey to her daughter the message that not only her father but also men in general can be taken as dependable love objects. [pp. 407–408]

Returning to his earlier model of how an unreliable father may affect orgasmic capacity, Fisher expands his thesis:

The writer earlier conjectured that if a woman has preexisting doubts about the dependability of love objects the process of becoming sexually excited is disturbing to her not only because it results in a less articulated perceptual "hold" on objects in general, but also because, while in this less articulate condition she has to "trust" the behavior of a man who, by means of his stimulating behavior, exerts control over her state of consciousness and the clarity of her object relations. Presumably, if she finds such conditions too threatening she will develop anxiety that inhibits the buildup of sexual excitement and blocks orgasm. It would be . . . accurate to characterize her concern as a fear of finding herself completely alone (without the support of a man who really cares). If so, one could expect that orgasm would be facilitated by any conditions that increase a woman's feeling that the man with whom she is having sexual intercourse can be counted on to be loyal and to maintain steadfast interest in her. [pp. 408–409]

He then proposes that women could be expected to improve their orgasmic potential under certain conditions, such as a long-term marriage with a reliable husband, and states that it should be possible to test these propositions. This is where Fisher fails to appreciate the profound nature of his own findings, and, as indicated above, has difficulty even accepting them. He has already correctly pointed out how small an improvement occurred after even five, ten, or twenty years of marriage in the Kinsey study. Psychoanalysis had been wrong about many things in relation to female sexuality; but Fisher's finding of the singular importance of the girl's sense of trust in her father is absolutely consistent with psychoanalytic theory, which stresses the importance of early family relationships for a later capacity for trust. The basic sense of trust, developed first in relation to the mother, and soon afterward in relation to the father, determines—as his findings show—a woman's capacity for orgasm with a male partner, thus confirming the basic theory of how internalizations of parental figures determine the later capacity to trust emotionally significant figures, especially when dependency is involved.

Fisher's hope for a correction of a negative experience with the father through a relationship with a dependable husband indicates his failure to understand the processes through which the unconscious influences all later attitudes. I would say that only through psychotherapy, plus later experience with more dependable men, can there be any significant change, because a woman's unconscious will not allow her to experience these male figures as dependable, and in any case most often will lead her to choose men who are undependable like her father (and sometimes like her mother). In Fisher's view, external reality can change internal reality, as if these fears were subject to rational thinking. Finding a caring and reliable man *can* be helpful, but only in addition to a lot of work involving reconstruction of the repressed components of the early reality, and insight into how old experiences distort current perceptions. The transference relationship in psychotherapy is the ideal place for this material to be revealed, elaborated, and understood. Even if there were insight, the level of anxiety at the point of increased sexual excitement that Fisher so sensitively describes would still be very difficult to overcome and control. Alcohol and drugs do not enhance this process for inorgasmic women. They may allow a woman to be more receptive to intercourse, but not more orgasmic.

Additionally, the danger involved in trusting a man in a dependent relationship can have the reverse effect on orgasmic capacity. The woman may be more likely to be orgasmic in a casual relationship, where trust is not really an issue, than in an emotionally meaningful relationship where she fears rejection. I know of women who can be orgasmic with men but cannot trust a man enough to live with one or marry one. It may be that, in these cases, the fear of intimacy is largely determined by having had a disturbed mother, whereas the father was more caring and dependable. Fisher studied only married women.

There are two other areas where Fisher's findings are weakened by his not focusing on what I believe are important factors. One is the relationship with siblings. Fisher never includes the possibility that a brother, or perhaps even a close boy cousin or childhood friend, might be influential, and I would be curious on this point. For example, an older brother who sexually molested his little sister might create a sense of unreliability as well as fear toward men, which could affect orgasmic capacity. I also wonder at Fisher's concept of sexual trauma, which seems limited. He includes under sexual trauma events such as menstruation, first intercourse, and abortion. Some of the research he reviews includes rape and forceful seduction. But, as we now know, a woman could only answer questions on such events if she had a conscious memory of them; and for many women the most traumatic sexual assaults are repressed. A powerful unconscious sense of guilt and shame in relation to sexual molestation may, in my view, affect a woman's sexual responsiveness without her being able to answer questions about it. Women who have been sexually molested do report sexual difficulties that they relate to the molestation. Fisher tells of one case, reported in the literature, in which a woman was finally able to reach orgasm, but only when she was on top of her husband, because in the reverse, she was always reminded of her father's forced intercourse with her.

Epp (1984) attempted to find a correlation between orgasmic frequency and reliability and assertiveness or unassertiveness in women. Her sample included 100 well-educated, professional women, of whom fifty scored as assertive and fifty as unassertive. In keeping with Fisher's results, assertiveness was not significantly associated with orgasmic frequency and reliability, and it was significantly associated with willingness to take responsibility for changing a nonorgasmic partner-sex pattern to an orgasmic one. Thus, the psychological factor of father relatedness is the best indicator of orgasmic potential; but a factor such as assertiveness might be instrumental in improving a woman's orgasmic potential if it leads her to seek help and make relationship changes. It is interesting to note that, although Fisher's focus is psychological, he does include some of the cultural factors that Chodorow and Gilligan have described. He notes that a fear of loss of love is an anxiety particularly characteristic of women and that several studies show women to be especially sensitive to potential separation from those with whom they have intimate relationships.

We might see here a connection between the significance of the father in orgasmic potential and the earlier connection of the girl to her mother, in which the extended dependency resulting from a failure to separate sufficiently from the mother may be transferred to a heightened sensitivity to rejection by the father.

The Hite report (1976) uses Fisher's research findings and quotes Fisher in a strongly cultural statement from his epilogue:

The psychological factors—for example, fear of object loss—which my work suggests may interfere with orgasm attainment in many women may exemplify at another level the general cultural feeling transmitted to woman that her place is uncertain and that she survives only because the male protects her. The apparent importance of fear of object loss in inhibiting orgasm can probably be traced to the fact that the little girl gets innumerable messages which tell her that the female cannot survive alone and is likely to get into serious trouble if she is not supported by a strong and capable male. It does not seem too radical to predict that when women are able to grow up in a culture in which they are less pressured to obedience by threats of potential desertion, the so-called orgasm problem will fade away. [p. 436]

MASTURBATION

The current attitude toward masturbation is very liberal, with sex counselors recommending masturbation as the primary means for a woman to establish knowledge of her body and what it takes to bring her to orgasm. But this thinking is relatively new, and old attitudes are slow to die. In one study of college-age women, 40 percent had never masturbated. Of those women who answered the questionnaire for the Hite report, 82 percent had masturbated and 95 percent could reach orgasm easily and regularly (Hite 1976, p. 59).

The issue of the relationship between masturbation and orgasmic success is one place where psychoanalysis and sexology completely diverge. Freud and Deutsch believed that clitoral masturbation was immature and would prevent the transition to the mature erogenous zone, the vagina. The girl had to relinquish masturbation in order to make this transition. In contrast, sex therapists encourage masturbation to help preorgasmic women become familiar with their genitalia; this includes looking at their genitalia in a mirror and learning to stimulate themselves in a way that results in orgasm. After orgasm has been reached in masturbation, the next step is to attempt it with a partner, through teaching the partner to manually stimulate the woman to orgasm. When this is accomplished, the goal becomes achievement of orgasm in intercourse, with stimulation of the clitoris. Of course, much of the difference between the two views rests on the finding of Masters and Johnson that all orgasm in centered in the clitoris, with the more recent modification that most women reach orgasm with a combination of vaginal and clitoral stimulation.

It is important to appreciate that there can be a difference between being orgasmic in intercourse, and feeling security and contentment in an intimate relationship with a man. There are women who can be secure and content in marriage because their dependency needs are met—a result of transferring an immature tie to their mothers to an immature dependency on their husbands. These women may be sexually inhibited and not orgasmic. On the other hand, there are women who have great difficulty handling the intimacy of a close relationship with a man, because of

anxiety-creating boundary problems resulting from a disturbed relationship with their mothers, and yet are orgasmically successful with men
because of having had reliable fathers. This is why good psychotherapy
(even with a woman analyst) can result in improved relationships with
men. Fisher's findings on masturbation are of interest because they show
the more powerful influence of the mother on this activity, and they are
compatible with the work of Torok (1970), which I reviewed in Chapter 3.
Torok views penis envy as a symbolic result of the mother's prohibition of
the girl's masturbation. The girl lets herself be deprived of her sexual
desire—of orgasm and accompanying sexual fantasies—because she needs
her mother's love. The result is that the girl remains dependant on her
mother, an appendage of her, reliant on her as the only source of pleasure.
This leads to an unfulfilled body image and an inability to develop a sexual
union with a male with full orgastic pleasure. The girl envys the boy and his
penis because she imagines he has the freedom for sexual pleasure that her
mother has denied to her. Torok reports that when a woman patient is
freed to masturbate through therapy, this is always accompanied by a
feeling of power. However, Torok does not take into account the significance of the dependability of the father.

In Fisher's study, the more a woman portrayed her mother as
moralistic, the less was her masturbation frequency and the less satisfaction
she received from it. However, masturbation was unrelated to how
moralistic her father was considered to be. This is the first instance in
which the mother's attitude correlated with some aspect of the woman's
sexual functioning.

Masturbation frequency was found to be positively correlated with a
mother described as behaving in a neglecting, egocentric, distant, hostile,
and nonloving fashion. In short, the more a woman depicted her mother as
unfriendly and neglectful, the more she masturbated. However, masturbation was not more frequent or more satisfying in those who perceived their
fathers as negative and unloving.

Thus, masturbation is a sexual act that has great pregenital significance relating to the nurturing bond with the mother, the mother's
capacity to allow her daughter to separate and individuate, and the
daughter's freedom to express autonomy from the mother. The woman
described by Torok, who gives up the autonomous pleasures of masturbation in order to hold on to the mother's love, is less likely to be able to
make a positive, autonomous connection to a male lover because of this
bond to her mother. Paradoxically, the girl who is rejected by her mother
may be in a better position to make a sexually gratifying connection to a
man, because her mother's neglect and hostility means there is no reason to
sacrifice her self-pleasuring for her mother's love. We can now see how, if
her father was caring and attentive, a rather disturbed woman could in

fact—because of her pathologically negative relationship with her mother—be in a good position to be orgasmic with a man. I would, however, expect that the neglect and hostility of the mother would nevertheless interfere with the sense of security and self-confidence necessary for a healthy marriage; this is born out by many of my patients, such as Rachel and Sandra, whose cases I discuss below. A possible pattern is the hostile mother; the masturbating daughter, whose masturbation brings her temporary autonomy; the mother discovering the masturbation and beating the daughter; which brings about a reuniting with the mother through a sado-masochistic connection around the daughter's sexuality. Such a pattern is frequently translated into masochistic relations with men or women in adulthood.

Clinical Examples

Let us begin with several examples of women patients who are orgasmic.

Mrs. R., a woman in conflict about having a baby, was unhappy as a child because of her parents' divorce. She lived with her mother, and so we could say she experienced separation from her father, but in fact she saw her father regularly every Saturday, talked to him on the phone, and always felt very welcome in his home even after his remarriage. She was always sure of her father's love and attention, and never had a problem with orgasm.

Sandra was a woman with a narcissistic mother who was neglectful and cruel. Yet Sandra loved her father, was close to him and proud of him, and felt sure of his love and devotion to her. Sandra had problems with intimacy in her relationships with men, based on her disturbed relationship with her mother, which had left her anxious, masochistic, and somewhat paranoid. However, she was fully orgasmic with men.

Rachel was a severe borderline patient with numerous symptoms. She was very depressed and often suicidal, had hypochondriacal delusions, insomnia, and extreme anxiety. She required medication and had been in psychotherapy her entire adult life. At age 50 she still required three or four sessions per week in order to function, and her dependency showed no signs of letting up. Rachel's mother was a very disturbed woman who was probably paranoid. She was extremely controlling, critical, and impossible to please. She was often angry and yelled in rage when Rachel didn't please her. Rachel's father was a successful professional man who loved her and was kind and attentive to her. His major failing was his inability to keep Rachel's mother from harassing her. He didn't stand up to his wife when she criticized and controlled him, either. The mother interfered in Rachel's relationship with her father by belittling the father to Rachel. Even in adulthood, with the parents on the East Coast and Rachel in San Francisco, the mother tried to prevent the father and daughter from speaking on the phone, carrying on about how expensive the call was. In spite of all her severe symptoms, Rachel was consistently orgasmic. She remembers frequent masturbation in childhood, when her parents would go out and leave her with a babysitter. She was anxious at the separation from her mother, and used the masturbation to relieve the anxiety and attempt a mastery of the separation through independent pleasure.

My clinical experience working with inorgasmic women validates Fisher's findings. Earlier in this chapter I described Tammy, who had been abandoned by her father; she was inorgasmic, and was overwhelmed with grief and anxiety when she did reach an orgasm with a man.

Penelope's father died suddenly when she was 9, and then she was sexually molested by a close and trusted friend of the family. Her trust in the dependability of men was traumatized twice, and Penelope remained inorgasmic with men.

When Clare was four her mother had a psychotic breakdown, was hospitalized, and never returned home. Clare was placed in a foster home until her father moved with her to the home of her paternal grandparents. But when the grandparents decided to move away after about one year, her father again placed Clare in a foster home and visited her on Sundays. She was very sad in the foster home and awaited her father's visits. Her foster father sexually molested her, and she was moved to another home with a widowed woman. Four years later, when she was 10, her father took her with him when he moved to California. She was happy with him at first, but then he remarried and had three sons, and Clare felt displaced. Her father was critical and even cruel and refused to help her go to college. She began work, married, and broke off all relations with him a few years later when she brought the whole family expensive Christmas gifts and she received none. She has married twice and had several long-term relationships with men, but has never been orgasmic with a partner.

Jeanine was so afraid of being unattractive to men that she injured her back in her efforts to lose weight. Jeanine had almost no sexual contact with men until her early forties, when she was in therapy and focused on this issue. Her father had supported the family and was physically present, but was so withdrawn and unaffectionate that Jeanine has no memory of ever being held, hugged, or kissed by him. She describes him as quite remote. When Jeanine was in college, her father died. Her mother was eager for her to make a good marriage, but none of the boys who showed interest in her were ever good enough to meet her mother's standards. Throughout her twenties and thirties she had sex only three times, with three different men. When she did recently get involved with a man she became aware of her terrible fear of rejection. She needed help in therapy to overcome years of sexual repression and anxiety about her desireability, but she was able to become sexually involved with a man who was very complimentary and reassuring, and she was orgasmic.

Jane was single until her early thirties and didn't date much after college. She had learned to masturbate to orgasm, but when she met a man and began living with him she was unable to have an orgasm in his presence, though he was patient and wanted to help. Jane had a number of symptoms of anxiety, such as smoking, nail biting, and difficulty making decisions. She was one of three girls and had an older brother. None of the three girls had successful lives, with both marital and career problems. The father, a successful professional man, was very strict and critical with them. They could never please him and he let them know he did not think much of women in general. He made belittling comments to them, about themselves and about women. The brother was successful in his career and in marriage. Apparently, the father's success was a good model for the son, who was the star of the family. The father was reliable financially, but apparently there was much lacking in his emotional relationships. His mother had become mentally ill and was hospitalized, and his brother was schizophrenic. I suspect he had a serious intimacy problem with his daughters due to the trauma of his mother's hospitalization, and perhaps to a problem with sexual impulses that forced him to keep them at a distance.

ORGASM AND WORKING-CLASS WOMEN—LILLIAN RUBIN

Fisher expresses concern at the lack of working-class women in his sample. Might there be differences regarding orgasm between middle- and working-class women? On this issue, Rubin's *Worlds of Pain* (1976) is a good resource. Rubin studied fifty white working-class families in which neither the husband nor the wife had more than a high school education, and a comparison group of 25 professional middle-class families in which both partners had at least a college education and the men were all in professional occupations. All lived within a radius of 50 miles from San Francisco. Only Berkeley was excluded, because Rubin considered the population there unrepresentative of that in the general Bay Area.

Rubin concludes that sexual behaviors that formerly were the province of the college-educated now are practiced widely at all class levels. Kinsey had reported (1948) that foreplay among high school educated males was very brief and perfunctory, but by the time of the Hunt study (1974), these men had "caught up" with college men in length of foreplay, variety of positions, and duration of coitus. According to Rubin the sexual revolution was very welcomed by these men, but often less so by their wives. The men were sometimes more concerned for their wife's orgasm than the wives themselves were. In comparing the two classes, Rubin found that all the couples engaged in the same kinds of behaviors in roughly the same proportions; but working-class wives expressed considerably more discomfort, especially about oral sex, saying they "hate it," feel "forced," "revolted," or "sickened," but give in out of a feeling of duty or fear of the husband's finding another woman who will "give it to him." Some women were more comfortable with the passivity of cunnilingus than with the activity of fellatio, which is so incongruent with their training in passivity. " 'How do I know he won't think I'm cheap?'—a question asked over and over again, an issue that dominates these women and their attitudes toward their own sexuality" (p. 141).

When *Worlds of Pain* was written, the working-class woman's abiding concern was with the distinction between the "good" girls whom men marry and the "cheap" girls who are sexually free and available. A woman's sexual naivete was her badge of honor, and so her sexual inhibitions and restraint were assurance to herself and her husband of her loyalty to him. The practice of oral sex clearly distinguished the working-class women from the college-educated. The middle-class wives were more relaxed in talking about sex, specifically oral sex, and in fact were uncomfortable if they felt inhibited, believing that this reflected some inadequacy in their personal sexual adjustment.

The formerly passive role of the woman in sex had changed by 1976, and the level of expectation for women included orgasm, by then a requirement of adequate sexual performance. This left some of the middle- and working-class women Rubin interviewed feeling "under the gun"— fearful and anxious if they did not achieve orgasm, making it a mixed blessing. It opened up the possibility of sexual pleasures but was also experienced as another demand. In Rubin's view, the women she studied were having more orgasms than ever before, and were enjoying sex more than women of earlier generations, but some experienced their ability to reach orgasm as more for their husband's benefit than for their own. The woman's failure is seen as a problem for her husband's sense of manhood. Here are some quotations from her subjects:

> I rarely have climaxes. But if it didn't bother my husband, it wouldn't bother me. I keep trying to tell him that I know it's not his fault, that he's really a good lover. I keep telling him it's something the matter with me, not with him. But it scares me because he doesn't believe it, and I worry he might leave me for a woman who will have climaxes for him. [p. 152]

> It's really important for him that I reach a climax, and I try to every time. He says it just doesn't make him feel good if I don't. But it's hard enough to do it once! What'll happen if he finds out about those women who have lots of climaxes? [p. 153]

> "All I know is, I can't turn on so easy. Maybe we're all paying the price now because men didn't used to want women to enjoy sex." [p. 153]

LATER REPORTS ON FEMALE SEXUALITY

The Hite Report

In 1976, Shere Hite published the results of a four-year survey of 3,000 women between the ages of 14 and 78; the women answered question- naires in which she asked detailed, intimate questions about sexual activity, sexual attitudes, and sexual feelings. Her results produced a figure of 30 percent for women who reported being able to reach orgasm "always" or "usually" in intercourse. However, this figure may have been inflated by the inclusion of women whose understanding of the point was question- able and who may have defined "in intercourse" to include all activity preceding penetration. The book is very comprehensive, but Hite's sample and methods have been questioned by some researchers. A spokesperson for the Kinsey Institute told me that the Institute does not use the Hite report as a reference, because it considers her methods questionable and because all her subjects are volunteers, but added that her results can be used in support of other research, though not on its own. Of course, other research relies on volunteers as well, so perhaps the problem is Hite's frankly feminist approach. Unlike "scientists," she states her values directly and often.

Hite is a proponent of the cultural explanation for inorgasmic problems in women. She asks the question,

> *Why do women so habitually satisfy men's needs during sex and ignore their own?* The fact is that the role of women in sex, as in every other aspect of life, has been to serve the needs of others—men and children. And just as women did not recognize their oppression in a general sense until recently, just so sexual slavery has been an almost unconscious way of life for most women. . . . our model of sex and physical relations is *culturally* (not biologically) defined and can be redefined—or undefined. . . . Lack of sexual satisfaction is another sign of the oppression of women. [pp. 419–420]

Hite asked her respondents if they liked vaginal penetration/ intercourse, and 87 percent said they did, including women who had never experienced orgasm in intercourse. The women gave as their reasons the affection and closeness of intercourse, rarely even mentioning orgasm. In response to the question "Is sex important to you?" answers were focused on emotional issues.

> Our sex life together is important because it makes me feel secure and wanted, and proves he loves me.

> Sex is to please him. What I like is the feeling of security I get when he holds me tight after. It makes me feel accepted and attractive.

> It reassures me I'm desirable, gives a deeper bond to a relationship.

> I've never heard a word of praise from my husband in twenty-one years except while having intercourse. While I resent this, I still love him, and I still enjoy sex with him—but only for this reason. [p. 425]

Quoting Hite:

> It is not the fact that women don't want or don't like intercourse that makes them sexual slaves (since they do like it), but rather the fact that they have few or no alternative choices for their own satisfaction. Sex is defined as a certain pattern—foreplay, penetration, intercourse, and ejaculation—and intercourse is always part of that pattern, indeed, intercourse *is* the pattern (at least insofar as it ends with male ejaculation, and this ends sex). This pattern is what oppresses women. [p. 431–432]

She relates the sexual freedom of women to their economic position in society: "You cannot decree women to be 'sexually free' when they are not economically free; to do so is to put them into a more vulnerable position than ever, and make them into a form of easily available common property" (p. 449). Hite's position is identical to the feminist analysis that women as a group are oppressed economically, culturally, and sexually by their dependence on men in a patriarchal society.

Dr. Ruth

Ruth Westheimer became popular on radio and television as a sex counselor; her book, *Dr. Ruth's Guide to Good Sex,* was published in 1983. She reports that research has shown that about 30 percent of American women experience orgasm during sexual intercourse, and that "this percentage appears to be growing as people become more sexually literate" (p. 103). This is typical of the sex counselor's approach, which believes so strongly in the viability of education as the cure-all for this problem. Westheimer says another 30 percent of American women need direct manual or other stimulation (perhaps by a vibrator) of the clitoris to reach orgasm. She says "some" of these women can be taught to have orgasms during intercourse, a major factor being the woman's own desire for orgasm. Another 30 percent do not experience orgasm at all. According to Westheimer, "most of these women can be taught to have an orgasm through direct stimulation of the clitoris, and some of them can then be further taught to have orgasms during sexual intercourse, again providing that they want to" (p. 103). Half of the remaining 10 percent are easily orgasmic, and may have an orgasm by tightening the muscles of their thighs while thinking erotic thoughts, and the other half are unable to have an orgasm under any conditions. Westheimer describes these women as "having deep-seated psychological problems, such as acute depression" (p. 104). It is not surprising that Westheimer and others who take the educational approach do not cite Fisher's studies and conclusions, because Fisher contradicts this approach with his findings of the centrality of the girl's relationship to her father, and the lack of correlation between sex education or sexual experience and orgasmic ability.

Warwick Williams of Australia (1984) shows a 50 percent success rate with couples in which the women were unable to achieve orgasm during intercourse without simultaneous direct clitoral stimulation, and worried about this, considering themselves inadequate. This is consistent with Barbach's (1976) 50 percent success rate after three months. Williams says he has been unable to elicit any consistent differences between the women who are successful and those who fail, but we are not told if he inquired as to the woman's relationship with her father. His program includes a wide variety of techniques, such as guided imagery, thought stopping, training in sexual rational thinking and sexual assertiveness, fantasy training, and vaginal sensation training, and various exercises in sensate focusing, sexual communication, and variations in pacing and approach.

The Grafenberg Spot

No definitive conclusions have been reached about the existence of a separate vaginal area that is sensitive enough to produce an orgasm independent of clitoral stimulation, and the issue remains controversial among sex researchers. Alzate (1985) concludes that most and probably all women possess vaginal zones, mainly located on the anterior wall, with a secondary location on the posterior wall, whose tactile stimulation can lead to orgasm. Other researchers have reported that some women experience a sudden spurt of fluid at the moment of orgasm, which is called female ejaculation. The apparent contradiction between this finding and the ample evidence indicating that coitus is an inefficient method of eliciting female orgasm might be explained, at least in part, by topographical and mechanical reasons, as well as by differences between male and female orgasm latencies (p. 271).

In 1950, Ernest Grafenberg, a gynecologist, described a bean-shaped erogenous area/zone in the anterior wall of the vaginal barrel midway between the pubic bone and the cervix, which is felt through the vaginal wall musculature. When stimulated, this soft mass of tissue swells and will activate an orgasm in response to prolonged stimulation. Perry and Whipple (1981) examined more than 400 women for the purpose of locating this sensitive area, and identified its location in each woman. However, two gynecologists trained by Whipple to identify the area found it in only four of eleven women examined. Some women subjectively report experiencing a vaginal-based orgasm that is lower in intensity than one clitorally stimulated.

Hoch (1983) declares: "The G-spot does not exist as such. . . . But rather, the entire wall of the vagina plus tissues between the urinary bladder and urethra region contain sexual nerve endings" (pp. 166–167). Hoch (1986) reports that 85 percent of subjects reported "high erotic sensitivity" on the anterior of the vagina. A 1989 study (Davidson et al.) involved distribution of a questionnaire to a sample of 2,350 professional women in medical, health, therapeutic, and sex education fields, which yielded a 55 percent return. Of the respondents, 84.3 percent believed that a sensitive area exists in some women in the vagina, and 65.9 percent experienced this personally, with 59.3 percent experiencing orgasm without clitoral contact. One is left wondering whether there are anatomical differences among women, whether women are very suggestive to gynecologist's theories, and whether psychological factors are at work in the so-called "vaginal orgasm" as well as in the clitoral orgasm. Even if both sources of orgasm are available to some women, the original Freudian theory that one is more "mature" than the other need not apply, because a more significant issue may be the ability of the male to maintain an erection long enough to allow the woman to achieve a vaginal orgasm. In such cases, it is the sexual maturity of the male rather than the woman's psychological qualities that determines the outcome.

THE FEMINIST MOVEMENT AND THE FEMALE ORGASM

Some of the early dissenters from Freud's theories about female sexuality, such as Josine Muller (1932), were proponents of the view that the vagina is cathected very early in life and that it is the most important erogenous zone for the little girl. Muller, who observed children as a general practitioner, believed this early cathexis is repressed and reinvested in the clitoris. This repression results in a narcissistic wound, which can then lead to penis envy. In Muller's view, women who can libidinally cathect their vagina have greater self-esteem and their penis envy tends to disappear. It is interesting that a recognition of vaginal sensitivity at one time was a feminist response to Freud, who did not believe in vaginal awareness until puberty, but forty years later some feminists do not recognize vaginal erotic potential.

Female Sexuality—Karen Horney

Karen Horney explored the problem of "frigidity" in women in several essays. In 1922, during her analysis with Karl Abraham in Berlin, Horney attempted a polite challenge to his theories of frigidity in women in her essay, "On the Genesis of the Castration Complex in Women." Abraham, in his paper "Manifestations of the Female Castration Complex" (1920), complains that women are rarely able to assume the normal position assigned to them because the wish to be a male prevents them from attaining a normal femininity. A women's penis envy, he claims, leads to various neurotic solutions, including frigidity and phobias—disguised revenge against her husband and all men. Abraham considers frigidity the least overtly violent but the most unconsciously vengeful of all such forms of revenge, and likens the frigid woman to the prostitute. The frigid woman emasculates her husband in retaliation for her failure to be given a penis, an ingenious strategy for sadistically diminishing the worthiness and significance of the penis. Abraham compares frigidity in women to premature ejaculation in men, in which the passivity of the male is the symptom of his sadistic-vengeful attitudes toward women. Abraham fails to draw a causal connection between premature ejaculation in men and frigidity in women. It is the wife of such a man who is often "frigid," because her husband cannot allow her the pleasure of extended intercourse. He is thus responsible for her condition.

Horney (1922) claims that repressed castration fantasies, based on love for the father, are of fundamental importance as a root of the castration complex in women. "It is wounded womanhood which gives rise to the castration complex, and that it is this complex which injures (not *primarily,* however) feminine development" (p. 51). This wounded woman develops a revengeful attitude toward men; she feels no guilt for this attitude, because she attributes the loss of her penis unconsciously to a sexual act with her father. Penis envy is thus the outcome of the little girl's disappointment in her sexual love for her father, not of a recognition of biological inferiority, as Abraham holds, and in this way is responsible for a subsequent attitude of revenge against her mate, who represents her father.

In "The Denial of the Vagina" (1933b), Horney concurs with Muller on the repression of vaginal eroticism, which she explains as a result of castration wishes toward the father, linked with oedipal frustration and fear of revenge. There exists in the girl a fear of genital damage inside her body, caused by the disproportion between the father's big penis and the girl's small genital. Thus, she represses her vaginal impulses and, for defensive reasons, transfers them to her clitoris.

In "Inhibited Femininity" (1926a), Horney reports a connection between frigidity and the impairment of other specifically female functions, such as menstruation. Fisher found no such connection. Horney also reports a connection between frigidity and disturbances of pregnancy and motherhood, including miscarriage, pregnancy complaints, nursing, and failure in a maternal attitude toward the child. Here again, Fisher (1973) found no such relationship. But such problems are not primary, in Horney's view.

> However, even where all these disturbances of female functions are absent, one relationship will regularly be impaired or incomplete— namely, the attitude toward the male. . . . Whether they reveal themselves in indifference or morbid jealousy, in distrust or irritability, in claims or feelings of inferiority, in a need for lovers or for intimate friendships with women, they have one thing in common—the incapacity for a full (that is, including both body and soul) love relationship with a heterosexual love object. [p. 74]

Again, in opposition to the findings of Fisher and others, Horney states "there is rarely serious nervous disturbance in a woman that is not accompanied by frigidity and its underlying inhibitions" (p. 82). She gives a classic description of the "masculinity complex" in women: a desire to be a male, envy of men, and a denial of femininity. A disparagement of men is a defense against a belief in male superiority. A woman's dissatisfaction with her lot in life is not explained by frigidity, but rather by her strong unconscious claims for masculinity, which then lead to frigidity. "Frigidity, in turn, is likely to intensify the above-mentioned inferiority feelings, since at a deeper level it unerringly is experienced as an incapacity for love. . . . In turn this . . . leads easily to a neurotically reinforced jealousy of other women" (p. 76).

It is surprising that Horney never mentions the girl's relationship with her father, specifically the father's attitude toward his daughter, which would be an obvious direction for a psychoanalyst to search. Is there denial here of the degree of rejection that some men visit upon their daughters? We know that Horney's father was a distant man, a sea captain who was away often on long sea voyages. Yet she does not explore this angle.

After a lengthy discourse on penis envy in relation to frigidity—again, a connection not found by Fisher—Horney returns to her earlier question of the frequency of the phenomenon of frigidity. She declares that the prevalence of frigidity is not reason enough to call it normal. She then redeems the essay by an attempt to integrate psychoanalytic theory with an appreciation of cultural factors, describing ours as a "male culture," not favorable to female development. "Firstly, no matter how much the individual woman may be treasured as a mother or as a lover, it is always the male who will be considered more valuable on human and spiritual grounds. The little girl grows up under this general impression. . . . The girl carries with her a reason for envy of the male" (p. 82).

Horney also finds a specific male component that contributes to the problem:

> An additional unfavorable factor lies in a certain peculiarity of contemporary male eroticism. The split into sensual and romantic components of the love life, which we find only occasionally in women, seems to be about as frequent in educated men as frigidity is in women. Thus, on the one hand, man searches for his life's companion and friend who is close to him spiritually, but toward whom his sensuousness is inhibited, and who, deep down, he expects will reciprocate with a similar attitude. The effect on the woman is clear; it can very easily lead to frigidity, even if the inhibitions she has brought with her from her own development are not insurmountable. On the other hand, such a man will search for a woman, with whom he can have sexual relations only, a trend he manifests most clearly in his relationships with prostitutes. . . .
>
> The extent to which the decisive effect rests with exogenous or endogenous factors will be different in each individual case. Yet

fundamentally it is a question of the joint operation of both these factors. [p. 83]

Horney describes the connection between the depreciation of women, envy of men, and the problem of frigidity. "Frigid women have a very ambivalent attitude toward men, which invariably contains elements of suspicion, hostility and fear. Very seldom are these elements completely overt" (p. 166).

In "Maternal Conflicts" (1933a) she states:

> The resentment against the female role comes out in teaching the children that men are brutes and women are suffering creatures, that the female role is distasteful and pitiable, that menstruation is a disease ("curse") and sexual intercourse a sacrifice to the lusts of the husband. The mother will be intolerant of any sexual manifestation, particularly on the side of the daughter, but very frequently on the part of the sons, too. [p. 180]

Horney struggled with the concepts of Freud and Abraham about frigidity in women. But she was never able to integrate the biological, psychological, and cultural factors involved, mainly because of the lack of accurate physiological information available at the time.

Among contemporary feminists, a common source of anger against psychoanalysis has been over the issue of the so-called "mature vaginal orgasm." What should be purely a medical issue became a political issue, as some feminists claimed that the vagina has no erotic value for women. Women, they said, agree to vaginal sexuality for cultural reasons only, as a way of pleasing and keeping a man—"sexual slavery," as Hite calls it (1976, p. 419).

Contemporary Feminist Views

The Masters and Johnson research results fueled the fire. Susan Lydon's "The Politics of Orgasm" appeared in *Sisterhood is Powerful* (1970).

> Woman's sexuality, defined by men to benefit men, has been downgraded and perverted, repressed and channeled, denied and abused until women themselves, thoroughly convinced of their sexual inferiority to men, would probably be dumbfounded to learn that there is scientific proof that Tiresias was indeed right [—that women experience more sexual pleasure than men]. [p. 219]

Lydon's thesis is that the notion of the vagina as the source of women's mature orgasm is a way of keeping women totally dependent on the male to achieve orgasm, thus adding sexual dependence on men to women's economic, social, and political dependence on men. She refers to Freud's belief in the superiority of the vaginal orgasm as "almost a demonic determination on his part to finalize the Victorian's repression of feminine eroticism" (p. 224).

Lydon complains that in sex education, children are told that boys have penises and girls have vaginas, while the existence of the clitoris and female pleasure in sex are never discussed. In the marriage-manual craze that followed the Kinsey report, the pressure on women switched from repression to a preoccupation with orgasm, bringing on not a revolution, but a new tragedy for women.

> So the sad thing for women is that they have participated in the destruction of their own eroticism. Women have helped make the vaginal orgasm into a status symbol in a male-dictated system of values. . . . Feeling themselves insecure in a competitive situation, they are afraid to admit their own imagined inadequacies, and lie to other women about their sexual experiences. With their men they often fake orgasm to appear "good in bed". [pp. 226–267]

Lydon praises the work of Masters and Johnson, especially their stress on the "infinite variety of female sexual response" (Lydon p. 222).

I have already discussed Mary Jane Sherfy's "A Theory on Female Sexuality," which also appeared in *Sisterhood is Powerful*. "Organs and Orgasms," by Alix Shulman, appeared in *Women in Sexist Society* (1971). Shulman decries the harmful "myths and lies" about female genital anatomy. Her main point is how sex education has ignored the clitoris and focused on the vagina, which she—like Lydon—claims functions in childbearing and to provide pleasure for the man, not for female sexual pleasure (p. 292). She quotes Masters and Johnson to support her cultural approach to female sexuality: "Sociocultural influence more often than not places woman in a position in which she must adapt, sublimate, inhibit, or even distort her natural capacity to function sexually in order to fulfill her genetically assigned role (i.e. breeding). *Herein lies a major source of woman's sexual dysfunction*" (p. 298).

Like Horney, she points out the role of the male for female sexual pleasure, again quoting Masters and Johnson: "Probably hundreds of thousands of men never gain sufficient ejaculatory control to satisfy their wives sexually regardless of the duration of marriage or the frequency of natural sexual exposure" (p. 298).

Shulman concludes: "In the process of exposing the myths and lies, women are discovering that it is not they who have individual sex problems; it is society that has one great big political problem" (p. 301).

"The Myth of the Vaginal Orgasm" by Anne Koedt, appeared in *The Radical Therapist* in 1971, and, as with the articles above, Freud and his followers are blamed for perpetrating this myth against women.

> Women have thus been defined sexually in terms of what pleases men; our own biology has not been properly analyzed. Instead, we are fed the myth of the liberated woman and her vaginal orgasm—an orgasm which in fact does not exist. What we must do is redefine our sexuality. We must discard the "normal" concepts of sex and create new guidelines which take into account mutual sexual enjoyment. [p. 128]

The first edition of *Our Bodies, Ourselves* (1971), a popular self-help manual published by the Boston Women's Health Course Collective, and read widely during the 1970s by women involved in the movement, takes a strong view on the pressures of orgasm.

> We are all so oppressed by sexual images, formulas, goals and rules that it is almost impossible to even think about sex outside the context of success and failure. The sexual revolution—liberated orgastic women, groupies, communal fucking, homosexuality—have all made us feel that we must be able to fuck with impunity, with no anxiety, under any conditions and with anyone, or we're some kind of up-tight freak. These alienating inhuman expectations are no less destructive or degrading than the Victorian puritanism we all so proudly rejected. . . . Great pressure is being put on us to be both independent (what modern man wants a clinging vine?) and a sex-kitten at the same time. [p. 9]

The book's prescription for nonorgasmic women includes a list of suggestions that encourage women to know themselves better, to be kinder to themselves, and not to have too-high expectations. The book also includes praise for Masters and Johnson and an attack on Alexander Lowen, a psychoanalyst, whose book *Love and Orgasm* appeared in 1965. The authors of *Our Bodies, Ourselves* claim it appeared in 1967, after the Masters and Johnson research; but they are in fact referring to a 1967 softcover edition, so it is unlikely that they are right in accusing Lowen of ignoring scientific evidence. Nevertheless, they are correct to be incensed by Lowen's views, which are strictly from the point of view of the male's pleasure. The quotation is from Lowen's *Love and Orgasm*.

> Most men feel that the need to bring a woman to climax through clitoral stimulation is a burden. If it is done before intercourse but after the man is excited and ready to penetrate, it imposes a restraint upon his natural desire for closeness and intimacy. Not only does he lose some of his excitation through this delay, but the subsequent act of coitus is deprived of its mutual quality. Clitoral stimulation during the act of intercourse may help the woman to reach a climax but it distracts the man from the perception of his genital sensation and greatly interferes with the pelvic movements upon which his own feeling of satisfaction depends. The need to bring a woman to climax through clitoral

stimulation after the act of intercourse has been completed and the man
has reached his climax is burdensome since it prevents him from
enjoying the relaxation and peace which are the rewards of sexuality.
Most men to whom I have spoken who engaged in this practice resented
it.

I do not mean to condemn the practice of clitoral stimulation if a
woman finds that this is the way she can obtain a sexual release. Above
all she should not feel guilty about using this procedure. However, I
advise my patients against this practice since it focuses feelings on the
clitoris and prevents the vaginal response. It is not a fully satisfactory
experience and cannot be considered the equivalent of a vaginal
orgasm. [pp. 216–217]

Once again, a psychoanalyst sticks his (or her) foot in his mouth. For
Lowen, the female orgasm seems to be a real bother. Can't these women
just have an orgasm in the easiest and best way for men, as we keep telling
them they should?

Vaginal Sensation—LeMon Clark

LeMon Clark, a gynecologist, reports (1970) that for some women, the
broader area of stimulation provided in penile penetration is significant
enough that clitoral stimulation alone may not feel satisfactory, although
orgasm is reached. Some of his patients reported less satisfactory feeling
when wearing a diaphragm.

It occurred to me that this might result from the rubber dome of the
diaphragm deflecting the penis so that it did not move the cervix as
much as it did without the diaphragm. Moving the cervix would move
the uterus and the broad ligament, both of which are covered with
peritoneum, one of the most sensitive organs in the body. This would
give a much broader base for sensation in the whole lower abdominal
area than mere stimulation of the clitoris alone. . . . I made [a dia-
phragm] with a dome as thin as the rubber in a condom, so that it would
not deflect the penis. This solved the problem for these women. They
enjoyed normal sensation with a diaphragm. [p. 26]

Clark also reports on women patients who, after a vaginal hysterec-
tomy, complain of no longer enjoying intercourse, feeling "dead" inside.
This occurs because they no longer receive stimulation of the cervix,
uterus, and broad ligaments (pp. 26–27).

A third piece of evidence for vaginal sensation comes from a woman
patient, who reported to Clark that though she had been fully orgasmic
with her first husband, who had a very large penis, she could not reach

orgasm with her second husband, whom she loved but who had a much smaller penis. She was left frustrated, and had become nervous and depressed because she didn't want to hurt her husband's feelings by telling him. Unfortunately, Clark does not tell us how he advised his patient. But the case is important because it deals with the size of the penis as a factor in vaginal orgasm—a most sensitive and unmentioned issue, which would not be significant if only the stimulation of the clitoris was involved in female sexual pleasure. In fact, penis size *is* a significant factor, and clearly has been a factor in the imposition of virginity on women, so that men need not feel threatened by comparison to other men.

Clark also offers the example of women patients who were inorgasmic even with a vibrator, but who reached orgasm with the combination of a vaginal vibrator and clitoral stimulation. The women reported from 40 percent to 75 percent increased pleasurable sensation when vaginal stimulation was combined with clitoral.

Feminist writers on this subject seem to deny that the penis is of any value to a woman's achievement of orgasm, or has any part to play in giving a woman sexual pleasure. This may be an overreaction to years of almost exclusive attention to the sexual pleasure of the male, but that in no way makes these statements either valid or helpful to women who wish to have a good sexual relationship with a man.

CONCLUSION

In conclusion, it seems fair to say that both psychoanalysis and feminism have been wrong about female sexuality. Neither group has done any independent research, and both have based their conclusions on a combination of insufficient evidence and a lot of biases: in the case of psychoanalysis, biases against women; in the case of feminism, biases against men. The sex researchers have been the most objective on this emotional topic; though some have tended toward an overly optimistic view, based on a strong belief in the value and power of education and training, with not enough attention to psychological factors. Some sex therapists (Williams, Barbach, Epp) do report about a 50 percent success rate for women who wish to achieve an orgasm in intercourse. All three groups have acknowledged the importance of cultural factors, with the feminists placing most emphasis on this influence, and the psychoanalysts assuming that biological and cultural factors are linked, are givens, and are not to be judged or changed.

The truth appears to me to be that biological, cultural, and psychological factors are all woven together in the creation of problems in orgasm for some women. The importance of the father's reliability to his daughter is consistent with both Fisher's research findings and a psychodynamic approach. This is the only psychological factor found to relate to the problem. To the extent that a cultural/educational component exists, it can be remedied with an educational/training approach. Women who are comfortable with their genitalia are more likely to enjoy masturbation and less likely to develop complications from early penis envy. To deal with problems chiefly psychological in origin, the woman requires psychotherapy combined perhaps with some educational material. Biological factors—such as women's association of intercourse with pregnancy and childbirth, the longer time needed for women to reach a climax than for men, and the internal nature of the female genitalia, which, unlike the male genitalia, are not visible—require education of the husband or partner, in order to elicit his cooperation and to reduce any sense of blame on the part of either partner. If the man suffers from a sexual disorder, such as premature ejaculation or the Madonna–whore complex, then he needs treatment: psychotherapy, training, or perhaps both.

It also seems clear that there are individual variations among women, which should come as no surprise. For some women there is great pleasure in intercourse. How much of this pleasure comes from her loving connection with the man and the narcissistic satisfaction and reassurance of pleasing him, and how much from vaginal sensitivity, cannot be determined with any certainty. But it is certain that between one-third and half of all women can reach orgasm in this manner, and it is both an emotionally and sexually gratifying experience. To rank these women as more mature seems to have no basis in fact. What is truly important is that a woman feel good about herself sexually and enjoy sexual connections, heterosexual or homosexual, with a high enough rate of orgasmic success to satisfy herself. Ideally, she should not be pressured to be orgasmic, either by her own sense of competition with other women, for the sake of some rating or scoring, or to make her partner feel successful. Her partner's sense of achievement, and his feelings of competitive success with other men, may be a desirable by-product for him, but should not be her primary motive or concern.

7

FEMALE HOMOSEXUALITY

One of the tasks implicit in object-choice is that it should find its way to
the opposite sex. This, as we know, is not accomplished without a
certain amount of fumbling.

—Sigmund Freud

THE PSYCHOANALYTIC VIEW

Sigmund Freud

Freud's view of homosexuality was very enlightened, and even radical for
his time. Unlike the process in regard to the psychology of women, where
Freud was culturally and internally bound, in the case of homosexuality
Freud's followers were actually more moralistic, critical, and prejudicial
than Freud himself. It took until 1980 for there to be a return to Freud's
nonjudgmental, scientific attitude, with an attempt at objectivity.

Roy Schafer (1974) describes the contributions of Freud to the
understanding of homosexuality and the moral condemnation so regularly
associated with it. Freud, he states, "had come to realize that genital
heterosexuality is a difficult, imperfect, more or less precarious achievement, and that this is so because it is a psychological as well as a biological
eventuality" (p. 343). Schafer refers to this as a "revolutionary discovery"

and states that because of Freud psychoanalysts "no longer presuppose any natural or pre-established culmination of human psychosexual development" (p. 345).

> Psychosexual outcomes other than reproductive genitality are called illnesses and arrests in development *only from the standpoint of the values and associated child-rearing practices common to most members of a society.* In speaking of perversions and inversions and their cure, we are operating in the realm of societal value systems concerning taken-for-granted evolutionary obligations; we are not operating in any realm of biological necessity, psychobiological disorder, or value-free empiricism. There is no established relation between these value systems and psychoanalytic insights, though there may be between these value systems and religion or existential choices. [p. 345]

Freud understood the intense revulsion toward, derogation of, and persecution of homosexuals as having three sources:

> a degree of precariousness in the heterosexual genitality attained by most nondeviant people; a greater or lesser dread common to these people of succumbing to modes of gratification that would disconfirm their heterosexual genitality; and some readiness on their part to project their repudiated desires onto others and then persecute them. This precariousness expresses various unconscious fixations on and regressions to homosexual and pregenital pleasures, and this dread and persecution reflect the intense, partly incorporated social pressures against assuming these deviant sexual roles. [R. Schafer 1974, pp. 345–346]

Freud's 1920 essay "The Psychogenesis of a Case of Homosexuality in a Woman," presents his understanding of the factors contributing to a homosexual outcome in an 18-year-old patient, and also lays out his views on homosexuality and on the treatment potential of such patients. In it, one is confronted with Freud's ambivalence and the inconsistency of his position on the subject. On the one hand, he retains his basic view of the original bisexuality of all human beings, and he is quite clear in stating that homosexuality is not an illness or a neurosis. On the other hand, he refers to heterosexuality as normal and homosexuality alternately as an inversion or a perversion. In describing his difficulties in treating this patient, who was brought to him by her parents, he states the following (this and succeeding quotations with regard to this case are from Young-Bruehl 1990):

> Further unfavourable features in the present case were the facts that the girl was not in any way ill (she did not suffer from anything in herself,

nor did she complain of her condition) and that the task to be carried out did not consist in resolving a neurotic conflict but in converting one variety of genital organization of sexuality into the other. Such an achievement—the removal of genital inversion or homosexuality—is in my experience never an easy matter. On the contrary, I have found success possible only in specially favourable circumstances, and even then the success essentially consisted in making access to the opposite sex (which had hitherto been barred) possible to a person restricted to homosexuality, thus restoring his full bisexual functions. After that it lay with him to choose whether he wished to abandon the path that is banned by society, and in some cases he had done so. One must remember that normal sexuality too depends upon a restriction in the choice of object. In general, to undertake to convert a fully developed homosexual into a heterosexual does not offer much more prospect of success than the reverse, except that for good practical reasons the latter is never attempted. [p. 246]

As Young-Bruehl (1990) emphasizes, Freud "understood neuroses to be based on repressed, unconscious sexual desires, not sexual desires declared and ardently pursued, as in this case" (p. 241). Freud viewed both homosexuality and heterosexuality as limitations of bisexuality. Yet he refers to the former as an "inversion" or "abnormality." He thus seemingly takes the stand that, although bisexuality is normal, a resolution of bisexuality in favor of homosexuality is abnormal. Freud offers an example of "normal" male bisexuality:

In all of us, throughout life, the libido normally oscillates between male and female objects; the bachelor gives up his men friends when he marries, and returns to club-life when married life has lost its savour. Naturally, when the swing-over is fundamental and final, we suspect the presence of some special factor which definitely favours one side or the other, and which perhaps has only waited for the appropriate moment in order to turn the choice of object in its direction. [Young-Bruehl 1990, p. 253]

Thus Freud anticipates Kinsey's six-point scale of sexual choice, which allows for a range of heterosexual and homosexual behavior. As to Freud's view of homosexuality as being free of repressed sexual desire, this too is invalidated by his position of a basic bisexuality. In the case of homosexuals, it is heterosexuality that is rejected and may be repressed. Ambivalence about a homosexual choice has been evident in many of my cases involving lesbian women. One woman patient was divorced by her female spouse, who wished to pursue heterosexual relationships and have a child. In regard to treatment, Freud describes the difficulty in treating homosexual patients who don't want to change and are coming for treatment under family pressure. But he does not in this essay mention the possibility of homosexuals coming for treatment for other issues: depression, anxiety, relationship problems, and so on.

Freud's case itself is most interesting. The young woman has fallen in love with an older woman of questionable reputation; she follows her around, living only for the moments when they can be together, although no sexual contact exists. The parents, but especially the father, are concerned for the family's reputation, as the daughter appears with this woman in public in an adoring demeanor. When, not by accident, the girl and her lady-love pass the father on the street and he gives them an angry look, the older woman rejects the attention of her young suitor, and the young woman makes a serious suicide attempt. Freud's analysis is that the beloved woman was a substitute for the patient's mother, but the slender figure of the older woman also reminded the patient of her older brother, an object of earlier love. The beloved thus combined both homosexual and heterosexual ideals, making the patient's love truly bisexual. Freud pinpoints the birth of a third brother when the patient entered puberty as the significant event in her homosexual choice.

> The girl we are considering had in any case altogether little cause to feel affection for her mother. The latter, still youthful herself, saw in her rapidly developing daughter an inconvenient competitor; she favoured the sons at her expense, limited her independence as much as possible and kept an especially strict watch against any close relation between the girl and her father. A yearning from the beginning for a kinder mother would, therefore, have been quite intelligible. . . . It was just when the girl was experiencing the revival of her infantile Oedipus complex at puberty that she suffered her great disappointment. She became keenly conscious of the wish to have a child, and a male one; that what she desired was her father's child and an image of him, her consciousness was not allowed to know. And what happened next? It was not she who bore the child, but her unconsciously hated rival, her mother. Furiously resentful and embittered, she turned away from her father and from men altogether. [Young-Bruehl 1990, p. 252]

Freud goes on to say that the girl then identified with her father and took a mother substitute for her love object, an overcompensation for her current hostility toward her mother. A secondary gain was that she left men to her mother, "retired in favour of her mother" (p. 253), and thus removed the competition between them. In addition, when she realized how much her homosexuality angered her father, she saw how much she could wound him and take revenge on him. Freud analyzes her suicide attempt as the embodiment of a death wish against her mother for the pregnancy, and an act of revenge toward her father.

Freud calls the question of whether homosexuality is congenital or acquired, "fruitless and inapposite" (p. 250). He describes his patient as having a strongly marked masculinity complex (she is "a spirited girl") and a pronounced envy for her older brother's penis. "She was in fact a feminist; she felt it to be unjust that girls should not enjoy the same freedom as boys, and rebelled against the lot of woman in general" (p. 264). He attributes her homosexuality to her strong mother fixation combined with her mother's neglect, and her comparison of her genital organs with her brother's. If this is so, in my view, it took place in a context in which the mother openly preferred the two boys. (Freud tells us that the mother "favoured sons at her [daughter's] expense" [p. 252].) But Freud does not discount the possibility of congenital factors.

> It is possible here to attribute to the impress of the operation of external influence in early life something which one would have liked to regard as a constitutional peculiarity. On the other hand, a part even of this acquired disposition (if it was really acquired) has to be ascribed to inborn constitution. So we see in practice a continual mingling and blending of what in theory we should try to separate into a pair of opposites—namely, inherited and acquired characters. [p. 264]

Freud makes another important contribution in this essay when he critiques the literature of homosexuality for failing to distinguish clearly between the issues of the choice of object, on the one hand, and the sexual characteristics and sexual attitude of the subject, on the other.

> It is instead a question of three sets of characteristics, namely—physical sexual characters (physical hermaphroditism), mental sexual characters, (masculine or feminine attitude) and kind of object-choice which up to a certain point, vary independently of one another, and are met with in different individuals in manifold permutations. [p. 265]

He accurately observes that what we recognize as masculine or feminine is not clearly demarcated, often being reduced to a distinction between activity and passivity. The common association of feminine traits with homosexual men and masculine traits with lesbians is a result of this confusion; and it is readily apparent to those who know homosexual men and women that there is a full range of so-called masculine and feminine physical and personality traits among them. The classic butch-femme coupling among lesbians has changed considerably, as lesbians have been influenced by the women's movement to discard dominant–submissive roles based on male–female coupling.

Helene Deutsch

Deutsch (1944) divides homosexual women into two groups. Those in the first group display pronounced masculine traits in all manifestations of life, including object choice; they also have a masculine physical structure, including a hermaphroditic character in some, and isolated aberrations such as an absence of breasts or hair growth in others. The second group includes women with no physical signs of abnormality, whose bodily construction is completely feminine, in whose cases the causes of homosexuality are obviously psychogenic. Yet Deutsch states that in the overwhelming majority of cases female homosexuality is psychologically determined, as most such women show no sign of masculine physiological characteristics, and, in any event, physiological traits generally share with psychological motives in the formation of a homosexual object choice. Deutsch describes her view of the psychological sources of female homosexuality:

> While we ascribe a primary character to this mother tie and support the view that in a large percentage of homosexual women the urge to union with the mother is predominant, analytic experience teaches us that this primary tie must be strengthened by other elements in order to infringe so powerfully and directly upon the woman's adult life. These additional elements gain their decisive strength during puberty. In the triangular situation, the mother's attraction and the girl's eternal longing for her must prove stronger than the biologic demand of heterosexuality. The father's favorable or unfavorable influence always affects the original mother tie during puberty. His love may be rejected by the girl as a result of fear; her disappointment in him, or his failure to gratify her, may influence her need for love in favor of the earlier mother tie. Her sense of guilt, and her need to reconcile herself with her mother, strengthen the attraction of the mother's magnetic field. [pp. 352–353]

Deutsch also sees a constitutional bisexuality as the core of sexual choice. She describes a common manifestation of intense love in puberty, where homosexual tendencies are directed toward a girl of the same age or a somewhat older woman. The love objects in these relationships are perceived as perfect beings. Deutsch believes that a positive and close relationship with another woman in early puberty helps to work through the normal bisexual tendencies and can lead to "normal" sexuality.

> This association is important, not only because it constitutes a protective shield against a regressive return to the mother, but also because the homosexual component develops more favorably than when it is

repressed and absent. In such a relationship the unusable surplus of homosexual tendencies can be best disposed of. This takes place partly by their gratification, partly by sublimation, partly by the acting out of the ambivalent feelings relating to the mother, etc. [p. 335]

Deutsch sees a fear of the father during puberty as either creating a masochistic tie to him or leading to the defense mechanism of identification with the aggressor—a frequent motive for homosexuality, where the sadomasochistic feelings are attached to a girl or woman. Deutsch also believes that one of the most powerful motives for female homosexuality is the opportunity it provides for women to alternate roles, one being active and sadistic and the other passive and masochistic. This alternation of roles can also be played out in a triangular relationship among three women. Deutsch fails to recognize that the alternation of passive and active roles can also occur between heterosexuals; though this probably occurred with less frequency at the turn of the century, when ladies were not supposed to move.

Deutsch reports a woman patient's successful treatment that resulted in her ability to actively engage in an uninhibited love relation with another woman. During her analysis, she was able to recall feelings of murderous hatred toward her mother. Between the ages of 4 and 6, when she was masturbating a lot, her mother had tied her hands and feet, strapped them with a belt to the railing of her bed, stood beside her and said, "Now, play if you can!" This caused, in addition to strong rage against the mother, an intense sexual excitement. The most dreadful element for the girl was the fact that her mother called her father in to witness this abuse, and he offered no help in spite of his tender affection for her. Although Deutsch never mentions it, I believe we can assume that the excessive masturbation itself was a symptom of the absence of loving care from the mother. The mother's sadistic solution to the symptom suggests a pattern of cold, rejecting, and hostile behavior toward the daughter, who tried to soothe herself with self-love.

After this incident, the girl stopped masturbating, repressed her sexuality, and repressed her hatred for her mother. But all sexual excitement was bound up with the mother's prohibition and with intense aggressive impulses toward her. This created intense guilt toward the mother, which the patient converted into masochistic love for her. Later, the fear of being "enslaved" to a woman, resulting from her forced submission to her mother, prevented her from having homosexual love affairs. This analysis of her fear of women cured her anxiety and depression, and she was able to pursue a lesbian relationship.

Deutsch says her patient "found happiness." Yet she draws the following conclusion:

In this case, analytic treatment did not lead to the patient's renouncing homosexuality and turning toward men; *thus its real task was not fulfilled.* But it succeeded in bringing the unhappy woman who was constantly on the verge of suicide to a point where, by mastering her fear of and her hostility toward her mother, she could achieve tenderness and sexual gratification. A better solution of the fatal mother tie proved impossible. [p. 346, italics added]

I would consider this case very successful. But the notion that the real task of analysis was not fulfilled since the patient remained homosexual reveals the ambivalence of the early analysts toward homosexuality, which surely reflected the attitude of the medical profession and of society. Later analysts who report treatment outcome also reveal ambivalence when the patient improves yet remains homosexual. It is only quite recently that this attitude has begun to change. We have seen how Freud (1905a) grappled with this dilemma:

We must learn to speak without indignation of what we call the sexual perversions—instances in which the sexual function has extended its limits in respect either to the part of the body concerned or to the sexual object chosen. . . . We surely ought not to forget that the perversion which is the most repellent to us, the sensual love of a man for a man, was not only tolerated by people so far our superiors in cultivation as were the Greeks, but was actually entrusted by them with important social functions. The sexual life of each one of us extends to a slight degree—now in this direction, now in that—beyond the narrow lines imposed as the standard of normality. [p. 50]

Freud (1905b) warned that it is "inappropriate to use the word perversion as a term of reproach" (p. 160). *"Psychoanalytic research,"* he states, *"is most decidedly opposed to any attempt at separating off homosexuals from the rest of mankind as a group of special character"* (p. 145, italics added).

Yet homosexuality *has* been viewed as a perversion, and perversions need cures. In psychiatric diagnostic categories it had been considered an illness until, due to pressure from gay activists within and without the psychiatric profession, the classification was eliminated from the *Diagnostic and Statistical Manual* in 1973; it now appears only indirectly, under the category "Other Sexual Disorders," as egodystonic homosexuality, "persistent and marked distress about one's sexual orientation." This is still a prejudicial remnant, because, as Marmor (1980) accurately points out, there is no category for "egodystonic celibacy or egodystonic states of being unmarried or of being divorced" (p. 401).

In spite of Freud's plea that we "speak without indignation" of sexual perversions, I believe the perversion of pedophilia, and also certain sadistic practices, do warrant our disapproval. The boundary of acceptable behavior in the case of consenting adults is often simple and clear, though sado-masochistic cruelty and exploitation should have their limits. However, children need protection. So do the mentally ill, who are frequent targets of sadists. We should also be indignant about psychotherapists who have sex with their patients; their behavior, like that of pedophiles, is dangerous, and patients need protection from it. It is a perversion of the trusted, curative role of the therapist.

SOME MODERN PSYCHOANALYTIC VIEWS

Judd Marmor edited two collections of papers on homosexuality: *Sexual Inversion: The Multiple Roots of Homosexuality,* published in 1965, and *Homosexual Behavior: A Modern Reappraisal,* published in 1980. In the preface to the 1980 volume he refers to the earlier book: "In the intervening years, however, there have been considerable advances in our understanding of the phenomenon of homosexual experience—biologically, sociologically, and clinically—so that the previous volume, a landmark in its time, must now be considered to be in large part outdated."

A comparison of the two collections reveals major changes in approach and attitude, if not always in etiology. In the earlier volume, Marmor finds

> no single constellation of factors that can adequately explain all homosexual deviation. The simple fact is that dominating and seductive mothers; weak, hostile, or detached fathers; and the multiple variations on these themes that are so often suggested as being etiologically significant in homosexuality abound in the histories of countless heterosexual individuals also and cannot therefore be in themselves specific causative factors. . . . We are probably dealing with a condition that is not only multiply determined by psychodynamic, sociocultural, biological and situational factors but also reflects the significance of subtle temporal, qualitative, and quantitative variables. For a homosexual adaptation to occur, in our time and culture, these factors must combine to (1) create an impaired gender-identity, (2) create a fear of intimate contact with members of the opposite sex, and (3) provide opportunities for sexual release with members of the same sex. [1965, p. 5]

In the preface to the 1980 volume Marmor confirms his belief that homosexuality should be viewed as "multifactorial" and includes chapters from religious and social action perspectives. However, a passage in the

1965 collection seems to seek the blame for male homosexuality in the behavior of women, especially those who do not conform to some ideal of femininity.

> The feminine revolution, the emerging dominant tendencies of many American women, the rise of "momism," and the diminishing importance of the paternal role in the home are other significant sociological factors that reverberate in intrafamily relationships and hinder the development of healthy masculine identifications. [p. 15]

Marmor does not specifically disclaim this prejudicial statement in his overview to the 1980 volume.

I referred in Chapter 2 to the belief by some that the women's movement was responsible for an apparent rise in impotence among American men. It is important to distinguish between problems with impotence and homosexual object choice.

Cornelia Wilbur

Marmor's 1965 collection contains two articles on female homosexuality. Cornelia B. Wilbur finds that a review of the theoretical and clinical concepts reveals sixteen different causes of female homosexuality. But she concludes that the most common constellation includes a "domineering, hostile, antiheterosexual mother and a weak, unassertive, detached and pallid father" (p. 280). Wilbur makes a number of negative statements about lesbian relationships. For example, "In some apparently stable female homosexual relationships, either or both partners secretly indulge in homosexual relationships on the side" (p. 279). This is rather startling as an indictment because one could easily and accurately say the very same thing about heterosexual relationships.

Wilbur also says that homosexual relationships "appear to serve a range of irrational defenses and reparative needs," another statement that could accurately be made about heterosexual relationships. "Frequent attempts to relate are frustrated by chronic ambivalence, hostility, and anxiety" (p. 279)—again commonly seen in heterosexuals who come for treatment. Homosexuality is a "pathological alternative," whereas heterosexuality is a "biologic norm" (p. 268).

Wilbur reveals that she has studied extensively only four patients, a small sample from which to draw conclusions generalizable to a whole population. This is a serious flaw in much of the psychoanalytic writing on this topic. Psychoanalytic theory has grown on the basis of clinical analysis, which reveals etiology in particular patients and is then drawn upon for hypotheses that may apply to other similar cases. This method of inquiry has often been critiqued by those who do not consider psychoanalysis a true science. In the case of homosexuality, the risk is particularly evident. Nowhere would we find a paper in which four African-American patients were analyzed, and then generalizations made to all African-Americans. However, Wilbur's most serious error is her statement that homosexual relationships are unstable, often transitory, and "do not contribute to the individual's need for stability and love" (p. 281).

The coup de grace is her concluding sentence: "With adequate motivation and cooperation, successful psychotherapy resulting in reversion to exclusive heterosexual behavior is possible" (p. 281). Who is cooperating with whom? Is the patient cooperating with the analyst's values and goals, or is the analyst serving the patient's goals?

May E. Romm

The second article on women in *Sexual Inversion* is by May E. Romm. Romm makes it clear that the choice of a goal in therapy is the patient's. The therapist should not seek "to remake [the patient] into a heterosexual individual. His aim should be to treat the patient with dignity and with interest in her problems whatever they may be and to help her to work through and to face and understand the vicissitudes of her past as they have influenced her present life" (p. 299).

Romm, like many other writers, cites Fenichel, whose *Psychoanalytic Theory of Neurosis* (1945) states that two etiological factors are involved in female homosexuality: the repulsion from heterosexuality originating in the castration complex, and the attraction through early fixation on the mother.

Romm comments on the relative neglect of female homosexuality compared to the voluminous literature on male homosexuality. She proposes the following reasons for this: (1) most writers on psychoanalytic and psychiatric subjects are men, and the fact that some women prefer women as sexual partners may be unacceptable to them; (2) homosexual women seek psychiatric help less often than homosexual men because society does not censure female homosexuality as vigorously; (3) sexual expression is not considered as important to women as to men. For women, sexuality is optional; for men, it is mandatory. Romm refers to Caprio (1954), in whose view man's unconscious refusal to acknowledge woman's ability to have sexual pleasure without his participation accounts for the absence of specific statutes against female homosexuality. In this regard, I viewed with some alarm and then with some amusement the fact that in Marmor's 1980 collection, an article titled "Psychodynamic Psychotherapy of Female Homosexuality" is misprinted at the top of every page, nine times in all, as "Psychodynamic Psychotherapy of Female

Sexuality." Many proofreadings by many editors overlooked that mistake, perhaps originally made by the typesetter. Like Wilbur, Romm makes some highly prejudicial statements in regard to the overall life adjustment of homosexual women:

> Homosexuals of both sexes are human beings who have given up hope of ever being accepted by their parents and by the society in which they live. They are basically unhappy because normal family life with the fulfillment in having children can never be within their reach. The label "gay" behind which they hide is a defense mechanism against the emptiness, the coldness and the futility of their lives. The claim that homosexuality is a way of life for persons who are more artistic, more sensitive, more creative than those who are heterosexual is a denial of their inability to test life on a responsible and mature psychophysiological level. [p. 291]

One is hard put to find in this statement anything but emotional, subjective hostility to those in our community who are different. Romm offers no objective, scientific basis for her conclusions. Are they based on the treatment of four patients, or perhaps ten? In any case, there are obvious responses to each of her points. (1) Many heterosexuals have given up being accepted by their parents, or by society, for good reasons; and many are unhappy with "normal" family life, as proven by the very high divorce rate. (2) Lesbian couples are now having children, either by adoption or artificial insemination, and some have had children from previous heterosexual relationships. Moreover, households numbering in the millions are headed by heterosexual women whose husbands have abandoned their wives and children to pursue irresponsible heterosexual lives. (3) Everyone hides behind defense mechanisms, including psychoanalysts; and to compartmentalize those who lead cold, empty, futile lives on the basis of their sexual orientation is hardly sensible. (4) In fact, many homosexuals *are* more creative than heterosexuals, a phenomenon worth exploring and certainly worth respecting. And so many adults are not responsible or mature as to make ludicrous any categorization of homosexuals in this manner. If all alcoholics, drug users, gamblers, and divorced, depressed, anxious, and otherwise unhappy persons were homosexuals, most mental health professionals would have gone out of the business of treating heterosexuals long ago. As to "testing life," one hardly knows what this means, other than that the author feels quite self-righteous about it. It is amazing that the authors who make such statements can at the same time describe the terribly unhappy, immature, pathologic heterosexual parents who have supposedly produced all these homosexuals.

In truth, homosexuals operate throughout their lives under the same burdens as all other nonconforming members of society. Racial and religious prejudices have historically isolated many minorities in their own communities, or ghettos, and often those with unpopular political and religious views have suffered the scorn and isolation of their "fellow men." Communists suffered this isolation and hostility in the United States in the 1950s and beyond, and the witch-hunt mentality against homosexuals carries many of the same scapegoat features. It is not a coincidence that in Nazi Germany, homosexuals as well as Jews, the mentally ill, gypsies, and Communists were all to be exterminated to produce a "pure" race.

In another part of her essay, Romm makes the statement that jealousy among homosexuals is frequently violent, with paranoid coloring. Perhaps, but as statistics indicate that between one-third and half of all heterosexual wives in the United States have been beaten by their husbands, one can hardly be self-righteous about that. Further, she says that depressions are frequent—a fact depressingly true for the majority of women.

Yet these statements that show so little compassion are mingled with others that show some understanding:

> When the female is rejected in her formative years by her parents; when she feels unloved, depreciated, and demeaned; when a male sibling is preferred to her; when she feels that her sex is a disappointment to her parents or when she becomes convinced, justifiably or not, that males in our society are the favored sex, she may react with feelings of inferiority and hostility toward men. She may then take refuge in psychosexual identification with the male and may assume a masculine role in a homosexual relationship. [p. 296]

Thus, in Romm, we see a mixture of clear-minded thinking and subjective prejudice that illustrates the ambivalence of psychoanalysis toward the homosexual in the 1960s. What about 1980?

Judd Marmor

In Marmor's overview to his 1980 collection, we find major changes from the introduction to the 1965 volume. One is the presence of a separate section on female homosexuality. Another is a section called "Homophobia and its Derivations"—surely a leap forward in fifteen years. On lesbian relationships, Marmor writes:

> Lesbians, like other women, tend to become aware of their sexual needs and to express them at a somewhat later age than men, and like other women, they tend to seek and hold to more stable and faithful

partnerships than do men. They are much less promiscuous than their
male counterparts, although they have a slightly greater tendency to
shift partners than do heterosexual females. As Shafer (1977) puts it,
"lesbian women . . . have internalized the sociosexual norms of combining love and sexuality equally as much as heterosexual women" (p.
362) and "being a woman tends to influence the sexual behavior of
women more than being a homosexual" (p. 355). [p. 16]

On the issue of why there are only about half as many female as male
homosexuals, Marmor proposes that it is less difficult in contemporary
society to achieve a feminine identity than a masculine identity; dependency patterns are more easily achieved than the patterns of competitiveness, vocational accomplishment, and self-reliance that are traditionally
required of men. He does note that these gender patterns are gradually
changing. He also notes that women can adapt more easily than men
because they can "simulate competence in the sex act." He cites surveys
that show that 70 percent to 80 percent of Kinsey group 5 and 6 lesbians
have experienced some heterosexual intercourse during their adult lives, in
contrast to only 20 percent to 25 percent of group 5 and 6 homosexual
men. (Kinsey [1948] develops a six-point scale in which 1 represents pure
heterosexuality, 6 represents pure homosexuality, and 2 to 5 represent
combinations in between.) In Marmor's discussion of etiology, he observes:

> A common finding in the backgrounds both of lesbians and male
> homosexuals is a strong antiheterosexual puritanism, stemming from
> either or both parents, that tends to color heterosexual relationships
> with feelings of guilt or anxiety. In these women, during their devel-
> oping years, physical contacts with boys were strongly discouraged,
> while "crushes" on girls were disregarded or covertly encouraged. [p.
> 17]

Yet so many girls are raised with strong prohibitions against sexual contact
with boys that other strong factors must be operative. Some develop a
secret sex life with men to avoid their mothers' disapproval. Marmor
acknowledges the influence of the women's movement in creating a
tendency toward lesbianism, and states that bisexuality in women has
become more widespread and acceptable.

In regard to homophobia, Marmor says that men and women secure in
their gender identity and/or heterosexuality are less apt to be threatened by
homosexuality. Also, those who belong to liberal religions or are not
religious are less homophobic than are fundamentalists. In my view, a very
important factor is exposure to homosexuals, in the same way as knowing
many African-Americans or Chinese or Latin Americans is the best cure for
racial prejudice. Prejudice allows one to make generalizations, to view the
other as "they." People living outside of areas where they have contact

with avowed homosexuals are more likely to feel sexually threatened by homosexuality, because they have not had opportunities to test themselves, to determine whether they have such inclinations themselves and whether those inclinations are more powerful than heterosexual desires. People who live in places like San Francisco, where gays comprise 20 percent of the population, may feel threatened politically; yet two avowedly lesbian women and one male homosexual have been elected to the nine-member Board of Supervisors. This could not have happened with the homosexual vote alone. It serves as an indication that exposure to homosexuals in the community gradually breaks down stereotypes, and therefore prejudice. One then tends to vote on the basis of political compatibility rather than sexual orientation.

Marmor refers to the ignorance factor in producing a fear that homosexuality is "infectious" and can be modeled. He calls this a myth, though his reference to the influence of the woman's movement in encouraging lesbianism would seem to contradict that view. Marmor claims that people do not "choose" to be homosexual or heterosexual, and that "in almost all instances" (p. 19) the basic factors are established before the age of 6. For this reason, "the legalization of homosexual behavior between consenting adults and the outlawing of discriminatory practices against homosexuals is . . . a mental health issue of the first magnitude" (pp. 20–21). Marmor issues a similar call to the psychiatric establishment. "Only when we totally free ourselves from the tendency to put psychiatric labels on homosexuals that singularly differentiate them from heterosexuals with analogous problems will psychiatrists finally become free from the age-old prejudice in this area" (p. 401). Marmor acknowledges that many psychoanalysts and psychiatrists (and we should add, other mental health professionals) who oppose discrimination against homosexuals, nevertheless feel strongly that it is a mental disorder. He cites Charles Socarides, a prolific writer on the subject, as an extreme example of this attitude. When the Board of Trustees of the American Psychiatric Association voted unanimously (with two abstentions) that homosexuality in and of itself did not constitute a mental illness, and recommended that it be removed from *DSM-II,* opponents gathered enough signatures to force a referendum of the entire membership. The decision of the Board of Trustees was upheld by a majority of 58 percent in favor, 37.8 percent opposed, and 3.6 percent abstentions, a decisive vote, surely, but one that indicated significant disagreement. However, that was 1974, and by now, 1992, it may be that the vote would be more favorable.

Barbara Ponse

Marmor's 1980 volume contains three papers about female homosexuality. The first, by Barbara Ponse, is a primarily sociological study called

"Lesbians and Their Worlds"; it explores issues of secrecy, "coming out," interactions, and life-styles. It also contains an interesting commentary on the "aristocratization of lesbianism," which Ponse defines as the attribution of special and desirable qualities to gay women. One aspect of this "aristocratization" involves attributing desirable qualities to women in general—particularly nurturance, sensitivity, and empathy, as well as strength and endurance, and, sometimes, competence and aggressiveness. Another element is the claim that lesbian relationships are superior to heterosexual ones. Relationships between women are idealized as more egalitarian, mutual, and sensitive, and as achieving greater intimacy. I stated earlier that I believed the Stone Center papers were biased in this direction. However, it is easy to understand the need for members of a devalued group to assert their value by exaggerated claims of superiority, and both women and homosexuals have been devalued for centuries.

Marcel Saghir and Eli Robins

Saghir and Robins report the results of their research comparing a nonclinical sample of 57 lesbians with a matched group (age, marital status, religious and socioeconomic background) of 43 heterosexual women. Two groups of men were also compared. Over three-fourths of the women in both female groups had never been married, while the rest were separated or divorced. Women in both groups had relatively high socioeconomic status. The results indicated that over two-thirds of women in the homosexual sample had been tomboys in childhood, versus only 16 percent of the heterosexual sample. In their self-masturbatory behavior, the two female groups tended to be alike and to differ from the male groups. Also, the female groups were alike in their overall sexual activities, including frequency, number of partners, and age of onset of sexual behavior, and differed from both groups of men.

The following patterns emerged from this research. The homosexual woman usually begins her relationship slowly, with a friendship and dating period. Such women often become involved with basically heterosexual women who are having difficulties in their heterosexual relationships. Heterosexual men are less likely to become involved in a prolonged homosexual liaison. Homosexual females rarely become involved in homosexual prostitution. There is an almost universal pattern of heterosexual dating among homosexual women between the ages of 16 and 19, ending by the age of 20 for almost half of them; by age 28, less than 10 percent still date men. More than three-fourths of adult homosexual women have had sexual intercourse when young, but they report a lack of psychologic and physical responsiveness and satisfaction rather than any significant manifest inner fears. About one-fourth marry, but ultimately the vast majority divorce. The men they marry are in one-third of the cases homosexuals. Of the heterosexual men, two-thirds are passive and uninterested in sex, while one-third are aggressive and interested.

In regard to psychopathology, close to one-third of the homosexual women and one-fourth of the controls had some form of psychiatric care, usually psychotherapy and counseling, at some point in their lives. The homosexual women did not suffer to a greater degree from neurotic illness, psychophysiologic reactions, affective disorders, psychoses, or other definable psychiatric problems in the form of hysteria, obsessional neurosis, anxiety or phobic symptoms, or paranoid reactions. However, the lesbian women did suffer more from alcoholism—close to one-fourth—and were more likely to use drugs. One wonders if this could be related to a masculine identification in these women. Another factor may be the frequent use of bars as a meeting place for lesbians, especially in areas where there are no organized lesbian groups and activities. It should be understood that before the recent openness of lesbian and gay men, the bar was often the only place where they could meet each other. Lesbians experience a strong need for community and connections to other lesbians because of the alienation felt from the rest of society. Depression was common in both groups, and was often related to traumatic life experiences, particularly following the breakup of affairs and love relationships. Suicide attempts occurred twice as often among the lesbians, usually during the peak period of conflict in late adolescence and early adult life, and particularly following the breakup of a relationship.

Parental loss was strikingly higher among the lesbian group than among the controls, with 39 percent having experienced parental loss prior to age ten, compared to only 5 percent in the controls. Of the homosexual group, 23 percent lost both parents, 12 percent lost only a father, and 4 percent lost only a mother. Thus, 27 percent had lost a mother prior to age ten, compared to only 2 percent in the control group. The causes of loss were divorce, death, and illegitimacy with placement in a foster home, in this order. Freud made this observation in 1905:

> In the case of some hysterics it is found that the early loss of one of their parents, whether by death, divorce or separation, with the result that the remaining parents absorbs [sic] the whole of the child's love, determines the sex of the person who is later to be chosen as sexual object, and may thus open the way to permanent inversion. [Young-Bruehl 1990, p. 144]

Also, two-thirds of the lesbians were either only children or had one sibling, in contrast to one-third of the controls. Both homosexual women and homosexual men had relatively few sisters, especially those lesbian women who were tomboys. The homosexual women had a history of emotional breakdown in their relationships with their mothers, often marked by distance and noninvolvement, while they were closer to their fathers.

The homosexual women were more assertive in their jobs and social lives, and in later adult life were not less happy or in more conflict, than the heterosexual women.

Saghir and Robins report an increased tendency for some heterosexual women to abandon that life-style and make a commitment to a lesbian relationship. They believe that this may partially reflect the increased independence and assertiveness of women in society. However, they consider these women to form a separate group; they do not regard them as homosexual, despite the choice of a homosexual partner, because they do not exhibit a lifelong pattern of homosexual preference.

Further evidence of a need for a change in attitude among professionals is offered in a chapter on psychological testing of male and female homosexuals by Bernard Reiss. Reiss concludes that there is no evidence of anything like a coherent psychological "syndrome" of female homosexuality and that homosexual behavior is not more pathological than heterosexual behavior. "That large numbers of mental health professionals still, a priori, identify homosexuality as pathology leads one to conclude that professional practice may blind one to the reality of experimentally established fact" (p. 308).

Martha Kirkpatrick and Carole Morgan

The final article about women in Marmor's 1980 volume is Kirkpatrick's and Morgan's "Psychodynamic Psychotherapy of Female Homosexuality." The authors state their view on etiology as follows:

> Current research on female sexual development shows that female gender identity may be more firmly fixed than male by the earliest experiences with mother, while for the same reason sexual object choice may be less firmly fixed, and intimacy with women on some level may be continuous as a natural part of a woman's emotional life. The sexualization of these experiences may not represent as much psychological distortion as in the male. In women, homosexuality and heterosexuality do not appear to be at opposite ends of a continuum as Kinsey et al. (1953) suggested they were. Rather, the two trends might be seen as running a parallel course, capable of intermingling and of changing positions of ascendancy in consciousness and behavior under certain circumstances. . . . The political lesbian and the new visibility of the lesbian mother further demonstrate this flexibility of object choice among women. [pp. 360–361]

Kirkpatrick and Morgan differentiate among kinds of lesbians, based on the meaning lesbianism holds for the particular woman:

> It may be a developmental phase relating to consolidation of feminine identity either in adolescence or in later life when that identity is threatened; it may be reactive as a means of restoring self-esteem and reintrojecting a loving, mother object in response to loss or disappointment in intimate relationships; it may be adaptive when heterosexual pairing is unavailable; it may be indicative of regression from the competitive anxieties of the oedipal period; or it may be a preoedipal gender disorder with a specific narcissistic defect. . . . We would like to limit our discussion of female homosexuality as a clinical disorder to this latter group. [p. 363]

The authors consider only this small group of lesbians to be pathological, as opposed to the other, "well-adjusted" lesbians, who are described as variant and reactive homosexuals. The essential features of this group are: a longing for intimate contact with a female, including sexual arousal, confusion about gender identity, a lack of pleasure in traditional feminine interests, inhibited capacity for sexual intimacy with men, and a lack of choice about the love object.

Kirkpatrick and Morgan report that women patients in this group show "an ambivalent and sexualized attachment to the mother who is idealized at the expense of the little girl's personal narcissism and regard for her own female body. On the other hand, the father is viewed as a depleted, sexually unsatisfying figure who fails in his protective role. He does not become a positive sexual object but may be the source of pathological identification" (p. 373).

The authors refer to McDougall (1970) for clinical examples. However, Marmor (1980) strongly disagrees with this approach, which he believes falls into the "trap of defining the psychopathology in these women in terms of their sexuality instead of seeing them as females who suffer from certain characterologic problems which are reflected in their sexuality also." He asserts that such disorders are seen frequently among heterosexual females as well. "Under these circumstances, to carve out a separate clinical grouping or entity for lesbian women with such problems and then label it as a clinical *disorder* called 'female homosexuality' seems to me to be a regressive step" (p. 399, footnote).

Of all the authors reviewed so far, Kirkpatrick and Morgan come closest to a feminist view of female homosexuality, and they can be called psychoanalytic feminists.

> Today, some women are finding a return to the primary source of femininity, represented by intimacy with another woman, to be their

way of breaking the hold of cultural stereotypes and renewing themselves as separate and complete individuals. Rather than an increase in
psychopathology, this may represent a healthy growth spurt previously
inhibited by a pathogenic aspect of society. The wider visibility and
acceptance of female homosexuality makes it possible to differentiate
the cultural from the intrapsychic sources of this behavior. [pp.
363–364]

They have returned to the Freudian approach of objectively describing homosexuality as an object choice, rather than subjectively con-
demning it as a pathological entity. They assert that if the relationship with
men is repeatedly disappointing, a return to a maternal object for intimacy
and erotic gratification can be a healthy alternative to either being alone or
to unhappy relationships with men.

In my view, identification with the mother has three major components: 1) mother as a maternal, nurturant figure, 2) mother as a housewife
or working outside the home, and 3) mother as a wife, the sexual object of
father. An identification with mother based on her role as a nurturant,
caring figure can be reproduced in a woman's desire for children and in her
relationship with her children, be she homosexual or heterosexual. It can
also be expressed in the choice of nursing, teaching, or social work as a
career, and, today, the choice of medicine as well. This differentiation
allows us to understand the variety of life choices by both lesbian and
heterosexual women, and the current trend for some lesbians to have
children. These women have both internalized the feminine ideal of
motherhood and have chosen to meet their emotional/erotic needs with a
woman. The daughters of lesbian mothers may choose men for their sexual
attachments, possibly depending on their experience with their own
fathers or other significant men. Lesbians are more likely than heterosexual
women to be in the work force their entire adult lives; they therefore may
not identify with a mother who was a housewife. Clearly we can find as
many variations among lesbians as among heterosexual women, permitting
such seeming anomalies as heterosexual women who, unlike their mothers,
have important careers and do not want children, and lesbian women who
want children and stay home to take care of them while their partners
work.

In an unpublished paper (1991), Kirkpatrick describes the results of a
research project begun in the early 1970s on the children of lesbian
mothers. The study involved forty children aged 5 to 12; twenty of them,
ten boys and ten girls, lived full time with single mothers who identified
themselves as lesbians; the other twenty, also ten boys and ten girls, lived
full time with single heterosexual mothers. There were thirteen previously
married lesbian mothers and twelve previously married heterosexual
mothers. Both groups of mothers reported marrying in an atmosphere of

love for their husbands and desire for marriage. Both groups had married at the same average age, and the average length of marriage was the same, seven to seven-and-a-half years. Beatings and alcoholism and/or drug abuse were present in 24 percent of the lesbian mothers' reports and in 60 percent of the heterosexual mothers' reports.

The only major difference was the reported reason for divorce. The lesbian mothers who initiated the divorce (all but one) stated that loss of intimacy or communication with the husband, not sexual dissatisfaction, was the motivation. This compares favorably with a study of married women who had affairs outside the marriage and reported that the primary dissatisfaction with their husbands was lack of emotional intimacy. The seven heterosexual wives who initiated the divorce did so because of the brutal or chaotic life-style of their husbands. Thus, more women in the heterosexual sample felt bitter toward men. As to motherhood, the number of children who were planned as opposed to unplanned was similar in each group, but only the heterosexuals reported that children (three) were unwanted. The lesbian mothers had breast-fed eighteen out of twenty children, compared to ten out of twenty in the heterosexual group.

The researchers could find no evidence of maternal inadequacies on the basis of sexual orientation. No differences in developmental psychological status, gender identity, or quantity or quality of pathology in the children were found. Kirkpatrick concludes:

> Clearly I was under the sway of the old myth that maternal interest and capacity evolved from the resolved oedipal relationship and subsequent heterosexuality. While my study was certainly not analytic, it further persuaded me that the primary origins of maternal desire are pre-oedipal, that they arise from the early dyadic relationship and have a developmental pathway of their own separate from sexual orientation. [p. 16]

Charlotte Wolff

Wolff, a British psychoanalyst, studied 108 English lesbians (1971). In contrast to Saghir and Robins and such other researchers as Bernard Reiss (1980), Wolff found that "the incidence of psychological illness, mainly anxiety neurosis, was astonishingly high among the lesbians as compared with the controls" (p. 159). Perhaps that can be attributed to the earlier date of her research, before the women's movement improved the atmosphere and allowed women to choose lesbianism with a political motive. We might speculate that these women form a mentally healthier group than the more anxious group of the 1970s and earlier.

Wolff compared the lesbian sample with a control group on twenty-

eight different indices. She found thirty-five lesbians who had had traumatic sexual experiences in childhood, as compared to eleven women in
the control group; and thirty who had had traumatic sexual experiences in
adolescence, as compared to four among the controls. There were fifty-six
lesbians with psychological illness, compared to fourteen among the
controls, including eighteen who had been hospitalized in a mental hospital, compared to two among the controls. There were sixteen lesbians with
alcoholism, none in the control group. The family history showed twenty-
five mentally ill, twenty-four alcoholics, and twenty-nine homosexuals
among the lesbians, with fifteen mentally ill, nine alcoholics, and one
homosexual among the controls, raising the issue of a possible genetic
factor.

In a test of reactions to stress situations, thirty-three lesbians reacted
well, compared to ninety-two controls; and seventy-three reacted badly,
compared to twenty-seven controls. The difficulty with these statistics is
that being a lesbian itself can be a source of considerable stress even now,
and was more so in 1971, so we cannot conclude that the high stress factor
is related to childhood experience alone.

The lesbians rated their parents' marriage unhappy in fifty cases, as
compared to twenty-three for the controls. The data on the mothers is
interesting. The age of the mother at birth of the subject was significantly
lower in the lesbian sample. Lesbians are significantly more often only
children or the oldest child, and significantly less often the youngest child.
The mother was the dominant parent more often among lesbians, and they
were more often the mothers' favorite than the controls. But as a whole,
mothers were regarded as less loving in the case of the lesbians. The mother
showed a preference for a son more often in the lesbian group, and was far
more often either indifferent or outright negligent in the lesbian group.
Although an equal number of lesbians and controls reported being the
father's favorite, only sixty-two lesbians described their fathers as loving,
compared to one hundred four controls. Fathers were deemed negligent by
fourteen lesbians and three controls.

Surprisingly, fifty-eight of the lesbians reported themselves to be
physically attracted to men, compared to only eighty-seven of the heterosexuals. Forty-eight lesbians and thirty-four controls were not attracted to
men. There was no significant difference between the two groups with
regard to the number of heterosexual partners. This leads to Wolff's thesis
that lesbian love relationships are more emotionally intensive than sexual
relationships for heterosexual women, with lesbians often having a broad
heterosexual background but lacking in comparable emotional intensity
with men.

Wolff takes a very positive attitude toward lesbians, in spite of her
focus on pathology:

The lesbian's refusal to be an inferior to man is absolute, while with "normal" women the rejection of man's superiority remains relative. Married lesbians often conform automatically to conventions, and are not always conscious of themselves as integral entities. My survey showed that a number of them only discovered their homosexuality after years of marriage, but when that happened, they changed in their attitude to their husband and—far more important—to themselves. They discovered their *selves,* and with it, their *absolute* rejection of being an object. They realized then that they had never felt their position as wives as genuine, but had played a part which education and convention prescribed for them. The unease they had always felt was only brought home to them when they experienced the spontaneity of homosexual society. [pp. 81–82]

The lesbian was and is unquestionably in the avant-garde of the fight for equality of the sexes, and for the psychical liberation of woman. She has the makings of the best soldier in the battle for a woman's right to independence . . . . A "normal" woman, conscious of herself, needs a far more complex mechanism to reconcile her wish to be a self-contained, independent person. On the one hand she must allow herself to be an object in order to get a man, on the other she will look down on herself for doing so. . . . She suffers from conflicting loyalties, one to herself, the other to her heterosexual instincts. [p. 80]

Wolff's cultural/feminist approach is in contrast to her psychodynamic approach, but the two can be integrated. Wolff believes that lesbian women make a much stronger emotional connection to their loved one than heterosexual women do, choosing from the heart more often than the head, as she sees in the cases of heterosexual women.

The stability of partnership between lesbians is endangered through their high degree of emotionalism. But true *emotion* is the key to their attachments and their search for fulfillment. It overrides reason and often plays havoc with their professional application and achievement. *Thus emotion is both the rapture and the danger of the lesbian's personal and collective life.* [p. 77]

Ruth-Jean Eisenbud

Eisenbud, in an article entitled "Early and Later Determinants of Lesbian Choice" (1982), sees lesbian object choice as a result of an ego development of precocious sexuality:

Primary Lesbian erotic love originates in a precocious turn-on of erotic desire mandated by the ego and it is progressive, not regressive. It occurs when the child has been excluded from "good enough" or "long enough" primary bliss and seeks inclusion by a sexual bond and sexual wooing. . . . Biological, genital sexuality is a resource available to the ego's diverse purposes. Once precocious sexual arousal is mobilized by the ego and used for organization of early pain and emotional hunger, the erotic feeling, together with the choice of object and interpersonal context, are internalized. When the inner love affair with a female love object becomes actualized again in later contexts, this should not be described as energy regressing from sexual feeling to oral dependency or to a fixation due to early seduction but as a replay of a primary, sexual, erotic feeling. [pp. 86–87]

Thus, Eisenbud sees the little girl's sexual approach to her mother as an effort to attain effective mastery, a method for forging a bond to the mother, and a means to arouse the mother in an "attempt at an erotic solution for miscarried weaning, envy, jealousy, insecurity and feelings of exclusion" (p. 98).

In most situations an only child or a first child (or a girl with brothers preferred or whose parents preferred a boy), the pre-Lesbian girl is faced by a closed alliance that excludes her and refuses her needed support, or with a felt lack of a cohesive group in a disturbed family after a close first year alone with mother. [p. 98]

The little girl is excluded by a new baby, because the mother dies, or because the mother withdraws from her after 18 months, resulting in grief, jealousy of others whom the mother values, and envy of penis, breast, or bottle—whatever brings close association to the mother. Eisenbud's lesbian patients remember rage and sexual arousal toward their mother, and ardently wooing, pestering, clutching, or attacking her.

The severity of the narcissistic wound of exclusion reflects the experi-ence of being discounted by one with whom there was an established mutual interdependency. . . . She is left helpless in her passionate jealousy. Unlike a little boy in the same circumstances, she cannot readily identify with father's power to re-establish her sense of effec-tiveness. Her ego then used sexual arousal, verbal and nonverbal expressions of physical love, in an attempt to create a bonding that will reduce annihilating jealousy and regain effectiveness. [p. 99]

Eisenbud points out that the factor of exclusion itself can serve as an aphrodisiac, and believes this is especially so in early same-sex erotic love. Turning to the father sexually is a later step, after some individuation, if the father is a stable force in the girl's life. Eisenbud proposes three reconstruc-tions of primary lesbian choice:

1. *Exclusion from being mothered.* The father and/or brother are neglectful or dangerous and no constant nurturing person is concerned with her. The girl tries to find a way to attract the mother's attention and arouse a response from a rejecting mother by a wooing approach, an erotic insistence on contact. Later in childhood she may champion, rescue, and protect the mother. The importance of the father's reaction when his daughter turns to him may be key to lesbian choice. Mistreatment or rejection by the father may result in her return to mother's body with an active sexual approach.

2. *Exclusion from identification with mother (a double bind and tomboy outcome).* This may be the outcome when the mother communicates to her daughter that she is supposed to be a little girl but must be active, independent, self-reliant, non-demanding, and a support to her mother. The double bind is that she is punished for her activity and independence. She does not want to be a man, she wants to be a woman with the power of a man. If the mother is a kind of reigning queen, giving and receiving attention from her audiences, the little girl is forbidden to compete or identify and must surrender to the mother's pre-eminence. She may then court the mother to be included as part of the entourage, making a primary lesbian sexual choice. As an adult lesbian she gives nurturance and a place on the throne to other women.

3. *Escape from inclusion, the active stance.* This child seeks individuation by a reversal of dependency, an erotic conquering and domination in order to overcome her mother's forceful coercion of her autonomy. "Who is to use whom becomes a burning question. Who is to be part of whom?" (p. 102). The hate–love affair with the mother must result in flight in order for her ego to survive. She must find a transitional object or interest, but the lesbian yearning remains binding with an undercurrent of bitterness and rage.

Joyce McDougall

McDougall's article "Homosexuality in Women" was published in Chasseguet-Smirgel's *Female Sexuality* (1970a). (See Chapter 3.) McDougall's views are also expressed in *A Plea for a Measure of Abnormality* (1980). Her theories are based on her clinical work with four homosexual patients and three others who were bisexual but were "dominated by conscious homosexual wishes" (1970a, p. 171). She also describes what she calls the *masculine woman,* and differentiates her from the lesbian woman. This is apparently based on two case examples. The masculine woman idealizes her father and models herself closely upon him, but he has never been an object of sexual desire. Her attitude toward her mother is closely veiled hatred. She believes she is different from other women—a castrated man—and denigrates all women. McDougall claims the source of these distorted beliefs is that the father is seen as so dangerously seductive that he had to be excluded as a love object. In the daughter's analysis the mother is revealed as once powerful and as having abandoned the daughter. The acceptance of an interpretation of penis envy serves as an "alibi" against a much deeper fear of women, especially the terror of ever being in rivalry with a woman.

McDougall summarizes her theory of female homosexuality (1980) as

> an attempt to resolve conflict concerning the two poles of psychic identity: one's identity as a separate individual and one's sexual identity. The manifold desires and conflicts that face every girl with regard to her father have . . . been dealt with by giving him up as an object of love and desire and identifying with him instead. The result is that the mother becomes once more the only object worthy of love. Thus the daughter acquires a somewhat fictitious *sexual identity;* however, the unconscious identification with the father aids her in achieving a stronger sense of *subjective identity.* She uses this identification to achieve a certain detachment from the maternal imago in its more dangerous and forbidding aspects. [p. 87]

The mother must be willing to allow her daughter to become independent of her and to help her in her sexual identification, acknowledging her as a sexual rival and accepting the daughter's love for the father. On his part, the father must be willing to offer his little girl his strength and love, and thus help her to disengage herself from her mother. McDougall concludes that it takes two problem parents to produce homosexual offspring.

McDougall describes some very disturbed homosexual women in whom, she proposes, homosexual behavior contributes to maintaining a precarious psychic equilibrium and ego identity, as the lesbian love relationship satisfies the longing for the idealized mother. In such cases, the source of the disturbance lies in the girl's ambivalent and sexualized attachment to her mother, who is idealized at the expense of the daughter's personal narcissism and regard for her own female body. The father is not a positive sexual object, but may be the source of pathological identification.

> Behind the conscious wish to eliminate or denigrate the father, all of my homosexual patients revealed narcissistic wounds linked to the image of the *indifferent* father. Strengthened by the conviction that the mother forbade any loving relationship between father and daughter, these women tended to feel that any desire for the father, his love or his

penis, was dangerous. Such a wish could only entail the loss of the mother's love and bring castration to the father. Thus the daughter's consciously avowed dislike of the father was experienced as a gift made to the mother. In turn, it gave rise to fantasies of a revengeful and persecuting father, and subsequently to the fear of men in general. [1980, p. 105]

The mothers are described by their daughters in idealized terms: beautiful, gifted, and charming. The daughter cannot in her own estimation come close to the mother. Yet there is no conscious envy of her, as she is seen as a victim of the father's domination, unfairness, and possible abandonment. Idealizing the mother, says McDougall, protects the daughter from hostile and destructive wishes toward her. "The daughter's wish is for total elimination of the father and the creation of an exclusive and enduring mother–daughter relationship," which is lived out in the lesbian bond (p. 108).

Unconsciously, the girl fears that she is indispensable to the mother and that her independence would be both disloyal and dangerous. Yet she feels that her body and her whole self have been severely rejected by the mother. McDougall describes two main poles in which either depressive anxiety or persecutory anxiety dominate, as a result of the pathological introjection of the father. This splitting into a "good sex" and a "bad sex" can lead to a paranoid attitude toward men. The homosexual attachment may serve to ward off states of depression or depersonalization and prevent suicide.

There is little doubt that McDougall is describing a severe borderline patient, who happens to have achieved a homosexual identity and object choice that protects her from either severe depression or paranoia. The question is whether she is describing all homosexual women; and the answer to this has to be no. One may describe heterosexual patients with severe splitting, fear of fusion, and borderline defenses, as well as serious depression and anxiety, without describing all heterosexuals. Thus, although McDougall's theories may be valid and interesting, it is doubtful if she is telling us about more than a small percentage of homosexual women. Others have made their object choice based on some combination of biological and cultural factors and family dynamics, perhaps the early loss of the mother. Rather than "Homosexuality in Women," a more apt title for the essay would have been "Borderline Disturbances in Four Women Homosexuals." McDougall shares the problem of other psychoanalytic writers who attempt too broad a generalization from a few case examples.

Charles Socarides

Socarides is author of *The Overt Homosexual* (1968) and *Homosexuality* (1978). In the latter volume he reviews the psychoanalytic literature and

presents his idea that in the clinical picture, female homosexuality is
basically masochistic, designed to temporarily ward off severe anxiety and
hostility toward the mother through unconscious guilt, which transforms
the hate impulses into a "masochistic libidinal attitude" (p. 133).

> The homosexual woman is in flight from men. The source of this flight
> is her childhood feelings of rage, hate and guilt toward her mother and
> a fear of merging with her. Accompanying this primary conflict are
> deep anxieties and aggression secondary to disappointments and rejec-
> tion, both real and imagined, at the hands of the male (father). [pp.
> 133–134]

Socarides states that deprived of their love object, homosexual
women very often become suicidal. The same problem of confusing
diagnosis with symptoms, and a lesbian object choice with diagnosis,
appears in Socarides's work as in other psychoanalytic writers. In fact,
many heterosexual women become suicidal, or at least threaten suicide,
when there is a loss or threatened loss of a love relationship. As research
has shown, lesbians are more like heterosexual women than like homosexual men. We must recognize that the diagnosis depends on the underlying pathology and that homosexuality is not the underlying pathology. It
is, as Freud said, the object choice, not an illness.

Elaine Siegel

Elaine Siegel (1988), who dedicated her book to Socarides, acknowledges
his value to her own work, which focuses on the preoedipal etiology of
female homosexuality. She describes his work as "masterful" and "sophisticated" and says her book is "respectfully" dedicated to him in "grati-
tude." I am struck by this adoration, and wonder if it provides clues to her
own theory-making. *Female Homosexuality: Choice Without Volition* is
based on her analytic work with twelve women patients, claimed to be the
largest sample treated by a single analyst. In a review of her book, Magee
(1991) quotes from Robert Stoller (1975) in a discussion of psychoanalytic
research about homosexuality:

> The desire to solve riddles—to search and discover . . .—is one of the
> keenest intellectual pleasures humans have. In this detective work,
> psychoanalysts are always at risk, . . . and in danger of succumbing to,
> the temptation of grand explanations. At those times, we substitute the
> vocabulary of theory . . . (as, for instance, when we say that homosex-
> uals have more archaic cathexis of X or Y than do heterosexuals). [p. 96]

Magee suggests that Siegel offers a "grand explanation" for female homosexuality.

> Although Siegel says she does not view female homosexuality as a single entity, her book certainly does, and characterizes it,—by its "earlier" origin and, therefore, its pathology—in order to distinguish it from another supposed entity, "female heterosexuality." Female homosexuality, says Siegel, is an unchosen choice, a choice made without the exercise of the will. This sounds dangerous and disturbed unless we remember that a choice shaped by unconscious determinants is certainly neither specific to female homosexuality nor necessarily evidence of disturbance. [p. 102]

Siegel (1988) finds the genesis of a lesbian object choice in narcissistic injury by a mother who didn't really love her daughter, resulting in massive failures of empathy. This produces a developmental arrest and fixation of a very specific type, in which the vagina and the inner space per se were not included in the inner representation of the body. "For them, this calamity had to do with their inability to take full possession of their vaginas. . . . Their basic endowment for self-love and self-esteem never blossomed. They were expected to fill their mother's needs, not their own" (p. 22). Siegel believes these women try to complete themselves with a same sex partner, "but the mirroring they received from their female lovers was as distorted as their primary, maternal experience had been, locking them into the never ending cycle of the repetition compulsion" (p. 23).

Siegel draws the following conclusions about her patients' parents:

> Both parents were regularly willing to sacrifice their daughters' developmental needs to their own inner drives. It did not occur to them to view their children as anything but possessions. The ruthlessness, coldness, and narcissistic impairment discernible in the actions reported by their daughters point to narcissistic personality disorders and possible borderline syndrome in some of the parents. [p. 223]

One would hate to be the parent of a lesbian daughter and have to read this. Yet again, it could easily be a description of the parents of many of my heterosexual patients. One wonders at its applicability to any but Siegel's particular lesbian patients as seen through the surely not entirely objective lens of their daughter's recollections. It is especially important to reiterate that these patients are lesbian women who have come for psychoanalysis, not for short-term counseling; and they are not lesbian women who feel no need for counseling at all, who, according to Saghir and Robins (1980), comprise two-thirds of the lesbian population. It is also another reminder of the pathology one can find in heterosexuals and heterosexual couples.

FEMALE HOMOSEXUALITY AND CHILD SEXUAL ABUSE

The Kinsey Institute researchers on homosexuality, Bell, Weinberg, and Hammersmith (1981), found that homosexual women were no more likely to have been raped or otherwise molested than heterosexual women, nor were they more likely to have been punished for childhood sex play with boys. Their work suggests that a homosexual orientation among females reflects neither a lack of heterosexual experience nor a history of particularly unpleasant heterosexual experiences. Among those who recalled having been sexually aroused both by a male and by a female before they reached age 19, the homosexual and heterosexual women did not differ in which type of arousal occurred first (pp. 175–176). These results are significant in apparently ruling out sexual abuse as a causative factor in female homosexuality. But of course even a comparable rate of abuse between the two groups means that as many as 30 percent of lesbians may have been sexually molested as children. This figure is likely to be higher among the group that seeks psychoanalysis or psychotherapy, so therapists need to explore this question.

Only Wolff, of the authors I have reviewed, makes any mention of sexual abuse in the backgrounds of her case examples. The two major sources I have used on child sexual abuse, Blume (1990) and Bass and Davis (1988), both deny any connection between sexual abuse and lesbianism. This follows from their view that being a lesbian is not an illness, therefore not a symptom of abuse or any other negative experience: it is a free choice to love women.

> It is true that being abused by men has influenced some women to relate sexually and emotionally to women rather than men. However, no one becomes a lesbian solely because she was abused by a man. After all, many heterosexual women were abused by men, and they continue to choose men as their mates and sexual partners. If abuse were the determining factor in sexual preference, the lesbian population would be far greater than it is now. . . . Being a lesbian is a perfectly healthy way to be, not another effect of the abuse you need to overcome. [Bass and Davis 1988, p. 268]

What is missing from this picture? What is missing is the possibility of sexual seduction and abuse by a woman. This experience may have included love and care or may have been coercive and sadistic, but in any case we cannot apply different standards to sexual exploitation of a child when it comes from a woman than when it comes from a man. The absence of the possibility of penile penetration makes abuse by a woman less likely to be physically traumatic. But the violation of trust and the betrayal of what should have been a care-giving relationship makes it emotionally traumatic. The sexual arousal and pleasure, and resultant guilt and anxiety, could burden the child, create repression or disassociation, and result in later symptoms. The young girl abused by her mother could also be prevented from developing a relationship with her father, if he is in the picture, as all her loyalty and emotional intensity is usurped by the mother.

"The Persephone Complex"—Eileen Starzecpyzel

Eileen Starzecpyzel, in an essay titled "The Persephone Complex" (1987), describes the effects of father-daughter incest on lesbians, using Chodorow's work on the early connection between mother and daughter as her model. Persephone, the daughter of the god Zeus and goddess Demeter, is violently abducted by her uncle, Hades, and held in the underworld with the permission of Zeus. Torn from her mother, raped by her uncle, she cries and mourns for her mother inconsolably. Hades eventually returns her to Demeter, but she is marked forever by her experience, remaining a powerful and mysterious figure in mythology. Her separateness is a source of creative and individual power in the world.

Starzecpyzel hypothesizes that incest affects the normal development of a girl as follows:

> The early loss of mothering, or severance of pre-Oedipal connectedness to mother, not only happens to boys in normal development, but also happens to a girl who has been victimized by father–daughter incest. It creates for the boy and the incested girl an unsatisfied longing for mother. Loss of and longing for the early sexual pre-Oedipal bond with mother may be a significant factor in the development of the choice of women as sexual objects for both a man and a lesbian who has been a victim of incest with her father. [p. 265]

She concludes that the break in the mother–daughter relationship caused by the father's seduction of the girl away from her mother gives the incested girl a unique psychological distance from her mother, and thus unusual independence, including the freedom to revert to the matrisexual bond that others must forego. Starzecpyzel's sample includes fifty patients from group or individual therapy, of whom 70 percent are lesbians. Starzecpyzel believes that the damage to the mother–daughter bond may be a significant contributing factor in the development of lesbianism in the incest survivor. She finds an intense longing for a nurturing, positive relationship with a woman to be distinctly separate from anger at and difficulties with men. Additionally, she believes that the incest survivor, after treatment, can in fact emerge with greater strength than can other women who have separation problems with their mothers.

The father who sexually abuses his daughter devalues the mother by keeping the child from being close to her. He teaches the daughter to be "better than" or apart from her mother, splitting them totally.

> The daughter has a profound sense of being unwanted, unloved, and unprotected. Because the mother feels powerless, enraged at her husband, and unable to keep her daughter for herself, she projects this sense of overwhelming badness to her child. . . . Furthermore, the enactment or threat of enactment, of the Oedipal wish to win daddy convinces the child that she is witch-like and evil for hurting mommy this way. [pp. 268–269]

This can result in a negative bond with the mother, or a pseudopositive bond in which the daughter sacrifices herself to her mother's well-being by mothering her mother. Underneath lies real abandonment.

> For lesbians, at least, it seems that this subconscious fear of mother's rage, this open encouragement to bond with the father, and the underlying strength of the sexualized attraction to and love of the lost mother, all form a powerful inducement to utilize the primary sexualized response to women that is an inherent part of the female experience . . . with eventual displacement onto a suitable lesbian later in life. [p. 271]

Starzecpyzel believes she has isolated five core issues that affect lesbians who have suffered father–daughter incest. Every lesbian incest survivor she has worked with is conscious of at least three of the following issues: identification with the father; protectiveness toward the mother; rejection of the mother; intense longing for the mother; and feelings of abandonment by the lost mother. Starzecpyzel claims that about 80 percent of the lesbian patients she has seen value the power of masculinity as a healthier model of adaptation than traditional passive female identity. In 80 percent to 90 percent of incested lesbians, she finds a strong conscious rejection of the mother and her model of femininity. We can speculate that this is a result of the demeaning of the mother by the father's turning to his daughter. Rage at the mother is "usually more defended against than it is for heterosexual patients because lesbians consider themselves woman-centered, and efforts to be politically correct may hinder free expression of anger at mother" (p. 278).

Considering the view that there is more merging in the lesbian couple, the notion that the lesbian is free to make a choice of a woman lover because in fact she is more fully separated from her mother leaves some confusion. Starzecpyzel ignores the debate over lesbian symbiosis and describes a differentiated woman who seeks to return to her first love, her mother, as heterosexual men do, and who is freer to do so because the mother–daughter bond was badly damaged. This implies that separation leads to freedom, and thus allows a reuniting that Starzecpyzel claims is not a regression but a "healthy reversion to the original matrisexual model that is a normal part of female psychology" (p. 281). It seems to me this concept conflicts with a basic premise in psychotherapy that damage does not lead to freedom, but rather to heightened defenses. Wolff (1971) describes the emotional intensity in the lesbian bond as based on the lack of differentiation in a same-sex couple. A damaged mother–daughter relationship is generally a poor prognosis for later homosexual or heterosexual relationships. It would seem that this issue needs further exploration, but Starzecpyzel's idea is a stimulating one, and the notion of healthy reversion takes a positive view as opposed to the concept of regression. It is necessary to be cautious, however, in any attempt to view homosexuality positively, that problem areas not be glossed over.

Starzecpyzel, a lesbian herself, is able to integrate a psychodynamic approach to understanding the etiology of lesbianism with a positive approach to a homosexual alternative. She provides an alternative to the too-simplified notion that if you search for causes you are biased toward an illness model of lesbianism. In my view, one can be interested in causes—and in fact must be to understand and help a patient become free of troubling symptoms—without falling into the trap of pathologizing lesbianism and maintaining that heterosexuality is a morally or psychologically superior position.

A Critique—Joyce McDougall

The view that sexual abuse is a significant factor in some cases of homosexuality leads back to McDougall's patients (1970). Among Starzecpyzel's lesbian incest survivors who do identify with their mothers, the father is described as having practically no redeeming qualities. Starzecpyzel believes that the father identification is submerged in bad father/good mother splitting. This would seem to apply to McDougall's patients. I was especially interested in McDougall's report that three of her four patients had an "intense preoccupation with vomiting" (p. 183). Romm (1965) also describes a patient with a symptom of persistent morning vomiting (p. 293). Romm's patient recalls never having received love from her parents as a child and describes her father as taking no interest in her except to tickle her and make superficial sexual passes at her girlfriends when she was an adolescent. She had just left a sadistic lesbian lover. McDougall's patients include Olivia, a young woman in her twenties who had such a severe vomiting phobia that it crippled most of her social relations and was one of her principal reasons for coming to analysis. Olivia says: "I can't bear the sound of my father with his *horrible throat noises* and coughing. He only does it to drive me mad. I can't stand looking at him. . . . I'm sure my father is responsible for my attacks. He tries to make me ill. You probably don't believe it, but *I know he would like to kill me*" (p. 183, italics added).

A second patient, Karen, says:

> "When I think of my father I hear him clearing his throat of mucus, blowing his nose, *making horrible noises* which seemed to spread over the dinner table and envelope us all. I used to think I would faint when he spoke to me, as though he were going to *spit at me*. I'd like to tear his guts out, filthy pig! *Makes you want to vomit.* He couldn't even eat without making a noise." . . . At other times she described a frightening fantasy which had persisted for some twenty years in which she imagined her father creeping up behind her to cut off her head. "I think *he must have threatened to kill me when I was little*. I would jump whenever he came up behind me. Always kept my distance. Would never sit beside him in the car and so on." [p. 184, italics added]

Eva says: "I can't describe the *terrible look on my father's face.* Even though I've done nothing I'm always afraid he will shout at me. My heart races *as though he's going to kill me* . . . He is brutal and disgusting" (p. 184, italics added).

McDougall:

> One has the impression of a little girl in terror of being attacked or "penetrated" by her father. The very intensity of her repudiation of him and her emphasis on his dirty and noisy qualities give us an inkling of the way she has used regression and repression to deal with any phallic-sexual interest attached to him. . . . The defensive value of this "impotent" father is clear: if he is castrated, there is less fear of desiring him as a love object. [pp. 184–185]

At another point she tells us that a recurrent fear of vomiting is in part a response to: "the unconscious injunction to *render up everything* to the mother—the introjected father as well as one's own essential femininity" (p. 201).

In another example she relates:

> One patient reconstructed one such "theft" [having been robbed by the mother of her feminine sexuality] when talking of a disastrous evening she had spent. She was the center of interest at a fashionable reception

when an attractive man entered the group and took over the conversation. Immediately overwhelmed with feelings of *nausea and suffocation,* she was obliged to go home. On her way she recollected on the situation and realized that she had experienced a moment of murderous rage and jealousy just before the onset of the symptoms. She suddenly had imagined herself *swallowing this man's penis without his noticing it and having to vomit it up when discovered.* [p. 203, italics added]

What is clear is that McDougall does not take her patient's fear of and rage and disgust at their fathers at all seriously! She even *denies her own impressions* of a little girl being attacked or penetrated. She has developed a complex theory that it all really means these girls are sexually *attracted* to their fathers. The more intense the fear, loathing, and disgust, the more sexual interest she must truly have in him. I seriously question this analysis. I think that in all three of McDougall's cases, and perhaps in the fourth of Romm's, the father forced his daughter to copulate him orally when she was a little girl, and the vomiting phobias are directly related to those orally traumatic experiences. Therapists need to be on the alert for symptoms relating to oral penetration and anxieties around bowel function as possible clues to oral or anal sexual molestation. Bass and Davis (1988) describe clinical work in which a therapist cures a woman patient of her bulimia by telling her to "get that penis out of her mouth another way" (p. 219). How many cases of bulimia might be related to forced oral copulation I cannot know, but it would be wise for the therapist to explore this avenue of repressed material.

Keeping in mind the references above to feelings of fear, loathing, and disgust in relation to sounds and facial expressions; the fear of the father "spitting," the aversion to looking at him or sitting near him; plus the fear of being killed by the father, let us examine the experience of an adult man having an orgasm in the mouth of a small girl. The following description, based on a compilation of clinical work and the literature, may be unfamiliar to most readers of clinical case material and is surely unfit for polite society. But an appreciation of the experience of sexual abuse is necessary if we, as therapists, are to avoid the kind of gross misdiagnosis illustrated by McDougall.

A man about 5′10″ tall, weighing about 170 pounds, approaches a small girl, his daughter. Try to imagine being approached by someone twice your height (11 feet tall) and four times your weight (600 pounds). He seduces her into sitting on his lap, or perhaps he lies down next to her in her bed and starts to stroke or caress her in an affectionate way. This is so rare in her life that she loves the attention and fondling. If he strokes or licks her genital area, she feels sexual pleasure and excitement that she is unprepared for, can't understand, and doesn't know how to handle.

He removes his penis from his pants, or takes his pants off, takes the girl's small hand and places it on his penis, instructing her to stroke it or pet it. She obeys him and hopes this means he likes her and will be nice to her. The penis engorges, becomes hard, and the little girl has her first feelings of fear. She is confused and uncertain about what has happened and what her part in it is. The father has become sexually aroused and shows signs of excitement that the girl finds disturbing. His voice tone changes, his heart is beating rapidly, his face becomes red, and he starts making strange sounds, such as groans, moans, grunts, or other noises. He then puts both his hands on the girl's head and pushes her face down on his penis. The girl sees and feels the rough hair in his pubic area and feels his hard penis force its way into her mouth. He may be on top of her, his huge heaving body pushing the penis into her mouth, or if she is alongside him or on top of him he forces her face into his groin and his penis down her throat. As the hard, thrusting penis penetrates her mouth and reaches the top of her throat, her natural gagging reflex is triggered and she starts to gag and choke, trying to vomit it out. Her little nose is her only means of obtaining air, but it may be pushed into the hairy area around the penis and she may not be able to breathe. She feels that she is going to die and that her father is killing her. As he reaches climax, her father makes noises that she has never heard before, but she has no way of understanding or appreciating that this is a normal human reaction to reaching orgasm. The expressions on his face, when she can see his face, may look to her like intense hatred or pain. She senses his agony and his pleasure; they are completely beyond her comprehension and only serve to further terrify her.

When she is finally relieved of the thrusting of the hard penis in her little mouth, she realizes that some smelly, sticky, mucus-like substance is in her mouth and could go down her throat. She wants to spit it out in disgust but may not be able to; she may start to swallow it, much to her further fear and disgust. When her father starts to relax he gets up and pulls up his pants. He will probably tell her that this is their secret, that she is a good girl, and that she must never, never, tell anybody about what happened. He might tell her of some terrible thing that would happen to her if she ever told anybody. She will probably completely repress this entire scene and have no memory of it, but she has been raped and can never be the same again. Maybe it will happen again, and each time it will be the same, except that from the start she will pretend she is not there, that this is not really happening to her; this will help her to survive. She may, after several such experiences, realize that what is happening will not kill her, but her father's grunts and facial expressions will still be frightening, and his penis and semen in her mouth will still feel disgusting. She will psychically remove herself from beginning to end, and will try to avoid her father as much as possible in the future. She may always associate sexual arousal with fear, secrecy, pain, and disgust.

Any reader who has had trouble believing in the terrible rage and fear of death that is described here must continually keep in mind the enormous difference in size between a 2-, 3-, or 5-year-old girl and an adult man. Dr. Michael Durfee of the Los Angeles Department of Health Services reported in 1984 that more sexual abuse was reported on 2-year-olds than on any other age group. Three and 4-year-olds were next (Blume 1990, p. 10). A recent report (Nihira and Chang 1990) from the Los Angeles County Department of Health Services confirms the 1984 statistics. It covers the reported cases of N. gonorrhea during the years 1981 through 1989 and includes over 6,000 cases of suspect child abuse reports per year from health professionals since 1985. A 1991 report of the Child Abuse Prevention Program states that "most of the alleged victims are very young with a peak incidence within the first three months of life" (p. 1).

These very young children are easy targets because they cannot articulate and will not remember. Anyone who has difficulty appreciating the sensation of the gag reflex might remember the feeling you had as a child when the doctor put a tongue depressor stick on the back of your tongue and asked you to say "ahh." In any case, I ask you to reread the quotations from McDougall's patients now and come to your own conclusions.

FEMINISM AND LESBIANS

Lesbians were acknowledged in the early writings of the women's movement, but they were never fully welcomed by heterosexual feminists because of the unfortunate reality that they tainted the movement in the eyes of men and the general public. It is of interest to note that a three-volume work, *The Woman Patient: Medical and Psychological Interfaces* (1978, 1982), edited by psychiatrists Malkah T. Notman and

Carol C. Nadelson, contains not one chapter on female homosexuality out of a total of fifty-four separate chapter topics. The word lesbian cannot be found in the index in any of the three volumes, and a brief reference to female homosexuality can be found in only one chapter, written by a male. Denial and avoidance of the topic was the best defense against the fear of contamination.

Martha Shelley

Sisterhood is Powerful (1970) includes one essay by Martha Shelley entitled "Notes of a Radical Lesbian." Shelley also has an essay in *The Radical Therapist* (1971), called "Lesbianism," which is similar in content and tone.

> The lesbian, through her ability to obtain love and sexual satisfaction from other women, is freed of dependence on men for love, sex, and money. She does not have to do menial chores for them (at least at home), nor cater to their egos, or submit to hasty and inept sexual encounters. She is freed from fear of unwanted pregnancy and the pains of childbirth, and from the drudgery of child-raising. [p. 171]

However, Shelley also describes the "penalties" involved in being a lesbian: the loss of the rewards of child raising (for some); competing with men on the job market while facing job and salary discrimination; facing the most severe contempt and ridicule that society can heap on a woman. She describes (1970) a scene that occurred in 1968, as feminists picketed the Miss America Pageant while hostile onlookers called them names such as "commies" and "tramps." It was only when they were called "lesbians" that some of them broke into tears. The popular confusion between feminism and lesbianism was common in the early days of the movement and continued for many years. I can remember being at a women's rally in Union Square in San Francisco in the early days; a young man walked angrily past me, saying "Why don't you just get yourselves a dildo!" I was shocked to realize that in his mind, being a feminist was synonymous with being a lesbian. As Shelley says:

> When a woman showed up at a feminist meeting and announced that she was a lesbian, many women avoided her. Others told her to keep her mouth shut, for fear that she would endanger the cause. They felt that men could be persuaded to accept some measure of equality for women—as long as these women would parade their devotion to heterosexuality and motherhood. . . . Lesbians, because they are not afraid of being abandoned by men, are less reluctant to express hostility toward the male class—the oppressors of women. Hostility towards

your oppressor is healthy—but the guardians of modern morality, the psychiatrists, have interpreted this hostility as an illness, and they say this illness causes and is lesbianism. [1971, p. 172]

"Straight women," she says, "fear Lesbians because of the Lesbian inside them, because we represent an alternative. They are angry at us because we have a way out that they are afraid to take" (1970, p. 347).

Keeping in mind that 1970–1971 was also a time of great political ferment on college campuses, with revolutionaries opposing the war in Vietnam and aligning themselves with the rebellion of African-Americans in groups such as the Black Panthers (Eldridge Cleaver ran for President in 1972), it is easy to see how while some feminists came to be characterized as liberal, middle-class reformers, represented by the National Organization for Women (NOW), others identified themselves as radical revolutionaries. Some lesbians considered themselves revolutionaries against the patriarchal system, and saw heterosexual women as tepid reformers. This antagonism caused splits in the women's movement for many years. I can recall attending a large gathering in 1972 to hear Gloria Steinem speak at Glide Memorial Church in San Francisco. A group of lesbians in the front row, represented by a spokeswoman, demanded that all the men in the audience be forced to leave so that this could be an all-women's event. Needless to say this caused considerable discomfort among the men and the women who accompanied them. At the suggestion of the chairwoman of the event, or perhaps it was Steinem, a vote was taken and a large majority of the audience preferred to have the men remain. When the vote was announced about ten lesbians stood up and marched out of the church.

Radicalesbians

"The Woman Identified Woman" by the Radicalesbians (1976), a group of six women who included author Rita Mae Brown, was a strong early statement about the role of lesbians in society and in the women's movement.

A lesbian is the rage of all women condensed to the point of explosion. She is the woman who, often beginning at an extremely early age, acts in accordance with her inner compulsion to be a more complete and freer human being than her society—perhaps then, but certainly later— cares to allow her. These needs and actions, over a period of years, bring her into painful conflict with people, situations, the accepted ways of thinking, feeling and behaving, until she is in a state of continual war with everything around her, and usually with her self. . . .

Lesbian is the word, the label, the condition that holds women in line. When a woman hears this word tossed her way, she knows she is stepping out of line. She knows that she has crossed the terrible boundary of her sex role. She recoils, she protests, she reshapes her actions to gain approval. Lesbian is a label invented by the Man to throw at any woman who dares to be his equal, who dares to challenge his prerogatives (including that of all women as part of the exchange medium among men) who dares to assert the primacy of her own needs. To have the label applied to people active in women's liberation is just the most recent instance of a long history. . . .

While all women are dehumanized as sex objects, as the objects of men they are given certain compensations; identification with his power, his ego, his status, his protection (from other males), feeling like a "real woman," finding social acceptance by adhering to her role, etc. [in Cox 1976, pp. 304–305]

This collective essay is written from a purely cultural/feminist approach to lesbianism. There is no mention of any psychological problem that determines the lesbian's attitude. She has looked around her, seen the position of women in relation to men, and rejected it, choosing to be her own woman by loving other women, and thereby loving herself. The message in this essay is that if a woman does not make the full commitment to other women of sexually loving them, she remains "male identified" rather than "woman identified," and thus denies herself and other women authenticity, pride, strength, and the achievement of maximum autonomy. "Until women see in each other the possibility of a primal commitment which includes sexual love, they will be denying themselves the love and value they readily accord to men, thus affirming their second-class status" (p. 306).

This statement is hard to justify. Men don't have to sexually love other men to affirm their status. Why should women? The problem of women undervaluing themselves was very real twenty years ago, and consciousness-raising groups were established for that very reason. The CR group had as its goal the eradication of internalized feelings of inferiority to men, the internal overthrow of patriarchal judgment and power. Emerging from the consciousness-raising experience, which took years to be effective, a woman could value herself and other women, and face men as an equal. The Radicalesbian philosophy is that if a woman relates to men it is a symptom of self-hatred. Such a viewpoint has been applied, just as erroneously, to cases of, say, a black having a love affair with a white. It might be valid if the black carried self-hatred, had not worked through feelings, and was choosing a white man or woman as a means of improving his or her status. However, a woman doesn't go outside her family to love a man, as a black does who loves a white. The woman has, we hope,

received love from men in her family, and carries that love into relationships with other men. The sense of man as alien, as oppressor, suggests the
absence of any warm, caring man in the life experience of these women.
Sexism in the culture, of which there is still no shortage, needs to be
separated from love and respect, or the lack of it, in one's primary
relationships. Of course the culture affects the family, but individual
fathers may truly be supportive of their daughters' ambitions and take
pride in their accomplishments.

The goals of the lesbians who wrote this essay are similar to the goals
of all feminists: the freeing of women from limited and oppressive roles
and relationships and from the traditional values of "femininity." The
difference between them lies in the means of achieving that goal. The
Radicalesbians believe that the goal can be reached only by separation from
men. Other feminists believe it can be reached in union with men. This
seems inconsistent to some lesbians, but not to the majority of feminists.

The Radicalesbians refer to the "delusion" that a woman can develop
a relationship with a man in any revolutionary sense, that he can be a "new
man" who allows her to be a "new woman." Relating to men "splits our
energies and commitments" (p. 307), leaving women unable to pursue the
goals of women's liberation. The result of this belief system is that only
lesbians can be true feminists. What is ignored is that authenticity is a
struggle in any relationship, even between two women, because the need
for and pleasure in intimacy is in a constant dialectical struggle with the
need for autonomy. This "splitting" mechanism attempts to create a pure
world of loving women, an ideal in the early years of the women's
movement. But the difficulties that developed in love relationships between women made clear the painful realities of how early life traumas and
current needs for control can make any relationship, no matter how well
intentioned, into a battleground damaged by mistrust, suspicion, disappointment, and even betrayal.

An analysis of this essay from a psychodynamic viewpoint finds the
bisexual triangle of childhood resolved by a total rejection of the father and
a turning toward the mother. The father is perceived as an oppressor, a
threat to the love and intimacy with the mother; and an attempt is made to
exclude him from the mother's care and love and keep the mother for
herself. This resolution may be entirely satisfactory for some women, but
their attempt to impose it on other women, with the coercive claim that if
other women don't conform to this model they are betraying the cause of
feminism, is unfair and manipulative. Feminists should respect each others'
choices. The unfortunate fear of lesbians in the early days of the women's
movement, which led to exclusion in some instances, should not be
reversed by lesbians who claim that heterosexual women harm the movement. Some feminists have succeeded in achieving relationships of equality

and mutuality with men through great efforts at consciousness raising and dialogue, and this should be respected. On the other hand, all women should acknowledge the tremendous amount of work lesbians have contributed to women's projects, and the special burdens of secrecy, discrimination, and structural oppression under which lesbians have had to live and work.

Sidney Abbott and Barbara Love

Woman in Sexist Society (1971) contains one essay on lesbianism, "Is Women's Liberation a Lesbian Plot?" by Sidney Abbott and Barbara Love. This essay also focuses on the resistance in the early days of the women's movement to acknowledging lesbianism. The authors recall that lesbians were referred to by a NOW official as the "lavender menace," a name first applied to Oscar Wilde. A NOW official once edited an official press release from the first Congress to Unite Women, held in the fall of 1969, deleting the names of two lesbian groups from the total of fifteen organizations attending the Congress. In the report on the Congress, two NOW women reported a prolesbian workshop motion tabled that other women recalled had passed. Some lesbian women resigned from NOW, protesting exclusion. Today, say Abbott and Love,

> conservative elements in the movement are still trying to keep the lesbians in the closet by saying lesbianism is not important and at the same time too dangerous to deal with. From motives of safety, not honest feeling, feminists dealing with the mass media still deny there are lesbians in women's liberation. . . .
> . . . lesbians are attracted to the women's movement, are active in it, and feel that they are in the vanguard of it. If women's liberation does mean liberation from the dominance of men, lesbians' opinions should be actively sought out, for in many ways the lesbian has freed herself from male domination. [pp. 602–603]

We can see here the common goal shared by lesbians and heterosexuals, and also the different means to the goal. Freedom from male domination may be reached by excluding men, but it can also be reached by not allowing oneself to be dominated and by maintaining close ties to other women.

Abbott and Love also write from an exclusively cultural perspective on lesbianism.

> Not only is the radical lesbian no longer ashamed of her commitment to the lesbian way of life, but after some self-searching and self-analysis,

she has come to realize that most of her problems are due not to any necessarily unhealthy traits in her personality, but rather to her social oppression. . . .

The problems of lesbians—guilt, fear, self-hatred—can therefore be regarded as part of a sociopathology, part of what is wrong with our society, preventing whole categories of people from being happy and productive. [pp. 606–607]

The authors, like the Radicalesbians, promote the idea of the lesbian as the superior feminist.

The lesbian has taken the ultimate liberty heterosexual women are not permitted: to live and love exactly as she pleases. She does not make emotional tradeoffs for the privileges of being a lady. For this she is violently hated and tormented. Lesbianism is the one response to male domination that is unforgivable. [p. 610]

No matter what the feminist does, the physical act [of sexual intercourse] throws both woman and man back into role playing: the male as conqueror asserts his masculinity and the female is expected to be a passive receiver. All of her politics are instantly shattered. [p. 618]

The depiction of sex with a man as oppressive is strikingly similar to Deutsch's view of intercourse as an act of female masochistic submission. This interpretation of coitus is certainly not the attitude my patients and friends have, and I don't believe most men today prefer a passive sex partner. There is a distortion here of an act of intimacy between a man and a woman that can be very pleasurable for the woman who experiences it, not as being conquered, but in reciprocal terms of giving and receiving pleasure in the context of a loving relationship. What is missing in the perspective of these writers is the possibility of the man being a caring person. He is seen in only one dimension, as exploitative, abusive, and power-hungry. Most women today appreciate that they need to be guarded in their relationships with men. We all know the statistics, and know individuals who have been sexually harassed, raped, beaten, or ruthlessly abandoned by men. That women need to be aware of the possible dangers in becoming close to some men should not force us to view all men in this light. Sadly, it reveals the serious traumatic experiences with men that the writers must be using as a reference point.

Adrienne Rich

Adrienne Rich (1977) represents a different point of view about the women's movement. She speaks for an integration of lesbians and heterosexual women for the purpose of working together for the benefit of all women. She opposes the appeal for lesbian separatism, and pleads for lesbians to work with other feminists in programs such as rape crisis centers and shelters for battered women, as well as on political issues such as abortion. Prompted by her disapproval of the gay male attack on Anita Bryant, she says that lesbians have been forced to live between two cultures, both male-dominated: the heterosexual patriarchal culture that has driven lesbians into secrecy, guilt, self-hatred, and even suicide; and the homosexual patriarchal culture, which reflects such male stereotypes as dominance and submission as modes of relationship and the separation of sex from emotional involvement—a culture tainted by profound hatred for women (p. 225).

> I believe that a militant and pluralistic lesbian/feminist movement is potentially the greatest force in the world today for a complete transformation of society and of our relation to all life. It goes far beyond any struggle for civil liberties or equal rights—necessary as those struggles continue to be. In its deepest, most inclusive form it is an inevitable process by which women will claim our primary and central vision in shaping the future. . . .
>
> All lesbians know the anger, grief, disappointment we have suffered, politically and personally, from homophobia in women we hoped were too aware, too intelligent, too feminist, to speak, write, or act, or to remain silent, out of heterosexual fear and blindness. . . . But I believe it [separatism] is a temptation into sterile "correctness," into powerlessness, an escape from radical complexity. [pp. 226–227]

> When we are totally, passionately engaged in working and acting and communicating with and for women, the notion of "withdrawing energy from men" becomes irrelevant: we are already cycling our energy among ourselves. . . . The meaning of our love for women is what we have constantly to expand. [pp. 229–230]

Jane Mara and Sandra Butler

Women Changing Therapy (1983) includes essays by two lesbians who give accounts of coming out experiences as an outgrowth of involvement in the women's movement. Jane Mara, a psychotherapist, writes:

> I languished for years in my marriage, being who I thought I "should" be, doing what I thought I was "supposed to" do and scared to death to pay attention to the voice inside of me that was screaming, "GET ME OUT OF HERE."

It took the women's movement for me to see that I had options. That I had a choice. What a revelation! Of course, then I had to be responsible for the consequences of my decision. One thing about being a housewife, I could always blame everything on my husband, and that's what I did, blame, blame, blame. I blamed him for my unhappiness because I didn't have the courage to say NO to the life I was living. . . . Most of all I was scared of being responsible for my own life. [p. 152]

Mara describes her move out of her marriage into the lesbian world:

There are numerous differences between this world and the patriarchy but the central one is the way power is defined and used. In patriarchy power means power over another; it is this that breeds all oppression. In the female-centered lesbian reality power comes from within. It is the power of centeredness within oneself, not the power of aggression and oppression. . . . There is no hierarchy, no division between leader and follower. In sharing power every woman empowered increases the power to each and all of us. [p. 154]

Sandra Butler (1983) describes an eight-year marriage begun at age 18, which produced two daughters but no sexual pleasure. Butler left her husband, started to support herself and her children, and became involved in new-left politics, which at that time included sexual liberation and a "frenzy" of sexual activity. But "none of this halting and sporadic sexual activity was able to mask my unspoken but growing feelings of being sexually used, dismissed, diminished and trivialized" (p. 106). She withdrew from politics and began to read the new women's liberation literature. She attended the first meeting of a newly forming women's group:

That meeting was for me the beginning of congruence, the beginning of speech and the beginning of community. The early awkwardnesses began to fade after several meetings and the trust never before experienced with other women began to form. I began to hear echoes of my own well-behaved compliance attached to the hopes of being acceptable . . . belonging.

It was the beginning of a new way to think about healing and nurturing. It was the creation of a new form and it was the genesis of my becoming whole. We struck the most delicate balance between demanding and insisting on the fullest and finest from each of us, and carefully and painstakingly helping each other move through our terrors and feelings of inadequacy. We were re-thinking what it meant to be fully alive. Fully human. A woman. And I was never the same again. [p. 109]

A year later she began college at age 35, her commitment to writing intensified, and she organized a teaching collective.

> I brought all these growing insights and budding strengths into my few relationships with men and found the magnitude of the importance of these changes in me, and their liberating qualities made no impact on the men other than to intensify their anger and insecurity. Now I had become the castrating bitch of their worst dreams. Here before them was a man-hating, ball-busting, demanding, insistent, "women's libber". . . . I immersed myself totally in the community of women and my heart and flesh responded. To all the women at first and finally to one woman in particular. And then another. And then a growing sense that this was a natural outgrowth of my path. I remember so clearly thinking how "natural" it all finally was. The congruence of work, thought, action, feeling, laughter and flesh, With women. . . .
> Each dimension of my life is grounded in loving women. Loving myself as a woman. And I will continue to write and speak and insist and struggle. A lesbian is a woman who loves woman. And I most surely do. [pp. 110–111]

Butler gives us a beautifully written description of her consciousness-raising group experience and her gradual evolution as a lesbian. She is an example of a woman who was dissatisfied with her relationships with men, for whom the women's movement provided an opportunity of trust and intimacy with women, leading to a homosexual choice in mid-life.

Kristiann Mannion

Kristiann Mannion (1981) offers a critical review of the research on lesbians by psychologists.

> The growth of serious research on this aspect of female sexuality is characterized by a highly identifiable progression from the individual case study, focusing on the internal forces that shape pathological deviance, to research that all but ignores the internal process of the individual, focusing on the social and cultural influences that shape the behavioral correlates of lesbian sexuality. This shift in the research is not accidental; it is highly reflective of the growing awareness that the lesbian is most typically a healthy individual who shapes and is shaped by her functioning in the heterosexual macrocosm and the homosexual microcosm. [p. 273]

This very thorough review reveals some interesting results and a few surprising conclusions. Extensive comparisons of lesbian subjects with heterosexual women failed to identify any personality characteristics in the lesbians indicative of psychopathology. In opposition to psychoanalytic theory, lesbians show no signs of serious oral regression or fixation. In fact, some researchers, using the MMPI, have found greater pathology in the heterosexual controls, who scored significantly higher on three scales classically indicative of symptoms relative to anxiety and neurosis— hypochondriasis, hysteria, and psychasthenia (Ohlson and Wilson 1974).

Mannion points out the problematic nature of many early studies regarding the control groups used. If the lesbians are working and the controls are housewives, the lesbians are higher functioning, comparing favorably with other self-actualizing persons. Self-reliance is high among lesbians, but it is hard to know if that is a core feature or a result of having to be self-supporting. Later researchers tried to control for this possible bias by comparing lesbians to control groups of single women. But in one study, for example, 68 percent of the lesbians were living with a lover, as compared to 24 percent of the controls, which may have been responsible for the report of greater interpersonal satisfaction by the lesbian group. One researcher found that single women living alone, regardless of sexual orientation, were the most psychologically homogeneous.

Another difficulty in the research on lesbians is how to separate innate features from the effect of living as a despised minority, with all the secrecy, shame, and guilt associated with being a lesbian in a homophobic society. Not surprisingly, feeling forced to maintain a secretive existence with family and at work is counterproductive to life as a healthy individual.

In reviewing the research on the family background of lesbians, Mannion describes the many difficulties inherent in interpretation of the data. Bene (1965) concludes that the difference between the relations homosexual and heterosexual women had with their fathers is far greater than that with their mothers; homosexuals more often had unsatisfactory relations with their fathers. Thompson, McCandless, and Strickland (1971) found that significantly more lesbians than controls had hostile and distant fathers. Other studies show disrupted mother–daughter bonds (Wolff 1971); but the largest number of studies show a lack of closeness and a degree of hostility by a father who has failed to meet the affectional needs of his child, and thus has played a significant part in the failure of his daughter to adopt a heterosexual orientation (p. 265). Nevertheless, some studies show that many lesbians report happy childhoods.

Of 205 lesbians in one study, 60 percent reported being close to both parents. One can conclude that family pathology is more predictive of psychopathology in general than future lesbianism.

Siegelman (1974) carries the analysis further and identifies lack of parental love, parental rejection, and excessive demands as being related to development of neurosis, while lack of closeness to parents, degree of family security, and parental friction are related to lesbianism, these factors being related to lack of appropriate heterosexual role modeling. [p. 266]

The difficulty with this conclusion concerns the children of lesbian mothers. Here we surely have a lack of appropriate heterosexual role modeling. Yet in a study by Green (1978) on the sexual identity of children raised by homosexual or transsexual parents, "the finding of appropriate gender identity in all but one of thirty-seven children defies psychoanalytic thinking and social learning theory" (p. 272). It behooves all of us in the psychiatric professions to remain humble when drawing conclusions about the relationship between family psychodynamics and a lesbian object choice.

Elizabeth Gibbs

Gibbs (1989) reviews the research on the children of lesbian mothers. She cites Hoeffer (1981), who compared the sex-typed behavior of children of lesbian and single heterosexual mothers and found that both boys and girls chose stereotypical sex-typed toys, and that the children's toy preference did not differ as a function of the mothers' sexual orientation. Kirkpatrick, Smith, and Roy (1981) and Golombok, Spencer, and Rutter (1983) compared the development of children of lesbian and single heterosexual mothers and found that sexual orientation of the mother was not a factor in the children's development of gender identity, sex-typed behaviors, or sexual orientation. They found no significant differences between the two groups of children on issues such as fears, sleep disturbances, conduct difficulties, and hyperactivity. Although there was a very low overall incidence of psychiatric problems, children of single heterosexual mothers revealed a higher rate of psychiatric problems and a higher rate of prior referral to a psychiatric clinic than children of lesbian mothers. The lesbian mothers were more likely to be living with an intimate, supportive partner, while the heterosexual mothers were more likely to be living alone. This points to the weakness in describing lesbian women as "single" in much psychological research.

This research has important social and legal implications in regard to the highly controversial issue of lesbian mothers receiving custody of their children in divorce battles. "Despite compelling evidence that lesbians can be competent mothers and that their children are not damaged, the courts are still hesitant to award custody to a lesbian mother" (Gibbs, p. 74).

In research on lesbian couples, sex was reported as extremely satisfying, with 70 percent almost always having orgasm with their current partner (Peplau *et al.* 1978); only seven in one study of 286 lesbian women had never had an orgasm. This compares favorably with the studies of heterosexual women reported in Chapter 6. In a study of behavior within the relationship, some women valued attachment more highly and others valued autonomy more highly. Those who valued autonomy more highly were likely to place career needs first, have a sexually open relationship, and express worry about having a dependent partner. Yet most of the women reported a high degree of closeness and satisfaction in their current relationship (Caldwell and Peplau 1979). In a study of personal ads in a lesbian periodical, compared to heterosexuals advertising in a singles publication, lesbians stressed occupational, educational, and intelligence characteristics, whereas heterosexuals mentioned personal appearance characteristics (Laner 1978). One could conceivably conclude that lesbians are more mature and substantial in their object choice than heterosexuals, at least those who advertise for a partner. This also has implications for the stress associated with aging. Laner also found (1979) that lesbians are less preoccupied with age than heterosexual peers. This could be related to heterosexuals' greater emphasis on physical characteristics.

We have found one or two articles on lesbians in the feminist collections from the 1970s, such as Morgan (1970a), Gornick and Moran (1971), and Cox (1976), books that I have used as sources throughout this book. In 1972, Martin and Lyon wrote *Lesbian Woman*. The 1965 and 1980 Marmor collections contain two and three chapters on lesbians, respectively. In 1987, the Boston Lesbian Psychologies Collective published a major collection of twenty articles on the psychology of female homosexuality, and in 1989, Rothblum and Cole edited a collection of seventeen articles, *Lesbianism: Affirming Nontraditional Roles,* with a wide range of subjects relating to the lesbian couple, the lesbian community, problems of coming out, and therapeutic approaches. This survey indicates the great changes that occurred in the 1980s, as lesbians asserted themselves in the academic and political worlds and in general demanded recognition for their strengths and the special issues they posed, which were recognized by psychotherapists as worthy of special study. By the 1980s, lesbian therapists were coming out of the closet along with their clients, and writing on the special needs of lesbians in therapy.

Audre Lorde

It is often stated that lesbians suffer double oppression, as women and as homosexuals. African-American women who are lesbians suffer the triple oppression of racism, sexism, and homophobia. Lorde (1982) writes of the hostility in the black community to the black lesbian. She decries the competition among black women for the available men, and the resentment toward black women who are feminists and work cooperatively toward common goals with white women.

> The development of self-defined black women, ready to explore and pursue our power and interests within our communities, is a vital component in the war for black liberation. . . . Today, the red herring of homophobia and lesbian-baiting is being used in the black community to obscure the true double face of racism/sexism. Black women sharing close ties with each other, politically or emotionally, are not the enemies of black men. . . . Instead of keeping our attentions focused upon the real enemies, enormous energy is being wasted in the black community today by both black men and heterosexual black women, in anti-lesbian hysteria. Yet women-identified women—those who sought their own destinies and attempted to execute them in the absence of male support—have been around in all of our communities for a long time. [pp. 20–23]

Lorde declares it is the right and responsibility of black women to work with black men to fight racism and to work with white women to fight sexism. She cites examples from African culture of close working relationships between African women, and of love/sexual relationships between women as well. Traditionally, she says, black women have always bonded together in support of each other for wisdom and strength and today have a right to "recognize each other without fear and to love where we choose" (p. 24).

CONCLUSION

It would seem that the underlying issue for lesbians, as for heterosexual women, is sexism: the patriarchal domination and belittlement and scape-goating of women, especially of independent and powerful women. Whether it be Mao's widow Jiang Qing in China, Eleanor Roosevelt or Nancy Reagan as assertive presidents' wives in the United States, Anita Bryant, or the thousands of demonstrators for women's liberation called "women's libbers," all feminists agree that being an active woman is risk-taking behavior, and one can lose acceptability by stepping out of line. The suppression of female ambition, talent, and intelligence has been a terrible crime and a loss to all humankind. Lesbians live under the double burden of being women and homosexuals, and thus are the target of irrational prejudice against both groups. For being independent of men and showing strength outside the protection of the family, they have been targeted as a source of danger to the patriarchal ideal and thus forced to the edge of society.

All of the research comparing lesbian and heterosexual women shows great similarities between the groups. Lesbians are more like heterosexual women than like heterosexual or homosexual men. One exception, according to some researchers, is that lesbians do not engage in prostitution with other lesbian women, whereas gay men and heterosexual women do transact sex for money.

How much of the etiology of lesbianism can be found in individual and family internal dynamics, and how much is more simply explained by a rebellion against the second-class citizenship that the young woman perceives as she develops in a sexist society, cannot be answered. This is not an either–or issue. Most likely some combination of both can be found in the majority of cases. But it is also likely that there are some "pure" cases on the cultural or psychological ends of the continuum. There are feminists who have succeeded in achieving relationships of equality with men, and perhaps this is becoming more likely, with changes in society that favor the equality of women. Yet a woman may choose to pursue a love relationship with a woman at any point in her life. Lesbianism is itself on a continuum, with some women maintaining close relationships with women that never proceed to sexual relationships but that are emotionally satisfying and enriching.

It is so common in psychiatric writings about etiology of a variety of disorders to conclude that the fault lies with a dominant mother and passive father. Psychiatric patriarchal bias has been most evident in the repetition of this view. So-called domineering mothers have been held accountable for everything from schizophrenia, lesbianism, and male impotence to all varieties of neuroses. Yet we never find writers proclaiming that a domineering father and a passive mother is a source of pathology. The legacy of the wicked witch is everywhere. One must conclude that when the male is dominant the situation is considered normal and healthy. Yet it is in families with domineering fathers and passive mothers that violence against women and children is most likely to occur, in the form of physical and sexual abuse. From a feminist perspective, the healthiest marital relationship would consist of cooperation between equals, each contributing and working together for the welfare of their children and themselves. It is interesting that some of our most famous men, such as Franklin Roosevelt, had ambitious, domineering mothers planning their education and spurring them on. Some of America's most accomplished African-American leaders, such as Jesse Jackson and Justice Clarence Thomas, were actually abandoned by their fathers and raised by their mothers. The currently popular literature on male bonding, and concern about fathers' difficulties in being close to their sons, draw blame on women as well. But to cast blame on women ignores the more probable cause—severe homophobia, which keeps men apart because they don't trust that an intimate relationship with another male, even one's own son, can remain free of sexual attraction or sexual abuse.

For a psychotherapist treating a lesbian woman, what matters is what troubles the patient—what she is in therapy for. The therapist should not impose his or her own agenda on a patient, and certainly should not consciously and surreptitiously try to change her sexual orientation if that is not her goal. Almost all the writers who report on treatment of lesbian patients are women, either lesbian or heterosexual, although some of the researchers are male. The pathologizing of lesbians has been evident in both male and female therapists. But perhaps equally important is the anxiety and thus discomfort with homosexuality that has limited therapists' effectiveness with homosexuals. Unfortunately, Freud's early theories about bisexuality, stressing a nonillness model, were not heeded by his followers, who then took part in training several generations of clinicians with a distorted and demeaning view of homosexuality.

Fortunately, the last decade has seen many positive changes in the field of psychiatry and psychotherapy, though surely we have a long way to go. In the meantime, lesbian patients are right to be careful in choosing a therapist who will not impose his or her own sexuality on her. The woman's movement has come a long way as well, now including lesbians in all aspects of feminism and recognizing their valuable contributions. Both psychoanalysis and feminism have a legacy of shame in regard to homosexuals, who deserve liberation from irrational and irresponsible moral judgment. The terrible burden of secrecy, guilt, and shame for lesbians must be appreciated and acknowledged by all feminists and all therapists, and these costly errors must never be made again. All feminists should come to the defense of lesbians at any opportunity when they are attacked in the workplace and in social and political life. Mental health professionals should be especially responsible for promoting the view of homosexuality, whether by choice or by necessity, as a valid, respectable way for an individual to seek and find love, intimacy, and happiness. This is respect, and not as some critics say, promoting homosexuality. This is an issue of civil rights and of freedom of sexual expression and fulfillment.

8

AN INTEGRATION OF FEMINIST AND PSYCHOTHERAPEUTIC VALUES

It is impossible to escape the impression that people commonly use false standards of measurement—that they seek power, success and wealth for themselves and admire them in others, and that they underestimate what is of true value in life. And yet, in making any general judgment of this sort, we are in danger of forgetting how variegated the human world and its mental life are.

—Sigmund Freud

One thing only do I know for certain and that is that man's judgments of value follow directly his wishes for happiness—that, accordingly, they are an attempt to support his illusions with arguments.

—Sigmund Freud

Implicit but not always explicit in the practice of psychotherapy are values and goals that provide meaning and direction to the therapy. The most basic is the value and goal of self-understanding, expressed in Freudian terms as: where id was, there shall ego be. This recognition of the presence of values in our work does not invalidate the concept of neutrality, but it does mean that as therapists we must examine how our values may influence our feelings about decisions our patient makes and behavior she or he exhibits. This is where the concept of countertransference comes into play, and our awareness of whether our reactions—

positive or negative—are personally or culturally determined by values that the patient may not share. Issues of class, race, and religious differences between patient and therapist may be involved here.

Even a reaction of neutrality can be influenced by values and needs examination. A neutral reaction may in fact be based on value concordance. Take, for example, a woman patient having affairs with several men. One therapist may be comfortable with this behavior and can maintain an analytic stance in a neutral manner, while another sees the same behavior as "acting out" or "promiscuous" and approaches it as symptomatic and in need of treatment. Defining a piece of behavior as a symptom is an expression of a value held by the therapist.

COURAGE AND DECISIVENESS

An example of the role of values in our work occurred recently in my practice, when a former patient returned to see me in a state of indecision and panic about taking a temporary job (four months) in another state. She was in her early forties, had never been married, and was very frightened about leaving her friends, her apartment, all that was familiar and desirable to her, for the unknown: a graduate-level teaching job in a small town, 150 miles from the nearest large city, where she knew no one. The decision was urgent, so we met on three successive days.

> In the first two sessions the patient expressed tremendous ambivalence and anxiety, could not make a decision, and was fearful of the move, but equally fearful of not taking advantage of what would be a step up in her career and a possible lead to better jobs in the future. She was afraid she would hate herself if she decided not to take the job, and was equally afraid of isolation and unhappiness if she did take it. She was so distraught she felt she was going crazy, and said if she were physically this ill, I would be putting her in a hospital. I said that the idea of a hospital might be appealing because she would feel contained there.
>
> The situation was further complicated because she had recently decided that she wanted to get pregnant, and she felt pressure because of her age. She feared there would be no appropriate men at the small-town college, whereas the Bay Area had more opportunities for dating. On the other hand, teaching was a better way to develop her career if she wanted to combine a career with single motherhood, and this job could lead to a shift to a teaching career.

In her earlier therapy we had dealt with many such decisions: she had agonized over them, asked advice from many friends, and then become fragmented with the plethora of opinions, losing a sense of the decision being her own because she had frantically sought help from so many people. We reviewed these past instances, which were comparable in terms of her anxiety and indecision, and recalled the various interpretations we had agreed upon. I commented that it would take a lot of courage to accept this job and make the move, that it was clear it was to her long-term advantage to take it, and that the issue was whether or not she had the strength to do it. I said I believed it was the healthy thing to do, but maybe it was more than she could handle. I suggested, since her ambivalence was so strong, that what she needed to do was to try to stop the fragmenting and look at both sides of the issue together, weighing and balancing the positive and negative, because there were losses either way. I suggested she go home after the second session, make a list of the pluses and minuses, and see if she could make her decision, and that we could meet the next day. I also said that in my experience, when a woman really decides she wants a child, she finds a way to have one, or to adopt one, and that the four months away would not stop her.

She came in the next day smiling, and told me she had made the list and the positives were so clear that she had decided to accept the position, and was pleased. She was still terribly anxious, but a male friend had said to her "It's better to swing and miss than to stand at the plate and watch the ball go by." I said again that it did take courage for her to make this decision. She asked, "Do you think I have the strength to do it?" and I said, "You had the strength to make the decision." She said, "I'd rather swing and miss then watch the ball go by."

Many values, implicit and explicit, were at play in this interaction. Karen Horney (1934) says, "For although in the last analysis sex is a tremendously important, perhaps the most important source of satisfaction, it is certainly not the only one, nor the most trustworthy" (p. 187). Her point is that for some women, marriage is not possible, and they should not minimize the value of their talents and abilities and deprive themselves of the satisfaction of achievement from work by overvaluing love relationships. Freud made a similar statement:

Just as a cautious business-man avoids tying up all his capital in one concern, so, perhaps, worldly wisdom will advise us not to look for the whole of our satisfaction from a single aspiration. Its success is never certain, for that depends on the convergence of many factors, perhaps on none more than on the capacity of the psychical constitution to adapt its function to the environment and then to exploit that environment for a yield of pleasure. [1930, p. 31]

For this woman, teaching had been the most rewarding part of her career. She felt much gratification when students came up to her and expressed appreciation for all they had learned in her class. A focus on the teaching aspects of her field could bring much satisfaction and, chiefly, human contact—especially important if she was not able to form a lasting connection with a man. The depth of her pathology was such that there was no certainty that she could marry or form a permanent relationship with a man in the future.

I thus expressed several values when I encouraged this patient to take the job. Job satisfaction was one; career advancement was another. A third value was courage. Courage has traditionally been a male virtue, not seen as a feminine trait. By valuing courage I am expressing a feminist value: that women need to be strong in order to be independent and to achieve something in their own right. For men, this is a given from childhood. For women it must be learned. It is interesting that the patient's male friend used a sports analogy in expressing his values—better to swing and miss than not to swing at all. Such an analogy is not likely to be used by a woman, yet it was one she could identify with.

This woman's continual indecisiveness about work was due to her pathology. In practice it led to an irregular income and dependence on her parents for financial help. Another value I expressed by supporting a decision to take the job is that of financial independence. I had also said that I thought her ambivalence about the move was related to how autonomous and independent she would be, getting away from family and friends and striking out on her own. She had used the word "adventure," and I repeated that it would be an adventure. Adventure has traditionally been reserved for men; women have been expected to live vicariously through the adventures of their husbands and sons. Thus, I expressed another feminist value by saying it is positive for a woman to be adventurous.

The issue of a single woman having a child or adopting a child also comes up in this example. Although I believe that the best situation for a child and the parents is a nuclear or extended family, with the participation of both parents and the availability of grandparents, aunts, uncles, and cousins, the sad reality for some women is that they do not marry and yet want a child very much. A single woman or a single man is entitled to have a child. There is no competency test for married persons having children, and we all know that many married persons who have children do these children great harm. Moreover, so many women who do marry raise children alone due to separation and divorce that we can no longer assume that marriage is a guarantee of coparenting. In my view, having a child as a single woman would be a tremendously difficult task for this patient, but with help she could do it. I would neither encourage her nor discourage her, but if she sought my help in planning for pregnancy or adoption I would offer her that help.

Would a traditional (nonfeminist) psychotherapist have handled this woman's dilemma any differently? We cannot know. But the independence of today's woman, and the many opportunities and choices available to her, are posing problems in therapy that involve value judgments as to what a woman's purpose is and what priorities she gives to her choices. A therapist can influence these choices because the therapist's values are expressed in the questions asked, the focus drawn, and the manner in which the patient's pathology is related to the external realities.

THE SOCIOLOGY OF VALUES IN PSYCHOTHERAPY

Many writers have expressed the idea that there is no such thing as "value-free psychotherapy." Among sociologists, Pauline Bart is one:

> Different psychotherapeutic orientations have different images of man, time focuses, concepts of society, assumptions of cause and effect, and orientations toward social change. These differences clearly reflect different values, hence the major conclusion of this chapter: Value-free psychotherapy is a myth. [1974, p. 9]

Bart quotes Thomas Szasz as saying "Value-laden psychotherapy is possible because the imprecision of psychiatric theory, especially the ambiguity concerning 'normality,' permits the psychiatrist's moral preferences to be enunciated in the disguise of scientific descriptions of fact" (p. 15). She also quotes K. Davis: "Such ambiguity has resulted in the mental health movement being in effect the Protestant Ethic writ large (p. 15).

Some sociologists view psychotherapy as a means of social control. Talcott Parsons (1951), for example, considers the process of psychotherapy "the case in our society where those fundamental elements of the processes of social control have been most explicitly brought to light. For certain purposes it can serve as a prototype of the mechanisms of social control" (p. 301).

The women's issue is really part of the larger issue of the explicit and implicit values conveyed to patients by their therapists. Such values can be revealed by the degree to which internal as opposed to external factors determine the therapist's focus in treatment. All agree both internal and external factors count: it is a matter of emphasis. Ideally, the two can be balanced. Issues of poverty, class, race, and gender may bring the values of the therapist to light—that is, not just how the therapist feels about these matters personally, but her or his belief system as to how these external conditions affect the patient's psychic functioning, and whether and how much this should be addressed in psychotherapy.

Erving Goffman (1961) cites the example of a therapist who viewed social problems or structural deficiencies in the society as merely a projection of inner dynamics. The therapist dealt with

> a Negro patient's complaints about race relations in a partially segre-gated hospital by telling the patient that he must ask why he, among all the other Negroes present, chose this particular moment to express this feeling, and what this could mean about him as a person, apart from the state of race relations in the hospital at the time. [p. 377]

How would various therapists respond to a woman who complained about job discrimination, sexual harassment on the job, or even battering by her husband? My approach is both to explore the external reality and take it seriously, and to explore the patient's inner reality. The patient's feelings might, for instance, be overreactive, with displacement from some other part of her current life or from past trauma; or there might be an underreaction, because of long-established defenses of denial and rational-ization due to the fear that complaining will bring retaliation. In the example cited by Goffman, the therapist's questions could be explored, as long as there eventually was an acknowledgment that the situation was discriminatory and therefore not acceptable. (I would wait with my acknowledgment in order not to close off opportunities for projections. The complaint can provide an opportunity for discovering what the patient projects onto the therapist as to his or her prejudices. The therapist might ask "How do you imagine I feel about this?" and "How do you imagine I feel about your complaining about this?") In any case, such questions do not rule out attention to external reality, and that reality might be a good jumping-off spot for exploration of earlier experiences of injustice and their effects on the patient, with a follow-up question as to what the patient would like to do about it.

I reported the following case in an earlier article (1988); it illustrates work with a patient that combines attention to both external and internal forces.

Assertiveness—A Case Example

Ms. A., a divorced woman of 30, had been in therapy with me for about a year, working on issues relating to her family of origin and to her dissatisfaction in her current love relationship. She was from a lower-middle-class background and had not been sent to college, in spite of what to me was clearly a superior mind. Ms. A. had worked as a secretary since high school and felt ashamed and inferior because of not having gone to college. She recognized how important it was to her to please her boss and be a devoted and faithful employee, for which she hoped to be rewarded by advancement and salary increases. In keeping with her wish to please, she worked very hard and put in extra hours without pay. In therapy she connected this with how she had tried to please her estranged father but never could. After some time passed and she did not get the longed-for recognition, she became depressed and acted out her anger against herself in self-mutilating ways.

My interpreting these symptoms as evidence of her anger at her boss resulted in her looking more clearly at her situation and recognizing that, rather than being rewarded for her hard work and dedication, she was in fact being exploited. She approached her boss and asked to be compensated for her overtime work. When he refused, she stopped working overtime. Once she was no longer trying to win her boss's love and was able to work through her anxiety about losing her job, through making him angry, she was able to go for legal advice and file suit against him to win her back pay.

After months of effort, she won her case and was awarded $1,000. In the meantime, she found another job. Her abilities were recognized and she was given specialized training, with which she has been able to advance herself to a semiprofessional capacity. In her personal life, she was able to leave the man she was living with, who was cold and depressed and couldn't meet her emotional needs. Eventually she married a successful and much more giving man.

The idea for legal action came from the patient and rather surprised me, but the groundwork had been laid by our work, which freed her to see the work situation as it really was, rather than imagining she could find the loving father she had longed for. Her success in her legal action added to her self-esteem and confidence, and helped her in later jobs to assert herself in seeking higher wages. In my view, successful therapy involves the interaction of internal change, external experimentation, internalization of the success of external change, and so on, as mastery builds ego strength. Where psychodynamically oriented therapy and feminist theory may differ involves a chicken–egg dilemma, with some feminists believing that external change preceeds internal change. The interaction is so delicate that it is not worth arguing over. For example, in the case of Ms. A., an external change, seeking psychotherapy, preceeded the internal changes resulting from psychotherapy; yet something had changed internally to trigger her decision to call a therapist.

To use a civil rights analogy, the 1954 Supreme Court school deseg-regation decision was a monumental external change, but it would not have been possible without internal changes by all involved: attorneys, judges, and black and white activists, who came to understand that separate-but-equal schools were still discriminatory. Once passed, the decision could not immediately be effective, because internal changes on the part of members of communities throughout the South were needed for it to be accepted and implemented—which took years. The Court's decision, by removing social sanction from school segregation, played an important external role in forcing attention to the conflict, bringing the power of the law (the superego) to it, and moving it in the direction of the values of the larger society. *De facto* segregation in the North became the focus next, and it became clear the reality was far from the ideal anywhere in the country. The external–internal battle has been waged continuously since then.

AUTONOMY AND GENDER—RACHEL HARE-MUSTIN AND JEANNE MARECEK

Hare-Mustin and Marecek (1986) also raise the issue of values and psycho-therapy. In an article on autonomy and gender, they too declare that value-free psychotherapy is a myth and that neutrality itself is a value.

> As an influence process, psychotherapy may do little more than teach the client the belief system and norms for behavior held by the therapist and by society. Certain basic premises of psychotherapy—that the examined life is the better life, that growth and change are better than stability and continuity—are so embedded in the therapeutic system and, in fact, in the American ethos, as to rarely receive comment. [p. 207]

They ask whether autonomy is an appropriate ideal for women, examine the nature of relatedness as well as of autonomy, and conclude that both values are complex and problematic. Humanistic psychologists, such as Carl Rogers, Abraham Maslow, and Frederick Perls, regarding self-actualization as a model of mental health, promote fulfillment of one's own needs "independent of social constraints and personal commitments" (p.

207). This individualistic philosophy has been criticized as narcissistic and encouraging of selfishness. Hare-Mustin and Marecek state:

> Psychologists' acceptance of autonomy as an indicator of mental health and a goal of psychotherapy may reflect the social status accorded to them as well as the sociocultural context. Autonomy and self-determination are upper-class values. They may be antithetical to the communitarian values of the working class in some societies and to the tradition of interdependence in certain non-Western societies (Hsu, 1972). The ideal of autonomy may well be imposed on clients by the therapeutic establishment. [p. 207]

This comment stands in contrast to complaints of feminists that therapists have not supported women's aspirations for independence and, in fact, have encouraged them to stay dependent for their life satisfactions on serving husbands and children. The promotion of autonomy has special meaning for women as it encourages women to fulfill their own dreams.

Hare-Mustin and Marecek also raise an interesting question as to the relation of autonomy to power:

> Moreover, autonomy and relatedness may depend more on an individual's position in the social hierarchy than on gender. As Zuk (1972) points out, those in power advocate rules and rationality, while those with less power espouse relatedness and compassion. For example, in marital conflicts, women often call upon caring while their husbands use logic. But in parent–child conflicts, women will emphasize rules and rationality while their children appeal to love and understanding. Thus autonomy and relatedness are transactional: whether a person expresses autonomy or relatedness reflects his or her relative power and status. [pp. 208–209]

The authors ask what a feminist therapist would do if a woman in therapy did not want to be autonomous, wanted to remain dependent. Is there a conflict between the promotion of a client's welfare and the principle of the client's autonomy? In my view, this is not a real dilemma, because only the patient can determine the goals of her therapy. Here neutrality must win out over the therapist's belief in what is "good for" the patient, as long as the dependency is not truly self-destructive but merely undesirable in the eyes of the therapist. "Nurturance entails beneficence as well as self-sacrifice. What is often overlooked is that beneficence involves power. Women as nurturers exercise power by determining what is best for those in their care" (p. 210).

I agree with this point about women as nurturers, but it does not apply in the same sense to psychotherapists. There is a lot of power in the role of psychotherapist, the power to help and to heal and to influence—but not the power to control. The patient chooses what information to reveal to the therapist and can withhold certain facts, thoughts, or feelings. The patient is free to leave and stop therapy or seek another therapist if she or he is dissatisfied. A child cannot choose another mother or father, and thus remains to some extent in the parent's control until maturation and financial independence. (Unfortunately, some women escape parental control by early marriage, and then find themselves in their husband's control.) Moreover, in the patient–therapist relationship, the patient is in financial control, as the therapist is employed by the patient—no minor matter. By paying for the service, the patient retains ultimate control. That is not to say that the patient's desire to please the therapist cannot lead to acceptance of the therapist as an authority, which, if it goes unanalyzed, can lead to abuses. In the hands of a disturbed therapist these abuses can be very serious, as in cases of sexual exploitation of the patient. If the therapist breaks the sexual boundary and involves the patient in sexual behavior, the balance of control is violated and the patient will feel much more dependent and vulnerable.

Hare-Mustin and Marecek continue:

> the achievement of autonomy may require the sacrifice of communitarian values and diminished capacity for intimacy. . . . Autonomy may be impossible for most women to achieve. Self determination depends on control of resources and most women lack such control. Therapy can expand women's awareness of choices and develop their courage to choose, but there are outer limits to what any therapist and client can accomplish. Even if autonomy were an appropriate goal for women, therapy by itself is not the means to that goal. [p. 210]

This raises the question of what is mental health, and is mental health for women comparable to mental health for men? The view of the therapist on this can affect the course of treatment dramatically. The second issue is, *who decides*? Does the therapist have the obligation and responsibility to decide what is mentally healthy for the patient, or is that where she or he must remain neutral? In the first case example I presented, I made clear my view that the job move would benefit the patient's mental health, but the patient had to decide which choice to make. In the second case, Ms. A., I interpreted her depression as a result of anger toward her boss, but it was the patient who chose the path of legal action, refused to work overtime, and sought a new job. The role of the therapist is to analyze conflicts, relieve anxiety, and thus make choice possible. If fear is so strong as to immobilize the patient and create depression or panic, then there is no alternative other than neurotic symptom formation.

ENCOURAGEMENT—MILDRED ASH

Mildred Ash (1974) also deals with the question of values in psychotherapy with women. Some of her case material may now be dated, but it is nevertheless interesting to review her approach. She states:

> Women aren't entirely the victims of culture, male prejudice or even feelings of inferiority. Women themselves have a hierarchy of values. The highest value is usually to make an association with a beloved man and create a family. This means that a bright girl may not be motivated to achieve very much scholastically or vocationally when she is at the age when men conventionally do so. Exhortation and preaching to such a woman would indeed be unprofessional and incorrect. Rest assured that the wish to seek other modes of expression will surface later in the lives of such young women. There is no need to force everyone into the same pattern. The therapist can help women understand that identity and self-expression are lifetime pursuits. [p. 412]

Ash goes on to say that therapists can "encourage" women patients, and that one of the tasks in treating women is to be aware of broader horizons for them, no matter what their age. While parents have been an important influence in a patient's past, a "good therapist can be influential at any point along the line." She also states, "As doctors we are taught that we can't make a diagnosis unless we think of it" (p. 413), and it is this key sentence that relates to values. What we "think of" is what we have become aware of and incorporated into our knowledge and value systems. It is here that a knowledge and appreciation of feminist theory and values is essential if a therapist is going to diagnose and treat a woman in a nondiscriminatory manner.

The word *encourage* can be a tricky one, because it is definitely not neutral. We need to recognize that it is one's value system that determines what one encourages or discourages. In the 1950s, psychoanalysts encouraged women to stay home and serve the needs of their husbands and children, which was believed to be their true nature and therefore what was best for the woman. I have stated that in cases of self-destructive behavior the therapist cannot remain neutral. Should we expand the definition of self-destructive behavior to include not getting an education, or not using the education one has? It is here that the value issue for women becomes one of individual development or devotion to family. The value of serving the needs of the family can be in conflict with the value of the individual woman's needs for exploring her own talents and potential. However, the conflict may be more in the mind of the woman than in reality, especially when we see women with teenaged children still fearful of leaving them for work outside the home. Therapy can help the woman examine her fears and determine alternatives. The same may be true for women trying to choose between career goals and marriage and children. These are not easy questions and there are no simple answers, but it is possible to work through the conflicts and achieve a resolution. Ultimately it is the woman's own choice where she places her priorities, and at what point in her life she places a family first, or combines family and independent work.

PSYCHOANALYTIC VALUES AND FEMALE PSYCHOLOGY—ETHEL PERSON

Person (1983) has contributed to our understanding of values in her article "The Influence of Values in Psychoanalysis: The Case of Female Psychology," stating that "science both is the product of cultural values and a contributor to the cultural evolution of values despite its 'objectivity' " (p. 624). She notes that psychoanalysis embodies values central to Western culture, such as the value of the individual and his or her welfare and a commitment to self-knowledge as an end unto itself.

In other cultures and at other times, the family or the state have been more highly valued than the individual. In China, for example, where the family was the highest value, the changes that took place under Communism were not as difficult as they would have been for Americans, because the seat of control shifted from the family to the state. There was no basic shift in the role of the individual, only in who the individual was subservient to. Person goes on to say that "values are not always easily separated from prejudice and bias" (p. 625). Freud believed that analysts were ethically neutral and that their observations were value free. However, as long as we, as therapists, believe we have something to say about what is mentally healthy, we are dealing with therapeutic goals. And as women's overall goals change, due to the influence of the feminist movement, feminist principles influence what the woman patient seeks from therapy. Whereas earlier women wanted help in being better wives and mothers, now many women seek to gain autonomy and self-realization by working through inhibitions in assertiveness and achievement (p. 39).

Women may also come to therapy for problems in relationships with men, as they used to; because no matter how successful they may be in their careers, many women still prefer the intimacy of a love relationship with a man to the life of a single woman. Wanting an independent career, with its financial and status advantages plus the satisfactions of the work itself, does not in any way diminish the desire for the warmth, comfort, and companionship of marriage for women any more than it does for men.

The relative value of children is another issue that many women must come to grips with, especially as they move toward the end of their childbearing years.

Person believes that Freud's systematic distortion in the case of female psychology "alerts us to the danger of using 'common sense' corroborated by cultural consensus to confirm scientific theory. Value bias lulls us into theoretical complacency" (p. 638). She reviews the dispute between Marmor (1968) and Barglow and Schaefer (1977). (I reviewed Barglow's and Schaefer's essay in Chapter 3.) Marmor comments on the change in *content* of what is considered feminine and masculine, and observes a gradual change in female gender-role patterns from the traditional patterns of Western culture. He notes that there are implications of these changing patterns both in theory and in psychoanalytic therapy. Marmor refers to Erich Fromm's observation that

> a psychoanalyst's value system would profoundly affect how he would treat a female patient who presented the problem of Nora in Ibsen's *Doll House*. If he held to classical psychoanalytical views concerning femininity, he would focus his interpretations upon her penis envy and her rejection of the "normal" feminine goals of wifehood and motherhood. On the other hand, if he were a feminist, he would, instead, focus upon her "healthy" rebellion against her husband's infantilization of her and would encourage her move out of the home as a laudable effort at self-realization. Still another alternative to these two extremes exists, however. One need not assume that motherhood and a fulfilling life in the outside world are incompatible, any more than fatherhood and such a life. . . . Women have alternatives now; they may or may not choose to combine them, and the choice is theirs. The task of the analyst is to help them make this choice freely, without guilt, and in relationship to the realities of their specific life situations. [p. 238]

Barglow and Schaefer do not believe that these are really psychoanalytic problems, seeing them instead as ideological problems.

> An analyst who, motivated by even the sincerest desire to reform society encourages changes in patients consistent with his own personal ideology must be said to run the danger of countertransference and transference interferences. An analyst's sympathy with the women's liberation movement (a sympathy we share, by the way) should not blind him to the fact that, for one patient, "women's liberation" might provide global rationalizations defending against recognition of intrapsychic responsibility for neurotic misery and thus reinforce avoidance of necessary psychoanalytic working through and constitute a resistance within the analytic situation. For another patient, it might

represent evidence of an ability to act on her own values and wishes. [p. 410]

One cannot disagree with the analysis of the risks presented here. But could it be that we are blind to our own biases even as we call other people's biases countertransference? An example of this took place in a course I attended at the San Francisco Psychoanalytic Institute during the 1970s. The question arose of a patient who requested a female therapist; our instructor, a male analyst with the Institute, suggested—correctly, I believe—that this request needed to be analyzed as to its meaning to the patient. I asked if, when a patient chose him as a therapist, he analyzed why he or she had chosen a male. The instructor was dumbstruck.

In my view, Barglow and Schaefer underestimate feminist-oriented psychotherapists' awareness of these issues, and the effort they make to bring in the feminist or social perspective in a manner not at all "blind," but in fact thoughtful and carefully executed. Jones (1990) gives a clinical example of her work integrating social and psychological dynamics in the treatment of her patient Teresa, and cautions therapists as to the risks involved:

> Clearly, social dynamics played a significant part in easing Teresa's movement into deeper psychological exploration and disclosure. At the same time, as the uncovering process was underway, it became apparent that social analysis was a two-edged sword, for it also threatened to defeat the discovery process by diverting Teresa from emotional experience to intellectualization. When clients are experiencing and revealing long-hidden pain, it's essential that clinicians remain sensitively attuned to opportunities for encouraging further exploration and expression of feelings. Referring to social realities at such times can shift attention from the experiential to abstraction and generalization. . . . discussion about society often provided a welcome relief and escape from internal pain. . . . To use social interpretation or other cognitive interpretations loosely at such times runs the risk of abetting rather than reducing clients resistance. [p. 402]

Any interpretation needs to be careful and sensitive, taking into account the patient's readiness. The rhythm of the session and the timing are both of great importance. This is true for interpretations relating to internal dynamics just as it is for those dealing with social dynamics. To assume that a feminist interpretation is countertransference, based on a wish to reform society rather than to provide the best interpretation to help the patient, is a bias, showing the value the critic places on internal dynamics to the exclusion of social dynamics.

Person states that "the serious potential for therapeutic bias in goal setting is sometimes underestimated'' (p. 629). In her opinion, Marmor was right, and Barglow and Schaefer have missed the point.

> An analyst's response (countertransference) must be permeated by his or her world view. Preferences and beliefs influence the therapist's judgment and may thereby slant interpretations or therapeutic emphasis. Therapists communicate their values not primarily with directives, but with silences, questions, and the very rhythms and cadences of the therapeutic hour.
>
> Sometimes directives are explicit. I have seen, in consultation and treatment, any number of women, particularly those now in their fifties and sixties, who were directly advised by analysts and psychiatrists that their feminine obligation, destiny or duty lay in preserving the marriage, not threatening their husbands, modulating their own sexuality, and so forth. . . . Although such inappropriate direct interventions are manifestations of countertransference reactions, theory has enabled clinicians to remain blind to them. . . . Furthermore, it may be that psychoanalysts tend to prescribe more goals for women than for men . . . [and] women may have sought such intervention in ''the transference'' more insistently than male patients. [pp. 629–630]

THE PROTECTION OF FATHERS—A CASE EXAMPLE

An example of male bias was revealed in my treatment of a woman patient who had previously been in therapy with a male psychiatrist. It became clear to me after several months of work that her previous therapist had misdiagnosed her. He had missed the fact that she spent a considerable amount of time living in fantasy, which she called ''listening to music.'' He had misdiagnosed her father as well. The patient's parents had had a terrible marriage, which finally ended in divorce when she was 15. Her older sister went to college, and she chose to live with her father because her mother was so disturbed as to be psychotic in the patient's estimation. The patient developed a very close, wife-like relationship with her father, which continued to the present. The patient was in her mid-thirties. She had never married or lived with a man, or even had a serious love relationship. Nor had she ever used her considerable intelligence to develop a meaningful career, in spite of graduate-level education. She was doing clerical work when her therapy with me began. She had her own apartment, but visited her elderly father frequently and took responsibility for his care. Her mother had died of cancer.

One day, in discussing her difficulties with her father, she described how hurt she had been when, after she spent considerable effort in making a quilt for him as a gift, his response was that he couldn't really use it as it would be too warm for him. This incident had occurred during her previous therapy, and when she told her therapist of her father's response, he said, "That's the way he told you he loves you." She was confused, but accepted her therapist's view that there was nothing wrong with the father's response and therefore she needn't feel hurt by it. I tried to conceal my astonishment and anger, but did tell the patient that I disagreed with her former therapist, and thought the father's response indicated hostility toward her. She was relieved at my interpretation because it made sense of her hurt feelings and opened up her relationship to her father to more realistic scrutiny. She was gradually able to see other ways in which her father was harmful to her through his criticism and belittlement, and to connect his discouragement of her independence and accomplishments to her difficulty in making a fulfilling life for herself. She was able to return to graduate school, get a degree in her chosen field, and move to New York City, where she got a very good job in her field.

Now we need to imagine why the male psychiatrist discouraged any examination of the true nature of the patient's relationship with her father. My hunch is that he was protecting the father for his own reasons. Was he protecting his own father, and letting countertransference bias his work because he could not look at the hostility in his own father? Was he himself a father, and was he protecting himself? In my view, there is a general bias in psychoanalytic and psychotherapeutic theory and practice against mothers and toward protection of fathers and other males. This has come about because males are more highly valued members of society than women or children. They are traditionally the "breadwinners," and the other family members depend on their financial support. Blowing the whistle on a father for incest, for example, can mean financial ruin to a family. Freud unconsciously protected his father when he protected Fliess and discarded the possibility that girls are the victims of real sexual transgressions by their fathers and other trusted men. Deutsch protected Freud by not objecting to his dropping her analysis, but she made no effort to protect her mother and spoke of her in the most angry terms. The bias against women and in favor of men throughout our culture has, not surprisingly, been a part of psychoanalytic theory, and feminist theory is a necessary corrective.

In the case of Helene Deutsch, her biases are evident throughout her work. Yet where has she been accused in the psychoanalytic literature of countertransference? For example:

> Woman's intellectuality is to a large extent paid for by the loss of valuable feminine qualities: it feeds on the sap of the affective life and results in impoverishment of this life either as a whole or in specific emotional qualities. . . . Everything relating to exploration and cogni-

tion, all the forms and kinds of human cultural aspiration that require a strictly objective approach, are with few exceptions the domain of the masculine intellect, of man's spiritual power, against which woman can rarely compete. All observations point to the *fact* that the intellectual woman is masculinized; in her, warm intuitive knowledge has yielded to cold unproductive thinking. [1944, pp. 290–291, italics added]

This is, quite frankly, appalling. I believe Deutsch confuses activity, assertion, and aggression with hostility. Perhaps this is so because her hostility toward her own mother was never worked through, and she was left searching for an explanation for her own conflicts and dissatisfactions. She makes the value judgment that the affective life is more valuable for women than the intellectual life, which is reserved in her value system for men. Perhaps she believed that she lost her emotional capacities because of her entrance into the masculine intellectual world of medicine. But this is not a tenable explanation for Deutsch or for any other women, just as it would not be for a man who pursued an intellectual life. If he was inhibited in his intimate relationships, we would explore the underlying sources of his condition and not dismiss it as a necessary result of his intellectual work. Why must objectivity in one's intellectual life preclude genuine emotional warmth toward loved ones? Men and women are capable of both. The splitting of intuition and objectivity is one of those dichotomies that ends up being a bias against women, who are thereby excluded from occupations with the most prestige and highest salaries. Keller (1985) describes this very well, as does Benjamin (1988). Perhaps Deutsch placed the blame for her miscarriages on her intellectual life ("cold unproductive thinking"). Surely we know of women in all professional categories today who are also successful mothers.

THE SPECTRUM OF VALUES, ETHICS, AND BIASES

Feminists and psychoanalysts share many of the values held by educated members of the middle class in Western cultures. In some cases, however, feminists may differ from traditionalists; in others, there may be no clear answer and each individual must determine values for her or himself. How this expresses itself in feminist psychoanalytic treatment as compared to traditional treatment can be gleaned from some of the excerpts cited so far, and in later examples in the companion to this volume.

The following lists represent an effort to find the values shared and to differentiate those that may not be shared, by psychoanalysts, psychoanalytically oriented psychotherapists, feminists, and analysts or therapists with a feminist orientation. Based on the assumption that there is no value-free psychotherapy or psychoanalysis, certain ethical values can be found in treatment and certain biases can be expressed. The question then becomes, how do we separate ethical principles of enduring value from Western, middle-class, or patriarchal biases? Is this even possible? These lists are not meant to be exhaustive, and they most likely reflect my own values. In lists II and III, it is possible to single out some items as feminist-psychoanalytic values. These are indicated with an asterisk.

List 1. Noncontroversial Values, Shared by all Groups

1. Verbal expression of ideas and feelings is better than non-verbal expression, with the exception of artistic expression. Artists must communicate verbally as patients.
2. Honesty and openness is better than concealment and deception.
3. It is better for children to be raised by both parents.
4. Adoption is better for children than remaining in an institution or foster care.
5. Relatedness is better than isolation.
6. Intellectual work is more valuable than manual labor, justifying a high hourly rate for sessions.
7. Being on time is better than being late to sessions.
8. Paying on time is better than paying late.
9. The therapist maintains anonymity and neutrality.
10. The therapist is professional in behavior and is not socially or sexually involved with patients.
11. The privacy of the patient is assured by the office arrangement and all communications are confidential, within the limits of the law.
12. Self-destructive behavior, such as excessive drinking or drug use, suicide attempts, repetitive abortions, sado-masochistic or criminal activity, is to be analyzed and discouraged, and is not a matter about which the therapist remains neutral.

List 2. Sometimes Controversial Values

1. Marriage, or a permanent relationship, is better than remaining single.
2. Staying married is better than getting divorced.
3. The individual unhappiness of a parent justifies divorce even if young children are being reared in the family.
4. Heterosexuality is preferable to homosexuality.

*5. A single woman can provide for a child's basic emotional needs.

*6. An abortion in the first trimester of pregnancy is the choice of the individual woman and is not tantamount to murder.

7. Extra-marital affairs are destructive to a marriage.

*8. Rape, wife-beating, incest, sexual molestation of children, and threats of murder must not be tolerated, and if they cannot be controlled by analytic work, hospitalization must be implemented. Victims should be encouraged to make police reports.

*9. Sexual involvement between patient and therapist is not acceptable, even once the treatment has been terminated.

*10. Having multiple sexual partners during single years is within the normal range of sexual behavior and is not "promiscuity" for men or women except in certain extreme cases.

11. Creative people such as artists, musicians, and scientists are exempt from the same standards of caring and relatedness as others because their work is of such great value to civilization.

List 3. Very Controversial Values

1. Communal child rearing is superior to the nuclear family.

2. Mothers who work outside the home are harming their children, who need a constant object for their development.

*3. A father's care is just as important as a mother's care in infant and toddler development.

4. Men who take care of children while their wives work are damaging their masculinity.

5. Women who earn more money than their husbands can cause a husband's impotence problem.

6. When there are children in a marriage, keeping the family together is more important than the individual happiness of the parents.

7. Women who express anger toward attitudes of male superiority are unfeminine and suffer from penis envy.

8. Girls who want to play sports are rejecting femininity.

9. Women who don't want to have children are rejecting their natural role and are self-centered, unfeminine, and uncaring.

10. A woman does not need to have an orgasm in intercourse to feel satisfied because she receives her gratification from satisfying her husband.

*11. Teachers, librarians, nurses, and social workers should receive salaries comparable to those of electricians, plumbers, accountants, and managers.

*12. Abortion in the second trimester is the choice of the woman and is not tantamount to murder.

13. Independence is masculine, dependence is feminine.

14. Aggressiveness is masculine, passivity is feminine.

15. Intellectual achievement is masculine, caring for others is feminine.

*16. Homosexuality is a normal form of sexuality, not a perversion. It does not imply pathological development. All humans are basically bisexual.

17. The therapist's sexual involvement with a patient may be therapeutic.

These lists do not differentiate between ethics and biases, and to do so risks the danger of confusing one's own biases with ethical principles. Nevertheless, I will attempt to make this differentiation by selecting certain values from each category that I believe professionals in our field can hold as ethical beliefs, both as members of a Judeo-Christian culture in the late twentieth century, and as physicians and other healers following a medical model of ethics. In List 1, numbers 10, 11, and 12 qualify as ethical values. In List 2, numbers 8 and 9 are ethical values. In List 3, number 17 is unethical. Other points center around three issues: the value of the individual's satisfaction in relation to family values; the value of women and children in relation to men; and financial values in relation to nurturing values.

LIVING IN MORAL PAIN—PETER MARIN

In an important article, Peter Marin (1981) describes his experiences with Vietnam war veterans; he calls their condition "living in moral pain." According to Marin, psychotherapists have trouble confronting two aspects of the vets' suffering: profound moral distress arising from the realization that one has committed acts with real and terrible consequences; and the inadequacy of the prevailing cultural wisdom, models of human nature, and modes of therapy to explain moral pain or provide ways of dealing with it (p. 68). Marin describes the symptoms these vets experience, now known under the diagnosis post-traumatic stress syndrome. He states that most psychological thinking about Vietnam has avoided the issue of judgment, because much of the research on Vietnam veterans has been funded by government agencies or by veterans' organizations.

> Several psychiatrists who work with the vets have told me that in this area as in any other, researchers tend to look for results and frame findings that will keep their funding sources happy. . . . One also suspects that many shy away from the question of moral pain simply because it is likely to open up areas of pain for which there is really nothing like a "cure." As one therapist told me regarding the atrocities and attendant shame that were sometimes discussed in his rap group: "That, my friend, is the hardest thing to deal with. When somebody brings it up we all fall silent. Nobody knows how in hell to handle it."
> [p. 74]

In a critique of psychoanalysis on the issue of the human conscience, Marin states that Freud separated considerations of psychological health from moral or social concerns in order to isolate the self in the therapeutic process. Also, morality itself was often treated in Freud's work as a form of social intervention or outside imposition. But "in its justifiable accent upon human need as opposed to social obligation, psychoanalysis established habits of thought that have now been honed in America into a morally vacuous view of human nature" (p. 74).

The ideal that therapy can help patients to avoid suffering ignores the tragic element in the lives of people who have been perpetrators or victims of physical violence. The effects of such acts cannot be escaped by therapeutic endeavors at reconstruction of memories, because the truth brings a tragic recognition that acts are irreversible, no matter how one analyzes them. For the perpetrator, there is no way to deny responsibility or culpability for acts that have affected others' lives. For the victim, no forgiveness or understanding can change the actual experience of having been helpless in the hands of cruelty and violence from another human being. "This is precisely the point at which the failure of therapy becomes tragic, and it is at this point that the future task of therapy becomes clear: to see life once again in a context that includes the reality of moral experience and assigns a moral significance to human action" (p. 77).

> The proper consideration for therapists and vets, for all therapists and all Americans, is "I-thou-they": the recognition that whatever we do or do not do in our encounters, whatever we forget or remember, whatever truths we keep alive or lies we fabricate will help form a world inhabited by others. . . . The responsibility of the therapist, then, neither begins nor ends with the individual client; and the client's

responsibility neither begins nor ends with himself or herself. Both extend far outward, from the past into the future, to countless other lives. [p. 80]

Victor Frankl (1962) wrote of the moral choices faced by all human beings, even the apparently helpless inmate of a concentration camp. Frankl focused on the meaning of one's life in relation to others. In my view, feminist theory is an attempt to bring some of these moral concerns about how we treat each other back into the psychotherapeutic endeavor—an attempt filled with the possibility of risk, but also with great potential for enlarging the scope of the therapeutic dialogue to include deeply human issues such as courage, responsibility to others, and the meaning of one's life and one's actions to a sense of integrity and relation to the human community.

In conclusion, feminism offers psychotherapists a new approach to women, which questions and discards many of the beliefs about women that have been part of our traditional culture and education. Basic to feminism is a valuing of women as individuals entitled to pursue their life goals, of which marriage and children may be a part, but not to the exclusion of other goals. The role of women in marriage is as an equal partner, not as "servant to the species," and this means the active participation of the husband and father in child rearing and running the household. Women are entitled to sexual and intellectual fulfillment, and this does not detract from their nurturing capacities. Female autonomy and female connectedness can coexist in a continual balancing of needs, goals, and values. Psychotherapists, in an attempt to remain neutral, have avoided the profound human question of doing good or doing harm that some of our patients confront. From a feminist perspective, harm has been done to women in society and in psychotherapy. Psychotherapists must take some responsibility for the harm that their patients cause to others less powerful, such as women and children; and must recognize that there are areas of human pain and suffering for which psychotherapy so far has no answers, and never will so long as it remains detached from moral and ethical considerations.

9

BOTH PSYCHOANALYSIS AND FEMINISM WIN WHEN THEY LEARN FROM EACH OTHER

As I write this book, the United States is engaged in a war against Iraq. Yet it does not really seem to be a war against Iraq so much as the war we should have fought against Hitler and the war we should have fought in Vietnam. Over and over we hear references to those wars, and at times others, as the journalists, generals, politicians, and other experts relive and try to rework the pain, humiliation, errors, and defeats of the past. Yet Saddam Hussein is not Hitler, Iraq is not Vietnam, the Middle East is a different part of the world, the air and ground forces have different equipment, and the American people have a different view of themselves and the world.

This is precisely the dilemma the individual is in as he or she tries to learn from and rework past trauma in the present. The cast of characters is different; the patient is an adult, not a child. And yet the heaviness of the pain, humiliation, frustration, and anger from the past colors all reactions and decisions, as if the past were alive in today's experience. The patient is not able to see the reality of the present in its uniqueness because of this tremendous need to right old wrongs, to correct past mistakes and injustices, and to finally achieve a sense of dignity, mastery, and control.

Both psychoanalysis and feminism have struggled to build a theory about the truths of human nature, and to achieve an understanding of human relationships—a formidable task. That both have made errors should come as no surprise. That both are evolving, changing bodies of theory and knowledge is a source of continuing intellectual ferment and discovery that brings emotional stress to those involved. You can't have change without struggle. You can't plant seeds without turning over the earth.

Ours is a very competitive society, and, perhaps because of our masculine value system, there is a great deal of posing of issues as either–or, right or wrong, winners or losers. I have attempted to explore an integration of psychoanalytic and feminist theories without there being any losers. Both sides win when they learn from each other. Both sides lose when they discredit the other. As in a good marriage, something beyond one and one makes two happens in a cross-fertilization of ideas and possibilities.

Psychoanalysis has represented a male view of personality development, in spite of the fact that it had important women contributors. Feminism represents a female view. I have often stated that "femininity" and "masculinity" have been seen as polar opposites, dividing what are basically human traits into two separate compartments. I don't believe human beings can be compartmentalized like that. Our basic biology certainly creates significant physiological difference between the sexes, but the differences that we have called "feminine" or "masculine" are largely psychologically and culturally determined. An integration of psychoanalytic theory and feminist theory parallels, on a theoretical level, what is happening in society on a practical level. Traditional boundaries between male and female roles and jobs are being crossed, and men and women are relating to each other more as equals, with a sharing of skills, talents, and ideas on all levels of society; from the home to the office, in government and academia. The progress is slow, but there is progress.

Sexual stereotypes are still alive and well. It is still more likely that a man will be able to admit to feelings of anger under the same circumstances in which a woman admits only to feeling hurt or sad, although she *is* angry. A woman is more likely to show sympathy than a man, although the man might feel just as emotional on the inside. What may be a difference of inside and outside, the true self and the false self, has been wrongly judged to be an innate difference. When men are in conflict, they turn their anger against the other, while women tend to turn it against themselves, by taking the blame and becoming depressed. This becomes a profound difference when, as therapists, we evaluate and work with individual men and women. The fact that men inhibit emotional distress and women inhibit anger is surely cultural. It is more dangerous to be aware of anger, however, when you are physically smaller and less muscular. Repressing anger and converting it into depression can be a protective device for women. And suppressing emotional response other than anger can be a protective device for men, who risk being called "sissy" or "wimp" if they show emotion. These internal/external differences are illustrated by the fact that nearly twice as many women as men are treated for depression, whereas studies have shown that rates of depression are identical for men and women. As therapists, that means we will have different jobs with men and with women: eliciting anger in the woman, while eliciting sadness and emotional pain in the man.

The issue of dominance and passivity is another area in which psychoanalysis and feminism have battled. There may be physiological differences in the hormones that make males more aggressive, and their larger size makes it safer for them to be more aggressive, but cultural factors are very powerful here as well. Unfortunately, psychoanalysis has defined female pathology based on the view that passivity is natural in women, and has labeled assertive, ambitious women as "masculine." Because of this bias toward male dominance, major tragedies of violence against women and children have been tolerated. The so-called normal, healthy, male-dominant family is precisely the family in which wives are battered and children are physically and sexually abused. Families with dominant wives have been decried as pathological; yet, in the mass of literature on the subject, it has not been easy to find experts who say that pathology in a family occurs when *either* parent is dominant or either is submissive. A domineering, angry, rejecting parent of either sex is frightening to a child; and a passive, withdrawn, nongiving, perhaps depressed parent of either sex is equally bad for a child's mental health. The notion that a passive father is more pathogenic than a passive mother is wrong. A healthy family, in my view, is one in which both parents work together, cooperatively, on the tasks of child rearing, housekeeping, and financial security, each contributing labor to the tasks and judgment to decision making. This is a family in which the children will benefit from the balance of skills and power between the two adults. The participation of extended family members adds to the balance and judgment needed in raising children.

In this book, I have engaged the work of biographers, sociologists, sex researchers, the law, political theory, psychological research, and my own experience to examine many issues important to feminists, psychoanalysts, and psychotherapists. Some of these issues are strictly questions of developmental theory, such as the debate over the preoedipal mother and revisions of oedipal theory. Other issues are much broader, such as pornography and abortion. These topics will be expanded in my second book, *The Technique of Feminist Psychoanalytic Psychotherapy,* which will focus on clinical examples to illustrate the integration of feminist theory into psychoanalytically oriented psychotherapy. Long case examples with extensive dialogue from sessions will be included, to show the questions I ask and the interpretations I make. These case examples will be organized under topics of great importance in the lives of women, including the mother–daughter relationship, the fears of women, the new woman, overeating, violence against women, women at mid-life and aging, lesbian women, and abortion. These topics all arise in psychotherapy with women, and sometimes involve questions of law, morality, and religion, as well as community values and standards. Feminist theory and psychological research are both valuable in untangling the web of conflicting and powerful emotions associated with these phenomena. Thus, in issues of broad societal interest, the best thinking of psychoanalysis, feminism, sociology, religion, and the law all need to be integrated to achieve the best possible solutions to complex problems.

As analysts and therapists, we are never without our personal reactions and biases. We try to remain neutral and wish to be scientific, but these are goals, not realities. Who we are as persons—our life experiences; our families, spouses, children, and friends; our class and religious background—all influence us as we listen to our patients. The older we get, the more wisdom we can bring to bear on our listening.

A patriarchal bias distorted the listening of the early psychoanalysts. But this has been corrected, under the influence of the new feminism, the sex researchers, and child observations. We now see modern psychoanalytic theory-building, which has eliminated those patriarchal distortions.

Just as psychoanalysis has been subject to revision, so too feminist theory is being debated among feminists. In this book, I have attempted to look at both feminist and psychoanalytic theory with a critical eye, to see what is valuable in each, and also what needs further research and debate and perhaps even elimination. Both sides have said some pretty outrageous things—psychoanalysts about women, feminists about men. I hope my work will contribute to a more reasonable debate, with each side truly hearing the ideas of the other in an atmosphere of mutual respect.

REFERENCES

Abbott, S., and Love, B. (1971). Is women's liberation a lesbian plot? In *Woman in Sexist Society,* ed. V. Gornick and B. Moran, pp. 601–621. New York: Signet.

Abraham, K. (1920). Manifestations of the female castration complex. In *The Selected Papers of Karl Abraham,* trans. D. Bryan and A. Strachey, pp. 338–369. New York: Basic Books, 1927.

Alzate, H. (1985). Vaginal eroticism and female orgasm: a current appraisal. *Journal of Sex and Marital Therapy* 11:271–284.

—— (1990). Vaginal erogeneity, the "G spot," and female ejaculation. *Journal of Sex Education and Therapy* 16:137–140.

American Psychiatric Association (1987). *Quick Reference to the Diagnostic Criteria from DSM-III-R.* Washington, DC.

Applegarth, A. (1977). Some observations on work inhibitions in women. In *Female Psychology,* ed. H. P. Blum, pp. 251–268. New York: International Universities Press.

Ash, M. (1971). Freud on feminine identity and female sexuality. *Psychiatry* 34:322–327.

—— (1974). The changing attitudes of women: implications for psychotherapy. *Journal of the American Medical Women's Association* 29:411–413.

Balmary, M. (1982). *Freud and the Hidden Fault of the Father.* Baltimore: Johns Hopkins University Press.

Bank, S. P., and Kahn, M. D. (1982). *The Sibling Bond.* New York: Basic Books.

Barbach, L. (1976). *For Yourself: The Fulfillment of Female Sexuality.* New York: New American Library.

Barglow, P., and Schaefer, M. (1977). A new female psychology? In *Female Psychology,* ed. H. P. Blum, pp. 393–438. New York: International Universities Press.

Bart, P. B. (1974). Ideologies and utopias of psychotherapy. In *The Sociology of Psychotherapy,* ed. P. M. Roman and H. M. Trice, pp. 9–57. New York: Jason Aronson.

Bass, E., and Davis, L. (1988). *The Courage to Heal.* New York: Harper and Row.

Bell, A., Weinberg, M., and Hammersmith, S. K. (1981). *Sexual Preference: Its Development Among Men and Women.* Bloomington, IN: Indiana University Press.

Bene, E. (1965). On the genesis of female homosexuality. *British Journal of Psychiatry* 3:815–821.

Benedek, T. (1959). Parenthood as a developmental phase: a contribution to the libido theory. *Journal of the American Psychoanalytic Association.* 7:389–417.

Benjamin, J. (1982). Chodorow's *The Reproduction of Mothering:* an appraisal. *The Psychoanalytic Review* 69:158–161.

—— (1988). *The Bonds of Love: Psychoanalysis, Feminism, and the Problem of Domination.* New York: Pantheon.

Bernal, J. D. (1953). *Science and Industry in the 19th Century.* London: Routledge and Paul.

Bernardez-Bonesatti, T. (1976). Unconscious beliefs about women affecting psychotherapy. *North Carolina Journal of Mental Health* 7:63–66.

—— (1978). Women and anger: conflicts with aggression in contemporary women. *Journal of the American Medical Women's Association* 33:215–219.

Blum, H. P., ed. (1977a). *Female Psychology.* New York: International Universities Press.

—— (1977b). Masochism, the ego ideal, and the psychology of women. In *Female Psychology,* ed. H. P. Blum, pp. 157–191. New York: International Universities Press.

Blume, E. S. (1990). *Secret Survivors.* New York: Wiley.

Blumenthal, R. (1984). Freud: secret documents reveal years of strife. *The New York Times,* January 24, pp. 13, 19.

Bograd, M. (1986). A feminist examination of family therapy: what is woman's place? *Women in Therapy* 5:95–106.

Boston Lesbian Psychologies Collective, ed. (1987). *Lesbian Psychologies: Explorations and Challenges.* Chicago: University of Illinois Press.

Boston Women's Health Book Collective (1984). *The New Our Bodies, Ourselves,* New York: Simon & Schuster.

Boston Women's Health Course Collective (1971). *Our Bodies Our Selves.* Boston: New England Free Press.

Broverman, I. K., Broverman, D. M., Clarkson, F. E., et al. (1970). Sex role stereotypes and clinical judgments of mental health. *Journal of Counseling and Clinical Psychology* 34:1–7.

—— (1972). Sex-role stereotypes: a current appraisal. *Journal of Social Issues* 28:59–78.

Brown, R. M. (1973). *Rubyfruit Jungle.* New York: Bantam, 1977.

Butler, S. (1983). Openings. In *Women Changing Therapy,* ed. J. H. Robbins and R. J. Siegel, pp. 103–111. New York: Haworth Press.

Caldwell, M. A., and Peplau, L. A. (1979). *The balance of power in lesbian relationships.* Preliminary draft. Los Angeles: University of California.

Caplan, P. (1984). The myth of women's masochism. *American Psychologist* 39:130–139.

——— (1985). *The Myth of Women's Masochism.* New York: Dutton.

Caprio, F. (1954). *Female Homosexuality.* New York: Citadel.

Chasseguet-Smirgel, J., ed. (1970a). *Female Sexuality: New Psychoanalytic Views.* Ann Arbor: University of Michigan Press.

——— (1970b). Feminine guilt and the oedipus complex. In *Female Sexuality: New Psychoanalytic Views,* ed. J. Chasseguet-Smirgel, pp. 94–134. Ann Arbor: University of Michigan Press.

Chehrazi, S. (1986). Female psychology: a review. *Journal of the American Psychoanalytic Association* 34:141–162.

Chesler, P. (1970). Marriage and psychotherapy. *The Radical Therapist* 1:16.

——— (1972). *Women and Madness.* New York: Doubleday.

Child Abuse Prevention Program (1991). *ICAN Data Analysis Report for 1991.* Los Angeles: Los Angeles County Department of Health Services.

Chodorow, N. (1976). Oedipal asymmetries and heterosexual knots. In *Female Psychology: The Emerging Self,* 2nd ed., ed. S. Cox, pp. 228–247. New York: St. Martin's Press, 1981.

——— (1978). *The Reproduction of Mothering: Psychoanalysis and the Sociology of Gender.* Berkeley: University of California Press.

——— (1989). *Feminism and Psychoanalytic Theory.* New Haven: Yale University Press.

Clark, L. (1970). Is there a difference between a clitoral and a vaginal orgasm? *Journal of Sex Research* 6:25–28.

Collins, G. (1985). Women and masochism: debate continues. *The New York Times,* December 2, p. 12.

Cox, S., ed. (1976). *Female Psychology: The Emerging Self.* Chicago: Science Research Associates.

——— (1981). *Female Psychology: The Emerging Self.* 2nd ed. New York: St. Martin's Press.

Davidson, J., Kenneth, C., Darling, A., et al. (1989). The role of the Grafenberg spot and female ejaculation in the female orgasmic response: an empirical analysis. *Journal of Sex and Marital Therapy* 15:102–120.

de Beauvoir, S. (1952). *The Second Sex.* Trans. J. M. Parshley. New York: Vintage, 1974.

Deutsch, H. (1925). Psychology of women in relation to the functions of reproduction. *International Journal of Psycho-Analysis* 6:405–418.

——— (1930). The significance of masochism in the mental life of women. *International Journal of Psycho-Analysis* 11:48–60.

——— (1944). *Psychology of Women.* Vol. I. New York: Grune & Stratton.

——— (1945). *Psychology of Women.* Vol. II. New York: Grune & Stratton.

Dicks, H. V. (1967). *Marital Tensions.* New York: Basic Books.

Dinnerstein, D. (1976). *The Mermaid and The Minotaur.* New York: Harper Colophon, 1977.

Dworkin, A. (1974). *Woman Hating.* New York: Dutton.

Ehrenreich, B. (1983). *The Hearts of Men.* New York: Anchor Books/Doubleday.

Ehrenreich, B., and English, D. (1973). *Witches, Midwives and Nurses.* Old Westbury, NY: Feminist Press.

Ehrensaft, D. (1980). When women and men mother. *Socialist Review* 49:37–73.

—— (1985). Dual parenting and the duel of intimacy. In *The Psychosocial Interior of the Family,* 3rd ed., ed. G. Handel, pp. 323–337. New York: Aldine Press.

Eichenbaum, L., and Orbach, S. (1983). *Understanding Women: A Feminist Psychoanalytic Approach.* New York: Basic Books.

Eisenbud, R.-J. (1982). Early and later determinants of lesbian choice. *The Psychoanalytic Review* 69:85–109.

Ellis, A. (1953). Is the vaginal orgasm a myth? In *Sex, Society and the Individual,* ed. A. P. Pillay and A. Ellis, pp. 155–162. Bombay: The International Journal of Sexology.

Elshtain, J. B. (1982). Feminism, family and community. *Dissent* 29:442–449.

Epp, J. M. (1984). *The orgasmic frequency and reliability of assertive and unassertive women.* Unpublished Ph.D. Dissertation. San Francisco: Institute for Advanced Study of Human Sexuality.

—— (1991). Personal communication.

Erikson, E. H. (1950). *Childhood and Society.* New York: Norton.

—— (1968). Womanhood and the Inner Space. In *Women and Analysis,* ed. J. Strouse, pp. 333–364. New York: Dell.

—— (1974). Once more the inner space. In *Women and Analysis,* ed. J. Strouse, pp. 365–387. New York: Dell.

Faludi, S. (1991). *Backlash: The Undeclared War Against American Women.* New York: Crown.

Family Therapy Networker, The (1985). 9:17.

Farber, L. H. (1966). I'm sorry dear. In *An Analysis of Human Sexual Response,* ed. E. Brecher and R. Brecher, pp. 291–311. New York: Signet.

Fenichel, O. (1945). *The Psychoanalytic Theory of Neurosis.* New York: Norton.

Firestone, S. (1970). *The Dialectic of Sex.* New York: Morrow.

Fisher, S. (1973). *The Female Orgasm.* New York: Basic Books.

Fox-Genovese, E. (1990). *Feminism Without Illusions.* Chapel Hill: University of North Carolina Press.

Frank, A. (1951). *Diary of a Young Girl.* New York: Modern Library.

Frankl, V. (1962). *Man's Search for Meaning.* Boston: Beacon.

Freud, S. (1900–1901). The interpretation of dreams. *Standard Edition* 4/5:1–713.

—— (1905a). Fragment of an analysis of a case of hysteria. *Standard Edition* 7:7–122.

—— (1905b). Three Essays on the Theory of Sexuality. *Standard Edition* 7:125–245.

—— (1908). "Civilized" sexual morality and modern nervous illness. *Standard Edition* 9:179–204.

—— (1917). Mourning and melancholia. *Standard Edition* 14:239–258.

—— (1918). The taboo of virginity. *Standard Edition* 11:193–208.

—— (1920). The psychogenesis of a case of homosexuality in a woman. *Standard Edition* 18:147–208.

—— (1923). The infantile genital organization. *Standard Edition* 19:140–145.

—— (1924). The dissolution of the Oedipus complex. *Standard Edition* 19:172–179.

—— (1925). Some psychological consequences of the anatomical distinction between the sexes. In *Freud: Sexuality and the Psychology of Love,* ed. P. Rieff, pp. 183–193. New York: Collier, 1963.

—— (1927). *The Future of an Illusion.* Garden City, NY: Anchor.

—— (1930). *Civilization and Its Discontents.* Trans. J. Strachey. New York: Norton, 1961.

—— (1931). Female sexuality. *Standard Edition* 21:223–243.

—— (1932). Femininity. *Standard Edition* 22:112–135.

—— (1937). Analysis terminable and interminable. *Standard Edition* 23:209–253.

—— (1956). An Outline of Psychoanalysis. In *Collected Papers* 23:239–258.

Fried, E. (1960). *The Ego in Love and Sexuality.* New York: Grune & Stratton.

Friedan, B. (1963). *The Feminine Mystique.* New York: Dell.

Gay, P. (1988). *Freud: A Life For Our Time.* New York: Norton.

Gibbs, E. D. (1989). Psychosocial development of children raised by lesbian mothers: a review of research. In *Lesbians: Affirming Nontraditional Roles,* ed. E. D. Rothblum and E. Cole, pp. 65–75. New York: Haworth.

Gilligan, C. (1982). *In A Different Voice.* Cambridge, MA: Harvard University Press.

—— (1990). *Making Connections: The Relational Worlds of Adolescent Girls at Emma Willard School.* Cambridge, MA: Harvard University Press.

Goffman, E. (1961). *Asylums.* Garden City, NY: Doubleday.

Goldin, J. (1955). *The Living Talmud.* New York: New American Library, 1957.

Goleman, D. (1984). Freud: secret documents reveal years of strife. *The New York Times,* January 24, pp. 13, 19.

—— (1988). Sex roles reign powerful as ever in the emotions. *The New York Times,* January 24, pp. 1, 13.

Golombok, S., Spencer, A., and Rutter, M. (1983). Children in lesbian and single-parent households: psychosexual and psychiatric appraisal. *Journal of Child Psychology and Psychiatry* 24:551–572.

Gordon, S. (1978). Helene Deutsch and the legacy of Freud. *The New York Times Magazine,* July 30, p. 23.

Gornick, V., and Moran, B. K. (1971). *Woman in Sexist Society.* New York: Signet.

Grafenberg, E. (1950). The role of the urethra in female orgasm. *International Journal of Sexology* 3:145–148.

Green, R. (1978). Sexual identity of 37 children raised by homosexual or transsexual parents. *American Journal of Psychiatry* 135:692–697.

Greenwood, S. (1984). *Menopause Naturally.* San Francisco: Volcano Press.

Grossman, W. I., and Stewart, W. (1977). Penis envy: from childhood wish to developmental metaphor. In *Female Psychology,* ed. H. P. Blum, pp. 193–212. New York: International Universities Press.

Grunberger, B. (1970). Outline for a study of narcissism in female sexuality. In

Female Sexuality, ed. J. Chasseguet-Smirgel, pp. 68–83. Ann Arbor: University of Michigan Press.

Haeberle, E. J. (1982). *The Sex Atlas.* New York: Continuum.

Hampson, J. L. (1965). Determinants of psychosexual orientation. In *Sex and Behavior,* ed. F. A. Beach, pp. 108–132. New York: Wiley.

Hare-Mustin, R. T., and Marecek, J. (1986). Autonomy and gender: some questions for therapists. *Psychotherapy* 23:205–212.

Havel, V. (1989). *Vaclav Havel: Living in Truth.* Ed. J. Vladislav. Boston: Faber and Faber.

Hayes, H. R. (1964). *The Dangerous Sex.* New York: G. P. Putnam's Sons.

Herman, J. (1981). *Father–Daughter Incest.* Cambridge, MA: Harvard University Press.

—— (1984). The analyst analyzed. *The Nation,* March 10, pp. 293–296.

Herschberger, R. (1970). *Adam's Rib.* New York: Pelligrini and Cudahy.

Hinckle, W., and Hinckle, M. (1968). A history of the rise of the unusual movement for women power in the United States 1961–1968. *Ramparts,* February, pp. 22–31.

Hite, S. (1976). *The Hite Report.* New York: Dell.

Hoch, Z. (1983). The G spot. *Journal of Sex and Marital Therapy* 9:166–167.

—— (1986). Vaginal erotic sensitivity by sexological examination. *Acta Obstet Gynecol Scand* 65:767–773.

Hoeffer, B. (1981). Children's acquisition of sex-role behavior in lesbian-mother families. *American Journal of Orthopsychiatry* 51:536–544.

Hollingshead, A. B., and Redlich, F. C. (1958). *Social Class and Mental Illness.* New York: Wiley.

Horner, M. (1972). Toward an understanding of achievement-related conflicts in women. *Journal of Social Issues* 28:157–175.

Horney, K. (1922). On the genesis of the castration complex in women. In *Feminine Psychology,* ed. H. Kelman, pp. 37–53. New York: Norton, 1967.

—— (1926a). Inhibited femininity. In *Feminine Psychology,* ed. H. Kelman, pp. 71–83. New York: Norton, 1967.

—— (1926b). The flight from womanhood. In *Feminine Psychology,* ed. H. Kelman, pp. 54–70. New York: Norton, 1967.

—— (1932). Psychogenic factors in functional female disorders. In *Feminine Psychology,* ed. H. Kelman, pp. 162–174. New York: Norton, 1967.

—— (1933a). Maternal conflicts. In *Feminine Psychology,* ed. H. Kelman, pp. 175–181. New York: Norton, 1967.

—— (1933b). The denial of the vagina. In *Feminine Psychology,* ed. H. Kelman, pp. 145–161. New York: Norton, 1967.

—— (1933c). The problem of feminine masochism. In *Feminine Psychology,* ed. H. Kelman, pp. 214–233. New York: Norton, 1967.

—— (1934). The overvaluation of love. In *Feminine Psychology,* ed. H. Kelman, pp. 182–213. New York: Norton, 1967.

—— (1937). *The Neurotic Personality of Our Time.* New York: Norton.

Hunt, M. (1974). *Sexual Behavior in the 1970's.* Chicago: Playboy Press.

International Encyclopedia of Social Sciences (1968). Glencoe, IL: The Free Press.

Jones, D. M. (1990). Social analysis in the clinical setting. *Clinical Social Work Journal* 18:393–406.

Jones, E. (1927). The early development of female sexuality. *International Journal of Psycho-Analysis* 8:459–472.

—— (1953). *The Life and Work of Sigmund Freud.* Vol. I. New York: Basic Books.

—— (1955). *The Life and Work of Sigmund Freud.* Vol. II. New York: Basic Books.

Jordan, J. V. (1990). Relational development through empathy: therapeutic applications. In *Empathy Revisited, Work in Progress,* No. 40, pp. 11–14. Wellesley, MA: Wellesley College, Stone Center.

Kaplan, A. G. (1990). Empathy and Its Vicissitudes. In *Empathy Revisited, Work in Progress,* No. 40, pp. 6–10. Wellesley, MA: Wellesley College, Stone Center.

Kaplan, M. (1983). A woman's view of DSM-III. *American Psychologist* 38:786–792.

Kashak, E. (1981). Feminist psychotherapy: the first decade. In *Female Psychology,* ed. S. Cox, pp. 387–401. New York: St. Martin's Press.

Keller, E. F. (1985). *Reflections on Gender and Science.* New Haven: Yale University Press.

Kelman, H. (1967). *Feminine Psychology.* New York: Norton.

—— (1971). *Helping People: Karen Horney's Psychoanalytic Approach.* New York: Science House.

Kernberg, O. (1975). *Borderline Conditions and Pathological Narcissism.* New York: Jason Aronson.

Kinsey, A. C., Pomeroy, W., Martin, C., et al. (1948). *Sexual Behavior in the Human Male.* Philadelphia: W. B. Saunders.

—— (1953). *Sexual Behavior in the Human Female.* Philadelphia: W. B. Saunders.

Kirkpatrick, M. (1991). *Reflections on maternal desire.* Unpublished paper. Los Angeles, CA.

Kirkpatrick, M., and Morgan, C. (1980). Psychodynamic psychotherapy of female homosexuality. In *Homosexual Behavior,* ed. J. Marmor, pp. 357–375. New York: Basic Books.

Kirkpatrick, M., Smith, C., and Roy, R. (1981). Lesbian mothers and their children: a comparative survey. *American Journal of Orthopsychiatry* 51:545–551.

Koedt, A. (1971). The myth of the vaginal orgasm. In *The Radical Therapist,* ed. J. Agel, pp. 127–137. New York: Ballantine.

Kohlberg, L. (1958). *The development of modes of thinking and choices in years 10 to 16.* Ph.D. Dissertation, University of Chicago.

—— (1981). *The Philosophy of Moral Development.* San Francisco: Harper and Row.

Krause, C. (1971). The femininity complex and female therapists *Journal of Marriage and the Family* 33:476–482.

Laner, M. R. (1978). Media mating II: "personals" advertisements of lesbian women. *Journal of Homosexuality* 4:41–61.

—— (1979). Growing older female: heterosexual and homosexual. *Journal of Homosexuality* 4:267–275.

Langs, R. (1973). *The Technique of Psychoanalytic Psychotherapy.* Vol. I. New York: Jason Aronson.

—— (1974). *The Technique of Psychoanalytic Psychotherapy.* Vol. II. New York: Jason Aronson.

Lasch, C. (1979). *The Culture of Narcissism.* New York: Warner Books.

Lederer, L. (1980). *Take Back the Night: Women on Pornography.* New York: William Morrow.

Lederer, W. (1968). *The Fear Of Women.* New York: Harcourt Brace Jovanovich.

Lerman, H. (1976). What happens in feminist therapy. In *Female Psychology,* ed. S. Cox, pp. 378–384. Chicago: Science Research Associates.

Lerner, H. G. (1977). Parental mislabeling of female genitals as a determinant of penis envy and learning inhibitions in women. In *Female Psychology,* ed. H. P. Blum, pp. 269–284. New York: International Universities Press.

—— (1988). *Women in Therapy.* Northvale, NJ: Jason Aronson.

Lever, J. (1976). Sex differences in the games children play. *Social Problems* 23:478–487.

Levine, S. (1971). Sexual differentiation: the development of maleness and femaleness. *California Medicine* 114:12–17.

Levy, S. T. (1990). *Principles of Interpretation.* 2nd ed. Northvale, NJ: Jason Aronson.

Lorde, A. (1979). Growing older female: heterosexual and homosexual. *Journal of Homosexuality* 4:267–275.

—— (1982). Scratching the surface: some notes on barriers to women and loving. *The Black Scholar* 13:20–24.

Lowen, A. (1965). *Love and Orgasm.* New York: Macmillan.

Lydon, S. (1970). The politics of orgasm. In *Sisterhood is Powerful,* ed. R. Morgan, pp. 219–228. New York: Vintage.

Maccoby, E. E. (1990). Gender and relationships: a developmental account. *American Psychologist* 45:513–520.

Magee, M. (1991). Book Reviews. *Clinical Social Work Journal* 19:99–102.

Mailer, N. (1971). The prisoner of sex. *Harper's,* March, pp. 41–92.

Mannion, K. (1981). Psychology and the lesbian: a critical review of the research. In *Female Psychology,* ed. S. Cox, pp. 256–274. New York: St. Martin's Press.

Mara, J. (1983). A lesbian perspective. In *Women Changing Therapy,* ed. J. H. Robbins and R. J. Siegel, pp. 145–155. New York: Haworth.

Marin, P. (1981). Living in moral pain. *Psychology Today,* November, pp. 68–80.

Marmor, J. (1965). *Sexual Inversion: The Multiple Roots of Homosexuality.* New York: Basic Books.

—— (1968). Changing patterns of femininity: psychoanalytic implications. In *Psychoanalysis and Women,* ed. J. B. Miller, pp. 222–238. Baltimore: Penguin Books, 1973.

—— (1980). *Homosexual Behavior: A Modern Reappraisal.* New York: Basic Books.

Martin, D., and Lyon, P. (1972). *Lesbian Woman.* New York: Bantam.

Masters, W. H., and Johnson, V. E. (1966). *Human Sexual Response.* Boston: Little Brown.

—— (1970). *Human Sexual Inadequacy.* Boston: Little Brown.

Mayer, E. L. (1985). "Everybody must be just like me": observations on female castration anxiety. *International Journal of Psycho-Analysis* 66:331–347.

McDougall, J. (1970). Homosexuality in women. In *Female Sexuality,* ed. J. Chasseguet-Smirgel, pp. 171–212. Ann Arbor: University of Michigan.

—— (1980). *A Plea for a Measure of Abnormality.* New York: International Universities Press.

Mednick, M. T. (1989). On the politics of psychological constructs: stop the bandwagon, I want to get off. *American Psychologist* 44:1118–1123.

Miller, J. B. (1973). *Psychoanalysis and Women.* Baltimore: Penguin Books.

—— (1976). *Toward a New Psychology of Women.* Boston: Beacon Paperback, 1977.

Millett, K. (1970). *Sexual Politics.* Garden City, NY: Doubleday.

Mitchell, J. (1971). *Woman's Estate.* New York: Vintage Books.

—— (1974). *Psychoanalysis and Feminism.* New York: Vintage Books, 1975.

Morgan, R., ed. (1970a). *Sisterhood is Powerful.* New York: Vintage Books.

—— (1970b). Goodbye to all that. *The every other weekly,* May 12, pp. 6–7.

Muller, J. (1932). The problem of the libidinal development of the genital phase of girls. *International Journal of Psycho-Analysis* 13:361–368.

Newman, F., and Caplan, P. J. (1982). Juvenile female prostitution as gender-consistent response to early deprivation. *International Journal of Women's Studies* 5:128–137.

Nihira, M. A., and Chang, A. (1990). *A descriptive analysis of reported cases of N. Gonorrhea in children under 12 years of age in Los Angeles County 1981–1989.* Los Angeles: Los Angeles County Department of Health Services.

Nobile, P. (1972). What is the new impotence, and who's got it? *Esquire,* October, pp. 95–98, 218.

Notman, M. T., and Nadelson, C. C., eds. (1978, 1982). *The Woman Patient.* Volumes 1, 2, and 3. New York: Plenum.

Ohlson, E. L., and Wilson, M. (1974). Differentiating female homosexuals by use of the MMPI. *Journal of Sex Research* 10:308–315.

Oremland, J. D. (1991). *Interpretation and Interaction—Psychoanalysis or Psychotherapy?* Hillsdale, NJ: Analytic Press.

Ortner, S. B. (1974). Is female to male as nature is to culture? In *Culture and Society,* ed. M. Z. Rosaldo and L. Lamphere, pp. 67–87. Stanford, CA: Stanford University Press.

Parlee, M. B. (1982). Chodorow's *The Reproduction of Mothering. The Psychoanalytic Review* 69:152–154.

Parsons, T. (1951). *The Social System.* Glencoe, IL: The Free Press.

Parsons, T., and Bales, R. F. (1955). *Family.* Glencoe, IL: The Free Press.

Peplau, L. A. (1972). The etiology of gender identity and the lesbian. *Journal of Social Psychology* 87:51–57.

Peplau, L. A., Cochran, S., Rook, K., et al. (1978). Loving women: attachment and autonomy in lesbian relationships. *Journal of Social Issues* 34:7–27.

Perry, J. D., and Whipple, B. (1981). Pelvic muscle strength of female ejaculators:

evidence in support of a new theory of orgasm. *Journal of Sex Research* 17:22–39.

Person, E. S. (1983). The influence of values in psychoanalysis: the case of female psychology. *Psychoanalytic Inquiry* 3:623–646.

Piaget, J. (1932). *The Moral Judgment of the Child.* New York: The Free Press.

Ponse, B. (1980). Lesbians and their worlds. In *Homosexual Behavior,* ed. J. Marmor, pp. 157–175. New York: Basic Books.

Prose, F. (1990). Confident at 11, confused at 16. *The New York Times Magazine,* January 7, pp. 23–25, 37–46.

Prozan, C. K. (1988). An integration of feminist and psychoanalytic theory. In *Women, Power, and Therapy: Issues for Women,* ed. M. Braude, pp. 59–71. New York: Haworth Press.

Radicalesbians. (1976). The woman identified woman. In *Female Psychology,* ed. S. Cox, pp. 304–308. Chicago: Science Research Associates.

Reage, P. (1965). *The Story of O.* New York: Grove Press.

Reich, W. (1942). *The Function of the Orgasm.* New York: Orgone Institute Press.

Reiss, B. (1980). Psychological tests in homosexuality. In *Homosexual Behavior,* ed. J. Marmor, pp. 296–311. New York: Basic Books.

Reuben, D. (1969). *Everything You Always Wanted to Know About Sex But Were Afraid to Ask.* New York: D. McKay.

Rich, A. (1977). The meaning of our love for women is what we have constantly to expand. In *On Lies, Secrets, and Silence: Selected Prose 1966–1978,* pp. 223–230. New York: Norton, 1979.

—— (1980). Compulsory heterosexuality and lesbian existence. *Signs* 5:631–660.

Roazen, P. (1985). *Helene Deutsch, A Psychoanalysts's Life.* New York: Anchor Press/Doubleday.

Robbins, J. H. (1990). *Knowing Herself: Women Tell Their Stories in Psychotherapy.* New York: Plenum.

Robertiello, R. C. (1970). The "clitoral vs. vaginal orgasm" controversy and some of its ramifications. *Journal of Sex Research* 6:307–311.

Robins, C. (1991). Hot and bothered. *The San Francisco Examiner, Image Magazine,* February 3, pp. 8–16.

Robinson, M. N. (1959). *The Power of Sexual Surrender.* New York: New American Library.

Romm, M. E. (1965). Sexuality and homosexuality in women. In *Sexual Inversion,* ed. J. Marmor, pp. 292–301. New York: Basic Books.

Rosenblum, B. (1983). Conformity in the collective. *The San Francisco Chronicle.* Book Review, p. 8.

Rosaldo, M. Z. (1974). Woman, culture and society: a theoretical overview. In *Woman, Culture and Society,* ed. M. Z. Rosaldo and L. Lamphere, pp. 17–42. Stanford, CA: Stanford University Press.

Rothblum, E. D., and Cole, E., eds. (1989). *Lesbianism: Affirming Nontraditional Roles.* New York: Haworth Press.

Rubin, G. (1975). The traffic in women: notes on the "political economy" of sex. In *Toward an Anthropology of Women,* ed. R. Reiter, pp. 157–210. New York: Monthly Review Press.

Rubin, L. B. (1976). *Worlds of Pain.* New York: Basic Books.

—— (1983). *Intimate Strangers.* New York: Harper and Row.

Saghir, M. T., and Robins, E. (1980). Clinical aspects of female homosexuality. In *Homosexual Behavior,* ed. J. Marmor, pp. 280–295. New York: Basic Books.

Schafer, R. (1974). Problems in Freud's psychology of women. In *Female Psychology,* ed. H. P. Blum, pp. 331–360. New York: International Universities Press, 1977.

Schafer, S. (1977). Sociosexual behavior in male and female homosexuals: a study in sex differences. *Archives of Sexual Behavior* 6:355–364.

Seidenberg, R. (1972). The trauma of eventlessness. In *Psychoanalysis and Women,* ed. J. B. Miller, pp. 350–362. Baltimore: Penguin, 1973.

Sennett, R. (1972). *Hidden Injures of Class.* New York: Knopf.

Shainess, N. (1970). A psychiatrist's view: images of woman—past and present, overt and obscured. In *Sisterhood is Powerful,* ed. R. Morgan, pp. 257–274. New York: Vintage Books.

—— (1984). *Sweet Suffering.* New York: Bobbs Merrill.

Shelley, M. (1970). Notes of a radical lesbian. In *Sisterhood is Powerful,* ed. R. Morgan, pp. 343–348. New York: Vintage Books.

—— (1971). Lesbianism. In *The Radical Therapist,* ed. J. Agel, pp. 169–172. New York: Ballantine.

Sherfy, M. J. (1970). A theory of female sexuality. In *Sisterhood is Powerful,* ed. R. Morgan, pp. 245–256. New York: Vintage Books.

Shulman, A. (1971). Organs and orgasms. In *Woman in Sexist Society,* ed. V. Gornich and B. K. Moran, pp. 292–303. New York: Signet, 1972.

Siegel, E. (1988). *Female Homosexuality: Choice Without Volition.* Hillsdale, NJ: Analytic Press.

Siegelman, M. (1974). Parental background on homosexual and heterosexual women. *British Journal of Psychiatry* 124:14–21.

Socarides, C. W. (1968). *The Overt Homosexual.* New York: Grune & Stratton.

—— (1978). *Homosexuality.* New York: Jason Aronson.

Starzecpyzel, E. (1987). The persephone complex. In *Lesbian Psychologies,* ed. Boston Lesbian Psychologies Collective, pp. 261–282. Chicago: University of Illinois.

Steinem, G. (1983). *Outrageous Acts and Everyday Rebellions.* New York: Holt, Rinehart and Winston.

Steiner, C. (1971). Radical psychiatry: principles. In *The Radical Therapist,* ed. J. Agel, pp. 3–7. New York: Ballantine.

Stepansky, P. E. (1988). *The Memoirs of Margaret S. Mahler.* New York: The Free Press.

Stern, D. (1985). *The Interpersonal World of the Infant: A View From Psychoanalysis and Developmental Psychology.* New York: Basic Books.

Stoller, R. J. (1975). *Perversion: The Erotic Form of Hatred.* New York: Pantheon Books.

Strouse, J. (1974). *Women and Analysis.* New York: Laurel Edition, 1975.

Surrey, J. (1985). Self-in-relation: a theory of women's development. In *Work in Progress,* No. 13. Wellesley, MA: Wellesley College, Stone Center.

—— (1990). Empathy: evolving theoretical perspectives. In *Empathy Revisited,*

Work in Progress, No. 40, pp. 1–5. Wellesley, MA: Wellesley College, Stone Center.

Symonds, A. (1971). Phobias after marriage: women's declaration of dependence. In *Psychoanalysis and Women,* ed. J. B. Miller, pp. 288–304. Baltimore: Penguin, 1973.

The Family Therapy Networker. Nov.–Dec. (1985). Vol. 9, No. 6.

Thompson, C. (1942). Cultural pressures in the psychology of women. In *Psycho-analysis and Women,* ed. J. B. Miller, pp. 69–84. Baltimore: Penguin Books, 1973.

—— (1950). Some effects of the derogatory attitude toward female sexuality. In *Psychoanalysis and Women,* ed. J. B. Miller, pp. 58–68. Baltimore: Penguin Books, 1973.

Thompson, N., McCandless, R., and Strickland, B. (1971). Personal adjustment of male and female homosexuals and heterosexuals. *Journal of Abnormal Psychology* 78:237–240.

Ticho, G. R. (1977). Female autonomy and young adult women. In *Female Psychology,* ed. H. P. Blum, pp. 139–156. New York: International Universities Press.

Torok, M. (1970). The significance of penis envy in women. In *Female Sexuality,* ed. J. Chasseguet-Smirgel, pp. 135–170. Ann Arbor: University of Michigan Press.

Turkle, S. (1985). Freudian apostle of passivity. *New York Times Book Review,* May 26, p. 8.

Van de Welde, T. H. (1930). *Ideal Marriage.* New York: Random House.

Vatsyayana, M. (1980). *The Love Teachings of Kama Sutra.* Trans. I. Sinha. London: Spring Books.

Weisstein, N. (1971). Psychology constructs the female, or the fantasy life of the male psychologist. In *Female Psychology,* ed. S. Cox, pp. 91–103. Chicago: Science Research Associates.

Westheimer, R. (1983). *Dr. Ruth's Guide to Good Sex.* New York: Warner.

Wilbur, C. B. (1965). Clinical aspects of female homosexuality. In *Sexual Inversion,* ed. J. Marmor, pp. 268–281. New York: Basic Books.

Williams, W. (1984). The practical management of the otherwise fully sexually responsive woman who complains of inability to climax during intercourse. *Australian Journal of Sex, Marriage & Family* 5:199–209.

Woolf, V. (1929). *A Room of One's Own.* New York: Harcourt, Brace & World.

Wolff, C. (1971). *Love Between Women.* New York: Harper and Row.

Young-Bruehl, E., ed. (1990). *Freud on Women: A Reader.* New York: Norton.

Zilboorg, G. (1944). Masculine and feminine: some biological and cultural aspects, In *Psychoanalysis and Women,* ed. J. B. Miller, pp. 96–131. New York: Penguin Books, 1973.

CREDITS

Excerpts from *Female Psychology*, edited by Harold Blum. Copyright © 1977 by International Universities Press. Reprinted by permission of International Universities Press, the editor, and the authors.

Excerpts from "Psychology Constructs the Female, or the Fantasy Life of the Male Psychologist," by Naomi Weisstein, in *Female Psychology*, edited by Sue Cox. Copyright © 1971 by Naomi Weisstein. Reprinted by permission of the author.

Excerpts from *The Bonds of Love,* by Jessica Benjamin. Copyright © 1988 by Jessica Benjamin. Reprinted by permission of Pantheon Books, a division of Random House, Inc.

Excerpts from *The Female Orgasm* by Seymour Fisher. Copyright © 1973 by Seymour Fisher. Reprinted by permission of the author.

Excerpts from *Love Between Women,* by Charlotte Wolff. Copyright © 1971 by St. Martin's Press, Inc. Reprinted by permission.

Excerpts from "Living in Moral Pain," by Peter Marin, *Psychology Today,* November 1981. Copyright © 1981 Sussex Publishers, Inc. Reprinted by permission of *Psychology Today Magazine.*

Excerpts from *The Hite Report,* by Shere Hite. Copyright © 1976 by Shere Hite. Reprinted by permission of Macmillan Publishing Company.

Excerpts from *The Feminine Mystique,* by Betty Friedan. Copyright © 1963. Reprinted by permission of Norton Publishing Company.

Excerpts from *Our Bodies, Our Selves,* by the Boston Women's Health Course Collective. Copyright © 1971. Reprinted by permission of the Boston Women's Health Course Collective.

Excerpts from *Feminine Psychology,* by Karen Horney, edited by Harold Kelman. Copyright © 1967. Reprinted by permission of Norton Publishing Company.

Excerpts from *Vaclav Havel: Living in Truth,* by Vaclav Havel. Copyright © 1989. Reprinted by permission of Faber and Faber Publishing Company.

Excerpts from 2 Live Crew, *Nasty as They Wanna Be.* Copyright © 1989 by 2 Live Crew. Reprinted by permission of Luke Records.

Excerpts from *Psychology of Women*, Volume 1 (16th printing 1965) and volume 2 (10th printing 1963) by Helene Deutsch. Copyright © 1944 and 1945 by Grune and Stratton, Inc. Reprinted by permission of Allyn and Bacon.

INDEX